Enthusiastic praise from readers of *FARM FRIENDS:*

Thanks to Tom Fels' *FARM FRIE*... ...unravel the importance and influe... ...t decade of our lives.

> —**Peter Goldm**... ..., Environmental Defense, former ...he Rockefeller Foundation and chairman a... ...EO of the *International Herald Tribune*.

Immensely enjoyable account of a modern rite of passage in which reintegration into society provided important new insights into social norms and expectations.

> —**Dr. Robert Cox**, professor of history, author, and head of special collections, W. E. B. DuBois Library, University of Massachusetts, Amherst.

I've been a Tom Fels fan for years. He writes beautifully because he thinks with profound clarity. This book— a journey, an elegy, an investigation— touches the soul of an era and, at day's end, the aching, searching American heart.

> —**Ron Suskind**, Pulitzer prize winning journalist, and best-selling author of *THE ONE PERCENT DOCTRINE*.

Make an exception and buy this book! Shop-a-lujah!

> —**Reverend Billy Talen**, author of *WHAT SHOULD I DO IF REVEREND BILLY IS IN MY STORE?*, *WHAT WOULD JESUS BUY?*, and spiritual leader of the Church of Stop Shopping

Flawless. You caught me in the act!

> —**Jesse Kornbluth**, author, journalist, NPR commentator, and one of the subjects of *FARM FRIENDS*.

Farm Friends

Farm Friends

*From the Late Sixties to the
West Seventies and Beyond*

Tom Fels

RSI Press

North Bennington, Vermont

RSI Press
Rural Science Institute / Famous Long Ago Archive
P.O. Box 816, North Bennington, Vermont 05257

Distributed by
Chelsea Green Publishing
White River Junction, Vermont 05001
1-800-639-4099
www.chelseagreen.com

CATALOGUING INFORMATION

Fels, Thomas Weston.
Farm Friends / Tom Fels (Thomas Weston Fels). -- 1st ed.

Summary: "The author, who lived on a commune in the Seventies, visits
friends he knew decades ago on the farm, curious about whether their
values and world view, their successes and regrets, and how they see
themselves, have changed,"--Provided by publisher.

ISBN-13: 978-1-6035800-3-8 (pbk. : alk. paper)

Memoir. Autobiography. Contemporary history.
America in the 1960s. Radicals. Back-to-the-land movement.

Printed in the United States of America

For

Eric Morgenroth, 1942-1965
Tom Britt, 1945-1968
Marshall Bloom, 1944-1969

who would have enjoyed these years.

Contents

Illustrations

Foreword

Readers with any direct experience of events that made the 1960s "the Sixties" will enjoy Tom Fels' memoir immensely just as they would enjoy the diary of someone who had been there and done that when there and that by this time carry more than just a slight patina of the illicit and the shared. Those for whom the Sixties is a more remote country will find out from Fels' remarkable book how the myth began, how its roots were put down in the lives of very real people who had no idea what they were doing when they did it, or how to do it, or why they felt so strongly that they needed to try.

I myself fall somewhat awkwardly into the former category. I was certainly there—that is to say, in the Sixties—and I did the things that Fels' book tells about, the things that the Sixties asked or demanded that so many of us do. But I always felt that I was only passing through, and that I had no idea where I was going or what I was doing. I cannot claim the Sixties as a place, a thing, or even a time that I had been looking for. Fels' book is so valuable and its heart is so convincing because he, too, I think, wondered if he'd caught the wrong bus, but realized before I did that there was simply no other bus to take. You might think, as I did for a while, that you were in the Sixties because you needed to escape the Fifties or because you wanted to avoid the Seventies. But Fels seems to me to have avoided both traps. He was in the Sixties because the Sixties were there.

Another way of putting this risks oversimplification but makes the magnitude of Fels' achievement in this book clearer. Many of us approached the Sixties as primarily a time of political protest. It was a rebellion, we say, that was set in motion by the civil rights movement and fanned to a flame by opposition to the Vietnam War. Some others of us see the same period as primarily defined by the rise of the so-called counterculture whose key themes were the rise of communities around pot, rock 'n' roll, sexual freedom and women's liberation.

These larger themes, the political and the cultural, still seem to have been often divergent in the Sixties, and doubtless they often truly were and indeed still are. The countercultural and the political aspects of the Sixties experience did find themselves often in conflict. But what Fels' fascinating story makes clear is the way in which the themes of political and cultural rebellion, despite the seeming conflict, were in fact joined at the hip, were ultimately the same cry for the same change speaking in ultimately the same voice, confronting the same enemy, and experiencing the same perplexing mixture of victory and defeat.

Both those of us who were there and did that and those who have only heard second hand that something extraordinary happened to a lot of people will find Fels' narrative a delicious and important read.

Carl Oglesby
Amherst, Massachusetts
December 2006

Acknowledgements

Many people have assisted in the effort to produce FARM FRIENDS. Foremost are those I have visited and talked to, whose portraits appear in these pages. Others include the family and friends who have supported this effort over the years, and those who have taken the time to read the manuscript, all or in part. Brad Marion deserves credit for taking on the large project of formatting the volume itself, and Margo Baldwin of Chelsea Green Publishing the task of distribution. My daughter Sophie has addressed some of the issues of publicity. My wife Jennifer has served an important role at home, assisting, supporting and facilitating the completion of this long and complex endeavor. The subtitle for FARM FRIENDS was suggested by the New York architect Peter Coombs, whose familiarity with the territory and always ready sense of humor led him to the phrase. My thanks to them all.

Author's Note

Writing about one's colleagues and friends over a period of time has necessitated some modification in the final form of FARM FRIENDS. Some of the book's subjects chose not to be identified or named. In other cases I made that decision myself. Generally, here, public figures are clearly identified while most others are renamed or their circumstances described in such a way as to protect their privacy. The tone of the various characters, their interactions, speech and acts remain as close as possible to the people and situations I have recorded. Their identities, however, for reasons of privacy and respect, are intended to remain unknown to the reader. In all cases, as in most memoirs, both people and events are subject to the author's imperfect memory, and their representation here should not be taken as the last word on the actual history of the time they depict.

A new edition of Steve Diamond's WHAT THE TREES SAID, the early history of Montague Farm referred to in the present volume, has recently been reissued in a new edition by Beech River Books (www.beechriverbooks.com).

The papers of Marshall Bloom are housed in the Special Collections department of the Amherst College Library. The new Famous Long Ago Archive, which focuses on the extended family of the Montague, Packer Corners and Wendell farms discussed here, is located at the Special Collections department of the W. E. B. DuBois Library at the University of Massachusetts, Amherst (www.library.umass.edu/spcoll/). Its main web site is http://scua.wordpress.com. Further news and information is available at www.famouslongago.org. A number of other persons and activities related to the extended farm family can be found through bibliographic research, as well as on the web.

Preface

From 1969 to 1973 I lived on a communal farm in the hills of western Massachusetts, not far from Amherst. I hadn't really intended to live there. Like many things during that difficult, disjointed era, it simply happened. During my last term of college, returning from a year off, I was invited to the newly purchased farm by a friend who had helped buy it. Though the college term was only five months long, I stayed at the farm for the next four years.

Ten years after I had arrived I set out to find what had become of my friends from that time. The results form the basis of much of this volume.

As the time and effort for this enterprise had to be fit in among jobs, travel, and family life over a period of years, the solution to completing this work was a method in which research and writing could be pursued when possible, and the parts assembled later. The structure of FARM FRIENDS reflects this. Part I introduces life on the farm and my first efforts to reconnect with my fellow farmers. In Part II the search continues as we catch up with four writers from the farm family who have relocated to California. Part III recounts my own story after the farm and brings the narrative up to the present. Each of these sections is comprised of a series of connected stories. Taken together these vignettes and their subjects constitute an interwoven narrative which ranges over a period of nearly fifty years.

The historical intention of FARM FRIENDS is to introduce a distinct group of people affected by the 1960s and its sources, and to recount from direct observation, assessment, and their own words how they went about living their lives in the wavering shadow of that era. A corollary purpose is to suggest the significance of this group. Its varied members, brought together largely through circumstance, eventually remolded themselves to adapt to the world they encountered and to serve the larger needs they each found. The apparent differences they developed, far from separating them, reveal a cross section whose associations reach out into society, providing a representation, virtually a core sample, of many of the prevalent directions and propensities of the time. FARM FRIENDS reports on this period using the farm group as a center. Later, the life of its author offers a more complete single example of the outward, but still connected, movement of the whole.

For the author himself, the personal purpose has been to understand his own life and times. As a young member of the counterculture there was nothing else about which I wished to write. As one now older, and having devoted many years to the investigation of the subject, there is little on which I am more qualified to write. As one seeking to continue to comment on contemporary life, I have needed to work through the questions raised here to move on to other areas, to understand earlier history in order to free myself from it. The book may be considered autobiographical to the extent that it attempts to explain one person's voyage through a particular era, what he saw, and how someone of his interests and concerns adapted to survive, become productive, and remain effective through what he perceived as adverse times.

Much has been written about the 1960s; a good deal of it, as it pertains to the farm group, is cited here. In FARM FRIENDS I have not, except as necessary, revisited sources readily available elsewhere. A selective bibliography is provided to pursue these subjects further, if desired. For the purpose of background, however, a brief overview of the farm's relation to those times is in order.

In the 1960s every year, often every month, was different. Time moved quickly, change was readily apparent, and lives, careers, and events unfolded with astonishing, sometimes alarming, rapidity. In 1960, while I was still in the midst of high school, in a burst of national exuberance, John F. Kennedy was elected president. The following year brought hopeful programs to advance the underprivileged. In 1962 we faced the Cuban missile crisis. In 1963, as I began college, our young president was murdered. 1964 saw a fractious Democratic convention and a further erosion of political and social ideals. By 1966 resistance was mounting to the war in Vietnam. 1967 introduced SGT. PEPPER, drugs, the San Francisco rock music scene and the Summer of Love. 1968: the Columbia revolt, the assassinations of Robert F. Kennedy and Martin Luther King, Jr., urban riots, and the announcement by President Lyndon Johnson that he would not seek reelection.

By early 1969, when I moved to the farm, America was facing the inauguration of a president it had rejected a decade before who represented many of the aspects of political life, and continuation of Cold War attitudes, the country's educated and concerned most abhorred. The war continued. Cultural and political heroes had fallen. The country seemed bent on pursuing a trajectory of thoughtless empire and consumerism not even beneficial to its own health–not to mention its dispiriting impact on those who intentionally disagreed. Under these conditions, opting out of the system–government, economy, mainstream institutions–seemed not only sane but perhaps even necessary. Compatriots left the country or went underground. Others changed their names or adopted lifestyles contrary to civility, reason, or responsibility as conventionally defined.

Our approach to alternative life, though certainly different from mainstream society, was on the relatively sensible end of this scale. Through ownership of buildings and land we protected ourselves from economic manipulation and social pressure. By locating in the country we removed ourselves from the world of trauma outside. Living as self-sufficiently as possible, through gardening, building, and mechanical repairs, we intended to learn what was needed to survive, and how to produce it. Conducting a colorful, unconventional, relatively satisfying life, we intended ourselves to be a model from which others might learn.

Reading through FARM FRIENDS you will encounter an assortment of those who participated in this grand experiment: a group of communal farms and independent freeholders sprinkled through the hills of western New England at a time of rampant social change and stress. You will also encounter them ten years later, around 1980, and eventually, along with the author, catch up with some of them today. New friends made along the way expand the farm family into the different areas we each faced, and exemplify its extension into the larger world. By the time you have met this diverse group, I hope you will be able to place them in the larger scene and draw whatever conclusions may be appropriate about them, the author, and the world they inhabit. I invite you to come along.

Farm Friends

In nova fert animus mutatas
dicere formas corpora…

My purpose is to tell of bodies
which have been transformed
into shapes of a different kind.

—Ovid, *METAMORPHOSES*

I

In the Beginning

Chapter One

The Farm

The Farm, 1969

If we were to listen carefully, we might be able to hear the roots of the farm at midcentury. Children born in the final years of World War II were listening to Elvis Presley and Chuck Berry, and later to Pete Seeger and "We Shall Overcome," and finally to MEET THE BEATLES. There were cheering crowds to hear "I Want to Hold Your Hand" at Forest Hills, and later, smaller groups gathered at home to listen to SGT. PEPPER. In the early days of the farm we might hear Bob Dylan's turbulent "Positively Fourth Street," or "Queen Jane Approximately," or "Sweet Marie" playing out of the farmhouse window. In the background would be some hammering and the sound of power tools. Noises from the kitchen: the sounds of canning, or of a meal in preparation. Later, one warm day in spring, we would hear NASHVILLE SKYLINE, when Dan Keilly pulled up in his new Dodge Power Wagon with the first copy of the record, and the more mellow "Lay, Lady, Lay" and "One More Night" resounded through our little valley, dispelling the dark mysticism of JOHN WESLEY HARDING. As we basked in the sun and smoked our own homegrown, we seemed finally to have made it across the first river and onto the solid ground on the other side.

Later, we would hear the sound of the old hog shed coming down, and of the new summer kitchen going up with its salvaged beams and siding. There would be the sound of the animals, and then of children. First, babies squalling, then children babbling, then talking, and eventually the sound of the school bus stopping at the door. There would be Marshall walking naked in the field behind the house (no sound), and Cathy breaking dishes and plates on the stone wall out back, screaming, "We have too much of everything!" There would be haying in summer and snow in the winter, picnics, dinners by firelight, and of course our own wine, sassafras tea, and fresh vegetables, and every day fresh meat, fresh eggs, fresh bread, fresh mayonnaise, fresh butter, fresh pies, fresh milk.

The greenhouse. A small, delicate wooden structure in two sections, covered with clear plastic and glass. The smoke from the wood fire inside merges with the cold morning mist. Outside, there is a hand pump over a deep, rock-lined well. Inside, the air is steamy and smells of earth. Rows of seedlings line the benches: flats of lettuce, cabbage, cauliflower, and broccoli; eggplant, peppers, tomatoes, and melons are in peat pots. The sense of life and growth is almost palpable.

Through the windows, above the flats, bare ground and dry brown grass are visible. Moisture drips slowly over the view of the red pump outside. This tiny world is our frail lifeline. Its tight balance barely betrays the staunch efforts that support it.

Inside the farmhouse the stoves have cooled. The night fires are now only coals to be rekindled by some early riser. The temperature is raised minimally over that provided by nature, just enough to avoid discomfort. People, capable of pulling up another blanket, or putting on a sweater, are less fragile than plants, and the house these cold spring mornings is often a good deal less comfortable than the greenhouse. Waking to this chill air and the smell of breakfast, one is reminded of the fragility of our lives, of the lively tension between necessity and the effort to placate it. Living in the farmhouse is rather like camping out year-round.

In various outbuildings are subsidiary scenes. Two people in the little house at the top of the hill; one in the garage, in its latest incarnation as bedroom and study. Somewhere in the woods a modern pioneer in a tent or lean-to; possibly, in some garret or loft, guests in sleeping bags. Out back the summer kitchen is deserted, still used as winter storage. The garden plot, plowed in the fall, is still unworked. No cars have been heard yet on the road.

The farm on which I lived was sixty acres of woods and cultivated land on a rural hillside. It harbored, on an average, eight to ten people, a dozen animals, four or five cars, one of which worked, a tractor, and some farm equipment. We grew our own vegetables, raised our own meat, and kept cows and chickens. We heated with wood and fixed our own cars; we were largely, though not completely, self-sufficient.

The farm embodied the ethos of the time, that unique wedding of dissatisfaction and ingenuity that we called the New Age. We were, or thought we were, the cutting edge of social change. There was a sense of purpose. The farm was a locus, a social node through which a great number of people passed. They were of many sorts. One would teach us the simple art of making a salad by pressing salted lettuce with a rock, while another would bring tales of the declining cities, plastic and degenerate.

The farm was a beautiful place. I use the word deliberately but with care. Dinners by lamplight before the fire were an everyday occurrence. It was a chore to milk the cow, but it was one we all enjoyed. Leaning into Dolly's milk scented fur and looking up into the beams of the barn, it was hard to believe anything was wrong anywhere. We had the best rural New England has to offer: an old house, an immense barn, a community of friends dotted along dirt roads in the wooded hills, and old cars and trucks in which to drive around and visit them.

Our gatherings were full of color and music. We enjoyed our home-baked, homegrown food, and visited one another in houses we had fashioned for ourselves. We undertook extraordinary projects: John made guitars, first in his room and later in the three-story shop he helped build. Tony planted an orchard and made maple syrup in the spring. Laz took up bookbinding. Dan made films. Everyone, it seemed, was an aspiring painter, potter, or weaver. We had the freedom to create our own lives and to make a world that worked.

FARM FRIENDS

*   *   *

Life on the farm in those days was certainly *different*. It was by prevailing standards entirely immoral and mostly illegal; yet it was a full, healthy, and relatively happy existence, and enough defenses had been laid (a mortgage, for example) to make us quite safe from harm. It was a world in which ten people, sometimes more, sometimes less, came between me and my morning coffee, and in which nothing of importance could be done without a discussion. It was a large household in which no one worked—regularly or sometimes at all. We never had any money, and rarely had even the prospect of any; where it came from when it did appear was one of the mysteries of the community, part of the shared faith that bound us all together.

The farm was a novel social situation in which partners were not permanent and marijuana replaced the cocktail. LSD and the highly prized mescaline were consumed as consumer goods were not. It was in this spirit that, in the early days of the farm, before piling into an old van to go to the movies, most members of the farm sampled their first batch of hash brownies, fresh and irresistible, leaving Irv and me, who had withstood this temptation, to figure out what to do as they later stumbled, one by one, out of the theater and onto a nearby lawn in varying states of altered consciousness. We, of course, in a very businesslike manner, simply got the van, piled them all back in, and started home, though the movie was only half over.

The farm was highly anti-institutional and antisocial. It embodied the strong feeling of disenfranchisement prevalent at the time. Cars were run on outdated, out-of-state plates, and were rarely either inspected or inspect*able*. A great cheer would go up as a ham or large cheese appeared from under a heavy coat or an electric drill or other useful implement was added to the farm's supply of tools, liberated from the local hardware store. When I took one of the farm family out to dinner in my hometown, during a summer when for a little while I had some money, it was all I could do to keep him from pocketing the silverware. "I *know* these people," I kept repeating in a desperate whisper.

Revolution was in the air, and the governed had taken the law into their own hands. Although it didn't look so at the time, this was much more an American than an un-American approach. The farm family was generally well educated and knew that it was the right of the people to meet threats to life, liberty, and the pursuit of happiness by altering or abolishing institutions and to institute others in their place, laying their foundations on such principles as might seem to them most likely to effect their safety and happiness.

But the political and social ethics of the farm, while in keeping with the letter of the Founding Fathers, were somewhat different in spirit, and more resembled the public views of the reformer John Humphrey Noyes (once a neighbor to our north) than those of Thomas Jefferson. The principal difficulty with our reasoning, often overlooked in the exuberance of our actions, was that we were by no means "the people." The majority of citizens, such as the owner of the hardware store, had certainly not agreed to our strategy. We fully intended to become the people, and to educate those around us, but as of the early days of the farm, we had only the considerable social pressure often leveled against utopian communities for our pains.

Practical problems were as pressing as moral ones. There was a farm to be run and a large household to be cared for. Food had to be cooked, the fires had to be started and kept up (and often started again) if we were to be comfortable. One's schedule was largely determined by others; one cleaned up after their pets, even if he had none of his own, and did their laundry, as they sometimes did his. There were cars to be fixed, and errands to be run when there was a car to run them in.

A typical morning for anyone unwise enough to rise early during our first winter might have begun with a blast of cold air. The furnace had gone out. His first impulse would be to go and start it up. Was there any coal? He would have to see. On his way to the furnace he would pass through the kitchen. It would logically occur to him that the kitchen stove, which was much smaller and easier to run than the furnace, and therefore more instantly gratifying, and which would, in addition, provide him with breakfast, should be started first, and this is what he would do. It would probably entail splitting some wood, and that would probably mean that he would have to go outside. It is easy to see why, if the dogs had been left in and there was a mess to be cleaned up, he might have told himself that it could be left till later. And so he would proceed through these simple steps to attain in perhaps half an hour a warm kitchen, and a little later some coffee, and midmorning a somewhat warmer though never truly comfortable house. By that time he would have somehow scraped together out of almost nothing a breakfast for ten people, and helped push the first car of the day over the brink of the hill in order that one of our number might get to town to earn a little money. If he were very unlucky, he might have found that there was no coal or wood, or that the car wouldn't start—but those were the bad days.

Of course, we enjoyed each other's company, and our life was often easier because of our collective strength, and cheaper because of our group buying power. We did things together that we could never have done alone, and there was a barracks-like camaraderie. If the good for the greatest number was not always good for you, it often was; if you were not the beleaguered early riser, you stood to benefit from his work. With money little valued, you were not expected to have any, and not having to work for it, you could do more ambitious things. Having to run a household, and maintain buildings and a fleet of cars and machines, you learned how to do those things. The farm was an experience I could have had in no other way. While it hastened me along a path already marked out, it jarred me into committing myself to it with more of a sense of tolerance and collective purpose than I would ever have discovered by myself.

Life at the farm was very uneven. One day fashionable New York journalists would arrive with a Czech film director in tow, or we would be regaled with tales of hobnobbing with the great figures of the New Age—the likes of Abbie Hoffman, Jerry Rubin, or Andy Warhol; another day a friend would visit and find himself helping us help ourselves to lumber at a construction site, or dodging the cops in an unregistered car on the back streets of town.

There was a great deal of uncertainty, and there was always the chance one of us might be caught at one of our antiestablishment games. People came and went at a dizzying pace. There was a great deal of rumor and politicking. Under these circumstances, life was not easy, nor, for that matter, in relating to others, was it always easy to follow. I went away for a few days and all my things were unceremoniously moved to another room. Irv, a staunch worker with experience in truck farming, who had worked hard to plan our first garden, was traveling at a critical period and found the plan entirely changed when he returned. A happy young man announced to me that the course of his life was now clear and purposeful, that he and his ladyfriend were planning to have a baby as soon as possible. She did, but it was not his.

Tim

"Life at the farm was very different from what I had expected," said Tim, a farm compatriot of mine, now a neighbor in Vermont, with whom I share an interest in art and writing and have sat many times discussing our days at the farm. "It was different from anything I had ever experienced. It was certainly different from the previous four months, a vacation from the job I had had in my year out of school which I had spent living alone by the ocean walking, writing, drawing, and playing music. Those had been very satisfying, productive months. When I moved to the farm, I fully expected them to continue.

"I spent my first seven months at the farm attempting to establish this continuity. But after two months I was forced to recognize somewhat after the fact that there had been no continuity at all, and that I was plunged into a world very different from the ideal or in some ways even the desirable one for me. I spent the next five months trying to correct my course.

"Once having realized how different farm life was from what I had expected, I conscientiously attempted to balance my own needs with those of the farm in order to arrive at a workable arrangement for both. But this was finally impossible, and my life at the farm became for the most part a fight to simply fulfill my own needs. This was so difficult that I could occasionally forget, or at least doubt, its importance; but whenever I succeeded, I was enough reassured to continue.

"My own needs were space, order, quiet, and a pace that suited me. On arriving at the farm this did not seem too much to ask. Rather, it seemed a negative demand that did not require much involvement or sacrifice on the part of my new comrades. This was a great miscalculation. Involvement was the very currency of life at the farm. People were incapable of not involving themselves, and were very suspicious of anyone not himself

The farmhouse in snow, Montague, 1969.

wishing to be involved. I left the farm after those first seven months rarely having enjoyed the peace I was looking for, and in fact feeling somewhat guilty for even wanting it."

The battle Tim waged to get what he felt were merely the minimal necessities of his life is instructive as a picture of life on the farm. He had come to the farm under an explicit promise from Marshall, the farm's mercurial, quixotic founder, that he could build a room for himself in the barn.

"This kind of space was important to me, and always had been. I was straight from a year in an architect's office, and as soon as I arrived at the farm, I set to work scouting out the barn and drawing plans. I even made a model. Then one night after dinner I presented my completed plans to the other members of the farm family. Every possible objection was raised, and in the end I was not allowed to build. It would be two years before I could finally build a house for myself, and even then it was over loud protest.

"I turned my efforts to securing some already existing space. Eventually, after a great deal of fuss, I was allowed to convert the garage, the print shop of the farm's former radical news organ, into a studio and bedroom. But even after I had moved there, I was plagued by the spirit of the community, in the form of Marshall himself, who seemed to be saying that such a private, ordered space and way of life did not suit the community's goals. Marshall would browbeat me in his inimitable way, cleverly poisoning whatever pleasures I had managed to obtain for myself. He would suddenly appear and unscrew a hinge from my door to use somewhere else on the farm, or build himself bookshelves in my studio as if it were a public space, clearly chastising me for not seeking approval for what I had done.

"But was Marshall the community spirit? The day after my last altercation with him over the use of the garage, Laz, the youngest and in some ways the most practical of our group, took me aside to say that I should keep up the good fight. He saw every such episode as a blow at disabusing Marshall of his illusions of utopian community, and helpful in moving us all on to more solid social ground. At the time, I found this encouraging, but eventually it became just another example of the many voices whispering in our ears, and of the difficulty of sorting them out in any meaningful way."

Such skirmishes were daily life at the farm. The pressures to abandon anything but the commonweal were very strong. Sam wanted you to help foment the revolution, to which Harvey added that you must do it while eating only vegetables. Tony needed help tearing down a barn. Janice was plucking chickens; if you were going to eat them, why weren't you helping?

"In the end, it did all seem to be worthwhile," Tim went on. "Once having created my own space and lived in it for a while, enjoying a place that reflected my vision and feelings, I reached a plateau from which the view was again familiar, quiet, and settling. My thoughts were genuinely different and more congenial to me than they had been under the stress of my first few months at the farm.

"In the garage I had visions of order. I saw the landscape through windows I had designed and built myself. I inhabited a physical space that had meaning for me, and which suited my needs. Such comforts should not be overlooked. Whenever the pressure of daily life dissolved into one of these islands of solidity, I flowered. Eventually I came to see that this was why my life at the farm was so difficult. My rhythm was not only different from the farm's, it was precisely the opposite. When life was going well on the farm, everyone was busy and productive, it was a beehive of mechanics, woodchoppers, farmers, carpenters, cooks, and musicians. At these times I could do almost nothing. Good times for me were the slack periods at the farm in which there were long, quiet days that went along in some sort of regular order. My rise always coincided with the decline of the farm, and *vice versa*.

"Life at the farm was concerned with survival. Subsistence was the order of the day; but my view was by habit longer both forward and back. One had to survive, of course, but one ought not to forget why one was trying to survive. At the farm the larger view was often lost. As one who saw himself not in the context of the particular daily drama of the farm, or even of the Movement or of the New Age, but as an individual with thoughts and feelings, I felt more akin to others of my kind than I did to those who happened to be nearby.

"My view was in fact much more like Marshall's, my friend and nemesis, than like that of the others in the farm family. Marshall's dream was a beautiful and haunting one. It was simply that we should endure, that we manage to be around when the smoke from our crazy, authoritarian, overmechanized age cleared, that we be an island in the midst of dislocating and cacophonous change of all that culture and community could and ought to be. That was why he had taken the farm family to the country, not to hide from the world but to be undisturbed by it in the pursuit of its own higher goals. The world was not trusted to know how important we really were.

"This was a good dream, and there was no way for Marshall to know at that time how easy it would be to carry it off. In 1969 the forces of evil seemed amassed undisguised. Nixon had just been inaugurated and LBJ was only recently gone—the farm's contingent to the In-hoguration (so designated by our compatriots from New York, the Yippies) arrived home a day or two after I moved in. The war in Vietnam continued, and with it the draft. Robert Kennedy and Martin Luther King, Jr. had been assassinated the year before; hippies were still pariahs who were laughed at on the street. How could he have known that we who had in horror opted out of this chaotic world would be the culture heroes of the next decade; that dentists and lawyers would soon be donning bell-bottoms and sporting beards; that from our very lives would come the marketing triumphs of the future? Marshall's vision was good, but it wasn't that good.

"It is one of the ironies of that time that we did succeed, but only at a very superficial level. We inadvertently helped fuel the system we were fighting, and were unwitting midwives to fortunes made in such fields as the human potential movement, the music industry, and the media. Ten years later, thanks to the kind of resistance Marshall fostered, we had devolved to a live-and-let-live situation in which evil was better euphemized, but a life of independence and culture had become more possible. The danger was then a new one, not obliteration but indifference and isolation."

"I did learn something from all the activity at the farm, something I have always valued. I was an island within this island; but there was a loophole within my otherwise quiet life, something I had discounted that turned out to be of great importance. I would call it motion, or resilience. I saw that the house and the barn responded to use. They were not inert. Floorboards and stair treads bounced back under the hard use we gave them. When something broke, we fixed it. I began to understand the life of the various objects around me, why they were used, what could be expected of them. I saw why in nature some materials persisted while others wore away. I better understood both the eternal and the present; my expectations became better attuned to practical considerations, the physical laws and local realities underlying experience became more clear to me. I saw for myself what T. S. Eliot describes so well in the opening lines of "East Coker": 'In succession houses rise and fall, crumble, are extended...'

"Before the farm I had lived in a world of undisturbed order. Any break in it was painful, and I thought irreversible as well. But the farm involved me in the ongoing processes of life more deeply than I had ever been, and from that point on I have always felt that whatever I enjoy or produce in my own cloistered life must in some way relate to the general, ongoing processes outside that small sphere."

"I was perhaps not the ideal farm member," Tim went on one night as we sat on the lawn of the farmhouse he keeps so neat and trim, "but then no one really was. I had come to the farm more or less by chance, but so had many of the others. It was in fact a tenet of the farm that you could come by chance and stay to become a full member of the community. This was, however, a nice matter, and the fact that one had come by chance and not design, or on one's own recognizance rather than as a friend of some particular member of the community, could, depending on the situation, work either for or against you.

"The people at the farm could be divided into those who believed that they (and thus others) had come there through chance or reason, and those who believed that they had been placed there through the workings of fate. The believers in fate neglected to observe that the two were, for all practical purposes, the same.

"To those who recognized it, this distinction was a basic one, part of a mythology that entirely underpinned life at the farm. While this mythology was an imaginative and artful construct, and could at times be a pleasure in its own right, it was at bottom an attempt to manipulate facts and to rearrange them to greater than natural advantage. It was an effort to improve on the intangible and immaterial aspects of our life with the same license with which we had begun to rearrange the physical and economic.

"Thus, if one had come to the farm by chance, and as it eventuated was well liked, could fix cars, direct plays, can prodigious amounts of peaches, or fall irrevocably in love with a member of the farm family, it was clearly sensed that he had come by fate, and the members of the farm family fell in, in ranks, behind him. If, on the other hand, one arrived, as many did, with his meager belongings in a tiny knapsack, a legitimate refugee from school, parents, job, marriage, or war, but overstayed the open but tentative welcome that the farm offered to any and everyone who appeared at its door, without managing to turn it into an event of cosmic origin, or at least of an obviously functional purpose, it was just as clearly sensed that this was simply chance, and after a brief but obligatory soul-searching, the members of the farm would set him on the road again.

"The burden of a mythology that bore such an ambiguous relation to the facts was constant uncertainty and an ongoing effort to extend and redefine the mythology itself and to correctly apply it to each new case that arose. Anything falling between the poles of felicitous fate and irksome chance provoked a great many problems. Much time was spent determining which was the preponderant quality among the choices that inevitably accompanied any important decision. Jim, let's say, was a nice fellow, but he didn't do any work. Did the pleasure of his companionship outweigh the liability of supporting him? Jack, on the other hand, worked incessantly, but he seemed to be out for himself. Would his motives become more enlightened if he were allowed to stay at the farm? Such questions would be, as necessary, sifted over in a New Age version of an executive session in the kitchen or in someone's room in the hope of fitting the fact to the fancy.

"However high the ideals embodied in the farm's mythology, its effect was to act as a constraint; it constituted a negative force encouraging conformity. It was always there as a tool, an extremely malleable one, to be used by whoever, or whatever group, was the dominant force at the farm at the time. It was an unspoken compact, an unwritten constitution that could be invoked to further one action or curtail another. There was a general sense to it, but it was a sense that underwent constant elaboration and redefinition according to particular needs.

"It was difficult not to run afoul of the mythology, since the only way to really know what it was in any definite, functional way was to be among the small group who were creating it at that time. It was best to play it safe. If it was time for farming and gardening, it was wise not to be seen reading a book; when friends came to visit, it was best to hear the news. There was no coercion, it was simply that to the farm family anything outside the mythology was of no real interest or importance.

"Of course, with views like these, I came up against the farm mythology with some frequency. That I could ever come to understand and appreciate it at all, despite my natural bent away from it, is evidence that the farm did me some good. I learned at the farm what I probably would never have sought to learn: tolerance. Because of my uneasiness with my supposed freedom, I learned to see the farm for what it was, rather than what it was supposed to be; and because I could separate myself from it, I began to enjoy it, albeit as an alienated citizen. It seemed a genuine irony to me that while farm members often played at tolerating my artistic and humanistic habits from the comfortable position of group doctrine, I was perhaps, from the more urgent and necessary position of self-preservation, tolerating them."

Raymond

I had been at the farm only two days when I met the source of the myth. His name was Raymond Mungo. The occasion was one of his frequent neighborly visits. The source of my immediate interest and curiosity in him was the description he gave— impassioned speech might be more accurate—of an Ashley wood stove, a piece of equipment that over the next few years would become an intimate part of my life, but which at the time I had never seen. I was intrigued by his ability to make it come alive. He evoked its power to great effect, and spoke of it with much feeling and obvious affection. His speech, given like most at the farm around the kitchen stove, centered on the words "space heater." By spinning around them in his own special way a web of inevitability, he painted a verbal picture of a machine friendly to man whose God-given, humbly accepted lot was to fill the whole space of a room, floor to ceiling, with a blessed, benign, even heat. His listeners were left, rhetorically, to wonder: How could it have been more aptly named; how could those words have found a more perfect physical embodiment? We were spellbound.

The more I thought about Raymond's story and became acquainted with the other stories, photographs, and conversations that flowed from the collective mind of the farms, the more I recognized in them signs of personification, anthropomorphism, fatalism, and superstition. Together the signs formed a trail that led directly to Raymond. Certainly, astrology, the *I CHING,* and the tarot were in the air, and there were other inventive souls at the farms who sparred with Raymond on the high wire of verbal and conceptual play, but Raymond alone made an entire life of telling stories and writing books. No one contested his vision; indeed, considering its resilient strength, chimerical variety, and disarming pervasiveness, it would have been unwise even to try.

Raymond organized nature around man, and particularly around familiar people and places, and especially, as ultimately became apparent, himself, and gave direction, purpose, and personality to such unlikely things as landscapes, dogs, cars, chain saws, and entire nations—not that these things do not have personalities or purposes of their own, but it is helpful in dealing with them to distinguish between those we can legitimately recognize and those we attribute to them for pleasure or effect. This was a line that under the implicit sanction of Raymond, and his companions in creativity, was rarely drawn at the farms. He was consequently a principal architect of the worldview of the farms, and hence among us, but largely unacknowledged by us, a person of some power.

A month later Raymond told a second story. He was going to drive to Vermont to pick up some friends and a few belongings, then to Maine, where they would stay at a rooming house run by an old woman he knew. Early the next morning they would take the ferry to Halifax and drive to a place where he said he wanted to buy an island. From there they would proceed across Nova Scotia to the Newfoundland ferry, and thence to Newfoundland itself, where he would buy "a hundred dollars' worth" of land, or about ten acres. Then they would run through the whole thing in reverse. The story was precise, with exact arrival and departure dates, allowance for time zone changes, and the correct price for ferry tickets.

There was much in this that was characteristic of Raymond at the time. The story was symmetrical and attentive to detail. There was a fascination with information combined with an ability to present it in a novel fashion. There was an aura of inherent organization that gave the listener the sense that he was operating in a familiar world. In addition, Raymond had recently sold his first two books, and actually did have the prospect of some income. But there was one thing of particular importance: None of what he described had happened yet. There was nothing in this story, or in most of Raymond's stories of that time, to indicate that there was any contingency abroad in the world. Everything, whether present or future, was announced with the same fervent certainty as a fact. Rarely in the rush of his monologue did anyone stop to think whether the details, which seemed a sign of truth, all fit, or whether the attractive symmetry could possibly have been imposed from without and not discovered within. We all knew that when Raymond returned from Newfoundland (he was at least going to go) the tale would be quite different, but until then the old one would stand just as it was.

And why not? It was a story. "Pisces will tell you he knows something, he saw something, when he only dreamed it," Raymond said later in his book TROPICAL DETECTIVE STORY (1972), in which he attempted to come to terms with this period of his life. "He's a terrible liar." Liar, storyteller: It's sometimes hard to know the difference.

There was in Raymond's telling of history this curious mixture of fact and imagination. No amount of information accumulated from the many sources so constantly arrayed before a man addicted to communication of all kinds—talk, letters, books, magazines, the telephone, even television—could stop Raymond from seeing the world as he thought it should be. No fascination with detail prevented him from rearranging individual details into wonderfully imaginative patterns of his own design. Though he had never been to Nova Scotia or Newfoundland, he had no trouble conceiving of the trip; he saw it in great detail—greater, in fact, than was really possible. This never bothered him; in fact, quite the reverse. In all the years I have known Raymond, I have never lost the sense that his current story was more real to him than anything else, and that it transcended anything that might ever really happen.

Raymond is under the artist's compulsion to order what he sees. He is deeply humane, driven by a belief in the good. He is a tireless, indeed compulsive observer of the world around him. These do not mix easily. How could a good man tolerate the world of the late twentieth century, with its inequities, its atrocities, its daily violence, and obvious inefficacy of positive, constructive energy, without in some way seeing it in disorder? How could someone who needs to create order do it under these circumstances except by inventing it?

None of this fazes Raymond. He indulges in an occasional reinterpretation or adjustment of the facts, but he knows them better than most of us. "I can be dishonest, too," said Henry Miller, one of Raymond's heroes, "if I believe that being so I can

Famous Long Ago Archive. Photo: petersimon.com

Raymond at his publisher, Boston, c. 1970.

do more good. Vision is the thing. The world of the spirit is too vast and deep for mere honesty to be of much value." In his long orations and well-meaning personalization of the world around him, Raymond much resembles Miller, who could go to Greece (in THE COLOSSUS OF MAROUSSI) and see only himself, as D. H. Lawrence could find only himself in Sardinia. At the farms Raymond turned everything into himself, and he didn't stop there but, extending his adventures, went on to annex Ireland, Seattle, and the Far East as well.

In our little tribe Raymond held the stature of a shaman. Knowledgeable, canny, unafraid, he is a man of principles and passions not emasculated by social institutions, and with the imagination to look beyond them when necessary.

Exactly one month later (the synchronicity would have pleased him), Raymond told a third story. He had attended a conference in Greensboro, North Carolina, and he regaled us with tales of intrigue, and infighting, and of course his own role in it. Then, turning back the clock a day or two, he pictured himself on the plane on the way to the conference. In high spirits he had taken a tab of THC, and for a while enjoyed his secret double flight. But on arriving at the airport, things took on a different cast. The woman who picked him up to take him to the conference was unbearable. The drug began to wear thin, and he was off on a bad trip. They got a speeding ticket. The motel owner was suspicious of him. Two people he knew at the conference wouldn't speak to him. Baffled and confused, Raymond retreated to a nearby cafeteria. There he was sitting, sipping a cup of coffee in a strange city, when out of nowhere emerged an old friend. He spirited Raymond out of the cafeteria and took him to his own place, where there were Dylan albums and, of course, marijuana, and there he stayed safe and sound for the next three days.

This did happen in some form, but it was a very personal story told with the force of cosmic truth, a good example of the teller's ability to *make* history by assigning values to facts. This is a delicate matter, much more so than spinning tales of things to come. We have a name for people who spin tales that move too far beyond established fact. At the very least it is fatalism. "Fatalism," says Lytton Strachey in EMINENT VICTORIANS, "is always apt to be a double-edged philosophy; for, while on the one hand, it reveals the minutest occurrences as the immutable result of a rigid chain of infinitely predestined causes, on the other, it invests the wildest incoherences of conduct or of circumstances with the sanctity of eternal law."

Nothing seemed to go right for Raymond in Greensboro, and when nothing goes right for Raymond, nothing is, apparently, right anywhere. The story is a New Age parable, as were many he told at the time. It was not told simply to convey what happened, but to suggest that in what happened there was an element of inevitability. By structuring what he saw through his own feelings about them, Raymond strove bravely to sidestep the evil force of random fate.

So would we all, if we could, and Raymond is more capable than most. But the result of Raymond's influence at the farm was a highly advanced form of Pollyannaism, for creating one's own world can become a trap unless one learns the important lesson purveyed to us by the great artists, divines, and thinkers of re-creating the world *that is.*

"It is curious, considering these differences," Tim went on, "that I did stay at the farm for so long. The reasons were partly circumstantial, partly something more. On the side of circumstance, living at the farm was convenient and inexpensive. It was a continuation of the rural life I had already grown to love as a boy in Vermont. It was a way of supporting an intellectual and artistic life without having to face the hard choices with which they are usually associated. While it was easy enough to see our life as a vow of poverty in the service of our ideals—as to some extent it certainly was—it was quite clear that there was for all of us a certain amount of convenience involved. We didn't have the money to live otherwise, and were not about to go to work to remedy the situation. Seen in this way, life at the farm was very much an extension of adolescence, though we were all convinced it was instead the first step to a new kind of adulthood.

"On the side of intention, the farm enacted the principles of the time. The attempt to be self-sufficient, to work in a group, and to challenge 'the system' wherever possible were all missions sanctioned by the prevailing ethos of our generation. It was a new and uniquely appropriate place to be. When I think back on it, it is hard to imagine any other way to have spent those years."

Liberation News Service

There was nothing coincidental about the farm's mission; it was to this that it owed its origin. The farm was the offspring, by violent birth (cesarean), of the Liberation News Service, a countercultural alternative to the major wire services, founded in 1967 by Raymond and Marshall. LNS flourished for a year before falling into the hands of political dogmatists, at which point, as farm legend has it, its more humanistic members pulled up stakes, and a certain amount of money and hardware from the service's New York headquarters, and relocated themselves on the newly acquired farms. The founding of the farm is a story in itself. In his book *WHAT THE TREES SAID* (1971), farm member Steve Diamond chronicled early life at the farm and recounted its origin in the ossification of political idealism and crumbling of its organizational structure in the late 1960s.

LNS was very much of its time. "During the sixties," says Raymond, whose first book, *FAMOUS LONG AGO* (1970), documented the founding, operation, and rebirth of LNS, "people didn't have any kind of private press, or people's press, so we learned that all you had to do to have a newspaper was to have some kind of printing equipment and start churning it out." LNS took this a step further, printing after the same fashion not a newspaper but a news source from which material might be drawn for any number of newspapers.

"Even if you were a plucky lad in St. Roué, Arkansas, bravely printing the *FUCK OFF* against overwhelming odds," Raymond continued, "and you had no local writers or designers, you could still fill your little newspaper with Liberation News Service. Scores of small underground papers would be fifty percent LNS, or seventy percent LNS, or in some cases almost completely LNS, because they were out in some small town in the Midwest and had no local news. They paid fifteen dollars a month for LNS and the fucker just kept arriving, you know, three, four times a week, big stacks of stories—"

Raymond's credentials for such an enterprise were excellent. "I started writing as a small child," he says in his later book COSMIC PROFIT (1980), "a family newspaper turned out on a kid's typewriter, letter by letter. I wrote through grammar school, and all through high school and college, working for and editing the school newspapers. In college I apprenticed in the summers with the daily newspapers. By the time I was twenty-one, I figured I had already written four or five thousand published news stories."

Some of the most notable of these stories, as well as a good portion of the early fame with which he has ever since had a well-publicized lover's quarrel, date from that twenty-first year and his tenure as the crusading student editor of the University *News*, in Boston. Born in Lawrence, Massachusetts (haunt of Jack Kerouac and, earlier, Thoreau) into the large family of a Catholic mill worker, Raymond, as a college senior, turned the *News* from just another college newspaper into one whose activities were themselves news. Under his editorship, he likes to point out, the *News* was the only college paper in the country to have its own correspondent in North Vietnam, and one of the first of any kind to call for the impeachment of Lyndon Johnson. Other issues dealt with in the pages of the *News*, besides the war itself were ROTC, university moralism and paternalism, sit-ins, workers' strikes, civil rights, sexual freedom, birth control, abortion, and drugs. This sudden burst of activity was not lost on the community at large. Early issues of Raymond's *News* are dotted with pictures of him on discussion panels, local radio, and TV. A November issue of the paper, reporting on a meeting for the parents of freshmen, quotes the president of the university as asking with evident anxiety that they "not be too disturbed" by editorials in the *News*.

These are days Raymond later recalled as having been "full of youthful passion," but he was a great deal more effective than many a passionate youth. Following his year at the *News*, he relinquished a graduate fellowship at Harvard to start LNS. With the News Service, Raymond and his associates did on a national scale what the *News* had done in Boston: represent the emerging viewpoint of a new generation. Again he rode the news to a measure of success and notoriety heady for a twenty-two-year-old. In only the third week of its existence, LNS estimated that its coverage of the "siege" of the Pentagon reached a million readers; by later in the year their readership had doubled.

But by that time internal political and personal struggles were beginning to divide LNS, and Raymond and a few friends departed for Vermont to found Total Loss Farm, one of the first and most successful of the new rural communes of the late sixties, and sister farm to our own. There he spent the next four years writing, chopping wood, boiling sap, smoking marijuana, and generally declaring the postrevolutionary life a reality and not a dream.

"When we lived in Boston, Chicago, San Francisco, Washington," he wrote in *TOTAL LOSS FARM* (1970), "we dreamed of a New Age born of violent insurrection. We danced on the graves of the war dead in Vietnam, every corpse was ammunition for Our Side; we set up a countergovernment down there in Washington, had marches, rallies, and meetings; tried to fight fire with fire. Then Johnson resigned, yes, and the universities began to fall, the best and oldest ones first, and by God every thirteen year old in the suburbs was smoking dope and our numbers multiplying into the millions. But I woke up in the spring of 1968," he continues in what is probably his most frequently quoted passage, "and said, 'This is not what I had in mind.' Because the movement had become my enemy; the movement was not flowers and doves and spontaneity, but another vicious system, the seed of a heartless bureaucracy, a minority party vying for power rather than peace. It was then that we put away the schedule for the revolution, gathered together our dear ones and all our resources, and set off to Vermont in search of the New Age."

Total Loss Farm

What Raymond had in mind was Packer Corners. Whatever the eventual fate of his move there, and of the many other moves inspired by it—for what could be a clearer demarcation line for the opening of the Me Decade than a political revolutionary leaving the heart of the battle to seek flowers and spontaneity in the country with his dear ones—we have to give him high marks for his decision to live out his beliefs.

Total Loss Farm, as Packer Corners is known to the world—and the name by which it was sold to the world as well, so that in saying it I feel almost as if I am pronouncing a synthetic invention like Spandex or Gardol—was a very different sort of place from the farm on which I lived. It was only twenty minutes away by car, and in many ways, to an outsider, looked and felt much the same, but there were subtle differences between them, as there are between any two families on any block. Their family, being largely old school friends, was more cohesive; their interests, being considerably more catholic, were more to my liking. Rather than the pure work ethic that prevailed at my farm, the revolutionary fervor at Total Loss Farm was tempered with a flair for storytelling, music, and drama. Books were written. Poetry was an acceptable *métier*. I have only good memories of Total Loss Farm; of Ray in the Green Room with its faded wallpaper, walls lined with books, his feet propped on the stove, coffee in one hand and joint in the other (it was a popular pose), spinning a tale; of dinners in fecund darkness, a kind of warmth never found in the most comfortably sheetrocked home of the nuclear family; of Richard opening the First Annual Variety Show, which included music, poetry, dance, and mime: "OYEZ! OYEZ! O Yez! O Yes! *O Yes!*" Nothing like that would ever have been heard, or even thought, at my farm.

THE FARM

One could not fail to notice the unique tone of Total Loss Farm. Even visitors fell immediately under the spell. In *FAMILIES OF EDEN,* his 1974 study of communes, Judson Jerome, who at other points in his narrative proves a rather too involved investigator, paints a good picture of what he saw when he visited "Beaver Road Farm," his *nom de dactylographie* for Packer Corners:

> There is an almost mythic, tragic air about the place because of the number of poignant events in their shared past (including close relationships with several neighboring communes) and the fantasies of high-strung, imaginative members. The living room contains a stage for performance and a loft that looks like a theatrical set. Around the property and buildings are signs and mementos with evocative histories. On a pasture hill visible from the house fluttered an abandoned Maypole from their Mayday festival (a gathering of the tribe), standing askance, its faded streamers fluttering, like a prop from a Bergman film. Here, more than at any other commune I have seen, the deeper cultural dimensions of the new age are apparent, encompassing a vision of evil as well as good, of ancient roots as well as future promise and a sometimes almost unbearably intense and vivid present.

At dinner he speaks of "a sense of stories lurking in the shadows beyond the yellow light."

This is perhaps the best we can expect from a sociologist who later tells us he is sitting naked at his typewriter, but it is not really enough. Every bit of Total Loss Farm and the area around it—in fact, anything that came in contact with it—was imbued with a mythological significance. Our mythology, which was largely derived from it, paled by comparison. The myths of Total Loss Farm were vastly more authentic, and had the mythic, poignant, imaginative, ancient resonance Jerome perceived. One could not start up the long dirt road from the apple tree, a road on which every turn had its name, and which passed over the stream in which Raymond—having committed the radical act of removing his thick glasses—had seen salmon, and tuna, and perhaps the universe, without thinking of the history of Colonel Packer and his family, and of the apocalyptic Christians who had inhabited his trees at some nearly forgotten time.

There was Mt. Muste, named for the civil rights leader, formerly a mere anonymous Green Mountain, and the eighteenth century cemetery that formed the opening scene of BURNT TOAST (1972), by Peter Gould, a farm novel that comes as close to expressing the mythic spirit of Total Loss Farm as perhaps is possible. There was the peach orchard; to hear the poet Verandah Porche talk about the peach orchard, you would have thought it inhabited by Demeter herself.

An overgrown farm road that disappeared into the woods above the farm, and ran right through the dooryard, was the Bloom Highway, on which, as if from nowhere, Marshall had once appeared, bouncing down through the field toward the surprised farm family in his green Triumph Spitfire. There was Bessie the black Jersey, and a flock of Peking ducks none of which were named Mao. The kitchen after its extensive New Age remodeling—old windows, natural wood counters, a special area for baking—became the Café Depresso. On one side, for the production of butter, yogurt, and cheese, with scallop-shaped milk skimmers hanging above waiting jars, was the Culture Counter. At the center was the wood stove that had won all our hearts: Home Comfort.

Life at Total Loss Farm was entirely allegorical. Everything had a name and a significance, even if it were sometimes only whimsical, in an attempt to imaginatively possess the object, experience, or person, or to free it from the grip of the system. A Nellybelle or Amazing Grace was somehow more bearable than another car, though it was really only an old Nash or Peugot. Even some of the people had new names: Verandah Porche, Hugh Beame, and Abraham Mazo will not be found on the birth certificates of any of the members of Total Loss Farm, though the people themselves are well known and have appeared in assorted books and articles about the farm.

THE FARM

I was as comfortable at Total Loss Farm as I have ever been anywhere. I could trip or get stoned and never feel threatened; I could stay for days and not feel unwelcome. I could drop in late at night, talk to Ray till dawn, and go on my way after breakfast, and no one thought twice about it; it happened all the time.

Total Loss Farm was the frequent target for a late-night jaunt from the farm. "Well, Stevie," Jeannette would say with a look too thoroughly suffused with cynicism to be entirely diabolical, "I wonder what Raymond's doing?" Jeannette was a veteran of the underground media scene who had moved to the farm with its founders. She and Ray were kindred spirits, and at this time of night—or, for that matter, at any time of day or night—found ennui pressing her hard, and would do anything to escape the pattern of good-natured indolence she had created for herself.

Steve would look up from the newspaper he was reading, check the stove beside him, and say as if he hadn't heard, "Dig this! Walter Jones is running for selectman; I can't believe it!"

"Owning a million acres isn't enough," explains Harvey from the other room, looking up from his book, "he wants to make the laws, too."

Jeannette thoughtfully sips her coffee and lights another Pall Mall. Steve, seeing the pack, takes one, too. Jeannette looks Steve in the eye; Steve squirms. Women were key to the farm effort, in the early days often carrying out the way of life about which the men only theorized. But Jeannette is an animal of a different sort. She doesn't buy any of that stuff about wholesome goodness. There is a silence in which only the stove is heard.

"I hear Phil has just been there," says Jeannette with a studied carelessness.

The thought of the dope Phil would certainly have laid on Ray brings a faint smile to Steve's face. "Well, it's only eleven o'clock. If we go up tonight, I guess we could be back for milking tomorrow afternoon. I wanted to talk to Ray about my article, anyway," he says, enthusiasm rising. "Let me see if the station wagon is here."

A half hour later would find them in the station wagon nearing Total Loss Farm, or, if the station wagon had been unavailable, perhaps in Irv's VW, putt-putting along in the vast blackness of night in the New England woods, the weak headlights barely piercing the dark.

"Let me see if we have enough gas to get home," Irv would say. He flips off the lights for a second on a straight stretch of road; Jeannette lights a match. Irv checks the gauge and flips the lights back on. "Looks OK," he says. The gauge works only when the lights are off.

Ray would receive them in style. He'd put on a fresh pot of coffee—about the extent of his domestic abilities—and roll a few joints. Jeannette and Ray would talk till dawn, people with something to flee from and time to kill. Steve would join them until sometime later, when he would go in hopeful search of one of the ladies of the farm.

In the morning any number of things might be going on.

Famous Long Ago Archive. Photo: petersimon.com

Snack time at Packer Corners, c. 1970.

THE FARM

Hugh might be building a boat, or a house, or a chimney. Marty might be adding to his cabin, writing an article, or working on a book. There might be fruit or vegetables to be harvested, or hay to be tossed. If it were winter there would be serious amusement. One summer morning I was handed the manuscript of BURNT TOAST and directed to a hammock hung between two apple trees, where I sat and read all day. When I commented on something I'd seen from my comfortable perch, the author admired the remark and wrote it into the book, where it remains to the present day.

Of course, this sort of reality spoils one. One looks at books or at the news somewhat differently if one has lived at their source. An "almost unbearably intense and vivid present" tends to make other less vibrant realities pale by comparison. At the farms we insisted on some kind of personal link. The farms were very much an endless, but not meaningless, series of acquaintances, courtships, school friends, family, business partners, potential literary characters, helpmates, and the occasional stranger who fit.

One can wonder about the meaning of these social chains, as Joan Didion does in THE WHITE ALBUM, but one cannot doubt their reality or effect. Jean, for instance, ended up living at Total Loss Farm for a decade or more, and later settled permanently nearby. But when she first visited there, she knew no one—not a single person. She visited there because she was a friend of Terry, who was a friend of mine. We took her there. Not only was she unfamiliar with this group of people, she was a visitor from England and knew, in this entire country, only Terry. That was enough. Soon after, she moved in. After her came her sister, Sandy. Sandy married one of the family from my farm; before long, they were well established on their own land near Total Loss Farm (close, as well, to a third farm to which Sandy's husband had earlier, close ties), had two children, and were a permanent part of the community.

The effect of Jean's acquaintanceship with Terry, whom she had met several years before, in England, was to change her life and that of her sister. The effect on Total Loss Farm of my acquaintanceship with Terry was to produce another member of their family and some permanent neighbors.

Of course, things like this happen every day. What is compelling about the way they happened at the farms is their concentration. The farms were a sort of modern *OUR TOWN* in which the connections were so tight, and the collective mind so strong, that what for many would be a random, once-in-a-lifetime event—meeting a spouse or making a good job connection—at the farms came to be a way of life. The life-blood of the farms was, in fact, a concentration of the very thing its members were originally fleeing—the American, and even global, middle class grasping and moving its members about through the tentacles of schools, and urban and suburban residential settlements. Despite their alternative appearance, the farms were, at least in part, really only the latest outer ring of this sector of American life.

Marshall

By way of contrast, four years before Jean moved to the farms, Marshall had spent a year in England. He had received a certain amount of publicity, and certainly Jean would have heard of him, but they never met, nor was there any indication that their paths would ever cross. The time was not yet ripe, the fatalists would say; your own brother who sleeps in the next room may be a stranger, responds the realist.

I met Raymond when I moved to the farm, four months after its founding, but Marshall, founder of the farm and cofounder of LNS, had been a friend of mine since my first days at college.

Marshall came from an upper-middle-class family in Denver which owned and operated a large department store. By the time Marshall moved to the farm, in the fall of 1968, his older brother had already joined the family business, and certainly Marshall was expected to achieve something on a similar scale.

The family was more than comfortable financially, and although Marshall was as serious a radical as any of the period, the money available to him, and his insider's knowledge of the world of commerce and the upper middle class, played an important part both in the magic of his character and in the more objective magic he was wont to produce, sometimes willingly, sometimes for lack of initiative on the part of his comrades, often less resourceful than he.

Even in the depths of his antiestablishment behavior, Marshall clung almost blindly to a number of middle-class perquisites. He was much attached to his Triumph Spitfire sports car, which he had had since his college days. Later he was accompanied, both in the car and out, by Max, an Irish setter as high strung as himself, who played a role something like that of a neurotic suburban housewife. Together they were a strange transfiguration of country-club life. When the farm mortgage became long overdue, and Marshall managed, miraculously, to pay it, it was more than once a trip to the local stockbroker's office to sell some of his dwindling inheritance that saved us.

Some of Marshall's daring and most characteristic acts were committed with the upper-middle-class persona so familiar to him as a blind. These exploits were heightened by their quality of being conscious travesties of middle-class life in America. He had the ability to use the system to his advantage, while simultaneously parodying it. Marshall was an astute observer and had noticed that respectability rested simply on a bond of mutual trust. Wherever he could establish his respectability, he correctly reasoned, his counterparts in the system would have too much of themselves invested in his credibility to allow them to question what he did, however unorthodox it might seem to be.

The guise that often best suited Marshall for his purposes— usually the acquisition of goods or services for his various revolutionary enterprises, which was doubly good because it struck at a group he particularly despised—was that of the rising hip capitalist. Due to a quirk in the styles of the time, rising young capitalists, such as the owners of head shops, purveyors of blue jeans and velveteen suits, or dope dealers, looked very much the same as rising young revolutionaries. By presenting himself whenever necessary as a scion of the system, merely an aspiring

Henry Ford or George Romney with long hair (Romney was a presidential candidate of the time from Michigan, and a lackluster successor to the legacy of Ford), he drew his unsuspecting victims into a relationship of apparent complicity. Together they became, so it seemed, co-conspirators in the great cause of the capitalist exploitation of youth.

When Marshall drove across the country in 1969, he thought nothing of pulling into a chain motel and explaining that he was the road manager for a rock 'n' roll band with some appropriately outrageous name like the Dead Fish. He would say that he traveled a day ahead of the band. He would make reservations for four or five others for the following night, order an expensive dinner to be put on his bill and a steak for Max, and spend the rest of the evening quietly in his room. The next morning he would be off early after a full breakfast, leaving fat tips all around, saying that he was going into town to make arrangements for the concert and would be back to meet the others for lunch. Off he would go in his forest green Triumph, leaving behind him an eager and expectant innkeeper, never to be seen again.

In a letter back to the farm from somewhere in the Midwest, he described the look of surprise on the face of a gas-station attendant as he simply drove off, after filling the car, without paying. Even the anarchistic Abbie Hoffman, author of *STEAL THIS BOOK*, has been quoted as admiring Marshall as a master thief.

This streak in Marshall amounted to a flair for the daring and dramatic, combined with a willingness and an ability to manipulate others. Others did what he did, but he did it with a great deal of style.

Marshall was not averse to extending this useful persona in whatever direction was necessary. He was able to obtain a car, a truck, expensive office equipment, and certainly more callously the services of others, by emphasizing the acceptable and exciting aspects of whatever he was doing, and de-emphasizing—one might with less sympathy say obscuring—the less acceptable. When he ran a news service for underground papers, he was a journalist in the service of truth and beauty. This was to a large extent true, but not in the way his backers and suppliers might have imagined. When he needed a mortgage for the farm, he styled himself a fugitive from Marxism trying to maintain freedom from political dogma. By locating near his alma mater, he courted the support of people who knew him from an earlier, more credible, period of his life who, having a personal investment in his career, wanted to believe what he said. Again his claims were by and large legitimate, but he certainly did not mention that in moving to the farm he would be abetting a bitter feud in the Movement, which was still his cause, and leaving behind a string of unpaid bills running into the thousands of dollars.

The mortgage for the farm, a legal agreement to ownership of a house and barn and sixty acres of land at a cost of twenty-five thousand dollars, guaranteed by the vice president of the college, was certainly one of Marshall's outstanding coups. He spent a good part of the next year fending off his old creditors (and simultaneously developing new ones), but he now did so from the comfort and distance of the farm. His problem was, as always, how to explain who he really was to people he thought could not possibly understand; and, one might add: How could he explain when he himself didn't entirely know?

These were some of Marshall's more celebrated traits and deeds, but he was much more than a con man. He was a deeply moral young man. The causes to which he devoted himself, and by which he largely defined himself, read like a history of the turmoil of the times: civil rights, campus revolt, the antiwar movement, South African apartheid, the underground press, the rural commune movement. He was an organizer, a facilitator, a tireless font of ideas and energy. He was willing and able to direct others, a thankless ability but one that considerably extended his province and the scale on which he could operate. He constantly looked ahead, planning his next moves and calculating the actual results of his present actions. He was careful and often cut his corners close. He was a political animal who saw meetings, committees, compromises, fiats, and coups as a way of life. He brought to the radical camp the talents of a deeply devoted executive.

The sum total of the manipulative abilities and the moral intentions peculiar to Marshall came to resemble the messianic fanaticism of which we later saw a great deal more than we had in 1969, when such attitudes were still associated with issues surrounding the Second World War. Marshall took some pleasure in his *deus ex machina* role and imbued his companions with an almost mystical sense of purpose and understanding that overrode other moralities and even other facts. We were removed from the dreary and the everyday into a more intense and pressing world of allegory and moral purpose.

The Sixties

Marshall's principal character during the six years I knew him was that of a radical. But despite his social, activist orientation, he was a lonely and unhappy person, an outsider much more content testing a bad system than benefiting from a good one. I'm not sure he could have survived happiness. His loneliness and unhappiness were a further motivation to work for the good of others, in part out of sympathy, in part as anodyne. He was happiest when he was making others happy; he was an altruist both by vocation and by his own assertion; but this, like other forms of happiness, was more brief and transient for him than for most. It was also a good deal more abstract. It troubled him, on looking over his life, how in the service of good he had so often managed to anger people, and more than occasionally to hurt them.

Marshall was a surprise choice to become the editor of the college newspaper. He hadn't come up the usual ladder, though his organizing abilities were recognized even at the time; he was his own principal supporter. From that point on, over the next few years, in whatever he did, he left behind him a trail of distraught opponents and confused detractors surprised at his power and tenacity. Often they did not understand what he was doing, or who he was, but hated him categorically for his personal manner and his penchant for moralistic self-justification, traits that seemed to combine the best, or worst, of Robin Hood and Machiavelli.

September 1963 to June 1966, the years I knew Marshall in college, were watershed years, the opening of what are loosely called the Sixties. Students only a year or two ahead of me were still drinking heavily, partying, and taking their fraternities very seriously. Those one year ahead of me, in Marshall's class, had already begun to waver. The classes after mine were decimated by

Famous Long Ago Archive. Photo: petersimon.com

Marshall Bloom, c. 1967.

plagues barely even known to me at the time: drugs, dropping out, politics, and war.

The change first seemed to reveal itself in Marshall's class. A small group, but one much larger and more articulate than any before, remained independent of the fraternities. Members of this group helped form a committee that was the forbear of our later campus political groups, through which students began to tutor in ghettos and assist in voter registration in the South. Looking back, this seems to be the sharp edge of a very large wedge.

In 1963-64, when I first met Marshall, the campus was still quite calm. The assassination of John Kennedy in November 1963, in the first term of my freshman year, though calamitous, could still be seen as a bizarre aberration, as the assassination of his brother Robert, and of Martin Luther King, Jr., four and a half years later could not. There was, however, a quality of foreboding. At the end of my first year of college, Freedom Summer came. I got as far as Washington before my parents found me and shipped me home. I was, however, committed enough to send SNCC (Student Nonviolent Coordinating Committee) my life savings instead of my body; I think it was about two hundred and fifty dollars. Over the Christmas vacation of 1964, a high school friend who attended Berkeley played me a record of speeches by Mario Savio and explained the Free Speech movement. When someone in Marshall's class was expelled from the college a little later for smoking marijuana, it was the first I had ever heard of the substance. Similarly, and under the same circumstances, LSD.

During those years political tension at the college increased tremendously, until from what had been an undercurrent in 1963 emerged full-blown demonstrations and changes in our way of life. In 1965-66 several hundred students banded together to form an alternative to fraternities and, with the college's rather unwilling consent, were given one and later two of the school's newest dormitories for their own use. When to our naive amazement the college invited Robert McNamara to be the speaker at Marshall's commencement in 1966, a demonstration seemed a necessity. At graduation, with the Secretary of Defense on the speaker's platform, members of Marshall's class staged a dramatic walkout that, as one of the first of its kind in the antiwar era, was reported with a large picture on the front page of *The New York Times*. These actions would have been inconceivable only two years earlier, and probably for some time before that.

After college Marshall studied at the London School of Economics. Study is perhaps a euphemism. He spent a good deal of his time staging demonstrations, and made himself visible enough to draw the censure of the British press and various public figures. Reports of the LSE revolt, often impassioned, took up a good deal of space in the London *Times* for most of the academic year 1966-67.

Returning to this country, Marshall became involved in the founding of LNS and settled into what was to be his most stable period. ("Bloom Go Home," the editorial headline of one British paper had read; but it was not external pressure that had prompted Marshall's return to the States but the fact that, as The London *Times* had noted with relief, the term was over.) He seemed to have finally defined himself clearly, to have recognized his strengths and found a sphere of activity large enough in scope, effect, and necessary outlay of labor to satisfy him. He became at that point the familiar figure many people at the farm knew.

Marshall was a brilliant, tireless, and utterly guileful organizer, but his successes belied his internal instability. Like everything that happened to Marshall in his frenetic, abrasive roman candle of a career, what happened to him at the farm happened very quickly. This was a time in our lives when entire chapters were compressed into a few months. A year after his hopeful move to the farm found Marshall again without hope. Though seen at the time as the beginning of a new life, it was for him really the beginning of the end.

Imagine a city boy, an intellectual, a genuine freak with a huge Afro and H. Rap Brown mustache, a student organizer, and neurotic political revolutionary getting on a tractor and trying to raise cucumbers for profit. Marshall had no preparation at all; he just jumped right in. He had no idea how to face the problems ranging from car and house repair to growing food and dealing with neighbors that make up everyday life in the country. He tried very hard. He put an immense triangular window in the barn and made a room for himself there; but the window, hand-crafted and personal in conception, always looked somewhat out of place among the classic, graceful lines of an aging New England barn. When he built a wood-box for the kitchen, it was with a bunch of odd pieces of plywood and sheetrock nails that bent before they were halfway in. The result, though functional, was a horror to behold.

The main difference, though, between the life Marshall had been leading and life in the country, the life he thought he wished to lead, was not physical but psychological: The results of his actions were now inescapable. The basis of the dream of life in the country was permanence, community, and a strong bond to the earth. It encouraged a willing acceptance of whatever was revealed to be true and good; less human control. But one could then no longer lead a hit-and-run life. It became increasingly hard to be a Pretty Boy Floyd, a people's outlaw, with a house, barn, family, and sixty acres of land.

The transition from citizens' advocate to citizen was neither as easy nor as logical as Marshall had thought it would be. It was difficult enough, though familiar, to defend the farm from bank and state, but it was harder to defend ourselves from the changes that the farm demanded of *us,* making us at one stroke landowners, taxpayers, and breadwinners. Marshall was not ready for these.

Even worse, the commitment to place and to a small community of people meant that it was time to face oneself. It would not do to bring one's hangups into paradise, and once having moved to the country, Marshall proceeded with precipitous alacrity to explore and, he hoped, divest himself of his own personal problems. This was most disastrous of all, because as with his material problems, his personal problems once revealed tended not to evaporate as expected into the crisp country air but to point back at him all the more clearly. In the simplicity of country life, Marshall's hypertension, his fixations, and various all-too-human flaws stood out even more clearly than they had when more of his time had been taken up with the business of protest and the diffusive diversions of urban life.

I think Marshall could have survived self-discovery if he had had the patience to wait it out, for although his time to deal with his difficulties had come, their own time had not. Had he waited only a year or two, he would have found a great deal more support for the problems he faced. His irony is largely, though not entirely, one of timing. But patience was not his strong suit.

Even had he survived, more serious problems awaited him. As long as his self-revelation and his attempts to educate others were limited to experiments in nudity, using an open toilet in the corner of the living room, and the exploration of homosexuality, most of us could bear with him. But beyond this treacherous passage, had he successfully navigated it, were the more pervasive and enduring sources of these symptoms: his need for others, and for their approval and love—directions that seemed almost entirely blocked for him—and determining the sort of life he might make for himself as an individual, exclusive of the causes through which he had previously defined himself.

Marshall's next crossroads might well have been the problem of doing good itself. He was unfortunately a perfect candidate for the kind of highly demanding, misguided guru of whom we saw a great deal more in the next few years. The thought would, of course, have repelled him, but the impulse might have been impossible to resist. The farm was for Marshall not the Garden of Eden but the Heart of Darkness. His saving grace was the time, which he himself chose to cut short, and his humanity, which might well have crumbled under the strain. I think if we can see his death by suicide in the fall of 1969, only a year after the founding of the farm, as at least in part the decision not to make this sort of demand on others, or on the larger culture—for he knew the keys to the public realm—we can all probably count ourselves quite lucky. I cannot imagine his wanting to die unless not only did his own future look bleak, but it appeared to him that he might be harmful to others; he could, perhaps, see an unwanted fate overtaking him. Both this accuracy and this concern would have been very much like him.

Haying

"What seems odd to me," Tim went on, musing, "is not the farm itself but my finding myself there, and my inability to

Cathy entertains a visitor from Packer
Corners, Montague Farm, c. 1970.

Famous Long Ago Archive. Photo: Tom Fels.

imagine having been anywhere else, when only a year or two before my farm experiences there were not even any farms on which to have them.

"The coincidence of my need for something like the farm, its appearance in the world, and its simultaneous appearance in my own life, is very curious, but it is a different one than it seems. My connection with the farm was only peripherally the outgrowth of my earlier radical politics, through my friendship with Marshall. What was truly coincidental, and for me fortuitous, was that someone whose values were intellectual, artistic, and contemplative could benefit from an arrangement whose aims were principally political and social.

"It was from a sense of this incongruousness that a large part of my uneasiness in being at the farm arose. For while an interest in such things as writing and painting was professed *pro forma* by most of the farm family, and was espoused more deeply by Marshall in particular, it was for most of them something foreign. When faced with an actual person writing a book or doing a series of paintings, or any of the other patently useless things such people do, their reaction was usually not one of interest or approbation but of opprobrium and accusation. Like many other people, they thought, judging by the spirit of the finished product, that such things were fun to do, and that the person who did them was probably just a self-indulgent, lazy soul who claimed to be working when he was, in fact, looking out the window. They had no sense of what the life of a writer or an artist was like; if they had, the condemnation it would have drawn from them would have been, I suspect, even more severe and puritanical.

"For my part, I was not much better. Vegetables were grown and appeared on the table probably, to my mind, by much the same miraculous process through which others imagined books and paintings to have been generated. I enjoyed working in the garden, haying, milking, and splitting wood in a way that I couldn't have if I had been working under the compulsion of community. But although I found at the farm only a place in which I could sometimes be myself, and did not particularly busy myself with the earnest business of deconstructing society outside or constructing the myth inside, it was the only place I can imagine having been myself at all in those years, and for this I will be eternally grateful."

"Farm life wasn't all bad," he said one evening, as we sat recalling a summer almost ten years earlier. Tractors and balers moving back and forth on the neighboring hill, like the keys of a typewriter across a page or teeth along a row of kernels of corn, had reminded us of our own farming experiences. "Mixed in rather unevenly with its general flow were some of the best experiences of my life."

We had spent the summer of 1971 haying continuously through the season in Gill, Massachusetts, making use of land lent to us by the owner, who could no longer keep it up. Each time we managed to finish the eighty acres comfortably curled into a bend of the Connecticut River, it was time for a new cutting and we would begin again.

"Day after day," Tim recalled, "we ferried ourselves, the hay, and various tractors and farm equipment back and forth over the ten miles that separated us from our workplace in sallies that were sometimes gay and raucous, sometimes grudging and subdued, depending on the progress of the work. Each morning we would arrive in Gill, gas up, tune up, and then mow, rake, bale, make repairs, load the hay, and ship it back to the farm continuously till dark. Each night we would lie aching and sweating in our beds with only another day of work to look forward to. The work was so continuous and protracted that day and night seemed by comparison to flash on and off at unexpected moments. Days in themselves long and tedious seemed at dusk to have been almost nothing, and so much like the ones preceding them and the ones surely to follow that they all merged into a single span of time over which day and night reigned as implacable but somehow arbitrary forces. You could not work at night; that seemed the only difference. Sleep was not restful, it simply restored in you enough energy to get you through till you reached your bed again.

"Despite the exacting quality of the work, it was a wonderful summer. There was in the steady, unfamiliar rhythm of night and day—unfamiliar because rarely have I had to abide by it so strictly—a sense of compression in my experience that revealed nature more clearly. After so many days the similarities distilled themselves into a unity. The usual sense of time gained from a daily life of errands, meals, and social obligations was revealed to be quite arbitrary when viewed against the inexorable movement of the planet. As we pitted our finite strength and endurance against the season, the day, or the cycle of a particular weather system, we could see what the real physical limits were.

"What was true of time was also true of the land. Sweeping over it again and again I began to feel it under me and to know it through the machines I was driving. Invisible and hidden in the grass below, the earth can be clearly felt once one has the feel of the tractor or truck in which one works. The sense of it moves up through the tires and, translated into whatever language that particular combination of bolts, springs, and gears gives it, can be easily read and understood through the hands on the steering wheel or the well-worn seat of the pants. Whether one swept alone around the irregular edges of the lower fields, under the benevolent, extended branches of maple hedgerows where the air was cool and the river near, or circled more regularly on the higher land, cutting together in formation, the red tractors moving in ever smaller figures toward the center, watching one another and feeling the heat move over us in waves, the smell of the gas and exhaust drowning the sweetness of the hay, the shape and feel of the land revealed themselves, both the particular place and the overall pattern formed by the movement of water over underlying rock as it made its ancient way downhill to the river.

"As we hayed I recognized a simplicity in life I had all but forgotten, or perhaps except in the smallest amounts never really known. The work reduced our lives to the bare skeleton of the social life. The farm became a bunkhouse and cookhouse to which we repaired only for functional reasons. The tractors and farm equipment became a movable camp, a place where we met each morning to make repairs and adjustments and to plan the day's work. Each morning this place, determined by the disposition of the tractors and equipment at the end of the previous day's work, was in a new location. As we grouped in or near it, tinkering, sipping coffee from a thermos, and waiting for the grass to dry, I would survey the new field we had begun, or were about to begin, from the fortress of amassed human strength and ingenuity that our little camp represented. At these times I felt we were not much different from a band of primitives stopping briefly in the shade of some skins stretched over a tripod of spears, surveying the land as we planned how to best harvest or hunt it.

Photo: Ira Karasick

Anna Gyorgy at the farm, c. 1974.

THE FARM

"On particularly beautiful days a car would arrive and Janice, Terry, Cathy, Susan and other women of the farm (for farm life did not preclude a division of labor but, rather, seemed to encourage it) would appear with a picnic that would be spread on a checkered tablecloth laid out over fresh-cut grass on a rise beneath a shady maple. Again the tractors would be parked. These places were rooms without walls that gained through use an identity that for me was permanent and unforgettable.

"I found in the landscape a delicate balance between man and nature. Farm roads led almost invisibly around and across fields, a double track closely following the undulations of the earth, rarely raised from it or cut into it like highways. Often they gave onto highways, small tarred roads, only through openings in the hedgerow, unmarked, where the road and the field met at the same level almost coincidentally. There were entire fields that matched the road exactly and could be entered, as any rural boy knows, simply by driving off the road at any point along the edge.

"There were small fields of gemlike beauty in which even at the center one felt the power of the looming hedgerows all around, fields that were isolated and quiet and were small worlds. They were entered by a break in the trees or in a stone wall, fixed geographical and social points unconnected to any road or lane. The landscape was a labyrinth, an endless chain of these interconnected blocks. From day to day they structured our experience as they had determined for years the daily lives of the farmers who had worked the land before us.

"What emerged from these places was an order greater than the one suggested by their simple, apparently natural appearance, and my haying experiences, besides being experiences of work, were experiences of order. As I moved from field to field through openings in the trees, along roads that existed only by virtue of memory and use, and traced in lines the shapes of fields again and again, cutting, raking, tedding, and baling, I began to see in farming immemorial structures of order, a pattern, a physical record of interaction between man and nature. In fields, roads, barns, mowing, and plowing were implicit lessons, as much the result of instinct as of learning, of space, volume, line, and economy. To farm the land was to unravel its history, to retranslate its features back into the experiences that had shaped them.

"As I swept around the fields, leaving behind me as I mowed a broad, even swath of fallen grass, and beyond it a wall of grass unmowed, and as the grass accumulated in curving parallel lines repeating the shape of the field and revealing the exact topography of the land below, I experienced the deep sense of satisfaction that the revelation of order brings, a feeling only entirely duplicated when I began farming on my own several years later."

Life at the farm went on and goes on still, but it could not long go on unchanged. Despite the success of the farm in creating a life on its own terms, the passage of time led some of its family to a growing recognition of the terms of life outside the farm, and this made it increasingly hard for them to tolerate a world entirely insular, self-made, and self-justified. This discovery left two alternatives: recognition of the larger, vastly more complex and heterogeneous life beyond our own fields and woods, or jealous retention of our sense of specialness, refusing to count ourselves with the outer world, at the price of increasing isolation and anachronism. This was a genuine choice, a difference that became increasingly pronounced among us. The members of the farm, indeed all who were a part of the New Age, can be divided along much the same lines as before, as believers in either chance or fate, into those convinced that its novelties and idiosyncracies constituted something genuinely new, and those who finally concluded on the basis of outside evidence that, all appearances to the contrary, nothing was ever really new. Those convinced that farm life was part of a grand new order of things clung to it and were, and often still are, under the influence of the New Age as style—something new, however transient, under the sun. Those for whom the transience and limiting sense of style were insuperable obstacles began to take the first steps in acquainting themselves with the ancient world they had so newly rediscovered, and braced themselves for another in the unending series of changes and adjustments that any honest confrontation with life constantly brings.

"Rejecting the New Age as style was an important step to take," said Tim, "and one entirely consonant with its philosophical message. Certainly it was a tenet of the New Age to face the world honestly and directly; but for some it was apparently a great temptation to stay in the niche created in facing the world at some particular time, even long after the transformation or subtle transfiguration of the specific problems they had faced.

"The error was, I think, imagining that there was somewhere new to go, someone new to be. This was understandable in light of youthful exuberance and hope, and the transient, ever-changing quality of the age, but less and less understandable in face of the world perceived, as time went on, with greater clarity and sophistication. As one saw more of the world, it became

Famous Long Ago Archive. Photo: petersimon.com

Party at Packer Corners, c. 1969.

increasingly clear that a closed system of myth did not jibe with the world as it really was; that while we had valiantly attempted to expand the provinces of work, and marriage, and to alter patterns of purchase and consumption, activities did still fall into just such categories as these, from which in the end there seemed no escape. A clearer vision of the world outside the farm (something not encouraged *at* the farm) revealed a system formed less from malice than from a kind of natural order, less from inordinate greed than from longings much like our own for privacy, comfort, individual freedom, and one's familiar or chosen way of life. Recognizing a natural order in the world entailed casting aside, or at least severely limiting, the human blame that was a cornerstone on which much of our little world was built. One had to conclude at this point that the search for new roles had been usurped by necessity, that we would have to take roles that were real and possible as defined not by self-proclaimed sages, social advocates, and ourselves, but by human and social necessity.

"As I considered life at the farm, and the future, in view of this change, it seemed to me that a coming of age was necessary if I wanted to preserve one of the important aims of the time, voluntary subsistence living; that the effort to simplify life in one sector—usually the material—was made only in order to do something better in another—usually artistic, intellectual, spiritual or political. One had to recognize the world as it was with all its contradictions and uncertainties if one were not simply to build oneself a gilded cage.

"I continue to live on a subsistence income, but I have had to abandon my preconceptions about the New Age and rural life to do it. One of the lessons of the farm and of my own later farming experience was that not all farmers are good, all employers and shopkeepers bad, that raising your own vegetables and chickens is more expensive than buying them. The value of subsistence living to me was that it enabled me to continue to do what I felt was important; I lived this way both before I went to the farm and after I left it. If one believes in supporting some higher purpose in one's life, it is the substance and not the appearance of it that really matters. The time and means to do what is important must be preserved; the farming and long hair go out the window. It was of course with regret that I left a life of such freedom and abandon, but it was only with the thought that I was moving on to something better, to do things that could not be done at the farm—that place where anything was possible."

Adhering to earlier ideals, and making them work in the world as it really is, is a challenge a great deal more difficult than making them work in a commune or any analogous organization in which, by imposing artificial limits and encouraging only selective recognition of anything other than itself, there is a great deal more control. It is a difficulty exaggerated both by the height of New Age ideals—peace, freedom, independence, equality, honesty, humaneness, community, justice, harmony with nature—and by the success experienced at the time in carrying them out. It was very difficult to move from a sphere in which a few farms formed a world, and the presence of a supportive counterculture was ubiquitous in the media and on the street, to one in which each of us had to make his own way. It did, however, seem to be a necessity, and it is from this we must derive whatever small pleasure and satisfaction we can.

As an adventurous attempt to mold a new way of life, the farm was laudable; but in resisting knowledge and reverting to a refuge from other similar attempts, it became, as I saw it, a dangerous self-indulgence.

But, though one had to see that the world was a jewel with many more facets yet to show, it is interesting to look back at a time when one was passionately attached to a single set of ideals and methods, a modern dogma, with an attempt at a rational structure to match. The change away from it is The Fall all over again in miniature. We had lost the garden. But we had at least seen the garden; it is this that gives the experience its importance. Without the fall from grace, the gaining of greater knowledge would not have been possible. To stay would have been to prolong and excuse a naive ignorance. It is stirring to have been involved in an attempt to create the garden itself, without which the experience of going beyond it could not have occurred. Too many people live never having tried their hand at such a garden.

The failure of the farms at that time, for me, was that those who stayed gave up a knowledge that seems essential to a life free of basic misconception and open to the deepest truths. That being the complexion of the farms, the cutting edge of the efforts to live out New Age cultural ideals, with some exceptions, shifted away from them, away from the literal, physical kind of independence of farming, gardening, mechanics, and the owning of land to a more mature independence of thought and character. (One can, after all, be a Marx or a Freud and live in the city in a rented apartment.) This was inevitable. We would otherwise be in the enviable position of having fixed and relatively simple solutions to our problems—a garden, an analyst, a large bank account.

Chapter 2

New York

New York, 1979

When I left the farm I entered upon a series of experiences, jobs, and situations of some variety, as matched, perhaps, the unsettled nature of the times. I restored a New England house, worked at farming and gardening, did carpentry and odd jobs, plowed gardens and hayed fields for a living, as well as a number of less picturesque occupations. By 1979, some ten years after the farm was founded, I was over thirty, married, with a young child, and held an office job at a small college. While my life was pleasant in some ways, and satisfying, in others it seemed very different from what we had then envisioned. There was little time to do what I wanted; relationships proved more difficult over the long run than they had in the blush of youth; the trajectory of independence and social change we had planned for ourselves in the New Age seemed to have faded substantially. From the isolation of marriage and my perch at a distant corner of New England, I wondered what had become of the others; where they were now; how they had fared. In the fall of 1979, a decade after moving to the farm, I set out to see what I could learn.

What surprised me from the start was that the best place to look for my friends from the farm was New York. Many of them had gravitated there. If they weren't permanently settled, they were comfortably camped; and if they had managed even more successfully to resist the magnetic forces of the city, they at least passed through it with some regularity. As children of the sixties, my farm friends had seen themselves as different. When I knew them they had been people who had not only given up but emphatically thrown away the chance to live the life of which New York was the acknowledged capital, choosing instead a life of quiet sanity, tucked away in the country, tending their much discussed gardens. In 1969, when I moved to the farm, or even as late as 1973, when I left, it would have seemed incredible that 1979 would find a sizable portion of the farm's freedom-loving family, for whom simplicity, privacy, nature, and independence were prized above any material thing, in the world's greatest city, a crowded, class-ridden, antibiological, materialistic commercial center of the very first magnitude. But, if this was a surprise, it was only the first of many.

I found Irv at a law office on the twenty-sixth floor of a building overlooking Broadway in the financial district. Below, the tall spire of Trinity Church was dwarfed by the giant edifices of business. Beyond the roofs of neighboring buildings Irv pointed out Ellis Island, through which his grandparents had passed not such a long time before.

Irv had been a serious farmer, builder, and mechanic, and it had been with some surprise that I learned that he had later gone to law school.

"We used to say that you should move to the country, and then find some way to make a living," he said in explanation; "but it seems better to make some money and *then* move to the country."

The law offices were done in a French motif, vacuously tasteful decor that might have suited the State Department or the kind of fancy restaurant of Howard Johnson's dreams. The echoes of fashion and Versailles were remote. In New York there is a new world behind every door. Leaving the office I reentered the world of the corridor, anonymous and public. The gold shaded lights stopped with the carpet at the door.

Later I went to Irv's loft for dinner. I called, as instructed, from a corner phone in the dark commercial district in the twenties. Maggie, with whom he shared the place, came down and let me in. There was nothing so civilized as a buzzer.

We had a late dinner and watched one of Irv's law professors on TV; he and Irv were writing a book. We talked about the farm; about the Vermont town we had each lived in for several years; about his early farming days in Pennsylvania. He recounted the true story of the farm's great yellow cat, Cuchulain, who ate Susan's sandwich, made from the last food in the house, as she prepared for her first day of work, an omen of what farm life would be like. He described a midnight visit from Marshall shortly before his death, an attempt to settle his debts, Irv thought.

"I just stood there cursing him," Irv said. "It was at my house in New Salem, do you remember that?" I said I did.

"I'm just going to wait here till you're through," Marshall had said.

"So I went right ahead," Irv continued, "and he did wait."

That's the two of them, unmistakable.

Late in the evening Margot showed up. I hadn't seen her in years. She had just driven down from her place near the farms. When in the city for her regular voice lesson, she stays with Irv. They settled in. Maggie shut her door with a suggestive bang. I decamped for the subway.

I found Susan at a fancy men's shirt store on Fifth Avenue near Rockefeller Center. She was upstairs, the receptionist for the wholesale division which operates the Shirt Shop's forty subsidiary stores around the country.

If the word "lifestyle" has any meaning, Susan had created one. The life she lived in the early seventies was something new, but it had the solid backing of her own integrity and singular sense of style. It was as gossamer as her old lace dresses, but as real as the chilly early mornings in her kitchen. She was a single parent living in a house of her own that she had helped renovate, a lover of rural life who could find *nothing* good to say about New York. On Susan, thrift shop clothes became elegant. She canned, froze, sewed, and baked; she wore long skirts and painted in her attic studio.

At the Shirt Shop, Susan worked in an open-topped cubicle about six feet square, a space about the size of the one in which she had once stored her unused Mason jars. She answered the phone she had once refused to own, sorted mail, and took messages. She dealt with her public—members of the company, salesmen, deliveries—over a small counter on one side of the booth. The room of which the booth was one corner had no windows; she had only the switchboard and a set of mailboxes to look at, and the elevator from which I had just emerged.

"This is just a job for me," said Susan, opening envelopes all the while, "but Mr. Levitt is really nice."

Mr. Levitt is the company's director; he founded the Shirt Shop forty years ago and now spends most of his time on vacation.

Susan has a degree from Smith College, an MFA in art, and several years' teaching experience.

"Mr. Levitt," she says, "was looking for someone intelligent to handle his appointments."

Those who receive appointments are ushered into an office two steps up from the rest of the work area. Passing through heavy double doors, they enter a room done in walnut Formica and black leatherette, materials that, like the rayon in Mr. Levitt's shirts, have the look of tradition but are greatly more serviceable. Mr. Levitt, as he swivels in his plush chair to gaze out the window, considering the comparative merits of various fabrics, or the cut of his fall line, or perhaps his cherished program for the education of executives in the ways of toiletry and dress, looks out upon one of the richest and busiest retail areas of the world.

"I never liked business," says Susan, "but I never really understood it."

This would be a good place to learn.

Even here Susan seems herself. She is appreciated, and manages to give up very little, considering the adjustment she has made. She paints at night and on weekends; to save money she shares a loft downtown with her brother; and she happily sends her daughter, who knew only the country, to a school in which there are eight first grades.

The windows at Andrea and Jack's are an ever-changing cityscape. In the early morning, light comes straight down the crosstown street below, throwing trim and ornament into relief. Smoke from many small chimneys drifts slowly in the wind, made luminous by the sun. I count fifteen wooden water towers.

In the afternoon, the backs of the aristocratic apartment towers on Central Park West loom above, monolithic sheets of reflected sun, like impregnable ramparts regularly slitted for defense. Two hundred feet above are rooftop gardens and airy living rooms I never expect to see.

At evening, the lights go down as on a scrim. As they fade to a Magritte luminescence, the stage set below is again slowly lit. Six or eight white town-houses appear by the light of street lamps, a storybook world below the looming shapes of black. At this distance they look miniature and remote.

I open the window a few inches for air. As I step back, I notice that in this space a man would just fit. A man does fit. He enters from the left and walks across the windowsill from east to west. From eight floors up I can hear the jangle of his keys and change.

As college students, Andrea and Jack and their friend Kate were radicalized by the Harvard revolt. They lived the artist's life in Paris. Andrea and Kate made a cameo appearance in one of the early books about the farm.

Andrea and Jack are now married and living in an apartment they own on the Upper West Side. As an editor of one of the most prestigious literary journals, Jack reviews and reports on important cultural figures to a national audience, a role for which, as a Harvard graduate and Rhodes Scholar, he is eminently well prepared. His office is being automated: no more erasures; no more typesetters. The thought of the lost jobs bothers him, but the change seems unavoidable.

Andrea gave a jolt of surprise when I asked to visit her at the hospital where she is finishing her medical training.

"No one has ever visited me at the hospital," she said, shocked, "not even Jack." Her reaction was divided between pleasure and skepticism. She wasn't sure there would be enough for me to see, she said in that way doctors have of describing medicine as if it were entirely inexplicable.

Certainly, the hospital was a different world. I entered behind a man who was unmistakably yellow. Faces in the crowded waiting room were anxious, attempting to master unfamiliar feelings and mask those less pleasant.

"They say he'll pull through," a woman says. The small group gathered around her looks skeptical.

This is Memorial, entirely cancer patients. Blackboards on each floor list patients on a scale from A to D, according to what measures are to be taken in the event of an emergency; D is little or nothing. Fifteen years ago, Andrea made her last visits to her father in this hospital. I remember a grateful poet saying once that a memorial hospital is a sign that points two ways.

The building is very new and clean. As we head from the elevator to the collective office of the doctors and nurses on the twelfth floor, a beaconlike set of windows with the seriousness of an airport tower, we encounter a woman tossing and complaining uneasily on a rolling bed stationed in the hall.

"Why hasn't she been moved yet?" asks Andrea.

"They're still out to lunch down there," answers a nurse.

" Call again." When we come back, she's gone.

We enter the tower. Another intern follows closely behind us.

"She's coherent, you know," he says, apparently continuing an earlier conversation about another patient.

"Yes," says Andrea.

"The family still thinks—" he goes on, but breaks off inconclusively. "But they haven't seen her," he goes on, his voice trailing off again.

"Have you thought of calling the family?" suggests Andrea, breaking an invisible, but apparent impasse.

"Good idea," he says. "Good idea!" he repeats, surprised and relieved, and steps to the phone.

As we leave the tower for lunch, we encounter an erect, grandmotherly figure. She has forsaken her porch rocker for a wheelchair with an IV bottle rigged up above her head. The equipment has a look of depressing utility and permanence; it will certainly outlive the patient. As a human figure against the blank, neutral hospital wall, she seems powerless and fragile; Goya takes over from Norman Rockwell. A few words are exchanged between doctor and nurse and we go on. She remains very still.

As we return from lunch, a nurse approaches Andrea: What to do about Mrs. B.; she's not used to solids.

"They're sending her home," says Andrea with annoyance. "You'd better see what she can take; there are no IVs at home, you know."

"Oh, yes." The nurse looks distressed. Doesn't look good for Mrs. B.

Jesse, our busy writer friend. First breakfast: Over hotcakes at a luncheonette on Columbus Avenue, he reads a sketch I have written of him.

"Good," he says; "good...excellent...yes!...You've got it just right. That's just the way I was—until last week."

Jesse: Second breakfast. We are invited to Janet's. I've never met Jesse's girlfriend. She has a tiny apartment near Andrea and Jack's and not too far from his own. At the top of a long flight of stairs is a living room. There is a small grand piano with a vase of roses on it. With the open window beyond, it looks like an early Matisse.

Janet is almost as gregarious as Jesse. We laugh our way through eggs, bacon, coffee, croissants, orange juice, and stories of old friends. She promises to read the sketch herself.

"I know I'll like it," she says, and I know she will. "I promise it an A. I have gold stars, too."

Late in the day, as I head back across 59th Street on the bus in the gathering evening, the trees in the park are a dark, romantic tangle recalling the charcoals of Seurat. Black shapes against the mauve, gray, and white of a winter scene suggest a delicacy and complexity in the city that I hadn't been aware of from afar. I feel New York growing on me. Idly I multiply the offices and apartments I have seen times the number of floors of various buildings and feel I have a better idea of what the city really is.

On an impulse I stop to see Alex, a friend of Terry's and visitor to the farms, at her midtown publisher's office. Up the elevator to the Nth floor. Step over an impromptu after-hours meeting: "We can't put it all aside for one book…" is all I hear. One book, I repeat to myself.

Alex is good enough to make time for me unannounced. We talk about publishing and writing, as we have for the past several years. Before I go, she takes me to the office of the editor in chief, who has gone home for the day. She quietly switches out the light. Suddenly, as if a curtain has been pulled aside, New York appears through the corner window wall: lights, and lights, and lights; bridges, buildings, and streets stretch before me in glittering profusion. It is breathtaking.

That fall and winter I made several more trips to New York. I had been told that Jesse's annual Halloween party was not to be missed, and one afternoon in late October I drove down for it.

At Jesse's small but dignified Upper West Side apartment in the Apthorp, disco blared from the stereo and there was hardly room to stand. The theme was Villains and Victims. A newly released film that aficionados said would never get out of New York was a victim: a woman wrapped in film accompanied by an ineffectual-looking man—her distributor. Another victim was simply a bride; women's liberation was still alive and well. Jesse and Janet were the blood-spattered murderer and victim of whom he had written in a recent article. A writer I knew who had just sold his first paperback and movie rights was there. His costume consisted of only a delicately drawn scar on his neck. It was somewhat unnerving. Some had gone to a great deal of trouble, others not. It was said not to compare to last year's party, when the winning couple came as the World Trade Center, and Paul Simon and Joni Mitchell were there.

Jesse, however, seemed quite pleased.

"Your piece on Jesse was perfect," said Janet.

"I don't mind if you use my name," added Jesse; "just spell it big."

The next morning found me on the guest bed at Andrea and Jack's. The phone was already ringing. I was reluctantly given another few days. Jack found six hundred dollars of uncashed traveler's checks forgotten in his desk. Feeling I had stumbled into an alien world, I made my way downtown.

I met Irv at his office for lunch. Lines were long at his favorite yogurt and salad bars, so we grabbed shish kebab from a street vendor he knew and ate as we walked. We looked at the architecture of the Wall Street area, and compared the merits of various new buildings. Irv expounded on the symbolic statuary of the old Customs House, and pointed out the Downtown Athletic Club, where he swims and works out.

After lunch he called his office, but found he was not needed. He wasn't needed later in the afternoon, either, nor was he needed in the morning. When I considered the tidy sum he was being paid each day whether he was needed or not, I thought law school hadn't been such a bad idea.

Real Estate

At 2:30 Irv had to be up in the West Village with Phil. Together with some others they were looking over a nine-story commercial property. Phil needs space for his business, Irv wants a place to live, others simply want to invest. This was the first I had heard of Phil in some time, so I went along. Phil had been a school friend of Jesse's and several others in the farm family. He had been a familiar visitor at the farm and was now a firm member of the farm family in New York.

Irv and I arrived first, then Jonathan, an architect and neighbor of Irv's whom he wanted to involve in the project. We were joined in short order by the superintendent of the building, and a representative of the owner. A minute later, Phil jumped out of an unmarked cab. He wore his graying hair and beard neatly trimmed; his tweed sports coat and clean Levis bridged the gap between the formality of business and his independent personal style. Phil and Jonathan were introduced and we went in.

Enthusiasm was high on the part of all involved, with the exception of the architect, who appeared dour and suspicious the whole time we were in the building; but it was Phil who was the most obviously engaged. With an incredible, though entirely unself-conscious, display of energy, he literally ran through the building. From top to bottom, from floor to floor, he disappeared around corners and into distant rooms long before anyone could catch up. He saw everything. He poked into bathrooms and closets, and when we got to the roof, he climbed to the top of the walls and peeked down on all four sides. The result of this burst of energy was quick comprehension. Much of the building was currently unused; the rooms were mostly large, if not vast. Unlike an apartment building with its many tiny spaces, it was not hard to get a good picture of it as a whole. He liked it.

After looking at the cavernous ground floor with its thick pillars and giant bays where a semi was being unloaded, we went up to the roof, then worked our way down again to the basement. The top floor was being used by a rehabilitation program. To get from the elevator to the roof we had to move through groups of helpless, retarded adults who acted much like slow-witted teenagers. Some were making and packing candles, but for the most part they were milling around, talking, and holding hands. They presented a strange scene. I've rarely felt more out of place than I did moving through this throng of otherworldly people, under the gaze of their curious, unveiled eyes, with a group of well-heeled men who intended to take the floor right out from under them. No one asked us what we were doing, it was so obvious that we knew and that, whatever it was, it was far beyond their control. We could as easily have represented the city, or the government, the army, or the mob as the owners of the building; it was all the same.

The view from the roof was open to the north and west. The Hudson was visible nearby, the cityscape quite open. The building was relatively new, built early in the century, perhaps in the twenties or thirties. It was of yellow brick and designed in a streamlined, modernistic style reminiscent of the Johnson's Wax tower of Frank Lloyd Wright. There were windows on three sides, with a good deal of light near the edges. The west was a blind, abutting wall, though whatever had been there had been torn down to make room for the playground that now took up the rest of the block. We inspected the roof itself, on which we were walking, then the water tanks and sprinkler system that were housed there. Phil was pleased, and said he'd heard that the sprinkler system was particularly good. Irv and Jonathan nodded in accord.

The seventh floor was a large, empty space, its old cedar paneling painted a dirty pinkish white. The scent of a perfume company lingered in the air, though there was nothing more than an old handbill to indicate that it had ever had any existence in the material realm. Jonathan continued to be skeptical. Phil continued to run around. Irv pulled some papers from the inside pocket of his comically ill-fitting suit and retired with Jonathan to a sunny window to discuss the building's balance sheet. The building was losing money, but as Irv pointed out, it was only half rented.

In the basement we noted the ample electrical service and the six-inch gas main. (By contrast, a typical residential line from tank to home is about one quarter of an inch.) The building was evidently well kept. The boilers were beautiful and clean.

We split up to discuss matters in private. The real estate man stayed with the superintendent; the rest of us went outside.

"What do you think?" Irv and Phil asked Jonathan.

To everyone's surprise, Jonathan produced a set of drawings of the building he had made for an earlier client. His whole act had been a ploy. He was already familiar with the building, and many of its advantages, as well as the problems that it posed. They discussed restoration, square footage, co-op, rental, building codes, and historic districts. The architect who when in the building had found only fault, allowed as how it was actually worth twice the price that was being asked.

"Seriously," he said, "I know fifteen people who would like to buy this building; but where are you going to get the money?"

They talked mortgages, refinancing, and investment.

The money was no problem, said Phil; he already had it. But he represented others; what would the return on investment be?

It was good. It looked, in fact, as if the building would be paying for itself in short order.

"It's not a bad buy," Irv said to me later, hopeful, as we headed for the Village for some coffee and a place to sit down and discuss what we had seen. "It's small, but it's very nice."

"What does it cost?" I asked.

"Two million," he said.

We broke up on a positive note. Jonathan and Phil—still running—went off in a shared cab to their next appointments.

"It's hard to get hold of Phil," said Irv. "He's so busy it's hard to even reach him on the phone, much less get him to go somewhere."

I guess two million brings him out, though I noted he could give it only an hour.

We found an Italian cafe and ordered coffee and pastry. "I like to walk," said Irv, as I recovered my breath. He spent his time looking over the women in the cafe.

According to Irv, Phil will be getting together most of the money. Irv wants to put in only a borrowed $25,000 in order to have a share in it, and to secure for himself a place to live.

"'Only?'" I asked. "'Borrowed'?"

"Sure," said Irv." That's not much. I can get as much as I want on credit."

He also wants to help his friend get a building. This is his deal. He found the building and has made most of the necessary arrangements. For putting it together he will be paid—if it goes through—a percentage of the cost. I saw that he is less involved as an investor than I had thought at first, and more involved in a procedural way, as a lawyer. A few deals like this, I thought, and he can stop going into the office at all. A year later he did.

Phil

I was not entirely surprised to find Phil on the New York business scene; but to fully accept it, some changes in my picture of him were necessary.

When I had first met Phil he was a bear of a man: heavily built, tall, wiry, and strong, his hair had been down to his shoulders and his face covered by a bushy, unkempt beard. I never saw him wear anything but a T-shirt and dirty Levis, and a pea jacket in season. He drove an ancient Volvo and was well started on his new vocation: selling marijuana.

Phil was then as unlike the well-heeled undergraduate he had only recently been as was possible. At first this metamorphosis was difficult to grasp, until the underlying law revealed itself. When the Ivy League accepts you over your competition of six to ten others, it does so only after a great deal of consideration. Men are paid to sit in offices, have meetings, lunches on expense accounts, make endless phone calls, and write numerous letters, just to sort people like Phil out of the batch. When the Phils do change their minds and decide to do things differently, you can be sure that they will do it with the same energy and ability that impressed these men, with the same canniness they used to excel at high school and do well on the college boards, and the same aggressiveness that helped them become head of the student council or captain of the hockey team.

Phil was, then, not just a freak but a freak with intelligence and drive. He liked what he was doing, and was willing to take calculated risks to increase his profit or his knowledge. He was not afraid to work, and his business quickly grew; he soon became one of Boston's largest dealers.

While Phil has always maintained a strict privacy about himself, he had at that time a sense of gallantry and good spirits about him that was common to a certain brand of dealer. He was aware of playing a part in the times, helping people learn and enjoy themselves. He himself enjoyed the satisfaction of beating the system at its own game: making money.

But while making money may have given Phil the impetus to go into business, it was only one of his real aims. For him it was bound up in the more challenging problems of learning to operate a business. Indeed, Phil made so much money, and was so unprepared to spend it, that it became something of a problem for him. The necessity to use it eventually led him to a larger project, and a more extensive education than had come to him through dealing.

Phil had his own interests; he made records, he owned some land, and he helped support his girlfriend and her children. He could be generous and public spirited. At a time when many of his friends were living hand to mouth, Phil always had a roll of bills, and could often be persuaded to part with some of them. Though in some ways a hip capitalist, he was also a dealer of the Robin Hood stripe who saw himself, as did many others at this point in their lives, as midwives to change, making not only money but history.

When enough money had accumulated, Phil saw that he could usefully expand his province. By moving to a larger, more public scale, he could recycle his money to create jobs, which would create goods and services that were both necessary and beneficial; the whole thing would keep itself going, and turn a profit as well. He had learned the cyclical model for a small business.

Phil brought some partners together, other dealers, for he didn't look so well off when he saw what was invested in even a small business, and bought a storefront, which he converted into a restaurant and bakery. It was named after a passage in

Confucius. The organization of this enterprise was an education in itself. High purpose didn't seem to create the picture of social harmony he had envisioned; in fact, it didn't seem to change anything. People weren't always to be trusted; there were endless changes and delays; poor work had to be redone and newly discovered regulations met.

Beyond the administrative, managerial aspects of putting the place on its feet, it was this experience with regulations that heralded an important change in both Phil's knowledge and his abilities. It involved him in a new, public level of activity.

In the world of dealing, Phil had had a great deal of personal control. Deals were made between individuals, and the rules were made up as you went along. In going aboveboard, his control was diluted; he had to go through the usual and proper channels: You could not run a restaurant on a main street in Boston without the right pieces of paper on the wall or in your files. These public channels wrought a surprising change in Phil. Suddenly he had an interest in meeting health and building codes: He needed them to get where he was going. Here was the hairy freak, the dope dealer, going down to City Hall for a plumbing permit. This was a change!

Phil was open to other ways of meeting the regulations as well, and this his rural friends found even harder to understand. In the country, where we still used outhouses and drove cars with plates that were handily out of state and out of date, we built without permits and flaunted our disrespect for local authority. Phil, in his cellar office, where crates of dope were mixed invisibly in among the building and food supplies, was simply paying them off.

We were shocked that Phil was paying off building inspectors, but we weren't shocked for the right

The name of Phil's restaurant in its original Confucian form.

reason. The problem for us was not that it was wrong but that these were representatives of the system, and that he shouldn't have been cooperating with them at all. It seemed to us that Phil had gone over to the other side. In fact, he was on the fence; looking too straight to his friends, he was also acting too loose for the comfort of the government.

This must have been a difficult time for Phil, yet it was also very instructive. Having been, as a dealer, on the wrong side of the law for the purpose of doing good, he was in an excellent position to see the arbitrariness, the moral unimportance of regulations and inspectors. He must have seen long before most of us that he would have to take the world as he found it, no matter how it looked to anyone else. Unlike the rest of us, he was forced to face something that was essentially just a mirror image of himself. Naturally, understanding their position from his own experience, he was willing to excuse the inspectors, to see them as people trapped in a system, rather than embodiments of it. Phil's friends living in the country, an environment over which they had a great deal more control, and which in its insularity protected them from having to move outside their familiar sphere, remained mired in their own system: alternative living. They were parochial, still largely unwilling to give others the benefit of the doubt that they themselves demanded. At the point at which Phil saw beyond the labels imposed by his subculture and began to do business in a real world with real people, he became genuinely more aware than many of his peers.

At first it seemed ironic that a dope dealer—and a successful one for whom a fifty-pound order seemed nothing out of the ordinary—should be the first among us to do business with the city and the government; he seemed to us the least likely person to be cast in this role. Certainly there is a genuine note of irony. On the other hand, it made so much sense that it is odd that we didn't catch it at the time. The dope business was, after all, just a business, and business was an enterprise to which Phil was eminently well suited.

On consideration, Phil was operating far outside the sphere of many of his peers. He was an entrepreneur of the classic stamp to whom independence, initiative, and risk were a natural way of life. His true peers were the few others in our large group who, like Phil, ran resistance for us, people such as Raymond, Marshall, Sam, and Dan who broke ground, and were always on the front lines making arrangements, signing papers, and making things work. In some measure they protected and insulated us. I think they understood and enjoyed this role. Of course, it was these people, who dealt so much with the outside world, who were the first to understand it. They could hardly have overlooked the discovery that the world outside was more real than the subculture they were helping to run, or in some cases even to create. They learned more about that realm than the rest of us; they became something of a countercultural managerial class. Because they were involved in the antiestablishment activities of running the counterculture, it was hard to grasp that behind their actions was a sense of political, social, and economic reality, and an ability to cope, that was central to their characters, and was more important than the alternative appearance of their lives. Beneath their actions, unorthodox by general standards, were motives and abilities that were really quite conventional.

Looking back, it was those who were the farthest out, who pushed as hard as they could, and tested the system the most severely, who were the first to come home to it. (Indeed, where else could one have gone; where were the others going?) In order to go farther, they had to seek out the standards to which they must conform. They pushed, and pushed, and finally broke down the wall. When they got through to the other side, what they found was not very different.

Phil functioned well in this new world. For a while he managed to survive in both worlds at once, dealing both food and dope. Finally, perhaps unjustly, he got busted, driving in his carefree way with a big bag of pills under the seat of his car. (Once when we were driving in Vermont, seeing a flashing light ahead of him, he jammed on the brakes, grabbed a big bag of grass, and sprinted for the woods, where he buried it under a rock. How many such bags are there around the country?) He stood trial, was convicted, and went to prison. When he came out, he went straight. He is married and runs his business in New York and is still the success he always was.

Others did not function as well as Phil in this new world. For some of these leaders (they would have resisted the label) the breakthrough to the real world was something of a shock. With all their energy geared to resistance, they were unprepared for the rather commonplace, inoffensive world they found outside the youth cult. Like Marshall, they broke down, or ceased to function in a useful way, when they found that there was no one to blame, or managed to perceive the true magnitude of the ingrained human problems they had set out to resolve. Often, like Raymond, they couldn't adjust to doing things "right," it was so much easier than what they had been used to, so much less energy was required.

Another group chose to continue to resist. They used this plateau of understanding to reembrace their earlier ideals. They stopped worrying about the police peeking through their windows and began to concern themselves with larger, more general social issues: politics, health, education, energy. Here their strength, resourcefulness, and expertise could again be of use.

Phil's colleague Pete belongs to a third group who continued to function successfully much as they had ten or twelve years ago. Marshall had championed Pete, along with Sam, Dan, and their friends, as earnest, hardworking young people. They had all met at the college, where Marshall in his senior year had been advisor to some of them as incoming freshmen. Though only three years his juniors, they appeared to him to be a whole new generation who would live out the revolution he had helped to incite. To them drugs, sexual freedom, and the new rural lifestyle were established facts. His relationship to them was almost parental.

Marshall would have been proud of Pete's success, his wiliness, and his ability to survive outside the system. He would have understood his human complexity. He would also have differed with Pete about many things, and would certainly have spent a good deal of time trying to convert him to more humanitarian ways.

Pete

Following our foray into real estate, Irv and I spent the evening with Pete at Irv's loft in the East 20s. It was November first, Bloomsday ten times over, the anniversary of Marshall's death, and we filled the time waiting for Pete by reading extracts from Marshall's journal, which had been typed up and distributed to his friends after his death. Later we were joined by Priscilla, a friend of Pete's who had come over to see him.

In 1979 Pete was still a major dope dealer. When he arrived, I saw that he was unchanged. He was loquatious, charismatic, energetic, and committed as he was in the days when he and Phil and Sam had all been close and seen themselves as harbingers of a new age. He is, in fact, much like Sam; they even share many of the same gestures. If you met them together, you might take them for brothers.

He walked right in and quickly made himself comfortable: The loft had been his before it was Irv's. He unpacked his briefcase and put neatly on the table a bag of Colombian marijuana, a biography of Meyer Lansky, and his address book. For the rest of the evening he was, on and off, at the phone proceeding with his business.

Between the shuttling of the phone between him and Irv— dope on the one hand, real estate on the other—Pete talked about life in south Florida, the dope business, and the coming of the revolution. When he was not on the telephone, or talking to me, he was talking to the others. We smoked some dope and snorted some coke that Irv had. The conversation that evening went something like this: Pete would be able to get together 25,000 pounds of marijuana in South America, but to do it he needed a DC-3; could Irv find him a bank? For various reasons Irv couldn't;

I think he pled that the climate for small loans was poor and interest rates high. Priscilla needed money to complete a radical educational film on economics, but Pete made out that he was broke. Later, though, he offered to fly her out to California so that they could hear Bob Dylan and Fleetwood Mac; he thought they could get backstage. Irv spoke enthusiastically about the building he and Phil were looking at, and talked on the phone to his connection inside the company that owned it. Priscilla turned herself on for Pete, but he didn't seem interested.

As the evening wore on, we talked more, and played more records. I asked Pete about his busts and the danger of his business. (He had been surprised at gunpoint by police at a suburban home he was using for a warehouse. Irv mentioned to me once in passing that he had lost a plane, as if it were a normal part of his business.) He shrugged it off, willing to take the risks. He held up his Meyer Lansky book the way a TV preacher might hold up a Bible, and told us all at some length what an amazing man he was. He showed me his own passport, so many times stamped with Colombian visas that he would soon, once again, have to get another.

I asked what he would like to do when the tension was finally over. He had at least admitted that there was tension, and made reference to the severity of penalties for "habitual offenders." He pointed out that he and Phil shared the experience of harassment and jail. "They tried to break our spirits!" he said with great emotion.

"Sail and dive," he said. "I'd like to play a lot of tennis, maybe write like you, or get into politics. Maybe I'll help Sam out, or some other good cause—really get involved."

All this frenetic, crazy, manic activity just to sail and play tennis? Politics—on dope money? Writing?

Pete is convinced he knows what's happening. "I know what's happening," he said again and again; "I know, man, I *know!*" He is convinced that the revolution is coming. He sees a lot of people in the course of his work, and feels he has a hand on the pulse of the land: Dope is spreading everywhere; people like it. They aren't voting, it's true; they're waiting for someone to vote for—someone like Sam!

Pete envisioned a spreading of New Age spirit that sounded, unfortunately, very familiar.

"First someone says, 'OK, it's going to work'; then another, then another." They all fall into ranks, and that's it; it's happened.

I reminded him of some of the problems of large groups, the Second World War.

This was different.

"You have to commit yourself," he said again and again.

I had doubts.

"That's OK, Tom," he said portentously; "that's what I expect at this stage."

Irv and I went to play ping-pong. In the huge loft the ping-pong table was barely noticeable. We worked ourselves into the game; it was sort of a dance. "When ya gonna wake up?" asked Bob Dylan again and again from the tape machine in his raspy, nasal voice. Pete was walking around doing a bass-guitar routine, as if the music couldn't really go on without him. Priscilla sat on the couch and watched him. We were all peaking on the coke and feeling good. I was sure this was the place for me to be on Bloomsnight.

I was watching Pete, too. Here was someone who had long ago handled more money than I would see in my lifetime. He seemed happy mixing business and pleasure. He had just flown in from the Florida Keys. He spent his time between his friends and his business, the phone and the music; there were the marijuana, the cocaine, and the wine as well. He was in very familiar territory. He made a lot of coded calls: "Hi, Phil? Can you come over? Bring your friend Rudy, too." We were already reeling from the effects of "Rudy" and smiled at his bag of tricks.

As a life of business, it was very pleasant. Pete is one kind of New Age executive: entertainment and pharmaceuticals, controlled substances. He spoke a lot about traveling, friends on the Coast, a party in Denver, back and forth to South America; that is really his life. As a life of pleasure, though, it was fraught with pitfalls. The business was really more important. He seemed isolated and remote.

Pete also had bits of news I needed to complete my picture of farm people in New York.

"Phil *believes* in Tim Leary," he said at one point; I later found that they were developing a close relationship. Then he told the story of how he and Irv had tried to persuade Sam to go to law school. Irv would have helped him get in; Pete would have paid. He wouldn't go.

"That's too bad," I volunteered, remembering some of my own conversations with Sam about the challenges of being effective in the public, nonalternative world, and missing the point entirely.

"No, no," said Pete, "he didn't *need* to go. He knows it all; it would have been a waste of time." To my surprise, Irv agreed. He said he'd had to study very little to get his degree.

We talked about the three-record set from the MUSE concerts, hopefully a solid fundraiser for the antinuclear movement. Pete and Irv are both peripherally involved in the development of MUSE (Musicians for Safe Energy), a protest group that is an outgrowth of farm activity. During the week of the concerts Pete had rented the entire penthouse of a downtown hotel.

"It'll be out by Christmas," said Pete.

"How could it?" said Irv. "The concerts were only in September."

"I don't know," said Pete. "I read it in the *Rolling Stone.*"

The subways closed, I finally found the right bus and was back uptown by 1:30.

In the morning I met Irv at Zabar's, a block or two from Jesse's. It was packed. After a brief tour of the store, which Irv thought essential (he considers himself my teacher in the folkways of New York), we piled into his battered old yellow station wagon and headed off to various errands. Later, after a brief stop at Irv's we picked up his friend Val and her grandmother and took them shopping as well—a set of tasks and *dramatis personae* that would help shape my next two days.

Irv

Of all the people I met at the farm, Irv was among the most congenial and interesting. He was resilient and adaptable, qualities which were a tribute and not a threat to his character. He had few preconceptions about himself and was a good and forgiving judge of others. It was impossible to fit Irv's ideas and experiences into some single and appropriate conception of the real person that he was, and he seemed to accept this, even to like it. He was the willing embodiment of impossibility, an improbable figure, a walking enigma.

Irv was short and heavy. He usually wore dirty jeans and a gray sweatshirt, and was himself often gray either from fieldwork or from farm machinery. But this was only a guise, for issuing from his mouth, in a difficult to identify patois perhaps associated with his Long Island roots, laced with Ds for the more recognizable *th* (dis, dat) were learned and imaginative statements of a high order. Stopping his work on the transmission of his truck for a minute to take a break, or perhaps just because he had something to say, Irv would hold forth on politics, psychology, religion, or history. His opinions were not only interesting but formidable. In his slow-moving way, he would patiently explain some aspect of Marx or THE BROTHERS KARAMAZOV, a twinkle in his eye, as he shook a thick finger at you to emphasize the point.

It was from this disjunction of appearance and substance that Irv had originally gained notoriety. In the superficial world of the college, to which we along with a number of others at the farms had gone, a freshman who quoted Bakunin, Kazantzakis and Jung from memory was enough to send most of the rushing chairmen packing. But Irv was not a bookworm. He was observant and thoughtful, and reading was only one of his interests. He was difficult to categorize, but that was part of his appeal. Irv was never satisfied with only half the truth, and despite his demeanor turned out to be a great deal more than a mere curiosity.

As Irv became better known, he was sought out by a different sort of people from the fraternity types who had assumed that he was destined for the front line of the football team. These were people who recognized his abilities, humor, and depth and became his friends. It was through these later friends that I heard of Irv.

These were peers from college, most of whom I have rarely seen again. But in the time I knew Irv, he did make two friends of whom I saw a great deal. Irv is not one to go only half way, and when he came under the influence first of Greg and then Aaron, it set him on a track that carried him along for several years.

Greg

Greg was a friend of Irv's from the college. He was a restless, romantic figure, utterly self-sufficient, and entirely without the need to court the approval of others. He did what he wanted. He was tall, thin, and good-looking; together he and Irv were suddenly Don Quixote and Sancho Panza.

Greg could be socially acceptable, and even socially adept when he chose to be, but this was rare. He was much more at home as a fun-loving joker, a devil's advocate. Beneath his controlled exterior, it seemed to me that time hung heavily on his hands, that his alternating mannerliness and amusing unmannerliness were equally facetious acts of boredom, attempts to fend off a case of terminal ennui.

Like Irv, Greg was an anomaly at the college. He was a reformed delinquent, something his graceful style, when he turned it on, made hard to believe. He was also a confirmed farmer. He sometimes used the period between classes and exams to go home to Pennsylvania to plant or plow. On the wall of his room were large road signs from his hometown, mementos of his old gang's final binge.

In recent years Greg's energy had developed along a more promising line. He traveled, and he paid for his trips by importing bric-a-brac that he then resold at a profit. His room was a storehouse of rattan furniture and tasteless carved idols.

Greg didn't go to the places everyone else did. While others traveled to Paris and London, basking in the overexposed aura of Western culture, Greg traveled to Central America, Morocco, and Arabia.

As a senior in high school, Greg had won a Rotary scholarship. In what he later said was merely an attempt to get away from school, he spent a year studying and traveling in the Philippines, speaking to Rotary clubs and learning the folkways of a foreign country. From then on he traveled whenever he could.

Irv accompanied Greg to Guatemala, and later on his own made trips to Central and South America. On one trip he got all the way to Tierra del Fuego. Irv's talk at the farm was constantly laced with stories of Guatemala, Cuzco, and Lake Titicaca. He loved to dwell on the primitive methods of travel in South America, and we all wondered how he had gotten anywhere at all: an ancient train that caught fire as it crossed the Pampas; hitching through Argentine cattle country; looking down into a steep valley from a bus teetering through the Andes to see the skeletons of other wrecked buses below. He told stories of the colorful markets; he had snapshots of himself in a bar in the *cordillera* that served home-brewed liquor, and developed the habit of keeping a macaw on his shoulder.

After college Greg taught school in the Middle East. When he came back, he had money in his pocket. He returned to Pennsylvania and decided to try commercial-scale farming. Irv joined him. In previous years, Greg's summer farming had been on rented land, so they rented a farm and equipment, collected some friends to help with the work, and spent the summer growing vegetables, mostly corn, for their roadside stand.

They worked hard, but had a good time and didn't take themselves too seriously. When the summer was over, they found that they had not made the great leap forward into commercial farming they had expected. With the money they had left, they built and outfitted a tiny house on the back of a big old International flatbed truck, furnished it with, among other things, carpeting, a wood stove, and two rocking chairs, painted it an unmistakable yellow, and headed for Guatemala. Late in the fall they returned, and one winter morning we woke up to find them parked in our barnyard. The furniture filtered into the house and eventually became community property. The truck became our indispensable farm truck. The walls of their mobile house became a hog pen. For the rest of my time at the farm, tasteless carved idols turned up unexpectedly in odd corners.

Irv stayed and Greg moved on, though he periodically reappeared. Once having arrived at the farm, Irv took things in hand, at least as much as this was possible there. He was a doer. In his time at the farm he built buildings, operated equipment and fixed it when necessary, and occasionally stopped to read or travel. He considered himself our farming expert, and on arriving at the farm he bought a tractor, and a plow and disk harrow to go with it. He wanted to continue to farm on a commercial scale, and heaped abundant scorn on backyard gardeners and back-to-the-land hippies. None of this went over very well with the others at the farm, who were both of these and decidedly noncommercial. Eventually, Irv felt his efforts to be thankless and that the rest of us lacked foresight, and moved to a neighboring farm.

Aaron

While still at our farm, Irv found a companion in his high work standards and his recast intellectual life in Aaron, a local recluse. Aaron was no ordinary recluse (in the sixties no one was ordinary), or perhaps—all recluses sharing the oddness of their habits—he was. Fleeing graduate school and a father who was a well-known writer and teacher, he had taken to the woods with the vengeance his highly developed interests and skills obliged. He was building an exact replica of a Colonial house in a remote clearing in the woods, and doing it entirely by hand.

This was the kind of effort Irv could appreciate. While Irv was unwilling to abandon his tractor and truck and thoughts of large-scale farming simply to comply with Aaron's purism, Aaron's integrity and tenacity appealed to him; he felt he could learn from him. I think Irv could see that while by one standard Aaron was thinking small, by another he was thinking big; for while he was focusing his entire life on a single building, and that, notwithstanding his socialism, only for himself, it would be a gem.

Everything Aaron did he did well, and he did everything. He sawed down trees and milled them into boards. He hewed his own beams. He routed and planed his own paneling and windows in the Colonial style. He split his own shakes and laid up his own masonry. He even made his own nails. Aaron's insistence on perfection was so great that I once helped him replace one of the principal beams of the house, which he had hewn by hand himself, and was already built into place, only because it had developed a slight twist.

Aaron was self-sufficient on a more challenging and total scale than we were at the farm; yet, since his system was geared to him alone, it was more realistic in its demands on him, and so he got much further with it toward meeting his particular needs. It was neater and worked better than our ill-defined subsistence, which tended to become merely antiestablishment and to have no more positive basis than our general disapproval of traditional middle-class American life.

Aaron made room for Irv in his work. Irv helped him tear down barns and houses for materials that Aaron sold, along with his own handmade beams and paneling, for decoration and restoration. He was well known, and his work was in great demand. Once in a while he and Irv would load up a truck and drive their handiwork down to Connecticut or Long Island, where the materials had been ordered by a contractor. They would remove slate from roofs and carefully store it; they cleaned old brick for reuse. They were particularly interested in beams, and in siding because it brought such a good price—even though a room paneled with old barn boards would have been totally anathema to Aaron. Old yellow-pine floorboards, first-cut from the New England virgin forest, pine such as we will never see again, went, naturally, to an old-yellow-pine-floorboard *specialist;* Aaron did things right. He and Irv were like a couple of squirrels storing nuts.

Aaron taught Irv how to use his tools, and to appreciate some of the finer points of building by hand. Later, when Irv built himself a house at the farm to which he'd moved, he used what Aaron had taught him. His tiny house had a slate roof, old windows, and beams pegged in place. It was a beautiful house; it sat on the edge of a tiny clearing in the woods and was as enticing as the gingerbread house of "Hansel and Gretel." It was a bit more forgiving than Aaron's.

But the house came later. Between Irv's move to our farm and his move into his own house was another period of his life when he left the farm and lived closer to Aaron. He had decided to go back to college and, needing to be alone to study, thought that this would be a good time to sample for himself the life of the recluse. He moved into a rambling old inn about a mile from Aaron's. Like Aaron's house, the inn was situated on a seldom used dirt road. It sat in a forest woven with a loose fabric of stone walls—evidence of the fields and pastures recently reclaimed by nature from the early settlers—in a town that had long ceased to have either a village center or a government, a backwoods settlement that had probably not appeared on most maps for a century or more.

Visiting Irv's house was like walking into one of the culture's abandoned rooms, one that had been boarded up for years. The forest was a thin haze of new hardwoods, tall, delicate, and evenly spread. They were so straight, thin, and even that they looked less like a forest than a heavy rain. The fields were still there among them: Nature had as yet woven only a thinly veiled present over the settlers' hard-earned past. There was still a sense of balance, as if either side could win.

I visited one day in January, but found that Irv was at the college. There was an immense log in the stove that indicated that he planned to be out most of the day. Having gone to the trouble of getting there, I decided to settle in for a while. There was always the chance that he might return. I took my time writing a note, looked at some of his books, and tried to take in the place.

He lived in one corner of the old inn. The inn was a long and vast building that had aged gracefully, but that in its simple and social elegance seemed to resent the unruly presence of the woods steadily encroaching on it from all sides. The new young trees seemed a threat, the sign of its certain doom. Forests, after all, continue to grow, while buildings, even the most solid, have only a half-life: From the moment of their completion, they begin to decay. The inn was still inhabited. Besides Irv, far at the other end of the building, lived another friend of Aaron's, but the empty

Photo: Courtesy Ira Karasick

Irv at a South American bar, c.1969.

rooms between were more than double the space the two of them had, put together.

Irv had an upstairs suite warmed by a benevolent Ashley wood stove. His many windows looked out into the surrounding trees. There were no other houses or cars for miles. There was snow on the ground and in the air; it was very quiet.

Stepping into Irv's house that day was like stepping out of time. Like many an old house, it had ceased to have a period; it just seemed old, and in seeming out of our time seemed, really, out of time altogether. Certain old houses no longer announce themselves as having been built in some particular century, or for some particular purpose; they read generically as human structures, as proportion, light, and materials. Irv's house and rooms seemed to have outlived temporality, and I thought perhaps Irv had, too. A few well-chosen books, basic clothes and supplies, a bit of food—looking at Irv's rooms, I thought he was, after all, a good recluse: He had pared life down to its essentials and had only succeeded in making it look better. On the way home I watched a flock of wild turkeys grazing in the woods.

After the inn, there was the period in which Irv contributed most heavily to the life of the farms. He helped design and build, besides his own house, a three-story workshop, and continued to farm and market crops, as well as to keep up the hundred other endless tasks of farm life. He soon tired of our nagging democracy, which, in good Greek tradition, leveled the outspoken as it quietly absorbed their ideas. Irv put out feelers and came up with a new idea, workable and bankable. He enlisted the fortune of his friends Oates, a lawyer, and Pete, the dealer in controlled substances, the ability of Greg, the farmer, and the interest and support of a prominent leader of the organic gardening movement, and bought a large farm in upstate New York to demonstrate the feasibility of organic farming on a commercial scale. This venture lasted several years, and certainly could have succeeded longer had not its founders moved on to other things.

Finally, perhaps under the influence of Oates, a Brahmin dropout who practiced law in his native Cambridge, Irv had a last card up his sleeve. Nine years out of college, with a resume that must have read like *HUCKLEBERRY FINN,* he graduated from Harvard Law School. Farmer turned attorney, he spent his first summer out of law school writing the constitution of a developing nation. When I tried to reach him at his office, I got one of his superiors.

"Ah, you want my friend Irv," she said warmly, wistfully, and I knew he hadn't changed.

Irv at Home

Back at home, in New York, we again enter the commercial building on 20th Street that houses Irv's loft. Getting in requires four keys, one for the front door, one for the elevator, and two for the apartment.

"Isn't that sick?" he says, looking at his key ring with perhaps fifteen or twenty keys on it. "I tried to get rid of some of these, but I realized that I use them all."

The door opens onto his large top-floor space. The loft is New York's answer to the rambling spaces we had in the country. There are a dining and a living area, a bedroom and study housing his large collection of books, and a curtained-off area in a corner that serves as a guest room. Even with all of this there is a lot of open space, and ample room for the ping-pong table. The place is comfortable, though without apparent style or the intent to express anything in particular. A macaw flutters among the pipes on the ceiling, and occasionally swoops down to light on a sofa, chair, or picture frame. Small change is scattered about: dimes and quarters apparently not worth picking up. On the table, among other papers, is the wrapper from $100 worth of new bills marked with the stamp of Irv's bank. A baggage claim indicates that Pete is back in town. In the clutter are some fairly large bills. There are two twenties in the dope box, evidently much used. The accoutrements of domestic cocaine lie nearby. Later, Irv finds another twenty, tightly rolled, gathering dust under the coffee table, and chuckles at the irony of losing money through sheer carelessness and neglect.

Irv loses no time in getting a long stick and poking the macaw out of the ceiling. Five or ten minutes are spent coaxing and chasing the bird from beneath chairs and atop tilting picture frames in a playful, yet intent effort at domestication and mutual understanding.

"Come on Sal...here you go, here you go...Goddamn it, come here! Pretty smart, isn't he?...Over here...that's it...No, no, no!" The effort reaches its long-sought-for climax when the bird sits on his shoulder.

This is apparently a serious and regular business between them, and means a lot to Irv.

"He's only done it a couple of times," he says proudly. They talk.

"Hello. Hello. Hello."

"Quack!"

Pure delight.

After the ritual of Sal's daily training, Irv turns to the other important aspects of his daily life: dope, cocaine, and rock 'n' roll. We turn on his stereo, indulge our bad habits, and then, after this brief stop at home, go out again.

Interlude: Laurel

I soon tired of shopping with Irv's friend Val and her grandmother—our mission of the day—especially since, being the only one without errands, I was often selected for guard duty, and spent a good deal of time sitting nervously in Irv's illegally parked car.

When we drove past Laurel's, a painter from the farm family, I bowed out. I called her from a nearby phone and dropped by for a visit. We went out to dinner at an artists' bar near her apartment, across from the American Thread Building, where in 1972 I had worked with the publisher and writer Paul Williams to try to get a new magazine off the ground. It didn't. At the artists' bar, paintings by someone Laurel reminded me had been a farm visitor hung on the wall. She clearly appreciated the bohemian ambience.

We talked about our lives in the years since we had last seen each other. She seemed happy and more articulate than I had remembered. Perhaps this had something to do with Werner Erhardt's *EST* program, of which she was a satisfied recent graduate. Laurel talked about the life of women at the farm, the freedom of relationships with its inherent loosening of the bonds of responsibility, and freedom of dress: the easily created dream world of secondhand clothing. Margot was the most obvious of this group: Her room had literally been filled with racks of secondhand dresses. We spoke of women's dependence on men at the farm. Since going there with me in 1970, she had always had a male in her life to do things for her. Later, she had been glad to be off on her own in Paris, after breaking off with an old friend of mine, though even there she said she could have "married a count and been set up for life." She valiantly resisted. Instead, she and her sister, who are financially independent, set up housekeeping in New York. Laurel supports her artwork by building museum exhibitions, and has had some success obtaining contracts for public art. Her sister, a curator, is planning to adopt a child.

After visiting with Laurel, I returned with Irv to the loft, and we settled in for a long evening. He had invited over his officemate, Chris, and his girlfriend. They arrived, and we proceeded with the business of the evening: dope, cocaine, and rock 'n' roll. Chris was half dead with a heavy cold, but we managed, mostly on Irv's indomitable high energy, to go through till 4 A.M.

Chris's girl was, however, very much alive.

"I was tempted to jump her myself," Irv said later.

I could see that this was a distinct possibility. I played ping-pong with Chris; he was so tense he could barely volley.

"A Vietnam vet," Irv had said to me in preparation for the evening, "crazy."

After ping-pong, there were forays into darts, and even talk of a visit to an after-hours club that didn't open till five. Irv had a great time. He was eager for company. He gloried in the spaciness of the night's activities, pointed constantly to the energizing effects of the coke, and announced each song on the long tape he had made as "a classic."

"Isn't it great?" he shouted later over the music. "Corporate America is paying for this lifestyle!"

Certainly Irv's style of life is a personal victory; about the rest of it I'm not so sure. I can't quite figure out what connection his life bears to corporate America. It does support him, yet he is utterly disdainful of other lawyers, especially young ones, and their habit of putting their work ahead of their private lives. He pits himself against them—rather effortlessly and indirectly, more by non-cooperation than by anything more active—and against his office, which he refers to with a series of four-letter words strung together to replace the long enumeration of impressive-sounding names; yet at times he savors the connection he has to them and to that world.

The difference is, I think, that he has a different kind of life and career in mind. He, too, often puts work first, but he works largely for himself and his friends, while the others are content to let someone else structure their lives.

"I'm the most competent person I know in the city," Irv had said to me unselfconsciously as we cruised along, moving uptown, in his old station wagon, the Yellow Blimp. And it is true. The farm people are in charge of their own lives, and sometimes those of others as well. If they do work for others, it is usually on their own terms; they get a reasonable return for their effort. They know how to do things. In contrast, other New Yorkers seem to enjoy paying for services, for having things done for them. Whatever good excuses they may have for this, it's a different kind of life. I often found Irv ferrying people around in his car as he had done for Val (a rare favor in the city), moving things for them, and in other ways manipulating the environment in a manner uncharacteristic of the city's upper middle class. This difference in outlook makes New York a natural sort of last frontier for farm people. It is an endless absorber of their energies; there is a great deal to do in the city, and money and progress to be made at a relatively low cost, if one is willing to work and to take a different approach.

On top of this, though, Irv's own style adds a personal touch.

"Know what Steve Krohn's doing?" he asks, as he bumps his way out of a parking space. The Blimp is invincible, and also expendable, and someone has made the mistake of double parking over it.

"I don't care," says Irv with a dismissive wave of the hand at the other car, as he neatly pulls his dented hulk out into the street with a scraping sound. The double-parked car, shiny and new, shudders perceptibly. "It's his own fault," he says of the car's unfortunate owner, and shakes a pudgy, scholarly, moralistic finger at my qualms.

"He's an Assistant Secretary of State," he continues, "and when he's done with that, he has a job teaching law at Georgetown." I register these changes.

Chris and friend leave around four. The subject of the after-hours bar is dropped. Irv rounds out the evening by reading to me from Hegel's *PHENOMENOLOGY OF MIND*.

"Let's see, here it is, the 'black cows' section. Listen to this: 'Beauty, powerless and helpless, hates understanding, because the latter exacts from it what it cannot perform.' Some people think this is really *it*, that this is where philosophy is at—particularly the 'Preface.' 'The truth is thus the bacchanalian revel,'" he continues, "'when not a member is sober...'" and on into the night.

Lawyers in Love

Sunday morning we slept late, delivered Irv's stereo speakers to Val, who was borrowing them for a party later in the day, and had brunch at the Kiev, at Second Avenue and Seventh Street, a favorite haunt of Irv's. Over the meal Irv discussed real estate with the man across the table from us, a complete stranger, and mentioned to me that Timothy Leary had been spending time with Phil.

In the afternoon we returned to Val's. This was the heart of the country: a tree-trimming party consisting entirely of attorneys, with a few friends, lovers, and children unavoidably sprinkled in. Eggnog, cookies, cocktails, trivia. A young man held forth on the presidential candidates, conveying a great feeling of his own importance. Another introduced himself to me as someone who sold vacuum cleaners.

"Not door-to-door, you know," he said; "nationally, internationally—marketing."

"I don't like the country," he explained to me very earnestly when he heard I was from Vermont. "For me the country is a Holiday Inn somewhere." He was quite serious.

Val's apartment was an extremely comfortable but understated place in a restored brownstone in Kips Bay, in the lower thirties. There was a fireplace, brick walls, and a roof garden. The brick gave it a warm tone, the fire made it almost homey. The view from the roof in the brown, foggy evening was breathtaking. The city looked like some lost canyon of Eliot Porter. I've rarely felt so much in the city, so much a part of it. At roof level there were no streets with which to orient oneself, just rectangular forms of differing heights, as if suspended. The evening lights shone warmly in the fog.

Val has a distinct interest in older men, but there were none at the party, perhaps due to the presence of her grandmother, with whom she seems quite close, and of whom she was extremely solicitous. Val's life seems strangely divided. Her apartment was more a part of her public life: presentable, neutral, passionless. The passionate side of her life, strong in Irv's knowledgeable assessment, was invisible. Val is wispy, thin, pale, wiry. She has a staying kind of energy rather than the assertive, muscular sort. I imagine she can bend iron when she tries—unhurriedly.

"Val's going to be unhappy," says Irv, and continues elsewhere his search for the perfect mate.

Conversation at the party ran almost entirely to work. Most put in long hours and endured awkward schedules. It sounded like a contest to see whose were worst. Most worked on weekends at least some of the time, but, as Irv pointed out, they like to. They are climbers, and that is the way to the top—one way.

"The slow way," says Irv.

They really did seem one-dimensional.

"I like to shock them," said Irv. "In Cambridge, when we were studying for exams, and we would come across a hard problem, I would say something like, 'Yeah, that's difficult. It's like trying to get all that hair out of your teeth after making love.' Or I'll wear my necklace to work—you know, the one made of shells. I'll go into a meeting, and one of those old farts will make some comment about it; but when I tell him it's a present from the president of the Marshall Islands, that shuts him up."

The attorneys seemed to work hard and without imagination. The same was true of their leisure. Being overworked, they wanted to do nothing the rest of the time, which is just what they seemed to be doing. Suddenly great expanses of golf course took on new meaning.

We waited out the party, unhooked the speakers, and went back downtown. At home again, Irv lectured me on the Spanish Civil War, "the greatest moment for the left in this century." We had a late dinner consisting entirely of parboiled, pan-fried cauliflower. Walking his fingers through an old atlas, Irv described some of his travels, from the Sudan to Patagonia. The train on the Pampas; dinner with a road crew in Argentina. At dark they simply took a lamb from a nearby field and roasted it whole on a spit over an open fire.

I commented on the difference in our present situation.

"Most of what I know," he said, "doesn't come from books."

Sam

I had made this particular trip to New York in order to talk with Sam. I had offered to drive him back to the farm so that we could have some time together. He was so hard to reach that I realized I would have to fit myself into his life if I ever expected to speak with him at all. He needed the ride; it saved him a bus ticket. The whole thing worked out well, and I congratulated myself for thinking of it. Others disagreed. "I think he took *you* for a ride," said Jesse's girlfriend, Janet.

We met at MUSE on Thursday afternoon. It was January 10, 1980. I waited more than an hour while Sam finished up business. I didn't mind, it was a chance for me to see what went on at MUSE, something I had not till then been able to do.

The office, which I had visited only briefly before, was papered with No Nukes posters, and ads for benefit concerts by a large number of musicians in a wide variety of places, from Seabrook to California, from Ireland to Australia. Some were attractive, others were not. They were often dramatic, sometimes more artful than informative, for those outside the immediate spell of reform. There were *Billboard* magazines everywhere. MUSE is one of those odd twentieth century hybrids: show business and politics; they were clearly tracking the progress of their record and their stars. There were a good many desks, eight or so, and all kinds of equipment—a photocopier, various radios and cassette machines. There was a sitting area with a comfortable and relatively tasteful new sofa and coffee table (more *Billboard* magazines). To one side was a windowless storage room that served as a design office for Jeannette. Opposite the front door was a conference room.

The tone of the place seemed at first businesslike. Unlike the farm's news service and other antiestablishment organizations I had seen, it had a certain executive grace. But, unlike the public spaces of corporate world, this one was overlaid with the paraphernalia of an obviously heavy workload. There was lots of paper on the desks; on the floor were stacks of solar-energy grant proposals to be filed.

There was also that tone so familiar to me from the counterculture, but entirely foreign to business, at least the public side of it, a kind of unfriendly exclusivity. It broke only after I had spent some time there. It lightened especially after I had taken part in the ladies of the office having presented Sam with his Christmas gift, a handsome wool shirt. They were very serious about it, and a little nervous; he was genuinely touched. As a witness to their emotions, I was accepted as a friend.

When I had come in, a meeting was in progress in the conference room. Under discussion was a cash-flow problem in units of tens of thousands of dollars. The staff could foresee income from the MUSE record but needed a hundred thousand dollars to get through the next month till it actually arrived. They were considering getting a bank loan for it but needed cosigners. They didn't want to strain relations between themselves and the musicians who were their principal backers by asking for further support.

Sam quickly ran down how the organization stood vis-a-vis the various "artists": So-and-so is in Phoenix in some kind of a funk; Graham heard *this* about us, and even though I talked to him and he realizes it isn't true, he's a little shaken. John is spaced out again; Jackson's touchy.

These were part of MUSE's stable: Graham Nash, John Hall, Jackson Browne—musicians of considerable stature. It was an impressive list.

"I don't want any trouble with Jackson," emphasized Sam, admonishing. "He's very important right now."

They hashed it all over. Later, before we left, Sam had a long phone conversation with a member of the MUSE board. It looked as if he had secured the loan. Feeling ran very high.

The subcurrent of the discussion in the conference room was where the money would go: so many thousands into the film, so many into releasing the tapes needed for the film (apparently, currently under some sort of lien), so many into running the office. There was also a lot of talk that sounded much like the office of any other nonprofit organization—getting names for a mailing list, xeroxing labels—but it was really more like a business than a group bent on reforming business. They discussed their "products" (T-shirts, records) and whether they should strengthen their "marketing arm."

By one of the strange paradoxes of our era, MUSE is in fact a corporation, and Sam, at thirty, a corporation president. While he is in some ways perfectly suited to the job, in others he is a most unlikely candidate. Sam is an activist and organizer, and the story of how he came to be the president of a corporation with offices on Fifth Avenue in New York is an interesting one.

Sam was one of the relatively large number of farm people who had attended the college. He and his group of friends had been just two years behind me, but I had known them only as names until they began to visit the farm in their last year at school. Marshall had been senior advisor in their freshman dorm, and upon graduating they followed his example, pooled their resources, and bought a farm for themselves in the town of Wendell, only a short drive away. Later Sam became involved with a woman at our farm and moved in to stay.

Through an era of disorder, and a time that has brought turmoil to many of his friends, Sam has remained little changed. There is a distinct line of continuity in his life that bears the unmistakable mark of character. While he has occasionally had to change his mode of operation, his underlying motives have remained the same.

I think Sam's character had been clear to him from an early age. He used to tell a story from his high school days that was indicative of this, but to appreciate it, it is important to know something about him.

Sam was as much of a local as we had among us. He had grown up, gone to high school, and worked summers on the fringes of the amorphous urban area just south of the college— our nearest city. His unassuming home was a short drive from the farm. His mother was a nurse; his father, a career military man, had died in service, leaving a small pension.

Sam knew the area well, and so added to his considerable talents an ability to be usefully realistic about the geography and the people around us, for whom he had developed a fraternal and benevolent kind of love. Sam was gregarious and fun-loving, and constantly out to catch you off your guard. He waged an ongoing war against pretense and propriety. When my mother came to visit the farm for the first time, Sam greeted her, suddenly opening the door with a great "Hello!" and a big kiss, and then disappearing past her just as quickly out the door to wherever he had been going. A minute or two later, when she had had a minute to collect herself, she turned to me and said, "Who *was* that nice boy?"

Sam was a hard worker and one of the few among us who had had previous experience farming. As transplanted urban- and suburbanites, bookworms, journalists, artists, and idealists straight out of high school, college, and even graduate school, we depended heavily on people like Sam to make our life work while we learned the ropes. Sam was more than willing to teach us what he knew; not only did he love farming and believe in country life, but he loved to teach. He was an inveterate observer of people; he wanted to see what you would do with what he had given you. He was constantly searching for that receding point at which he had taught or given you as little as possible, from which you could then go on to do as much as possible. He didn't do this out of smallness but on the frugal New England principle that it should take as little effort as possible to prime the pump before it began to work under its own power. There was a touch of the evangelist in Sam. He wanted you to learn to learn; he would never tell you how to do something but, rather, how to find out how to do it.

While this attitude encompassed farming, it was not limited to it. Sam observed people under a variety of conditions. His principal tool in these observations was money. Through friends Sam had access to considerable amounts of money, and he dispensed it in a watchful way he might well have learned from the enigmatic Guy Grande in Terry Southern's THE MAGIC CHRISTIAN. Sam had earned his way through college with a house painting business that intersected, through his friends, with the burgeoning underground economy of the day. During this period Sam was an enterprising young man who had started his early businesses with a loan from the college's financial aid office. Naturally, he wanted others to be enterprising as well. He was a generous soul who wanted his friends to see just how easy and how much fun it was to be a productive member of society. He developed what seemed to me to be a technique of staking people to whatever it was they thought they needed. As he knew, this was only what they needed for the moment. He would then wait to see what happened when they needed more. Would they look for a way to earn it or save it? Would they find that they hadn't really needed it at all, but merely desired it? Would they, under the pressure of desire, come back to Sam for more money? If so, he remained interested in the continuing, unfolding story, but he was disappointed that the recipient hadn't learned anything from his or her first loan. In a similar way, he preferred buying things on shares with people, even though he could often afford to buy them outright himself. Sam was a student of human nature; only his disinterest and genuine concern for others saved him from simple voyeurism.

This habit of Sam's was little noticed, it was a game he played mostly for himself, but his money was certainly noticed. Ten people living on less than five hundred dollars a month notice someone who is willing to buy farm equipment, help pay the bills, or offer employment for a few weeks painting houses. To us, Sam was both peer and patron, and at a time when one still glanced frequently over one's shoulder at authority, someone questioning the system with Sam's thoroughness and passion was a comrade in arms as well.

It was no small set of contacts back then that left Sam with enough loose change to buy such things as a hay rake and baler. He was a student of the types of work he pursued. He traveled often to keep up his connections, and he knew the technical and management side of painting houses at home. He enjoyed the drama and tension of business transactions. He always pushed things to their limits. He loved risk, and I think felt that a life without it was inexcusably lax.

Just as he bartered away relatively small amounts of money in teaching and learning about individuals, Sam gambled much larger sums to find out about society at large. He valued knowledge and experience far more than he valued money. I suspect that it was not a subsidiary but a central aspect of his business to find out what he could about the world around him. I think he felt that he learned, one might even say earned, as much from negotiations that were never completed as from ones that were. In the case of the latter, he simply confirmed what he already knew: that he had performed correctly and could expect to make a certain amount of profit. But in the case of the former, if something went wrong, or there were bargaining or other complications, he stood to learn something priceless about human nature, the limits of trust, or perhaps about the workings of the social and legal system with which, in his playful way, he was constantly sparring.

Sam enjoyed the high stakes of these business games of his early years, which were simply commerce with the added ante of his ongoing challenge to accepted mores—not, after all, such an unusual stance either in business or in our own way of life. He was well aware that despite its component of dream, and its sometimes theatrical demands, his life as an entrepreneur was real. In Boston he once showed me, with professional pride, a small roll of bills packed tightly into a frosty plastic bag in the freezer of an apartment in which he was staying. "Just in case," he said, and waited a few well chosen moments in which I could take in his tattered jeans and dirty T-shirt, "ten thousand dollars."

Harold

What was Sam's story? He had worked for several years for an old farmer named Harold, driving tractors, operating farm machinery, tossing bales, climbing the silo, milking. He had liked Harold and often spoke of how hard Harold worked, and how much respect he had for him. For Sam, Harold was the image of purity, strength, and vitality that made up the model citizen. One thing Harold always did for himself, and that Sam did not do, was to spread the poisonous herbicides and fertilizers. One day while doing this, Harold became unconscious and fell off the tractor, which simply rolled over him and continued mechanically on till it reached a stone wall at the end of the field.

Harold recovered from the accident, but the seriousness of what had happened was inescapable. The youthful Sam drew conclusions from it that have guided him ever since. What particularly bothered him was the wantonness of the destruction. Here was someone leading a model life, doing what was asked of him, cooperating with the system—which was more than Sam himself would have asked—and what was his reward? To be poisoned in his work. What was this system, Sam asked in righteous indignation? Who was running it? Who was asking Harold to risk his life, and why?

At this point I imagine the only Sam I ever knew to have been born, crystallized into a person of deep moral concern as a butterfly might emerge from its cocoon. It is this moral sense that provides the continuous thread woven through all of Sam's characteristic deeds, from his evangelistic teaching of rural life to his altruistic life in business, from his serious farming days with us to his later political work. He insists that we be accountable for our actions, that our motives be responsible and humane.

The Tower

In the early morning darkness of Washington's birthday, February 22, 1974, the political spirit of the farm, which had lain dormant, suddenly burst forth again. Whatever small amount of peace the back-to-the-land farmers had achieved was immediately and irrevocably shattered. As Sam described it in a later published statement:

> I'd been a physics and math major in college. I actually *liked* nuclear power. I'd heard about the safety controversy but never gave it much thought until the local utility decided to build a

nuke in my backyard in 1973. At that point I began to read everything I could about nuclear power, which was about all I did for eight months.

Then they built this tower, a 500-foot weather-monitoring rig. When I first saw it, I said, "Somebody's gonna knock that tower down." Eight months later, somebody did—me....

On a cold, crisp night, I took a crowbar and unscrewed the bolts supporting the tower. It was easy. Then I walked to town and turned myself in to the police.

"The tower," as the event is called by all those familiar with Sam, touched off a far-reaching series of events including a trial, Sam's self-education at law to prepare for it, and the consequent founding and administering of various antinuclear protest groups, foremost among them the Clamshell Alliance and MUSE.

The act of creative civil disobedience that immediately propelled Sam to the status of "heroic eco-activist" (after which any public mention of his name was invariably coupled to the epithet "tower-toppler") was accompanied by a four-page typed statement turned in at the police station when he reported his crime. Comparing the fight against nuclear power to the antiwar movement of the sixties and early seventies, he said he believed it was a vast issue involving this time "not just the destruction of Vietnam, but the possibilities of nuclear holocaust and destruction of the entire world." In clear language, Sam set out his rather daring purpose: to take the issue of nuclear power out of the hands of private power companies and the government and bring it to the judgment of the public itself through a jury trial.

"With the obvious dangers of a nuclear power plant," he wrote, "with the biological finality of atomic radiation...a clear duty was mine to secure for my community the welfare and safety which the government not only refused to provide, but has conspired to destroy....Through positive action and a sense of moral outrage," he concluded, "I seek to test my convictions."

They were duly tested in a two-week trial in which Sam defended himself and was finally acquitted—on a legal technicality, however, rather than on the moral issues he had hoped. The tower had been identified in the indictment as "personal property," but it was clearly real property owned by a corporation. The indictment was therefore incorrect, and Sam, who had risked five years in prison for his act, went free.

It is often stated in the voluminous material by and about Sam that the tower was a symbol and an arm of the nuclear power industry, entirely mechanical and impersonal. (Steve Diamond, in an article on Sam, talks about its "icy beam.") But it is interesting to note that in every description of his first perceiving it, including his own, it is clear that he was personally offended by it. It was an intrusion into a world, and a geographical and social territory, over which he and his peers believed they exercised more influence and control—their "backyard." It is ironic that while it was

Sam Lovejoy, c.1970.

disallowed as the personal property of the power company, it was the subject, the victim one might almost say, of the very personal reaction Sam had to it. While he saw himself as deputized to act for the community, the very human outrage that he felt provided the crucial emotional spark for his later physical deed.

Sam's act was courageous, outspoken, and fiercely moral, but another part of him was also operating that night. Only someone with Sam's knowledge of mechanics could have seen how simple it would be to topple the tower. As well as interpreting the tower as a symbol, as well as reacting to it as an intrusion, he was capable of seeing it as a construction put together by men and clearly susceptible to being taken apart by one. Beyond its imposing presence and height, he could see to the three turnbuckles on which it depended for support.

In perceiving this, Sam identified the power of the individual as it lies latent in various Achilles' heels of industry, commerce, and government. Though Sam's act was seen by some as anarchic, it lay well within the tradition of American rebellion. We lived then in an era of the widespread taking of hostages, hijackings, and assassinations. (Recently, it seems to have returned.) What could be more characteristic of the times in which he acted than the effect of smaller groups and individuals aimed at leveling the larger?

Certainly anyone who can fix a tractor or a baler or put up a barn can take down a weather tower. The important ingredients are mechanical knowledge and physical work. To Sam it was a matter of scaling the fence and having the right tools for the job. As he later said himself, it was surprisingly easy. Looked at from this vantage point, it is the limited, controlled quality of the event that is striking. As Sam would tell me later, non-violence was his tool, not terrorism. Sam could easily have gotten away, as did others of the time, and gone on to topple more towers and throw other wrenches into corporate machinery. He did not. For, if the important elements were available to many, the critical ingredients—the inspiration, courage, and purpose—were his own.

FARM FRIENDS

*   *   *

Sam may have been a major in physical science, but his heart lay in the political branch of learning. To this end, the tower became the seed for a much larger attempt at influence and public education. The events surrounding the trial were filmed by farm family members and formed the centerpiece of *LOVEJOY'S NUCLEAR WAR* (1975), Green Mountain Post Films' second work, a sixty-minute color documentary directed by Dan Keilly depicting the story of Sam and the tower, and pointing out the obvious dangers of nuclear power. The film was well received, won awards both in the United States and abroad, went on tour, and finally became permanently available for rental and sale to educational and political groups.

With this activity and success, the budding activists, filmmakers, and writers of the farms diversified, bought a house in a nearby town for use as offices and for film work, and formed a non-profit organization in order to centralize their resources, efforts, and finances, and to move their work out of their homes. The Center, as it was called, and the farm, with their small income drawn from such diverse sources as organic vegetables, hay, documentary films, and other unlikely enterprises, became one of the bases from which the Clamshell Alliance and other protest movements were launched.

Organizing is a slow process, but on May 1, 1977, less than three years after the trial, "the Clam" succeeded in rallying some 2500 highly dedicated people to sit in at the site of the construction of the Seabrook, New Hampshire, nuclear power plants. More than 1400 of them were arrested, causing the state of New Hampshire an unprecedented and widely noted amount of time, trouble and cost, first in incarceration and then in the clogging of the state's court system.

In a full-page editorial on July 4, 1977, *Barron's,* the business and financial weekly published by Dow Jones, quoted the socialist paper *In These Times:* "The mass sit-in at Seabrook, N.H., nuclear construction site...marks a new phase in the democratic struggle against corporate power." The paper's editors noted the Alliance's vow to work both "inside and outside the system," and wondered nervously, "Will elements in the Clamshell Alliance force it to drop nonviolence and initiate Left mass action?" Sam, along with Harvey, also of the farm, was described as an "experienced radical" who in the bold language of business and finance had "invaded the premises of a power plant...and caused a weather tower to crash to the ground."

The editors of *Barron's* may to some extent have been indulging their sense of paranoia, but their perceptions were not entirely unjustified. It was a new phase in the life of our generation, benefiting from more than ten years of political and social action, from newly developed resources and tactics, and an ability at organizing and publicity well honed since the days of civil rights and anti-war protest. "The Clam" became a model for other local-based nuclear protest groups. Suddenly there was the Pacific Alliance, the Abelone Alliance, and a host of other activist groups. Farm members like Sam, Anna, Harvey and their peers, who saw themselves as skilled organizers, could now claim serious validation of their work, and be judged successful at it as well.

Demonstrations continued. The various alliances protested their local nukes. Green Mountain Post Films marketed its work on nuclear power, completed new projects on the Vietnam War, and became distributor of other energy and politically related films and books. Solar power gained in credibility and technology; another New Age of interlocking activities again seemed to have dawned.

The final phase of this series of developments, in the late 1970s, was nothing less than an all-out assault on the public consciousness, in the name of No Nukes, through the use of entertainment and the media. This was Musicians United for Safe Energy, or MUSE. In September 1979, only half a year after an accident at Three Mile Island raised the nation's nuclear consciousness by a quantum leap, and two years after the demonstration at Seabrook, Sam and his colleagues parlayed their reputations, their abilities, and their energy into a five-day festival of music and speeches planned to generate interest in and funding for the antinuclear, pro-solar movement in the United States. The talent offered was some of the top recording stars in the nation. The place was Madison Square Garden.

Sam in New York

"Yeah," says Sam with unstudied negligence as we begin to talk in rush-hour traffic on the West Side Highway. "The concerts spun off to a record, and the record spun off to a movie. The concerts produced so much interest in the rock 'n' roll field that now they want to do more concerts, because there are more artists."

He explained that MUSE Incorporated is the production arm of the organization, which generates capital through entertainment, while the MUSE Foundation exists to disburse it. Sam is president of the corporation and a member of its board. He is not on the board of the foundation, although because of his role in the corporation he is influential in it. His duties at MUSE are much the same as those of any other chief executive officer. He runs a tight meeting, and speaks familiarly of his board.

"MUSE is organized as a two-headed monster," he said with typical idiosyncratic informality and humor, "which is real important to the way it operates. The thing is, you're dealing with producing concerts for a political purpose. There's a big difference between having a foundation head on and having a production head on, in terms of the hassles and the subject matter and everything, right? These artists do want to help, but you know, they go on tour for six months, they're in the studio for nine months; their schedules are eccentric and eclectic, so income isn't stable. You make a lot of money, then for six months nothing will happen, then suddenly four people will approach you to do concerts and you can only do one of them. So, there's a lot of suspended animation.

"There's also a lot of loose ends and cleaning up. Everything's in transition. It's a new organization, it's less than a year old. The people were hired under the guise of putting on a concert, but things have grown, so you've always got to be calculating what the personalities involved can actually do and what they can't, either because they're not skilled or because they might blow it or don't have the contacts. It's going to take several months for the thing to come down to earth."

"When it does, will you be there?" I asked.

"Well, I've got to do the film; that won't be done till May, maybe June; and I've got to make sure that as I phase out of any roles in MUSE I leave behind a design, pure and simple.

"I'm interested in the organizing side, the politics, the local groups, the strategy. It was fun. The concerts had to happen. They needed my name to give them credibility to raise money in the name of the No Nukes movement. You know, if they didn't have some name, then all these rich people wouldn't have given the money: 'So, you've got the artists; how do I know this has anything to do with No Nukes?' But I'm not interested in the rock 'n' roll world, the whole commercial side of it."

"But," I said, "if someone wanted to run a second Woodstock—for which MUSE offers something of a tenth anniversary celebration—mightn't he well come to you?"

"Oh, I'm not interested. I'd never do it. I've learned a lot about the business, and I guess I'm not that bad at it, but I'm just not interested in it. There's very little information in that whole area that I find useful or enjoyable.

"The artists are interesting. I am sometimes *shocked* at Jackson Browne; he is so smart, so bright; he has a synthetic brain. He can space away on you, or at least that's what you think, for a whole hour, in the middle of a meeting on things that you think are important, or even that you might think *he* thinks are important, because they might have to do with music, or artists, or arrangements for the concerts. You'll be discussing some issue that needs resolution, and all of a sudden Jackson will open his yap, synthesize every thought that's been thrown out, add some point, say it *completely*, and resolve it, and not take thirty seconds. I mean, just like *whang!* He has such a clear mind! Every now and then he does it. The trouble is, not necessarily can you count on it. I've gotten to sort of pray for it. Sometimes it doesn't happen when you think it should; but maybe it's just foolish on my part to expect it.

"Anyway," he continued, "I think I can phase New York down to about half-time, through the spring till the movie's out, then I'm going to phase it out totally. I'll go to a board meeting once a month or something, if that's necessary—whatever.

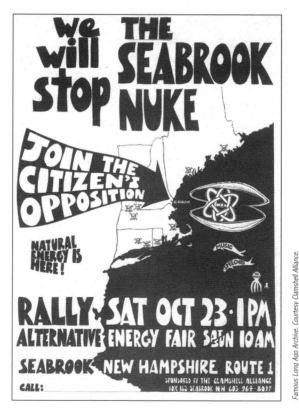

Poster for Clamshell Alliance
Alternative Energy Fair,
Seabrook, New Hampshire, 1978.

"I want to do local work. You know, I'm just real interested in organizing in Franklin County. To me, one county and 65,000 citizens is an incredibly large responsibility, a large bite to chew when you get into nitty-gritty organizing.

"I'm also real interested in South Africa. It might sound corny, but I've always been interested in foreign policy and international affairs, and I really think there's something sitting there that's unfinessable. It's not like the power politics of Iran, Afghanistan, Israel, the Middle East, Vietnam, or any of that; it's just racism, pure and simple. It has its own dynamic. It is untimeable, it could blow up on any spontaneous spark. If it did, the world would destabilize very fast! If a race war broke out in South Africa, it would be as destabilizing to the world as if Russia attacked western Europe. It would throw a wild card into everything. So I'm real interested in that."

"How would you approach it?" I asked.

"Oh, just start getting environmental and antinuclear people helping on South African issues, by making connections, by starting to develop black-white connections in America."

"Would you go there?"

"Oh, I wouldn't last very long there; I seriously doubt if I could get a visa. They're not going to let *me* in. I've got all the baggage and none of the connections of Jesse Jackson."

"It brings up an interesting question, though," I said, as we crossed over into Riverdale and started to head north. "Through MUSE, as a group, you've made an immense number of connections, and had what I would have to call remarkable success. You accomplished a lot. On the other hand, when you stack it up against the opposition, it's only a beginning. It's extraordinary what you're undertaking to do. If you consider your current work to be one end of a lever, the object you have to move at the other end is very, very large."

"Oh, yeah. In a lot of ways, in terms of economic and political power, of psychic power, nuclear power is probably ten times more important on every level to all the sickness that we're fighting than the Vietnam War—easily. The industry's bigger. You're dealing with the atom. The atom is all power politics wrapped up into one little simple thing; you know: The bomb is the essence of international reality. The profits are astronomical. The corporations that are involved are way more highly connected and sophisticated. You're not talking about arms merchants, you're talking about GE, Westinghouse, the entire utility industry and the entire oil industry—because there's no such thing as an 'oil industry' anymore: It's 'energy.' They control two thirds of all the uranium, they control over half the coal, well over half the natural gas. So, you know, I mean in terms of just power and the fight, by comparison organizing against the Vietnam War was almost corny.

"Also, in terms of strategy, you have the potential for wiping out an entire industry. If it happened too quickly it would cause a depression. You can't deny Westinghouse a third of its income, GE a good deal, a big chunk for the utilities industry, and then all the other spin-off realities; you can't just deny 'em that, they'd crash. The utilities borrow most of their money from the banks, to the tune of hundreds of billions, so in many ways anything less than a crash would be hard to pull off. So it's not going to happen, and that's it. You're right, they have a lot of power."

"Of course by becoming a force in the economy or the political scene," I considered, "you become part of the rivalry. Your enemies are now much more powerful than ever before. Doesn't it scare you?"

"Let 'em kill me. I mean, to be perfectly blunt, let 'em kill me. It would be the most important message that ever got stuck on the antinuclear movement. Let me tell you, I'm wimpy; when you come right down to it, I'm actually quite wimpy. I talk civil disobedience, not armed struggle. So if they're going to blow me away, then, dammit, there's a few million people out there that better learn pretty quick about the reactionaries, the sickness, the radical right in America. If they're willing to kill me, Sam Lovejoy, then there's a few million people that better get their shit together, and do it within hours, 'cause I ain't any great shakes."

"But, of course," I said, "they learn from you. I saw in the paper the other day that the power companies are creating little information teams to speak directly with the public. That's turning your own tactics back on you. They're saying, 'You're not the only ones who can talk to people.'"

"Yeah," answered Sam, "but it's *re*active. It's hard to run around and be totally pro-nuke; there's just too many people who will say, 'What about Three Mile Island?' There's nothing they can say about that. On another level, there's nothing cuter than to have a rock 'n' roll album out there. The Atomic Industrial Forum has no capability to go out and get twenty rock 'n' roll stars to do a megaconcert and release an album that's going to be able to compete with it or communicate with *us.*"

"'The *GE ALBUM,*'" I imagined out loud.

"Yeah, right. Who's going to be on it, Glen Campbell?"

"You know, it's just a fact," he continued. "Us young kids basically all agree on certain things, and every poll indicates it. Young people tend to be more tolerant and to support a lot of other culturally necessary things. These are indicative of what their political mind is—especially with a little education. They look differently now at sex, drugs, and gays; they believe in a fair shake economically—that everyone should be able to have a job."

"Yes," I admitted, "but it's not always that clear. When I look at Phil and Pete I see something of a New Age business ethic merging into the system. But by the time a fellow like Pete gets a pocketful of money, he's going to want something to spend it on."

"Right. It's funny," he said. "Pete, of course, now makes his money quite differently from Phil or me—you know, Phil has gone into the sound recording business—but they are very similar in the way they look at money. I'm not that kind of businessman: If Phil's business were my business, it would be completely different. In terms of a comparison between MUSE and Phil, though, in a lot of ways it's similar. We still play our power games and everything."

*   *   *

"I've been having this hassle with a guy," Sam continued by way of illustration, as we began moving through the more open countryside north of New York. "I needed him to sign a piece of paper. I needed it in December, except that the need for this piece of paper got delayed until January. He refused to answer every telephone call; I had called on and off starting around the middle of November.

"The requirements are, basically, to regain ownership of some tapes. The tapes are important to the movie. The studios are not stupid, and they want to know what's going to be in a movie. When it comes to artists, they need releases; when it comes to property like film or tape, they need to know that you own it or control it. So, I needed a piece of paper that very clearly gave me control over these 24-track tapes.

"Anyway, to make a long story short, this guy kept jerking me around for a month and a half. Tuesday it became very obvious to me that he was continuing to yank me around, and I needed the piece of paper. It wasn't a question of his having me send him a letter and then he would read it and write something up. Uh-uh.

"So yesterday afternoon I jumped into a cab and I went there. They gave me this incredible song and dance, and this and that and everything. So I told 'em, 'Look, I'm going to come trooping in here tomorrow morning at nine o'clock, and I don't give a damn what you do, tell this idiot that he's going to call me tonight at six at this number.' Meanwhile, the guy's Mr. Bigwig Businessman and all kinds of ego and everything.

"So he did call me at six, and he says to me, 'You own the tapes.'"

"Well, it just so happens that the tapes are being held in the vault of a recording studio, and the paranoia about hot tapes is very real. So when somebody delivers a tape to a recording studio vault, the security is exceedingly high. And it is literally the case that even though this recording studio knows who I am and what my role is, in actuality they are being right in refusing to turn these tapes over to me. I can't blame them; it's their job to protect them. There's no other way around it than to have pieces of paper and a security system tight enough so that no one ever has to worry. Probably if I had wanted to, I could have screamed at the top of my lungs and scared the shit out of them. But if the word goes out, you know, that they gave Sam the tapes just 'cause he screamed at them—and who the hell is he—artists who are big time might never go there again, just 'cause they heard it once. So I can't blame 'em, and I didn't want to put them on the spot.

Official Program for the MUSE concerts, 1979.

"So this guy called me up at six and he said, 'Oh, they're your tapes, they're your tapes.' I said, 'OK; I'm going to hang on this phone, you're going to call the studio, and you're going to ask them a very simple question: "Would you turn over those tapes to Sam tomorrow morning?" and then you tell me what they say.' So he got back to me in thirty seconds all humiliated. 'Gee, well, Sam, uh, no, they won't.'

"So then I walk into his office today at eleven. I was actually going to try and be friendly, now that I'd gotten personal contact after two months with this jerk. I was going to have him just sign the piece of paper and have it sent down to the office by Friday; I could give it to the movie kids by Monday, and that's all that was necessary.

"Instead what happens is that the secretary has the nerve to lie to me and say that this guy Larry isn't there. But as I was walking into the office, I had seen him, glancingly, walking down the hall.

"So, because she lied to me, they lost any chance they'd had of giving them another day of friendly elastic. I walked right down through the office, with everybody looking at me and saying, 'Where are you going? Who are you?' I said, 'I don't even want to hear it. I want to get into Larry's office, the president of your stupid organization, and I'm going to sit there till he signs these three pieces of paper'—copies, you know; three copies of the contract. I walk into his office, pull out the *Times,* and start reading.

"Ten minutes later his secretary walks in: 'B-but there's going to be a meeting in here.' I said, 'I don't give a goddamn; that's great, that means Larry's going to be walking in. I'm staying here till he signs these three pieces of paper; it's that simple.'

"About ten minutes later, in comes Larry, all condescending. 'Oh, how can I help you?'— feigning friendliness and everything. I just handed him the three pieces of paper and said, 'Sign these *now.*'"

"Why was he holding out on you?" I asked.

"Well, once you get something from someone, especially in New York, they don't want to hear about it. I gave him something, he had his fun; now he's got to clean up the loose ends, and that's the last thing on his priority list. On the other hand, he's got to watch his back. This has to do with rock 'n' roll, and there are a lot of famous musicians on those tapes.

"I told him, 'Look, you jerked my chain around a little too long, that's why I'm sitting here. If you'd continued to jerk my chain, I can only tell you that, you know, the artists that are on those tapes would have ended up hearing about it—and not from me.' I had no interest in causing the guy any trouble; I couldn't care less about him.

"But it's true. If Jackson Browne calls up Linda Ronstadt, and Linda Ronstadt calls up the Eagles, and John Hall calls up James Taylor, which is Carly Simon, what you've basically done is short-circuited this company that makes its money mixing and producing radio rock 'n' roll shows. If the signal goes out, 'These idiots don't know what they're doing; don't ever deal with them again,' to Jackson, Linda, the Eagles, and James, it would probably neutralize twenty-five to fifty percent of all the musicians in the country, *just on their word.*

"So, I just said that to him directly. I said, 'Hey, if this had gone on much longer, let me tell you, I doubt you'd have had any more radio shows. You just damn well better start growin' up.'"

"Sounds as if he were testing you."

"He lost."

Chapter 3

Evenings in the City

Uptown

Here I sit at my desk, before me some artifacts: a little yellow page from a notepad printed "GOLD," with various boxes marked off for OPEN, CLOSE, BID, OFFER, and the other categories of the Exchange; a matchbook from Plato's Retreat; an airline stub marked DENV; a currency wrapper stamped with the seal of the Chemical Bank of New York. There is also a copy of Steve Diamond's new book, *PANAMA RED*, and the MUSE record, as well as assorted photocopies and notes.

On a Thursday in late fall I finished up the work I was doing, packed, and drove back down to the city. I was tired and battling a cold. I had arranged to stay at Irv's, but when I got to the city, *sacrebleu,* no Irv! It was a dark late afternoon in December. It was raining. I was on the street. I put the sleeping bag and briefcase that were all I had into an open-air phone booth—they don't even get you out of the weather anymore—and made it my mobile office. I called everyone I could think of, but no one was home. I crossed the street to a nondescript American restaurant for dinner, feeling very lonely.

The meal revived my spirits. I found Jesse at home and headed uptown from 8th Street on the subway.

Jesse was out, but with the key he left, I unlocked the apartment and jumped as fast as I could into a hot shower. I had been driving for four or five hours through the worst sort of slippery 32-degree snow and rain. The constant tension had drained whatever energy I had. Cars slid off the road all around me, but I had pushed on, purposefully, down the Taconic Parkway. Now, just having a roof over my head was a delight. I made myself comfortable and enjoyed it.

I settled into one of the director's chairs that have always been a favored feature of Jesse's decor, and gazed out the windows. After the long drive from the country, the many nighttime windows across Broadway filled the view like a massive, glittering curtain, dotted with colors, dropped from above. Behind me were the dark parquet floors of Jesse's apartment. The walls and ceilings were painted two delicate shades of white. The room was edged with lovely neoclassical moldings and pilasters. At one end was a gracious but nonfunctional fireplace with an electric outlet in the middle. In the center of this spare but well-organized space were three shiny new ten-speed bikes, neatly lined up. To one side stood a vase of purple irises on an antique wooden pedestal. Positively 79th Street.

Jesse

Jesse is a writer I had first met when he moved briefly to the farm shortly after I did in 1969. He was a recent graduate of Harvard, and before that of Milton Academy. Most of his friends were either Milton or Harvard, or, as in the case of his brother Rocko—perhaps his closest friend—both.

Before coming to the farm, Jesse had had an apartment on Green Street in Cambridge, which on leaving the city he had bequeathed to his brother. After Jesse's arrival at the farm, Green Street became our informal Boston office. We would stop there when we got to town, get our messages, use the phone and the kitchen, and occasionally crash for the night, to the occasional surprise and probable discomfort of Rocko and his roommates. Through Jesse and Green Street I met people who later became friends and to a greater or lesser extent members of the farm family: Rocko, Carl, Mac, Phil, Stephen, and Laurel and her sisters and mother. (Carl later moved to the farm. Mac married a friend of mine. I would see more of Phil and Stephen in Vermont, and I would later live with Laurel.) Some of Jesse's friends, like the future financial writer Jack Egan, the producer Andy Solt, and the medical guru Andrew Weil were never much more than names to me, though through farm connections they showed up occasionally in my life.

Perhaps the most exciting bit of news from Green Street in 1969 was that one of Jesse and Rocko's friends was going to be the first American to record for the Beatles' new label, Apple Records. He was dating Laurel's sister. It was the first time I had heard his name: James Taylor.

From Green Street we would visit Phil's restaurant, or sell the *Green Mountain Post*—the farm's magazine—in Harvard Square, at that time overflowing with a bountiful array of countercultural types, or we might simply go on to the various individual friends we had come to see. Mostly, we went to the city for fun and relief. We would sell the magazine and use the proceeds to treat ourselves to dinner or a movie. Occasionally it did not work out: A parking ticket or fine for street vending could wipe out the earnings of several days.

At the time he moved to the farm, Jesse was already something of a celebrity. He had a book in print and had published articles in several national magazines. While these were for the most part products of "straight" publishers such as Viking Press and *Look* magazine, Jesse's subject had always been the counterculture and the underground press. This was, after all, what was happening at the time, and in the new, burgeoning McLuhan era media and culture had become major subjects of journalistic focus. Of Jesse's two principal articles of that era, one is on the demise of the revolution, the other chronicles the co-option of the underground press by the forces of commerce. His wit has always been acerbic. "Do you dig it when they burn you?" he had asked succinctly, in the argot of the day, in his 1969 *Antioch Review* article "The Underground Press and How It Went."

These were views he shared with other members of the farm press corps, who were themselves refugees from blind politicization and commercial co-option of the revolution. But Jesse, the visitor, saw what was happening at the farm and in the underground press more clearly than many of the people who lived there and were still part of it. He had the reporter's eye for taking in a scene, and the critical distance to assess it. While he, too, could conjure up from his own experience a moving passage on what the sixties had really been to those who had participated in them—a realization that life could be beautiful, and people happy and free, a philosophy that he saw often summed up in one word, "love"—he concluded more realistically than others at the farm that we had been at that time "overstimulated, living in a prolonged ecstasy." He saw the coming crunch of idealism clashing with harsh reality.

"You can't go on repeating the love-word indefinitely if you want to sell papers," he wrote, prophetically.

"Very intelligent," said an older woman meeting Jesse for the first time in Vermont, "and *very* cynical."

Jesse Kornbluth, jacket photo from NOTES FROM THE NEW UNDERGROUND, Viking, 1968.

Courtesy Viking Press. Photo: Sandy Noyes.

[121]

At the farm Jesse was perceived as too slick and commercial to be taken seriously. Over the years, however, he has usually had the final word. "As the belts pull tighter," he wrote in 1969, "we'll see who really wants to live." For someone who had once called himself "a schmaltzy young man with a quick typewriter," a product of the 1968 Harvard revolt who had dreamed of someday being appointed Minister of Psychedelic Culture, this was quite a sound assessment of the next decade.

Jesse was a journalist and was interested in the farm mostly, or perhaps only, because it was news. As soon as he saw that no news was being made there, he left. One day he and I drove up to my hometown in Vermont. Jesse was taking his driver's license test. At 23 he was still oriented to urban life and only then learning to drive. He needed a friend licensed in Vermont to go with him. While we were there, we went to a party. He met some people he liked. Not long after that, he moved there himself. He stayed for several years.

When I was ready to leave the farm in the late summer of 1969, in what was to be, over four years, the first of several terminal fits of pique at communal life, Jesse was already settled in Vermont. He had a large apartment, and was happy to have me take over the third floor, for which he had no use. I cleaned it up and painted it, relieved to be free of the farm and on my own again. We shared this apartment on McCall Street, in Bennington, for the fall, until I returned to the farm in January 1970, a year after I had first moved there.

At McCall Street, a period when I had personal work to do and needed to get away, I was appreciative of having a place to go. At the same time, I was at first surprised when I noticed that someone I had only recently met had moved to my town, drove a car identical to mine, worked with someone I knew, and was living with a personal friend. In a certain sense, I felt it was fair to say that I had contributed something to Jesse's life as well.

At McCall Street, Jesse supported himself as a chef at the only local restaurant with any style. He spent his days cutting beans for *salade niçoise* and deftly flipping *omelettes fines herbes* and mixing the *mousse;* but when he came home, he would cook rice and vegetables in sesame oil diced with his macrobiotic knife, and never had a dessert that I can remember. He devoted most of his conscious effort to writing screenplays and smoking the best dope he could buy. I, in turn, spent my time practicing music, writing, and drawing. I was living on savings from a summer job as an architect.

Various people passed through McCall Street. I got to know Stephen, with whom Jesse was collaborating in his writing, and Carl, another writer, who actually moved in for a while. Jesse met some of my friends: Sandy, my musical partner—intending as I then did to become a professional musician in order to support my writing; Mary, who attended the nearby college and later married Rocko's roommate; and Cora, with whom Jesse later lived for several years. It was not rare for Phil to appear from Boston with his good Colombian grass and bag of pills. There was a great deal of mescaline around in those days, and we made some memorable trips, often in the hills, farms, and orchards that surround the town.

The living room, where we did most of our smoking and socializing, was painted a vivid sky blue, to which I added a large set of paper clouds on the wall, supplying a playful extradimensional aspect. It was furnished in the manner of the time with only homemade slipcovered mattresses and a glass-topped coffee table of Jesse's design; but despite our meager resources, Jesse had made sure that everything matched, and the room was well supplied with his good stereo and large collection of records. We passed many a long evening there, and occasionally a day, listening to the Rolling Stones and Junior Walker, very stoned.

McCall Street was very much of the times, and just as much *of* Jesse. "He turns everything into Cambridge," people at the farm complained, but that didn't stop them from enjoying a visit there when they wanted to get away, or to partake of some free dope and savor a bit of Jesse's irresistible repartee.

From Vermont, Jesse moved to New York. For the past several years he had been making frequent trips there. His agent was there; the publishers were there; his parents and brother (then in medical school) were there; finally, it seemed *he* ought to be there. He moved several times in the city before finding the apartment he now had at the Apthorp, where he had stayed several years and planned to buy into the building.

Theories of Jesses Past

Jesse's apartment is one of the most pleasant I know in the city. As I sat in it and looked around me, waiting for him to return, I considered him as I had thought of him over the past few years, before my recent visits to New York.

He had started off at a run with the avowed intention of getting ahead and staying ahead; and to my knowledge, as his apartment and the life he had made for himself showed, the moribund normalcy he so much feared had never caught up. But in this race, who was the winner, and what was the cost?

Jesse's warm kindness and deep generosity are indisputable. These, together with his intelligence, are the luminous parts of his soul shining through his daily acts; they are consistently present through the years. Despite this, I could think of no one among those I knew well of whom I had really known less than Jesse. Most of him had been so entirely obscured from view by his cynicism and unfailing affability that he seemed like a tree draped with Spanish moss, the covering having become so singular and distinct that the supporting form beneath was lost to the eye.

But a tree was hardly the appropriate image for one so constantly in motion as Jesse. He worked extremely hard at his writing, and when not writing, he was doing something related to it: research, promotion of himself or his work, or scouting the world of publishers, editors, actors, and producers he hoped would provide advancement and work. Over the years, when I would visit Jesse in New York, he always seemed to be on his way somewhere: to the West Coast to do a screen rewrite, to the

Hamptons for the weekend, out to lunch to discuss a project, to a screening, to a conference with his agent, to dinner with his present or intended future ladyfriend—usually someone in some way connected with his work or his vision of himself. When I called him, he could see me only at times inappropriate to his other business. On weekdays, we would go out to breakfast; he did have to eat, and we could get a few words in between bites. On weekends, Sunday was better than Saturday, morning better than afternoon or evening. I tried never to stay more than an hour.

This urgency lent a special tone to my visits with Jesse. It took me a while to get used to the small amount of time allotted me. At first I was surprised, and checked an injured sense of self-importance; later I saw it as a variant of the restaurateur's ploy of producing a tiny table and deftly placing it in the center of an impossibly crowded room, making you doubly pleased to be seated at all.

This is a gambit I once heard ascribed to Vincent Sardi—as a college classmate of my father, Sardi figured in several family stories—but there is certainly something broader about human behavior in it, and Jesse, another confirmed New Yorker, is well aware of such ploys. Like many a New Yorker, Jesse says he lives in the city because he has to. Perhaps he really does; the great communications node is particularly convenient for his work. But it also suits him. He was a strange sight at the farm with his modish clothes, cut off from all he thought he was missing in the world outside. I once watched him sawing wood; the dust got on his coat and he stopped. He lasted only a few months.

What was curious to me was that all of Jesse's motion, or perhaps commotion, didn't seem to get him anywhere. I often wondered how it was that someone working so hard didn't seem to make more progress. Certainly there was a healthy, almost obligatory amount of exaggeration in his shop talk, but that seemed to be part of the business he was in. Contracts and projects never panned out; the screenplay that would make it big was always just around the corner; his story for *Esquire* would put him on the map as a journalist, but it was canceled and came out instead in *New Times*; a budding romance with a movie queen was never mentioned again. These were vintage Jesse and were in themselves interesting enough; they represent some part of his charm—"all the news before it happens," as *Avatar,* the underground paper he once sold, used to say. But even factoring these out, there seemed to be a good deal of space between the places he intended to reach and the ones he really did. What lay under this barrage of hopes and expectations, this blanket of tentative future laid over the actual present?

One thing it provided, it seemed to me, was privacy. By postulating success, and acting on it as if it were already his, he in some way already had it. More important, publicly declaring himself a success alleviated the pressure he felt to succeed, and allowed him to turn his attention, privately, to the more pressing

Author profile for Jesse's feature on Muhammad Ali, *New Times,* 1974.

matter of the work that would actually get him there. Jesse did not merely feign involvement in the professional and social life he led; he had both a genuine interest in and ability for them; but they seemed only the means to an end: the perfect actualization of himself. Being one of Jesse's admirers, I considered this a lofty goal, and was more than willing to forgive him his high level of dream, even when it crossed confusingly with reality. I agreed with his mentors, the filmmakers Marshall Brickman and Woody Allen (about whom I would soon hear), whom he quoted with glee: "Act like an artist and they'll treat you like one."

More surprisingly, along with what he might have felt to be the less satisfactory aspects of his professional performance, this blanket of projections obscured Jesse's accomplishments, as well. This seemed unfortunate, but I saw that it, too, had a purpose: to make the most of his attainments. His recent article in a national magazine seemed to be more significant if it were only the first chapter in a forthcoming book; the screenplay on which he was working was more impressive if it could be linked to a Hollywood name or a large sum of money.

Ironically, what was hidden in this inflated rhetoric was a career and a body of work that did Jesse great credit by any scale more reasonable than the one he usually applied to himself. He did write for national magazines; he had published a book; he had written a number of screenplays and rewrites, and even made money at it. He was an extremely versatile author willing to write for readers and viewers and not for himself alone. Then, as now, he did this well. What he had obscured, then, was his success, which was not small. I concluded from this that Jesse did not want us to see his success, partly because in his generosity it embarrassed him, partly because as an aspirant to wealth and fame it was not yet enough. In addition, the myth of adversity added to his stature: It suited him to be viewed in this light. The Jesse who worked so hard and achieved so little was a rhetorical device to shape our picture of him, a place at which he could hold the line at a firm point as he built his next bulwark. This seemed to be taking some time, but then, it was that period in our lives when we were taking the time to build.

This was one view. Another was that Jesse didn't have so much control, that he was struggling to pull himself from a mire of his own making. Just as his personal mark is his generosity and willingness to be accommodating—he would not be satisfied to give you only the shirt off his back, but would probably stuff a few dollars into the pocket as well—his professional mark is his willingness to please, his versatility of medium, style, and content. His belief is that to be successful he must gratify: A movie that doesn't make it at the box office doesn't make it at all; a book that is remaindered may do worse things for your career than no book at all. His whole effort to write is upbeat, and by some standards not artistic but merely businesslike. If he could write the series of Horatio Alger novels again, he would; if he had a surefire television series like *ALL IN THE FAMILY* up his sleeve, he would sit right down and write it. Professionally, Jesse is eager to please. He believes, probably with good reason, that when he finds his vein, the mining of it will be relatively easy.

Jesse has always worked very hard at the homework of staying ahead of the public's taste. He watches the media and the street carefully for signs and portents. He is as good at this as anyone I know—much better, in fact. I have never met anyone else whose allusions so constantly refer not to something I have seen or read but to something I *will* see or *will* read, who is so aware that he is creating the future.

But, I wondered, can the future be fashioned out of scraps of the past, however recent? In keeping himself in trim, waiting for his shot at the title, I feared that Jesse gave up a better chance at shaping the future, for he positioned himself as a follower rather than a leader of the ideas and events he expounded. He seemed intent on cheating time, and the result of this—because time cannot be cheated, though it may be bent to advantage—was that while one could be quite sure that Jesse would never arrive first at the scene of cultural genesis, being too busy at the last, one could be very sure that he would always arrive second, long before most other people had noticed that anything was even happening. These work habits were, as you will, Jesse's blessing or Jesse's curse.

His book might have offered him an early clue. From the first it lent the familiar meteoric tone to his career. Published while he was still a senior in college, NOTES FROM THE NEW UNDERGROUND (1968) was a collection of the writings of others. With it he attempted to ride the timeliness of the subject—the underground press—into the field of interest he judged the larger public to have in it. It was a good idea, or concept, as he would say, but the broader public did not have the projected interest in alternative culture, and the book never sold well. However, neither Jesse's game plan nor its results seemed to have changed much since. To me he seemed continually to work harder and harder at the same impossible plan. Eventually, I felt, he became its victim. A disinterested look at his situation might have suggested a relevant analogy: A rising star appears to proceed ever more slowly. Or, more chastening still: Meteors do not rise at all; by nature they fall.

Jesse always gave the public a good deal of weight in his thinking, but he did not give it much credit. He was too busy, I thought, giving people what he felt they ought to want, to realize that what they really craved was the one thing he wouldn't give them: some part of himself. By and large this is what people do want. Entertainment must be diverting, but it must have some measure, however deeply hidden, of underlying humanity, something to draw us into it. With all of Jesse's ardency reserved for the production of his work, he rarely gave himself the chance to develop a message of his own. As I saw it, through pursuit of an elusive quarry, his own bearings seemed to be lost. In the service of giving the world some pleasing entertainment, he devoted his attention to removing from his work with almost surgical care any trace of his own motivation or taste; and while he offered the public as the cause for this, they would be as capable as anyone of sensing its mechanical quality, as their representatives, the producers and editors with whom Jesse often wrangled, had often already perceived.

I thought there was no way Jesse could get ahead of the game without staking something on it himself. He could continue to be a bellwether, keeping enough ahead of the public to make a career in journalism, but this was only a matter of days, weeks, sometimes even hours. Or he might succeed on a one shot, hit-and-run basis, as he had spent ten years trying to do in writing screenplays.

But real subjects have real sources; they represent genuine needs, desires, or events. They form attitudes and attract interest because there is something in them that is actual and necessary, even if it is only the fit of whimsy of roller disco—a subject on which he once wrote. They burst onto the scene unexpectedly, much to the chagrin of those who follow such developments, and owe their gestation not to agents or promoters (who will not, however, hesitate to capitalize on them), but to some innate value attached to them by particular people.

Jesse's work had always seemed to me to be a grasping at these gems of value, but because it is a peremptory seizing and not a rooted flowering, it had often been of necessity a scattered, rearguard effort. In his proteanism he seemed to outrun even himself, and to bury in his prodigious efforts the one sure seed of success—his own feelings and interests.

Late Sixties to West Seventies

These observations had constituted my view over the few years that Jesse had been in New York and I had been in Vermont, and I had seen him only rarely. When I would visit, he would just have written a new disco song, or talked to a producer, and letters on his playful American Myth & Metaphor stationary lay on his desk. But now, in the early eighties, as I saw him more, the pieces of his career fell somewhat better into place. As I sat in his apartment and read some of the articles and papers he had left out for me, I saw the volume of his output and realized that many of his projects had panned out. What I had seen as a deadly running in place had, in fact, been more like a necessary and life-sustaining treading of water. By dint of volume of work and sheer attentiveness to the market, he had managed to stay afloat, and had often done much better. Others who had started with him had long since dropped by the way: Stephen was in law school; Carl was teaching; Phil was in business; Rocko was a doctor.

I had underestimated just how much work—how many drafts tossed into the wastebasket and inconclusive conferences with the moguls—it really took to succeed. At the time I had actually believed Jesse's upbeat assertions that he was almost there, leading me to think he was misjudging his progress; but I suspect that from the beginning he himself had already known how hard it would be, and he had persisted. His *Esquire* article had once been canceled, but now he was in the magazine. His stint of cover articles for *New Times* now seemed not a substitute for appearing in the larger magazines but, rather, an ideal apprenticeship for them. Despite a pile of unproduced screenplays, he still writes them, and was even from the beginning, if not yet in the big leagues, at least onto them. A letter from Paul Newman in 1972 had been brief but did ask if he had any new work he might read—but Newman was a long way from Jesse's apartment in Vermont. In 1979, when I dropped in on Jesse in New York, the actor Elliott Gould was actually there.

Jesse's work habits and sense of time were different from my own, but they were hardly an aberration. I came to see that they were the regimen of many ambitious New Yorkers. In the city it was not unusual to have, as Jesse did, two phone lines, an IBM Selectric word processor (a fancy electronic typewriter then a new marvel), and a heavy schedule. I realized that Jesse really had not had time to see me: I had no contracts to offer, no concepts to chew over, no "elements" to represent.

Occasionally Jesse would offer me, by way of explanation and education, a share of his own work.

"I have three assignments due on the same day next week," he said to me on one of these visits. "If you can think up a song that fits," and he went on to describe the format of a new radio show that required a song one could act to, "that would be great. Call me before the weekend." But that is not my kind of work. I once took him an article, destined for *New Times,* for editorial advice. By the time he was done making it upbeat and suitable for publication, there was nothing recognizable left.

I had been worried that Jesse would settle for a secondary role, that there was no room in his writing for his own thoughts. As it turned out, I needn't have worried. He had once told me emphatically that I would never see *his* real thoughts for 98 cents on a newsstand paperback rack (translation: today, $4.50), but it was my mistake to think that one's thoughts must always be expressed literally. A look at much of Jesse's work reveals his interests between the lines.

I had doubted the reality of the agent/promoter and his world, but I had not seen that it was simply a different world. What had looked implausible in Vermont looked very possible in New York, where I saw that one could make a living playing off an event or idea and its later publicity. This capitalizing gap turned out to be the key to understanding Jesse's world. He knows the media business, the communications industry—movies, books, magazines—backward and forward. He knows how long it takes to get things into print, onto TV or film, and he operates in that journalistic profit margin between. These are things I would never have known had I not seen Jesse at work.

When Jesse returned that night, we walked the few blocks to the Museum Café, near Andrea and Jack's and across from the Museum of Natural History, for drinks and a midnight snack. He was tired and beleaguered, having been out on an assignment.

"Now I know why writers drink," he said, alluding to his recent profile of John Cheever for *The New York Times Magazine.* ("The presence of alcohol," Cheever had said, "like a knowledge of Latin, is immediately noticeable in a man's prose style.")

Jesse treats. "I expense it all," he says in explanation.

We talk about my own writing.

"Here's something for you," he says in his droll manner. "The coat I was arrested in for selling *Avatar* just ripped and I'll have to throw it out." He holds it up like a piece of evidence. It's hard to believe that Jesse was a part of the underground press in Harvard Square—or that it was a dozen years ago.

Jesse relates his major projects for the spring: a profile of Marshall Brickman for the *Times Magazine* in February; a profile of *Playboy*'s Christie Hefner for the cover of a new women's magazine; an article on sperm banks for the April *Esquire*. A crime thriller is due out in March: Jesse is the writer; the protagonist will be stopping by to visit later in the month on his way to Allendale,

Jesse on Marshall Brickman,
New York Times Magazine, 1980.

the fashionable prison for perpetrators of white-collar crime. Other projects are in the works.

He has just returned from interviewing Marshall Brickman, Woody Allen's collaborator, whose first film, *SIMON,* is soon to be released. They've enjoyed each other. Jesse plays me part of the tape. "I'm just clowning around here as much as possible," says Brickman. "Yes, and I want to be your straight man as much as possible," counters Jesse. The two were made for each other.

Indeed, Jesse is cast in the Allen-Brickman borscht-belt-gone-to-Harvard mold. Much of what he would later say about Brickman and Allen in his published profile would serve to describe himself as well. He appreciates their sharp, cynical, literate wit, quotes them to advantage, and adds a few lines of his own. Like the Brickman Jesse describes in his days with the Tarriers, a popular folk group of the sixties, he, too, is bored with only a moderate level of success. Like Brickman and Allen, he sees the universe as the sort of place "in which God is basically an underachiever."

"Woody is the funniest person I've ever known," says Brickman on the tape. "To walk along the street with him is a hilarious experience." One could say the same of Jesse. Jesse is so sharp, and has a mind so well ordered, that at first one mistakes his incisiveness for randomness. It seems impossible that someone could be quoting Thomas Wyatt, Bob Dylan, Lama Govinda, and Hugh Hefner all in the space of a few minutes, all perfectly to the point, and all presented with such wanton disregard for context that you seem to be hearing them for the first time. In the months we shared in Vermont and Massachusetts, I found that this was a habit I enjoyed getting used to. I have yet to tire of it.

On the way back to the apartment we bought the paper, the earliest possible edition of the *Times,* near midnight. Tonight's news is tomorrow's idea, which may be next week's article or pitch. If you're not on top of it and out in front right away, forget it and go ahead to the next paper.

Jesse has finally found mainstream. Next week he'll be talking to Woody Allen; in September he had the cover article in *Playboy,* and there is another piece in the works. He seems much in demand, and finally, to some extent, content with the progress he is making. "Success is having all your phone calls taken," he says with satisfaction.

While at Jesse's, I looked through his recent work for *Playboy*, as well as some drafts for future work, and letters. I was trying to get a fix on his involvement with them. Certainly, writing for *Playboy* on a regular basis is the public side of the success signified in having all his phone calls taken. He now has some clout: *Playboy* is one of the best-paying and best-selling of current magazines. Yet there was the nagging question of exploitation. I was curious to see to what extent complicity was a necessary ingredient in his success.

Jesse's September article, "Women of the Ivy Leagues," seemed a model of being both involved in and beyond the reach of exploitation, and a benchmark for the consciousness of some members of the farm group. On the one hand, Jesse chides the Harvard *Crimson* for "moralizing" about the exploitation of women, taking the high line that women are capable of fending for themselves, and that their participation is not possible without their cooperation. On the other, there are the ten or a dozen pages of typical *Playboy* photographic fare, probably of more interest to the typical reader than the accompanying article. Despite this, the article comes off as peculiarly appropriate, and as Jesse would ask: Does it matter? The world will continue to turn; if he hadn't written it, someone else would have.

A letter Jesse showed me on his desk outlines his next assignment: swinging, for "Sex in America: Manhattan," an installment of one of the magazine's regular features. It described what he was to cover, and how much he was to be paid. It included this advice: One of the guidelines for this piece is restraint of judgment—if people enjoy doing it in front of strangers, fine. Everyone deserves to be famous for fifteen minutes of something. You are not required to personally participate in the activities—this is not New Journalism. For that the pay is less, if it's paid at all. It concludes, "We will send you a formal Sex in America contract to sign."

Restraint of judgment has an awful ring to it, though, of course, it could pass for an ideal as well. I guess it seems an independent confirmation of the restraint of judgment in the service of commerce I have always feared for Jesse. The lines seem hard and patronizing, apparently handed down from a position of strength, yet one that betrays uncertainty and perhaps a posture of self-defense. Though they commission a writer, they show little sensitivity; there is a clear tone of philistinism in them. Their view of New Journalism also seems to constitute a benchmark: The totally professional attitude has returned—keep a clean nose; we want only what we're paying for.

They needn't have worried. Jesse described to me his visits to Plato's Retreat, one of the clubs he had covered, and concluded, "My advice is not to sleep with anyone on whom you haven't done a Dun & Bradstreet report." He was serious. He later married a scion of the Cox Communications fortune.

I queried Jesse on the subject of the farm people in New York. His thoughts were undivided. He described MUSE and the entire antinuclear movement as a backwater, and saw the move to New York as having left most of the farm people unchanged.

For me," he said, "Soho is the farm."

To Jesse idealistic energy invested in pure food, public welfare, and home-brewed arts is misguided.

"Those people don't deserve serious attention," he said. "By merely surviving, they believe they are successful. In the sixties, people moved to the farms because they wished—to paraphrase Thoreau—to lose deliberately. Now, having invested a decade to failure, they are not likely to think of the support system they have built up as anything less than extraordinary.

"I went to the farm because I, too, wished to lose deliberately. It wasn't phrased quite so accurately then. I think I said that I did not wish to win in a society that made heroes of beasts and was bent on the destruction of anything that looked like civilization. But looking back, I see I was projecting. Their apocalypse was really my apocalypse, their rage for power was truly mine. What a child I was!

"Fortunately, rural life was so offensive to my middle-class, upscale agenda that I was forced to move to New York to get down to my real work. I discovered that given a choice between totalitarianism and indoor plumbing, and freedom based on an outhouse, I voted with the "pigs." I no longer feel guilty about it and, in fact, have become so much a part of "them" that I now wish indoor plumbing on everyone."

Jesse Kornbluth, civil rights cover story,
New York Times Magazine, 1989.

Downtown: The Exchange

The next morning I went from Jesse's to see Susan's brother Michael at the Commodities Exchange. When I had visited them at their shared loft, I had become intrigued with his stories of his work and fascinated with the commercial aspect of New York. I thought it was important to see, because through Michael it was part of Susan's New York. It was also of interest because through Michael and Susan the farm group was tied into larger currents in American life. The two of them had grown up in Muncie, Indiana, the city that served as the source for MIDDLETOWN, the important sociological study of midcentury American life conducted and written by the parents of future activist Staughton Lynd.

At this time, the Commodities Exchange was located on the eighth floor of Number 4 World Trade Center in a large space especially designed for it. As I stood outside, waiting for Michael, I could hear a dull roar.

I called in from the front desk, and after some delay he appeared.

"Sorry," he said. "There was a rally, and I was really busy. I forgot you were here!" I borrowed a tie and signed the guest book, prerequisites for entry, and we went in.

On entering, what I saw was a large room perhaps the size of a football field, full of people, mostly men, rushing, shouting, and pushing. The floor was littered with thousands of scraps of paper. There was an incredible amount of activity; confusion appeared to reign. It was, as Mrs. Mallard said, no place to raise ducklings.

What was happening here?

What was happening, Michael explained to me, was something a long way from the confusion I perceived; it was, instead, a paragon of organization. The walls were lined with telephones, arranged in a serrated fashion around the perimeter of the room, like the duodenum, to increase the surface area of the work space. This created many small, open-topped, cubicle-like spaces that entirely circled the room. The walls of these cubicles, which were like short, dead-end alleyways, were made up of several smaller booths, eight or ten to each space—four or five on each side of the tiny aisle. There was just room to pass in and out, bumping shoulders. Each booth was manned by a team of brokers and clerks, and consisted only of phones and a tiny flat surface on which to write. Each booth was perhaps two or three feet across, but they had anywhere from four to twenty phones. They were entirely open, and there was no place to sit. The brokers were mostly young; the job takes a certain amount of sheer physical energy. Above the booths were the boards, where transactions are displayed. In the center of the room were the pits, where they take place.

Over the phone, a clerk takes orders to buy or sell whatever commodities he deals in. Michael's group deals in cotton and orange juice. For each order they mark up a little note on a preprinted pad, and their runner takes it over to the appropriate pit, usually not more than a few feet away, to their broker. The broker, who actually transacts the business, has a pack of these little notes in a clip. One side of the pack is printed *BUY*, the other *SELL*. Keeping his eye on the board, he, along with the other brokers in his pit—and similarly everyone else in the other pits—attempts to buy low and sell high. When the runner brings him a slip he adds it to his pack; when he makes a sale or a purchase, and executes an order, he marks the slip, and sends it back to the booth with the runner. At the booth it is tallied and recorded; the buyer or seller is then notified over the phone of the purchase or sale.

The boards above are marked off into months. What are bought and sold are commodities "futures": cotton to be delivered in April or June, for example, though bought and sold in December. Under each month is a series of prices. The prices change constantly. According to scarcity, plenty, season, and economic and social climate, the market is generally high or low, good or bad for a period of days, weeks, or even years. According to the various sales, and the day's news, prices change every few minutes, often several times in a minute. These changes create the margins on which the brokers exist, and on which at times fortunes are made—and lost.

The pits are the unique characteristic of the Exchange. They occupy the center of the room and are the focus of all other activity. There is one pit per commodity—one for cotton, one for copper, one for silver, and so on. There are perhaps twenty-five in all, with a board for each. The pits are small amphitheaters, circular bowls sunk into the floor, lined with bench-like risers on which to stand. Each has a raised desk manned by employees of the Commodities Exchange Center (CEC), an independent agency whose employees record the transactions and ride herd on the bidding. In each pit are from ten to fifty men, depending on the commodity and the day—today there are many in gold, few in orange juice—shouting to one other, buying and selling their orders. The bidding is competitive and lively. They shout so much that many of them are hoarse. If you have any fears that man's primal competitive instincts are dying, a visit to the pits of the Exchange might be reassuring. (The human background of such concentrated economic activity is treated in Frank Norris's novel about the Chicago commodities exchange, THE PIT.)

The market rallies and falls; the action in the pit is both a source and a reflection of it. While I was at the Exchange, there were several strong rallies. Gold set a record at somewhere near five hundred dollars an ounce, and this influenced other commodities as well. When a rumor spread through the room that Iraq had invaded Iran everything went crazy. (This was the fall of 1979; there were American hostages in Iran, and gold was moving into an historic ascent in price.) The excitement was contagious. One could watch the news move through the room. It was clear how responsive this vast human machine really was. The noise went from a dull to a deafening roar, and the running and pushing increased like molecular activity with the application of heat. As the bidding got louder, brokers lost their voices entirely. Sometimes it became so loud and confused that a CEC supervisor would ring a bell and say, "OK, OK, take it easy!" and for a minute they would let up. The rumor later proved false, but that didn't affect the trading that had gone on that day. It was already a matter of record, published in the evening papers. Dog had already eaten dog.

To me, the Exchange seemed a giant synapse. Something was really happening here; you could see it. Vast amounts of goods and money were being actively exchanged. According to conditions of society, of nature, even of the people in the room, prices went up or down. As prices of commodities went up or down here, they would rise and fall in the products made from them—dye for cloth, cloth from cotton, clothes from cloth. According to the prices of the transactions made here, the board changed, and the board itself is hooked up *all over the world.* (The board records the prices paid in the most recent transactions, as well as the allowed "limits" within which the prices are allowed to fluctuate, and the high and low from the previous day's trading.) The information affects markets, prices, products, interest rates, and other sectors of commerce.

Here was power and effectiveness. When a gold broker screamed, or croaked, "Five even for five April! Five even for five April!" Michael told me, one translated as follows: The broker is bidding to buy five lots of gold, at 100 ounces each, times the current price of some five hundred dollars. This comes out to two hundred and fifty thousand dollars, and most of the gold lots were larger than five. These men have the goods in hand, as it were, though it's only on paper. The excitement is tremendous. As they rush from the phone to the pit and back again to the phone, acting as agents for the nation's growers, manufacturers, importers, wholesalers, and investors, the economy actually *happens.*

Of course, the people who work here know this. The action is all out in the open. It's a big machine, and they're all parts. Whatever style or method they develop comes out of the demands of this specific workplace. Because of the tension between phone and pit, there is a lot of running and bustling. Because of the bustling and the system of notepads, there is paper all over the place. At the end of the day the pits look like a carnival site, deserted and covered with old ticket stubs from the shooting gallery and Tilt-a-Whirl. It is not uncommon for a disgusted broker to rip up his notes, throw his newspaper into the center of the pit, and simply walk away.

New ways of functioning have also developed here. It's a rubber-meets-the-road situation with very clear rules; any way in which you can increase your effectiveness within that set of rules is fair game. There are all manner of gadgets and techniques for doing this. People stand near their desks—on the phone, watching the board, talking to other cities—engaged in arbitrage: using the minute differences in the various markets in other cities to find a margin of profit. One man was seated in an upper gallery with a headset on, which left his hands free to figure or signal. He studied the board and communicated to someone somewhere about it in an unending stream. He looked entirely passive, even a little bored; he was perhaps too good a piece in the machine. Two others spent all their time plotting the price of gold on long pieces of graph paper. By noting each price change in a tiny square, they came up with a table on which the up or down movement of the market was very clear. At any time they could see "the day at a glance," and their colleagues frequently checked their chart. Unfortunately, this offered no guarantee that the trend might not be reversed at any moment.

Seeing the Exchange taught me something about business and the economy, and about the lives of some people I knew. For my urban lawyer and business friends, a career at the Exchange would have been a real possibility, something they might have been exposed to, something their parents or mentors might even have suggested. Compared with law and business, the market offers another viable way of tapping into commercial energy, and of making a good living. Yet, despite the money obviously in evidence, it is abundantly clear why they hadn't chosen it, why Michael and his friends seemed, in fact, somewhat out of place. The Exchange is so straight. It seems to favor the preppy, postadolescent, hale-fellow-well-met types who return to the suburbs by train and car, or by taxi to an undistinguished but very comfortable apartment with an expensive stereo. It's like a college fraternity gone wild. It favors a practical, highly competitive, game-playing set of mind. It requires expertise, but there is no larger content. It asks no questions that are not entirely commercial.

The Exchange is a certain kind of business, and it attracts a certain kind of people. According to Michael, it is a port of entry into New York business and finance. It brings southerners to trade cotton and orange juice, Texans in oil. There is the traditional preponderance of Europeans in precious metals. From a large but local enterprise, moving to the Exchange would be a logical next step into business on a national scale, where one's knowledge of a specific market and type of goods can be leveraged to greater advantage. Entree is the hundred thousand dollar cost of a seat on the Exchange—the license to do business there. The Exchange is, I thought, just one kind of business: noisy and loud. Banking must be very different, as is Irv's quiet law office—taxes, mergers—or the life of an executive, or something as different as manufacturing.

I was also intrigued by the role of the CEC. No one questioned the imposed "limits" on trade or the actions of the CEC officials that clearly affected trading. Unlike the countercultural world with which I was familiar, people here were perfectly happy to operate within prescribed guidelines.

As I walked to the employees' cafeteria to discuss with Michael what I was seeing, I noticed behind the great board wall of the Exchange an open door. I peeked in.

It was a room of medium size, perhaps thirty feet square, entirely full of wires. There were rows on rows of circuit banks, and miles and miles of wire for the telephones and vast accounting mechanisms of the Exchange. The room was unassuming, painted a serviceable gray with a ceiling of hung tile. It might have been a boiler room or large closet. Some tools and spare parts lay carelessly on the floor for the occasional repair. There was no one in the room.

I was awestruck; I hardly dared enter. It seemed odd that this door to the very nerve center of the Exchange should be left casually open and unattended, for what the Exchange was to its sector of the economy, this room was to the Exchange: its electronic heart. I walked in and stood in the middle of one of the aisles. Banks of circuitry rose on each side. I just stood listening to the slow, irregular clicking, trying to imagine the volume and the kind of information passing through those wires.

Interlude: Janet

The next morning I did some copying and read more of Jesse's articles and letters. Phil, who had expressed reluctance to speak to me, was still on my mind, though I felt a bit better about it than I had the day before when we had spoken. I packed, but before leaving Jesse's for a few days downtown with Irv, Janet called and we had a long talk. As always, she was very funny, but she was depressed. At 31, she felt she still hadn't made it. Her apartment was unpresentable for the kind of socializing she wanted to do, and she was ready to switch jobs. She described her pattern of working for a few months at a time, then changing jobs.

"You get tired of the act," she said, "and they get tired of your act. It's best to move on."

She was neither young nor famous. A friend of hers had recently had a blind date. It turned out to be John Connally, the outsized, Lyndon Johnson-like former governor of Texas. Janet was a bit shaken. Somehow it confirmed her sense of insecurity: not that it hadn't been her, but rather that it might have been, or perhaps both.

Jeannette

Monday morning I called Jeannette and arranged to have coffee. I walked over from Irv's. On the way, I picked up a copy of

Steve Diamond's new book, *PANAMA RED* (1979), to read at home. Though I hadn't seen Jeannette in two years, she was cordial. We talked, but of course, as I should have known, we never got to coffee.

Heir to the tradition of Poe, Bierce, and Baudelaire, Jeannette was the farm's chief cynic. She was the unlikely daughter of a French admiral, one of the European Union's chiefs of staff, and later a diplomat. Jeannette had had an upper-class youth, complete with large house, servants, and a Renault Caravelle when she went away to school. It is hard to imagine, but she must have attended parties in a formal gown. She went to school in Asia, where her father was stationed, and was properly trained to carry out her nation's work in its empire. By profession she was an engineer. She once told me with a characteristic mixture of amusement and awe that she had built a bridge in Burma.

Since then she had come a long way. At the farm she had left her past farther behind than any of us, by virtue of both geography and sheer change. She was five years older than most of us, and ten years older than some. Her attitudes were more developed; she was more purposeful. In choosing a life of apparent degeneracy and mere subsistence, she was making more of a conscious choice; she had left behind a life matured to a point most of us hadn't yet reached—and that had been several years before she had come to the farm.

Jeannette had moved to this country to work on a new bridge in the American west, but soon found herself involved in something more interesting: an intense, messianic commune family on the East Coast. She had managed and designed their newspaper. The paper was not an ordinary underground rag, it was well written and illustrated, beautifully designed, and reasonably well printed. It bore some of Jeannette's other hallmarks as well: her dry humor and unique way of turning a phrase. These were qualities she later brought to the farm magazine, which is still sporadically published as a journal of alternative life among its far-flung friends.

To appreciate Jeannette and her work requires, as Jesse has said, "patience, a great deal of empathy, and a taste for whimsy." But Jeannette has a bent for classic design, a sense of balance and proportion that seems nearly perfect. I can think of no one whose eye I more trust. She has a similar way with words. She makes them do what she wants; she coins phrases. Once Jeannette has put something into words, it is impossible to forget, or to say another way; it is fixed. Sometimes she does this by a mere shift of emphasis, sometimes by giving her words a slight twist of meaning, or by dredging up some wonderfully arcane or outdated term. Her trace of a solid French accent lends an additional *frisson* to what is already said in mock seriousness.

Though apparently absorbed and musing, Jeannette is always alert. She is one of those people for whom daily life seems to be merely a distraction from something infinitely better and more interesting, but that—except under the influence of helpful drugs and diverting pastimes—lies most often just out of reach. She could as easily raise the ante of a conversation unexpectedly in the

A characteristic example of Jeannette's work, from an early issue of the farm's magazine, *Green Mountain Post*, Spring 1970.

BUGLER BUGLER

Can't afford a half-buck for a pack of tailor-mades which your friends smoke right up anyway? The answer is not to work more, but to spend less. After a few months nothing'll be the same.

Famous Long Ago Archive.

back of a pickup truck bouncing down a dirt road as she could in the more propitious circumstances of the dinner table or a weekend party.

These were qualities that attracted emulation. There was no dearth of people willing to help Jeannette with the farm magazine, or eager to sit down with her and do up a joint, hoping that some of her magic would rub off. Being around Jeannette, it was hard not to want to be like her. Many of the residents of the farm, and even casual visitors, found themselves slipping into her infectious, lyrical cynicism.

Jeannette's opinions, grounded in her cosmopolitan, highly educated sense of the world, were more sweeping and dramatic than most. She believed that the world was in a stage of decadence, degeneracy, and decay comparable to Rome. She referred to New York as Babylon. With views such as these, Jeannette's motivation for anything but comfort and pleasure were, naturally, low. She was an inveterate loafer. I picture her most often by the stove in the kitchen, coffee in one hand, a Pall Mall in the other, quietly observing the daily ritual of food preparation, or in her room, on the mattress that served as both bed and sofa, smoking a joint and talking earnestly, gentle but intense.

It was one of Jeannette's early-summer pleasures to sit in the strawberry patch with a bowl of fresh cream and honey. She once announced at breakfast that she would be staying in bed for the day. When someone asked why, since she wasn't sick, she answered, feigning surprise, "But that's the best time to spend a day in bed!"

In another, Jeannette's habits might have been unbearable; in her, they were a pleasure. Where another might have been proud, Jeannette was unpretentious. Where her humor might have worn thin, it was always fresh. Where she might have lectured us all on the basis of experience and age, she was too jaded to make the attempt. Jeannette was wise, original, and sentient. No one minded if she stationed herself by the stove to comment in mock acerbity on the all-too-human scene that passed before her; rather, it was a privilege for us.

Jeannette finally left the farm to pursue an interest in classical music, but after several years' study, found she wasn't suited to it. (Her time at music school was not wasted, however; her Chopin CDs now produces a line of tapes and disks of rare performances by keyboard masters.) This loss of hoped-for change was not her first such disappointment. On her thirtieth birthday, at the farm, she had changed her name to Lilly Stillwater and adopted the calm, organic lifestyle that ought to have gone with it, only to be deeply disrupted shortly after by the growth of a consuming passion for the music of Tina Turner.

When Jeannette left the farm, I was very sad. At that time she was one of the few people of her kind in my world. It was a puzzle to me why friends were constantly disappearing into distant cities to lead lives I never saw.

When Jeannette later arrived with Raymond at my house in Vermont, on one of her infrequent visits, they wanted only to borrow the car and to have directions to the nearest bar. Jeannette has stopped talking, at least in public, just as some people stop writing or painting. She prefers to live. At the time of my visit to her apartment she had been making the gay scene in New York. For a living she was laying out a glossy skin magazine. More recently she had become involved, with others of the farm in New York, in the antinuclear movement, which once again had galvanized community energy and claimed her attention.

Jeannette's tiny apartment on Carmine Street is a fifteen minute walk from Irv's, where I was now staying. In style of life it is worlds apart from Jesse, leaving Irv about halfway between. The woman with the perfect eye for design, and the invisible third eye her acolytes all seek, doesn't devote much time to housekeeping. She is unconcerned with what she would call "the material question"; a powerful fragrance of cat piss sets the tone.

To some extent this is intentional. Jeannette would be very uncomfortable in the kind of uptown ease described in "The

Editor Goes to a Party," a parody of *The New Yorker* that appeared in her commune's newspaper, in which Mrs. P., "a supporter of leftist causes," demands of an unregenerate feminist, "Young lady, just what is your name, education, and cultural background?" In our picture, the feminist is Jeannette.

Her apartment consists of a kitchen, a bedroom/sitting room/dining room, and a workroom. The latter is set up for both design and film. In this tiny space she can lay out a magazine, develop a photograph, or edit a film. In the living area, amid peeling paint, a simple palette-on-the-floor, and a Mexican blanket on the wall for decoration, are a good stereo and some records.

Jeannette rolls a joint and pulls out the MUSE record— actually a three-record set. I had heard it for the first time at Irv's. Jeannette was involved in the MUSE concerts, as were other farm people: Sam, Dan, Chuck (today Dan's business partner), Steve, Harvey, Irv—peripherally, even Pete and Phil. Sam is, of course, a prime mover behind this entire branch of the antinuclear movement, and responsible, according to Irv, for the success of the MUSE venture, from making sure the musicians showed up at the concerts to record contracts and production. They are dealing with public figures of some stature: Crosby, Stills and Nash, James Taylor, Bruce Springsteen. Jeannette helped design and produce the record; she is very pleased with the results.

Jeannette has always believed in the efficacy of "the magic" of the farm group and, for that matter, others like it. This time the magic has really come through. The success of MUSE is a far cry from old cars and wood fires. According to Jeannette, the concerts grossed one and a half million dollars. The quarter million cleared after expenses went through MUSE to antinuclear and pro-solar groups at the local level through a process of grants. The concerts were backed by individuals; she said Pete was among those whose gifts had helped support them. The advance on the record was three quarters of a million; this was invested in the film.

"The record gamble is paying off," she said cautiously, but with a note of satisfaction, speaking of high finance with the same understated sagacity that once characterized her writing and talk on the economics of subsistence living.

It certainly is. The record is very good. It's out in time for Christmas, and it's getting excellent exposure. It's on sale, and occasionally sold out, all over the city—and perhaps in other parts of the country. It was featured in ads in *The New York Times;* it was the loss leader at the discount record stores. According to Jeannette, MUSE has a particularly good contract and makes more money than usual on each record sold. The film is now up for sale to a producer and distributor who will edit and market it; that income will open another round of funding for the grassroots groups.

Jeannette had just returned from the West Coast, where she had spent two months working on the record. She pointed out the high quality of the recording and talked about how the record was actually created from the live tapes of the concerts: Graham Nash and Jackson Browne, MUSE principals, worked on it on their own. Jeannette chuckled appreciatively as she described their "fixing" it where necessary by dubbing themselves in. She described with awe Graham's private studio and other particulars of the music scene in LA. For Jeannette, former devotee of Tina Turner (and Chopin), involvement like this is a dream come true. I thought of how it must have thrilled her and Sam and the others to hear the music they had helped to produce. Their involvement must have heightened the heady pleasure of the rock concerts and all their attendant activity.

At Jeannette's it struck me for the first time, when I considered the whole MUSE scene and Jeannette's involvement in it, that it pays. There are salaries; they are self-employed in New York. This is nothing short of remarkable. Add to it that their source of income is protest, and that they have contrived to maintain intact their alternative style of life, and their accomplishment becomes even more clear. (Actually, despite the amount of time they spend in the city, Jeannette is the only one of the farm-turned-MUSE staffers who makes New York her full-time home.)

But, though it is remarkable that people with so few resources of their own have, by shrewd manipulation of the assets of others, managed to make a stand in New York, the entire effort follows the guidelines that have always governed efforts of the farm. You can't go to the city, Jeannette had written from the farm in 1969, because to live there you would have to have a job. By employing themselves, they could now go to the city but avoid what she had then called "the degradation of working for another person; or worse, a soul-less company." By being a soul*ful* company, MUSE in many ways served to resolve for Jeannette and others the dilemma of, as she had put it, "being torn between seeing the fall of Babylon as a participant or an observer." They moved from the latter to the former by simply applying what they had learned in rural living to the new challenges of finance and urban life. They have generally come out ahead. When I mentioned this to Harvey later on, he just shrugged it off as inevitable. "It's the farm way," he said.

I wondered, now that the concerts were over, the record on the racks, and the movie nearly out of their hands: What was next? It seemed that the rest was up to the accountants.

"Do you have any future projects in mind?" I asked, naively thinking they all might like to take a break for a while.

Jeannette is a good judge of shock value.

"It's a presidential year, Tom," she said, and waited for me to put the pieces together.

Politics

I took a deep breath.

I think I would never have believed it. It took the farm's own Jeannette to tell me that Jerry Brown, California's scion of the United States of Consciousness, was the philosopher king.

"We can now see," Jeannette continued with great seriousness, conjuring up the perspective of distant epochs, "that government should be run by experts and presided over by someone"—she searched for the right words—"with a broader outlook."

This move from the negative, protest side to the positive, electoral side of the political scale was surprising enough; but I wanted to know, if this change were granted, was Jerry Brown really The One? There was no doubt in Jeannette's mind. She pointed out, in reasoning now familiar to me from other farm-MUSE people, that those who had been the youth of the New Age would soon be a voting majority, and that Jerry Brown was the only politician of national stature willing to espouse their views.

Jeannette averred that Jerry Brown's consciousness was very high. She put it this way: "Jerry and Linda are really *in love.*" (By Linda she meant the singer Linda Ronstadt, with whom Brown at the time was pursuing a much-publicized friendship.) "It's love that moves the planets, and if it moves the planets, it certainly moves *us.*"

The criterion of being capable of love as a qualification for the office of president of the United States struck me as the ultimate extension of the youth cult into age and public life; and while I found it—all things being equal—a romantic, hopeful, and rather charming idea, things are unfortunately not usually equal.

"What about problems beyond our personal control?" I asked. "Missile proliferation, mad Iranians?"

"There will be times, we realize," she said, "when he won't be able to express himself."

I took another breath. These seemed to me to be among the most revealing words I had yet heard from my old friends. The point at which one is no longer able to express oneself is the point at which he accedes to larger forces. To all intents and purposes, the battle is then already lost. Did not Lincoln and Churchill "express" themselves? FDR, Ralph Nader, Sam Lovejoy? What happens when the dictators of the world decide to express *them*selves?

These are knotty questions. Certainly, behavior is often imposed by circumstance, and we are not always—we are rarely—in control. Lincoln did not contrive the circumstances of the Civil War, nor Churchill World War II. They were not, in an important sense, expressing themselves as they pursued these enterprises. Their importance rests on their prosecuting necessary, often dire, actions on the basis of principles—principles that we perceive as, on balance, good and humane. They were, ironically, laudable in part because they were *not* expressing themselves. They were, however, through their actions, helping to express something larger embodying national sentiment—figures who in the words of Carlyle's first lecture on heroes, in 1840, "have shaped themselves in the world's history." Their fame could also be attributed, beyond their substantive importance, to the attractive, but to some extent adventitious, element of the personal style that they brought to the larger prosecution of principle, people Carlyle can only explain as being somehow "sent into the world" for this particular mission.

Courtesy Random House. Photo: Dorothy Tanous.

Jacket photo from *BROWN*, by California journalist
Orville Schell, Random House, 1978.

Expressing oneself, while a high calling in the arts, is often a dubious distinction in the realm of politics and public events. It seemed to me that Jeannette had her proposition framed in the wrong terms. Not being able to express himself would be the norm for the new president; the question was: What was his underlying character, what were the convictions that would prove unshakable in the face of extreme duress? I wasn't sure the capability of falling in love with a rock star was quite enough. That presented a picture of a man who, when faced with the difficulties of public life, retreated into the personal. How do you respond with love—effectively—to an invading army?

I felt that Jeannette was acceding to the obvious contradiction that "love" today was just a cover for a very ordinary world view in which coercion and force, love's opposites, were entirely appropriate tools. I have since come to see that this is not an uncommon outlook. In this view, the individual, and even the far larger groups of which he or she is a part, are seen to have little or no control: Pain must be endured, and pleasure taken as it is meagerly meted out. In regard to daily life, it is the world of accepted contradictions: the bar, the prostitute, the many regrettable, though not necessarily reprehensible, acts we often feel compelled to perform.

But Jeannette is a very capable thinker. While in condoning the way of the world she represents a complete turnaround from the accountability demanded of public figures in the not far distant past, this does not represent much of a change in Jeannette herself. She has always appreciated such contradictions. I'm not sure if others of the farms share the detachment that makes her own views, if to my mind somewhat irresponsible, at least consistent.

Still, I was shocked. Here was someone who still talked about the atrocities of Vietnam, civil rights, and the antics of Richard Nixon, telling me that Ted Kennedy would never make it to the White House because he was a poor public speaker and couldn't think on his feet—someone who seemed to have abandoned the ideal for a totally practical view. (In the case of Teddy: If the man can't get elected, he's useless.) It all reminded me of a friend who runs a local government and maintains a clean public image, to the extent, for example, of taking people to court, who likes nothing better than to get stoned. There are two views. One is that this is an ethical problem, the other that it is simply the way of the world. Jeannette has always had the effect of heightening my awareness, and she left me this time with a new appreciation of the way of the world.

As I talked with Jeannette about her life in New York, things became more difficult. Again, as Phil had, she brought me up short.

"Information about us is fuel for future enemies," she said.

This seemed an ultimate dodge, of sorts. Is it true? There is enough damning evidence in any number of books and articles, if anyone cares to look. In fact, this is a problem for the future politicians of the farm group: Their past is already well documented.

The cat-and-mouse nature of this game bothered me, but I could see that there was a real issue here. It's the question of privacy, with the demands of business and politics added in. In this new New Age, strategies are very important; the battles are specific rather than ideal; time and the arsenal must be deployed to best advantage. If this is one's approach, there is a rationale for secrecy.

The MUSE machine and Jerry Brown have some earlier parallels. The McCarthy campaign of 1968 was another idealistic assault on the practical—as with Adlai Stevenson in our parents' generation, an attempt to get a decent public figure elected to office. And there was that other revolution, the one that occurred in 1776. Here again, today, are grassroots people, citizens not yet politicians, self-taught, deeply devoted, rooted in self-determination, independence, and free enterprise (of their own description) *willing to break laws.* To them, taxes and the authority of government are not sacrosanct. (Several of the farm family are tax resisters who would have felt quite at home at Boston's Tea

Party.) They condone illicit businesses and living outside the law, all in the service, they would say, of principles beyond those merely civil and legal. Or is this just their own view?

And so I leave Jeannette, having recently finished the design for a Jerry Brown fundraiser—"Protect the Planet/Serve the People/Explore the Universe"—and moving on to lay out some printing for the Mungo for Governor campaign (state of Washington, the opponent Dixie Lee Ray, a major proponent of nuclear power): "No Nukes, *NO NUKES* / Be Yourself / Legalize Pot / The Party Party: Vote For Mungo And We'll All Have A Ball"—and on it all goes.

Evening in the City

When I next returned, the scene continued much as it had before.

My own habits remained the same, as well. As I drove down to the city, I listened to a tape I had just made of some music I was learning. Somewhere along the scenic drive down, I added a few new songs *a cappella*. Later I played them back and sang harmony. The weather was beautiful. The sky had the excitement of an ever-changing canvas by Turner or, perhaps more appropriately, by the area's best-known artist, Frederic Church, whose house was nearly visible from the highway.

By evening I had neared the city. The air, even in New York, was crisp and clear. As I swung under the bridge, reflected perfectly in the water below, it radiated the presence of an immense rigged ship. Across the river in New Jersey, not far from where Edison himself had worked, lights sparkled by the thousand. As always, it was dramatic.

With a bottle of wine I had brought as a gift, I proceeded with my few belongings directly to East 20th Street, where I was expected for dinner. I found a parking place on Broadway within sight of Irv's windows, parked, called in, and within five minutes was upstairs in the loft.

Irv was working on dinner with Marion, a lawyer from his office. Harvey and Jeannette called and were invited. Jonathan was also expected, to discuss the building he was looking at with Phil and Irv.

Dinner was duly prepared. Harvey came. Irv fixed him a separate vegetarian dinner. After a few terse exchanges, Harvey, never one to mince words, again disappeared into the maelstrom of New York for a meeting on Agent Orange. Harvey has been brought in as a writer to planning sessions for the class action suit being brought by Vietnam veterans against the government. Dan Keilly has been introduced as a filmmaker, and Irv as a legal consultant. Sam is to be at tonight's meeting as well. This is the business of protest, the sort of thing that brings them to New York. The next morning Harvey, whose principal residence is actually Ohio, would be back on the road in New England, near me, to give a lecture on the college circuit about nuclear power.

Jeannette and Jonathan arrived after dinner. Until Jonathan left, the subject was the building. The burden of this part of the evening was that Irv and Jonathan come to workable terms with each other. Phil, who had been the financial source in this deal, had not come through; they were now left to shift for themselves.

"I didn't mind that he didn't come through," Irv said to me later, "but he took too long not coming through."

Time was running short, and something had to be done. If they wanted the building, they needed to raise the money from some other source and work out their respective percentages in the deal. In thinly veiled language, this is what they did for most of the evening.

"Well, I think the work on the building ought to be reflected in the ownership," Jonathan would say in a very reasonable, casual tone.

"No, I think if you do work you should be paid for it," Irv would correct him, saying not what it sounded like, assurance that he should be adequately paid for his time as an architect or contractor, but rather that he should be compensated directly and not through ownership, which later might prove to be of considerably more value. They both knew the game very well.

Because of Phil's defection, the essence of the building is now time. Marion, who has been introduced into the scene because she is planning to get into real estate law, listens in as they work out details.

Irv states the situation. The owner is interested, but for him it is small fish; it's up to them to make it work.

"Look," he says, "here's a four-million-dollar building we can pick up for two million, if we can get together a hundred thousand dollars; but we've only got two days to do it. We've got to sh—" The rest of what he says is indistinct. Considering the level of smoke, coke, liquor, and rock music that seem the favored working conditions for the young in New York, this is not surprising.

"We have to what?" says Marion, dutifully attempting to take in both the scene and the dialogue. All of this is obviously strange to her. Throughout, she chimes in with advice that even I can see is neither particularly complex nor helpful. She is just trying to understand what she is seeing.

"We have to shit or get off the pot," says Irv, repeating, and going on without thinking much about it.

"Oh,...oh yes," says Marion, bravely, looking unconcerned. This is not the boardroom that her recent years in law school had prepared her to expect.

Serious Discussion

Jonathan's contribution to shitting or getting off the pot is that he thinks he can raise the money. He has a business acquaintance who is looking for a tax shelter. He has just sold an oil company for 43 million dollars. This news is greeted with general interest, but not with the awe and sense of wonderment that might once have attended it. The building should be perfect for him, and clearly vice versa. This gives Jonathan a good deal of clout in the negotiations. In the end some percentages are worked out, and he spends five hours the next day talking to his friend.

They need only a hundred thousand dollars now in order to secure their bid for the building, but they will need much more later. They will have to make up the remainder of the two million dollar purchase price, and with renovation, interest, and other related costs, it will take several million more to float the project.

But there is money to be made as well. Irv figures that if the building goes co-op, he stands to make eight hundred thousand dollars; if it goes to apartments, an income of two hundred thousand a year.

Irv originally found the building and, notwithstanding Jonathan's promised money, continues to direct the negotiations. He has done most of the legwork and paperwork so far: collecting facts and figures, doing financial projections, meeting with the owners. This maintains his stake in the deal. In contrast, Jonathan had known of the building but never pursued it. In New York, it's taking action that counts.

Irv's incentive is income for himself. For him, money is a means to an end. He talks to Jeannette about the study and writing he would like to do someday, which, as a practicing lawyer, it is now impossible for him to do.

"Some say do it now and live simply," he says, echoing his own earlier words to me. "I say, get the money together and then do it."

Jeannette nods as she does to most such assertions, seeing in them idealistic dreams that will never come to pass.

Jonathan's view is different. For Irv there seems an ultimate use—however distant—for his machinations; for Jonathan it is a ceaseless game. In the end, it is a serious one.

In discussing the risks of construction, Jonathan and Jeannette, trained as an engineer, each has something to say. Jonathan talks about cutting corners; non-union labor saves about fifteen dollars a square foot. At the mention of this, I flinch. Labor is an issue of the not-so-distant past.

The talk turns to building failure. Jeannette and Jonathan agree that the recent, much-publicized collapse of the Civic Center in Hartford was caused by a fault of design rather than of construction.

"Now, those engineers are completely out of business," says Jonathan. "They might as well go fishing. And why? Because someone in the office slipped up, that's all."

It's a game played for high stakes.

"I have a million dollars' worth of insurance," he says. It sounds like a lot. "And what's it going to cover? My big toe.

"I do ninety buildings a year, a hundred million dollars in construction. What's a million dollars going to do for me? And for this I pay fourteen thousand dollars a year.

"I get sued for five million dollars all the time. If someone asks me if I'm insured, I say no. They don't sue.

"If I get sued," he says, suddenly turning very serious, "it's Brazil for me." We all laugh until we realize he is being absolutely serious.

"There's a lot of new construction in Brazil," says Jeannette, hopefully.

It seems strange to me that the system, as it is, so much encourages people like Jonathan to take risks, to be daring and wily, even to thrust others aside in the service of their own success, but in turn to step on them, offering them only Brazil, if they fail. I guess that *is* the system we were all fighting: Winner take all, and nothing if you lose. I can't say it's a club I'd rush to join.

Of Captains and Fleets

As the dope and coke were flowing freely, Jeannette stayed very late. I asked her about MUSE and her own life. She spoke passionately about nuclear power and Jerry Brown, shedding some light on her own motivation for involvement.

She pointed to the horror of the nuclear threat, asserting that the arms race will inevitably lead to nuclear war, unless we make an effort to stop it. The main device for stopping nuclear power was Jerry Brown, but in the end, the candidate was seen only as a tool.

"It's important to have someone like Jerry on the team," she said. Referring to Brown's involvement in the race for president, she noted that that position offers the opportunity to shape "one of the most important media presences in the world." She described California, for reasons of size, economic power, and groundbreaking social and cultural attitudes, as the most significant state, and Brown as, of course, its leader—recently reelected, Jeannette emphasized, by the largest plurality in the state's history.

Jeannette was adamant that we in the East pay more attention to Jerry Brown. She almost pleaded.

"Keilly's on," she said. Irv and I pricked up our ears. Dan is discriminating.

"Really?" asked Irv, surprised.

After a few tentative remarks about how helpful this might be in the upcoming primary (Dan is from New Hampshire), Jeannette backed off a bit.

"He's involved *psychically*," she corrected, cautiously.

Irv snuffled. This is not a language for which he has much tolerance.

Certainly, Jerry Brown as an embodiment of California could in some ways be seen as a wave of the future. But it is also true that for a group of experienced media junkies, attachment to a presidential candidate is itself an ultimate sort of trip.

Jeannette, however, is involved with these issues in more than just a psychic way. She has done design work for Brown; she goes into her MUSE office every day. She described MUSE as having many of the same needs and responsibilities as any other organization.

"Yes, there is a lot of money involved," she says, "but the money is in direct proportion to the hassles."

MUSE has to deal with fifteen hundred local energy protest groups; there is a vast amount of overhead on any income they make.

"We printed the wrong 800 number for the Energy Hotline in the concert program," she says by way of example. "That was good for a few calls a week for six weeks. Someone has to deal with those things."

Jeannette is totally devoted to the MUSE network and Jerry Brown. I asked her why.

"By virtue of birth and education," she explained, "my family is entitled to direct captains and fleets. 'Send that ship to Portugal and not to London,'" she commands in a haughty voice, pointing an outstretched arm, feigning the demeanor of a captain of industry. "'We'll pick up cargo there and send it through the Canal.' But, why do it, Tom? It just leads to more of the same."

Jeannette has always taken great exception to more of the same, perhaps because there is no place in that world for people like herself.

Record cover from the MUSE / No Nukes concert series, 1979.

"From that point of view," she continued, "the work I do is an obligation." She's out to change the system, substituting love and happiness for unnecessary greed and death.

"It's been a long fight," she says.

We sit and listen to Phil Ochs sing about Medgar Evers.

Yes, it has. Civil rights, Vietnam, personal freedom, feminism, nuclear power: a revolution in values. Or has it always been there? Certainly, the way we see it has partly to do with our own perception of time. Gandhi; the Second World War: We are not the first to deal with these issues, even in our own era. But whatever the specifics of the issues of this time, Jeannette identifies with them strongly.

And what does Jeannette do for herself? Why New York? Where is the action from which she is never very far?

"What do you do here?" I asked.

"Girl patrol," she answered, and she winked.

One of the more interesting bits of gossip during the evening was Irv's description of Pete's latest business scheme: making money off the delegates to the Democratic convention here this summer. This is enterprising, if a far cry from the moralistic MUSE of which he is an avid supporter, and for which many of his friends work. Pete is supposed to be coming to dinner tomorrow, so I can find out more about it then. He's bringing someone to consult with Irv, one of his "people," a woman from Colorado with "legal problems."

"That's all I can say," says Irv, and perhaps it is. Pete is never publicly specific about his business. Today he called Irv but wouldn't leave his number, and wouldn't say where he was staying. Often he operates under an assumed name.

We were up late. No one here seems to even think of going to bed before twelve. As Irv said, "If you need to sleep, you'll never make it in New York." Jeannette nodded knowingly.

But then, as our mutual friend Tony pointed out a day later when I saw him at the farm, where he still lives, not everyone in

New York lives this way. This is a particular sector of the population, a relatively comfortable group free to schedule its own time.

I was up till five, then up again at seven to move the car. I didn't do much during the day, gathering my energy for the next evening.

Interlude: Janet and Samantha

In the morning I had breakfast with Samantha. She is a friend of Irv's from Cambridge, the former manager of a restaurant in Harvard Square for which Irv is legal counsel in exchange for now little used meal privileges. He is currently handling a liquor license case for them. He plans to get one of his ex-professors to plead the case in court.

"It's the only way to get their attention," he says. His former teacher is a widely respected expert on the Constitution.

Samantha is the young, energetic job hunter in the big city. She wants to get into what she calls "communications" and has interviews at magazines ranging from *Seventeen* to *Food Preparation*, with *Family Circle* thrown in between. She wants to write and edit. She has energy to spare. Samantha is about twenty-three. For her New York is hopeful, the chance of a lifetime.

I had lunch with Jesse's friend Janet. She spoke mostly of hard times, the impossibility of supporting yourself and doing anything else of value.

"'Power corrupts,'" she quoted. "Once you get a good job, it takes you over. Once you get money, you need more."

Despite her difficulties, I was struck by her humane values and genuine compassion. When I recounted our inspection of the building in the West Village, she was alarmed at the attitude of Phil and Jonathan, and seemed sincere in saying she would never kick anyone out of a building. It was almost the only kindness I had seen in my visits. But then, she herself is feeling oppressed by some of the conditions that define life in New York.

A day or two later, when I spoke with her on the phone, her mood had sunk even further. Beginning with what was at first just an amusing riff on royalty, simply a humorous vision of wealth and ease—the Museum of Natural History as a castle: "I'd settle even for one wing"—she moved on to a psychotic fantasy of how she might attain wealth and her desired castle by taking over an orphanage. The route was through a charity organization.

"I think I might enjoy the work," she said slyly. "I'm good at fund-raising, and society is always amusing." The only problem was how to get rid of the children.

Was Janet going over the edge, or was this just a new level of the cynicism she shares with Jesse?

Jesse is now writing on sperm banks, and I wasn't entirely surprised to hear Janet say that she liked the idea of test-tube babies. At thirty-one, she is unhappy not to have achieved success. She has just broken up with Jesse. The only thing she can see ahead for herself is a single life of less than ample comfort. Giving up on males, she chooses the lab.

"It frees up the family unit," she says, testing the sound of the phrase.

Her views are, indeed, a bit different than most others connected with the farms. She announced that she refused to take the subway.

"After a day of work, it's an insult," she stated unequivocally.

"A rather distasteful attitude," remarked Susan, the public-spirited downtown artist, when I repeated it to her.

A case could be made that Janet is an older and wiser Samantha, that Samantha is Janet prior to disillusionment. There is some truth to this, but there are important differences, among them Janet's intelligence, a quality that often brings with it its own challenges in dealing with the daily world.

Pete's Enterprise

When Irv came home from work, he and Samantha and I went shopping at Balducci's; the famous market is only a few blocks away. Beautiful produce, dripping-wet greens, fancy cheese, fresh-cut meat and fish, a bakery; Balducci's is itself a reason to come to New York. Everything is there for the colorful, exquisite, fantastically expensive meal; it's commerce with style.

By chance we met Val there, as well. After a vain search for the Swiss white wine she needed for fondue, we gave her a lift home. No number of wine clerks or friends could convince her that nationality was of no great concern in a cooking wine.

"But it says 'Swiss' in the recipe," she complained, a literalist to the end.

At Irv's we didn't start cooking before eight, didn't begin eating before ten. Irv was there, of course, and Samantha; Pete, again in from Denver, and his operative-friend Madge; Irv's friend Joey, a lawyer, and his ladyfriend, whose name I never did catch. Jeannette, always in search of company and a good dinner, was there as well.

Pete and Madge were at first subdued. Later Pete warmed up, and Madge and Irv spent an hour on the sofa in what was apparently legal counseling. Joey and his friend seemed heavily self-involved and jittery, as if either tripping or extremely self-conscious. Something in Joey's manner made me look at him with suspicion. He carried on as if he were very, very stoned, yet he was extremely sharp as well. This was a confusing combination. For some reason, he seemed to be disguising his alertness and intelligence. Why? He was black and evinced an aristocratic air. From his speech, he appeared well educated. Irv said his mother was a judge. What did he make of this scene? In some ways I felt sympathetic to him, an outsider in a tight circle, but he was extremely distant.

As the evening took shape, we all sat around Irv's table smoking and drinking wine as we waited for dinner. In front of me, I fingered one of the wrappers from Irv's bank bills lying casually on the table. Soon Pete had the floor. He was talking about nuclear power and hustling converts for Jerry Brown. It was the first time I had heard anyone speak of Brown outside the charmed, private circle of MUSE—Joey and his friend were entire strangers to all but Irv. This scene could have been dismissed by an outsider as excessive exuberance on the part of Pete, except for one thing: During Pete's rap, Jeannette was on the phone in the next room speaking for a good half hour to Jerry Brown.

Let me be clear about what I was seeing; for, even with my background in the unorthodox sixties, in 1980 this was still surprising to me. A dope dealer was stumping for a presidential candidate in front of some Wall Street lawyers, and the candidate himself was actually on the phone in the next room.

The New Age was going public. In the electoral process it had found an overt channel for its energy and a legitimate way to increase its influence. Obversely, a scion of the process, however marginal to the mainstream, had accepted them. Neither had really changed. Closer observation would reveal that Jeannette was using Jerry to stop nuclear power and bring about a climate of greater tolerance and cultural awareness. Sam was using nuclear power to educate people socially and politically. Jerry was using Jeannette and Sam to try to get elected. Pete, who represents a point of view more at home on the right than the left, was standing behind the New Age because it was good for business, and his business supported his style of life. He embraced Jerry Brown (surely, unbeknownst to the candidate) because he was the most powerful, visible figure presently willing to espouse the liberated values of the New Age. They all fell for each other. Was it a tragedy or a comedy? I wasn't sure.

Consider the wide set of connections that made this scene possible. Irv knew us all. Irv, Pete, and I were college friends; along with Jeannette, we were members of the farm. On one side Irv's connections went out through Joey and his friend, and many others like them, to the straight world of business and finance. Through Pete they extended to, for lack of better words, the underworld and crime. On the farm side, Irv's connections reached to the grass roots of cultural and political unrest in the late sixties—campus upheavals, civil rights, increasing racial and sexual tolerance, the shift away from material values, wholesale dropping out and rejection of the system. On the MUSE side, his ties now reached to presidential politics. The proximity between the presidential candidate and the underworld was particularly unsettling, an ultimate sort of contradiction.

Pete took it upon himself to speak for our generation. He seemed to feel entirely comfortable in this role. Much as he had in earlier conversations, he described how we would eventually rule, how it made statistical sense. The stoned and the free would run the country.

"You bet!" he added with relish.

In this he saw Jerry Brown as a possible ally, a temporary front for the aspirations of his group, our generation. But he was only a front. The real push was for Sam as a future candidate, probably for president.

Pete carried on at great length, and with considerable conviction, and occasionally some humor. His rap was cut with the social paranoia typical of the New Age: Billy Graham used his powers of persuasion to convince Eisenhower to run for the presidency (a recycled version of a recent article in *Esquire*); the Dulles brothers as archvillains. He went off on a tangent about the new boom in fallout shelters, an offshoot of international tension in Iran and Afghanistan. He described the new, improved shelter:

"Of course, they'll be replacing all that old canned food," he mused. "Dried food is better. Anyway, it's less bulky, it gives them a few extra inches for the Betamax." He winked to emphasize the humor of his sociological analysis.

Occasionally, I was simply shocked.

"I have this friend in the Panamanian government," he said at one point, with no special emphasis. I thought: That must be handy.

"Yeah, he was with Carter when he was down there. He's the head of the army. He's a funny guy, though. He's really nice, you know, *really* nice; I like him a lot. But he's a stone killer. Funny, you wouldn't think..."

He stopped for a minute to contemplate.

"I've never seen him kill anyone, you know, but I've seen him talk about it. His face just changes; it sort of goes blank."

Yes, Pete's something: something else. He's tough and callous. On top of that persona is layered a social conscience, but the connective tissue is rather thin. Before going to the college, he spent three years in the Army. Sam said it this way: Pete has been educated by the people around him; he's been fortunate in his friends. Underneath he is very different.

"Yeah, he goes through all sorts of changes," Sam once said to me, meaning that there is conflict and the need for constant readjustment; he straddles two worlds.

"He has friends who educate him; otherwise, I think he'd be way out there in never-never land. Money attracts a certain kind of people."

He would except himself, of course.

Jeannette and Pete had a lot to say to each other. They spoke in private. Because of the babble in the room, I wasn't part of the conversation. They spoke with great interest; their appreciation and mutual respect for each other was apparent. In some ways, they are similar: survivors, outsiders in society devoted to pleasure and aware of life's ironies. Each respects the different strengths and achievements of the other. For some in the extended farm group, Jeannette and Pete represent "what's happening;" though not personally close, their paths put them always out in front.

Pete particularly distinguished himself, and made himself a great deal clearer to me, when he began describing his business venture at the upcoming Democratic convention. He tried to explain it to the visiting lawyer and his friend, who couldn't seem to grasp it or, if they grasped it, believe it.

"A lot of money is going to be spent at the convention," Pete said, assuming that the implications of this would suffice to show what sort of thing he had in mind.

"Really?" they said, as if the business side of the convention had never entered their heads. "On what?" What sort of thing did he have in mind?

The word he used was *escorts*.

"When people come to town, they like to enjoy themselves, they don't like to just sit around in the hotel alone. The escorts are to accompany them."

But this seemed to be not clear enough.

"Escort them to what?" said Joey, feeling apparently that he was finally getting to the bottom of this evasive subject—or perhaps, as I imagined, encouraging him to speak more clearly for the record.

I was sure that the answer to his question was "beds," but Pete was way ahead of me.

"Why, escort them to their *wallets!*" he said with a great guffaw.

And what was Jeannette talking about with Jerry Brown? Jerry had called to say how much he liked some design work Jeannette had done for the New Hampshire primary. Jeannette also likes it, and so is particularly pleased.

"I'm so happy, Tom, I almost don't know what to do," she said. She floated around. She had put a lot of time and thought into the work.

"These candidates can be difficult," she chuckled.

Jerry had also complimented Jeannette on the work she had done for their pre-Christmas Linda Ronstadt concerts.

"He says they could have sold six times as many units as they had printed," says Jeannette, displaying a mixture of pride and regret.

Jeannette has made it onto the chests of progressive Californians, and the fence posts of New Hampshire—a measure of public acceptance, a milestone in the marketing of her exceptional ability in design, a personal victory. It's a long way from the underground press to the New Hampshire primary.

During the evening, Irv spoke occasionally about Phil.

"He's been up three days now," he said. "Phil is always drugged up, that's the only way he can stay awake so long." I remembered his startling energy when we had looked at the building in the West Village.

"Did he enjoy himself at your house?" he asked Pete. Phil had vacationed with Pete in south Florida and the Keys. I could envision the scene: aging dope dealers and their wives, silvering hair, soaking up the sun.

"Yes," said Pete, "we did a lot of drugs."

On the subject of the building, Irv said, "Phil is a Neanderthal when it comes to finance. He wants every penny accounted for before the deal goes through. No loose threads."

I can see the point. There is a difference in their methods. But there is a difference in their aims, as well. Irv is speculating from nothing, he has no real financial base; for him, it's all gain. For Phil, what's important is investment: He's got the money, and always works from a solid footing. Perhaps the Neanderthal outlook should not be slighted. Irv lives on extended credit and a midrange, five-figure salary. Phil runs a business for which, according to Sam, he has been offered six million dollars.

And so I leave New York. I clutch my mementos. As I leave the tunnel at the western end, I look back at the whole skyline of Manhattan. It is breathtakingly beautiful. It is 4 P.M. on a clear afternoon less than a week from the shortest day of the year. Thick yellow-orange sunlight bathes the buildings. The World Trade Center and the Empire State Building gleam. The water is clear blue: a postcard view. Eventually, all but the tallest disappear behind the low rise of New Jersey hills. Finally, as I head north, they all vanish.

I am left with many questions. Irv and Jesse were both surprised that I had thought I might enjoy this personal foray into history, the participant-observer relationship. Now I see why. I wonder about letters I've sent to Pete: Was this "cool"? I wonder about ever getting through to some people—Phil, Sam, Jeannette.

As Raymond says, "I don't know what I will believe next."

II

Garden of Eden

Chapter 4

ASA ELLIOT

The Pacific High Way

California, Winter 1980

Interlude: Waiting

Following my visits to New York, I decided to seek out four writers I had known at the farm. All had been productive, and published accounts of people, places, and events relevant to the farm group. I thought that this would make good comparative material: ready-made commentary from an earlier era with which to contrast their current opinions and lives. All lived on the West Coast and knew each other. With a small amount of money I had put aside, I planned a two-week trip to see them.

In February 1980, I bought my ticket and set out from Vermont for the airport in New York. Taking a ride with a neighbor, I stopped on the way at the Millay Colony, in the hills outside Austerlitz, New York, to visit a mutual friend. In the reading room, I checked into the current era.

I found, in *Ms.* magazine, the "Decade of Women" issue, the suggestion that at Christmas time women "Give yourself the gift of sanity by: a) telling everyone to bring a dish for Potluck Holiday Dinner, b) asking your family to do all the present-buying and wrapping as their present to you, c) leaving town." The "improvements" outlined in women's work included a photo of a woman state trooper. Another issue, "80 Women to Watch in the 80s," included the president of Max Factor. Clearly both the anger and the goals of our era persisted, though still in a somewhat unformed, chaotic state.

Later, the friend with whom I was driving recounted her recent love affair with a renowned scholar the age of her father. I remembered his name from one of my college texts. It was a very romantic tale. The setting was a boat on the Nile. They were well matched. (They later married and spent many happy years together.) This seemed a more promising approach.

Waiting for my plane, I spent the next day at Irv's, in the city. Greg was also visiting, with his family—his wife, Alexa, and his son Nikolai or, as they liked to call him, Nickle.

To the parents of a child, Irv's loft certainly took on a different look. Greg and Alexa call it the Towering Inferno, after a recent film of the same name, in layman's terms: a firetrap. There is also the matter of bird droppings. Irv loves Sal, his pet macaw, but Greg and Alexa now think in terms of health. Nickle is a toddler who might pick up anything. And of course there are the roaches.

Greg and Alexa have moved out of upstate New York, where they've been living. Greg was lured to the city by a job in a university admissions office, which has since fallen through. They're both very dispirited. They're without a home, living between Irv's temporarily vacated apartment and her parents' house in Teaneck, New Jersey. In New York, they have to move the car at 8 o'clock every morning, worry about spending money, look for jobs, and take care of their child. They are very conscious of the new pressures of parenthood. We spoke about the sixties. It was generally looked upon as Neverland.

"How could we have known what was coming?" asked Alexa. "'You can do what we've never been able to do,' our parents said. They overeducated us, got us interested in the arts, and gave us a taste of freedom, and we acted on it."

Alexa and Greg felt betrayed by this idealism, which they now considered to have been puerile and unproductive.

"But it had a lot to do with the times," said Alexa, in explanation. "It was after the war; there was plenty." The economy was growing, she suggested; now the boom is over.

The boom in agriculture is over, too. They had been farming in upstate New York. But, poverty is setting in. They describe the area where they were living as depressing and depressed. There is nothing to stay for. Greg wants to sell his share of the farm he bought with Irv and others.

With Irv I looked at photos of that farm and other chapters of his not so distant past. It was like a brief miscellany of the world we shared. A corn dolly made by someone, we couldn't remember who; Aaron's prodigious junk shed; snapshots of Irv, Maggie, and her sister at Aaron's house. Our neighbors Hugh and Mary and their dogs. Aaron's back wall: half shingled, books piled in front of trim, red windows. His front door: *Dominus Providebunt.* (Always the scholar, even in the woods.) Irv with his MUSE T-shirt under a wool jacket. Cows. A pig. Piles of squash. Dan and child. Pete, also in a MUSE T-shirt. Jeannette in a *beautiful* MUSE T-shirt—presumably one she designed. Pete again, talking, as always.

Connecting

The day before, I had spoken with Steve Diamond, Asa, and Asa's wife, Louise, about the current weather in Los Angeles and the advisability of my trip. These were some of my proposed visits out west. I spoke longest with Louise, whom I hadn't yet met. She was loquatious and nearly hysterical. She described the torrential winter rains I'd been hearing about, closed roads, and collapsing houses. Her father, who visits only once a year, is so disgusted that he's going home early—and standby, at that. She described with evident horror a neighboring home at which a large portion of the mountain on which it was built had slid into the swimming pool. Another neighbor called to say that some of *her* mountain had slipped down over the road and trapped the family. Asa, on the other hand, had told Louise that the storm had changed the landscape back into something with which he was quite familiar: the long, muddy road up to Total Loss Farm.

At the airport, there were many more experienced travelers than me. Next to me was a conversation about a scheduled work "rotation" that allowed two women to feel at home in both San Francisco and New York. "I don't have to cut my strings," said one. "It makes it so much easier to be here if you know it's all arranged for you to leave," agreed the other. I hadn't been on a plane in ten years.

It was a bumpy ride to California. The storms that had so disturbed the state were moving east. Between clouds, patches of civilization would appear briefly below like brush fires in the night. As we approached the Coast, Los Angeles stretched on, and on, and on. The lights, arrayed in an orderly checkerboard pattern, seemed endless.

At 12:30, Steve Diamond, always a night owl, met me at the airport. We stayed up talking till 4 A.M.

First, though, he took me to the ocean. He is a believer in connective, symbolic experiences. I hadn't been to California since my sole earlier visit as a child more than twenty years before. The ocean was roiled from the storms, but the air was clear. There were palm trees. The low buildings nearby displayed a Spanish stucco style. Though it was dark, we got out and I touched the water. I had arrived.

Steve is pleasantly chauvinistic about California. When I commented on how unchanged our old friends still seemed to be, he said that, on the contrary, out here he feels very different.

To me, though, he seems much the same. He is involved in efforts to legalize marijuana—he recently attended a conference on the subject in Holland. He is, however, amassing considerable girth. This in itself differs from our frugal communal days.

Steve mentioned that Sluggo—our farm friend Harvey, writer, activist, star of the after-work softball leagues—has a sizable following.

"I met someone when I was living in New Orleans," he said, "this awkward young girl. She was completely in awe that I knew Harvey Wasserman. 'Oh, yes, I know him very well,' I said." (In his voice a distinct echo of Dylan touched this caustic phrase.) "Haw, haw! It was all I could do to keep from laughing!" Even among idealistic farm members, activists, and fellow writers familiarity can, apparently, still breed contempt.

Asa

The next day, Steve gave me a ride to Asa's office.

Asa was a friend of ours from farm days. In the late sixties and early seventies, he had lived in a little sod-roofed cabin at Grasshopper Farm, a neighboring communal group next door to Total Loss Farm, and one of the sister farms in our close New Age *karass*.

(*Karass* is an important term coined during the era of the sixties by Kurt Vonnegut, both a hero to our generation and a visitor to the farms. It describes a loosely knit group, usually larger than a family but generally smaller than a university or a town. The *karass* conveys a sense of like-mindedness, voluntary affiliation, and personal relatedness among its members. For youth of the New Age, it offered the flexibility needed to replace the outgrown ties of the nuclear family.)

Like most of the farms, Grasshopper consisted of an old house and barn and the many outbuildings and acres that had once constituted the foundation of a life in New England agriculture. Unlike most of the other farms, however, Grasshopper's was a large and stately house in excellent condition. Its land was gracious and well kept. I always assumed that in recent years it might have been the summer house of an out-of-state family. While the residents of Grasshopper drove the Volvos, tractors, and trucks we all did, their Volvos, tractors, and trucks were new. And while Asa lived in a grass-roofed cabin, it was the only one I knew that housed a grand piano.

FARM FRIENDS

Members of Grasshopper Farm were typically well-heeled and financially stable, but, like the rest of us, they were engaged in living outside the system. Though grounded in business and inheritance, they fought with their families and moved in alternative directions from those of the past. One member was a professional photographer, another a successful journalist and writer. A third became a painter. Regular visitors included recording artists of national stature. Buildings were built, businesses started, projects published. Among their family and friends were the proprietors of some of the new, successful alternative businesses in the area. Later some of these enterprises were expanded to a regional and national scale.

Although Asa was a bona fide member of this close-knit group, he appeared to have less family support and to be more on his own. He was more cautious in displaying his urban roots and more committed to the communal, sharing, nature-loving aspects of intentional collective life. He had come to Grasshopper, and to the larger farm group, as one of a number of associates of Raymond, through the university newspaper that had originally drawn all these friends together. As a freshman Asa had been the newspaper's new young star reporter. A talent for photography helped complete his qualifications for journalism. In the farm community his writing and photographs continued to play a strong defining role in his identity.

As a summation of his abilities and a contribution to the life he enjoyed at Grasshopper, Asa undertook, in the early nineteen seventies, to write a personal history that explained how he, and by extension others of our generation, happened to be living in the country and fleeing life in the system—life in Long Island in particular, the community in which he had grown up and lived before meeting Raymond and his friends at the university. Published under an assumed name to protect his parents, *THE BLOOM HIGH WAY* (1972), a novel illustrated in part with his own photographs, was a 400-page paean to the youth culture of our time. Witty, sentient and literate in the sardonic, tongue-in-cheek manner one might expect of a precocious college dropout in his twenties, the tale of Asa's thinly disguised autobiographical protagonist, Ethen Bloom, is, as its jacket accurately announces: "the story of young people growing up in the 1960s—suburbia, radical lifestyles, the generation gap, Vietnam, student protest, LSD, dropouts, living in communes." "This very personal novel," it continues, "is directed to 'America's middle-class parenthood' and to those of his New Age generation."

With a few obvious lacunae (including the music scene he loved and the advent of feminism), this list constituted a reasonable summary of the first twenty-four years of Asa's life, and the lives of most of us. Indeed, in pictures and in words, he recounted where we had been, what we had liked and disliked, how we had felt confined, and how we had broken those social and generational restraints to help create a world, we thought, of greater possibility and hope.

Long Island had been one of the major areas of American postwar growth, and the university in Boston one of the epicenters of protest and countercultural change. Asa's peer group, about two years younger than my own, had experienced the years of drugs and Vietnam, and the farm family through which he had chosen to drop out (or, from our point of view, drop in) was a magnet for those willing to work at creating a new sort of cultural and political life in the United States. In THE BLOOM HIGH WAY Asa demonstrated that he had been present at the creation of most of these novelties, or at least had become involved soon thereafter. For a young writer, it was an impressive entrance.

While the book was welcome reading to those of his generation, the painful honesty of THE BLOOM HIGH WAY did not make it a best seller among the parents he sought to inform. Although the book was envisioned as an account of the feelings of the young generation, addressed to the one that had come before, its abrasive refusal to cede any territory—emotional, political, or social—surely offended, or would have offended had they read it, exactly those he was trying to reach. Indeed, rather than a disinterested explicator of his generation, Asa came across as its unquestioned advocate. The waves he made, anticipated in his adopting a *nom de plume,* were both considerable and deserved, according to the values he himself had set out, and the battle lines he had drawn.

THE BLOOM HIGH WAY aggravated rather than assuaged the generation gap of which Asa so eloquently spoke. His mother, whom he both loved and questioned, was highly distraught at the picture it revealed. His father, of whom Asa was extremely critical in the book, was discreetly discouraged by the family from ever seeing it at all.

The Bloom High Way

To me, THE BLOOM HIGH WAY and Asa's story represented, and still represent, a skillfully drawn *précis*—however lengthy it may seem—of the monumental social and cultural warfare we had all experienced over the past few years. In its pages a new generation was introduced, rules were recognized and broken, parents reacted and overreacted, and internecine family conflict reached levels that now, in retrospect, seem astounding. Among the characters in THE BLOOM HIGH WAY, immense energy is expended on discussion of such things as proper dress, length of hair, and the privilege of borrowing the family car. To youth growing up, however, and to parents and siblings defending the demise of their values—and in some cases their property—these were, at the time, not unimportant matters.

THE BLOOM HIGH WAY is largely about personal freedom and about the author-protagonist Ethen's self-declared "rights as an individual" coming into collision with the beliefs and values of his fifties-style American nuclear family. In part it is the story of his growing up, in part the story of his father and his father's personal limits both as a parent and a person.

The differences between Ethen and his father, while typical of the era, are unusually severe. This situation is well described in the book, though it is unclear to a reader whether or not the author, so deeply involved in his subject, was aware of this reportorial veracity at the time he was writing. What a reader does pick up on, even years later, is Ethen's attempts to deal with the ego conflict his father feels at his son's resistance to authority, and his father's lack of awareness of the change occurring in the society around him. (In fairness, many parents of the time were far from up to speed on this.) The book is really a plea for understanding; at the same time, it offers few concessions in return. Given his father's closed attitude, this can readily be understood; in view of the author's stated humanistic values, however, it is harder to accept.

According to Asa, Ethen wants to be able to talk to his parents, but can't: The barriers of generation and personality are just too high. In a poignant scene, Ethen, his brother, and his mother sit at home watching the popular British film THE LONELINESS OF THE LONG DISTANCE RUNNER on TV. When it is over, he understands and is inspired by it, while his mother dismisses it in the typical middle-class materialist terms he hates.

In the movie's conclusion, the main character, a reform school inmate, is about to win a footrace that will bring him a coveted prize and personal power. Instead, at the last moment, he slows down and drops out, leaving victory to the rival school.

> "So, what did he accomplish?" Mrs. Bloom asked.
>
> An instant later her sons realized something of what was different between them and their parents. She didn't understand what seemed so obvious and out-front to them. It wasn't that he was trying to accomplish anything (and even if it had been, what would winning a race be accomplishing?!). It was somewhat to the contrary, in that this young kid in a reform school was refusing to sell out his personal freedom for anything; not even for his own physical freedom.

"'It's the system,' he started to say to his mother, 'he didn't want to work for the system...'" but his mother instead deflects such substantive issues by attributing the difference in their views to the influence of foreign films: "'Either they're depressing, or they're all full of dirt, or they're so slow moving that I'm surprised I didn't fall asleep,'" she says. This obfuscating, disconnected attitude reminds Ethen by association that his mother recently offered the ultimatum that if he didn't cut his hair he was no longer entitled to use the family car—hers. This circumstance soon leads him, against his parents' wishes, to buy one of his own, creating one of the many scenes of family dysfunction that make up the book.

Later on, Ethen is referred by his mother to an excerpt from the writing of the sociologist Ernest van den Haag. Although Ethen dismisses it as further brainwashing from the system, the words of this conservative academic, in fact, capsulize the effectiveness of the rebellion Asa and other suburban youth conducted against the views held by their mothers and fathers:

> To be a hippie is guaranteed to upset one's parents, to worry them and make them angry," suggests van den Haag. "When every ambition may have parental support and monetary backing, ambitionlessness is the one way left of getting parents riled....You want me to be neat? I'll dress in the least neat way possible. You want me to use my brains for success? I'll use them to find new ways to fail...I will not be a scholar, or a monetary success. I will be an ambitionless nothing. I will not even be a failure—for a failure is one who tries and does not make it. If I tried, you would not let me fail.

In Ethen's middle-class home—with its two color and two black-and-white televisions, all appropriate kitchen appliances, an electronic garage door opener, a gardener, and a Cadillac and a Pontiac, both new—the truth of van den Haag's observations seems perfectly applied. How could people who have had to work for these things—his parents—not value them or want to pass on to their children the opportunities they have had to acquire them? In Ethen's mind he may be winging it and feel himself inventive and independent; in hindsight, as the aptness of a sociologist's published observations show, he and many other of us were playing it by the book.

In a sense, *THE BLOOM HIGH WAY* is a modern *Bildungsroman,* taking us from the birth of its protagonist to the present moment, through the trials of early adulthood to life on the rural farm from which he was then writing. In its attitudes, language, experience, and influences it reflects the society and culture of which it was the direct result.

In *THE BLOOM HIGH WAY* Ethen hits all the major points in the life of an American boy of his era (and by extension and reversal, those of the American girl as well). As a youth he discovers *SUMMERHILL* and *PEYTON PLACE,* but they are taken away by his parents. The advent of Elvis and the Beatles is described from a front-row living room seat at the *ED SULLIVAN SHOW.* He loses his virginity, smokes his first dope, and takes his first acid. He has his draft physical (no girls here). As mentioned, though forbidden by his parents, he buys a car. Later, he describes a long and tenuous road trip of the sort that most of his generation experienced at one time or another: As the trip progresses, the car falls apart, storms are encountered, safe haven is rejected, but in the end our heroes safely arrive.

However personal, questioning, and intense, the book is a catalogue of widespread postwar adolescent attitudes: dislike of double standards, eschewing inconsistency, reluctance to plan ahead, not wanting to be forced to do things on others' schedules, fighting the repression perceived in parents, schools, and organizations. All the familiar language of the era is there: hair, appearance, dropping out, drugs, hippies—the full antagonistic vocabulary of resistance, experimentation and change. Besides experiences of family and growing up, cardinal points of the larger subculture appear as well: Dylan's "Desolation Row," the siege of the Pentagon, Timothy Leary, Lyndon Johnson, the drug experience, the underground press.

If Asa excels at one thing beyond the overall picture he ably paints in his book, it is his appreciative encomiums to the drug experience. His many explicit references provide a good description of marijuana, mescaline, and LSD, as well as instruction and education for those unfamiliar with their delights (and traumas). In touting these he clearly portrays a more innocent era. How this might all play out is not his concern.

Wilshire Boulevard

At the time of my visit in the winter of 1980, Asa's office was on Wilshire Boulevard and Sixth Street, in Santa Monica, about a quarter of a mile from the ocean and the Pacific Coast Highway. It was an ordinary storefront—California ordinary: a new building, neat and clean. There were about twenty-five desks. Asa and his wife were salespersons for Spring Realty, a company with some thirty offices, "specialists in Los Angeles locations and lifestyles," as they described themselves in one of their brochures. The open waiting area was graced with a tank of tropical fish and copies of *Palm Springs Life.* Asa had a desk in a booth of his own, a sign of some kind of achievement, as there were only two of the more private booths among the many other open desks. Some of the brokers were formally dressed, but jeans and boots predominated. To my New England eye there seemed to be a low threshold of self-consciousness. Middle-aged women dressed like high school girls. To an easterner, Californians seemed to wear their bodies in a more casual way.

Asa had a "Million Dollar Club" plaque by his desk.

"With houses at five hundred thousand," he said, "it's not that hard."

We walked two blocks toward the ocean to have lunch at Zucky's, a favorite local sandwich shop. Asa talked a lot about real estate, and about Los Angeles as a great place *for* real estate.

"The population here has been expanding since the 1860s," he explained, "and it hasn't stopped. It won't stop. LA is Dream City. It draws new people all the time. Even with all the building that's going on, we're far short of the housing we need, and there's no end in sight.

"I came to LA with some screenplays and treatments to sell. I came very close to making it, but"—and he made the motion of a pen with his hand—"no one ever signed the paper. I never made a cent. I sold some photographs, but it was never enough to live on—$75 at most when I was doing well. So I ended up waiting on table.

"It didn't take me long to figure out what was happening in real estate. I would see friends who had paid $20,000 for a house turn around and make an $80,000 profit on it in one year. Sometimes it was a lot more. I figured I was pretty foolish to be waiting on tables when that was going on."

So he got his license. He chose his present agency because it offers a good commission on sales: dollars and sense. Eventually, he'd like to put together enough money to do the buying and selling himself.

"I'm helping these people make money," he said. "If I had the down payment, *I* could be making the money. A lot of people make a comfortable living out here just by buying and selling now and then."

I had come to California to see how people's lives had changed, or not. In view of his marriage and new obligations in real estate, I asked Asa, did he still believe in, and manage to enjoy, the "personal freedom" about which he spoke so strongly in *THE BLOOM HIGH WAY*, with its rural and countercultural values, some ten years before? His answer surprised me.

"I have more freedom now than I used to," he said. "It has a lot to do with real estate, with the kind of work I've chosen. I'm my own boss; I can pick my own hours, and take a vacation or a day off when I want. If I don't like someone, I don't have to deal with him.

"We had freedom at the farm, but it was of a different kind. We had no money. We never knew how we would be able to afford to fix the car or buy our food.

"We used to think money was the least important thing; now I can see that it's the most important. *Money buys freedom,*" he asserted. "I can have the car fixed; I have a place to live; I don't need to worry about those things."

It was clear to me from his descriptions of his work and future plans that he now had free time. Time to do what? I asked. Time to do more deals, he said, so that he can set himself up with a good income, then he will write. Writing is now "on the shelf," he said; "not even on the back burner—*on the shelf*," he repeated for emphasis. Writing is a full-time job, he said. In order to plan for full time writing, he is now engaged in full-time work.

I asked him about goodness. In THE BLOOM HIGH WAY Asa says that we are all good, it's just circumstances that make us bad.

He chuckled. "I've met my share of bad people out here," he said.

I wanted to explore this a little more deeply.

In his book he had described a fiasco that he called the "wedding freakout," in which various of his acquaintances, gathered together for the marriage of a friend, were betrayed by drugs, and perhaps each other, but were, in his view, ultimately redeemed by the difficult experience. What was the lesson to be learned from this? Is it right to let people suffer through such traumas?

Famous Long Ago Archive. Photo: petersimon.com

Asa during his farm days, c.1970.

"As we go through life," he said now, "we face fifty or sixty years full of situations we can't control. It's valuable to see that, to learn to let go and stop trying to control everything."

We talked a bit about the antinuclear movement in which many of our earlier friends are involved, and about a broader range of politics. He felt that the issue of nuclear power was in the hands of dogmatists and had been blown out of proportion.

"Sam and those people still have the battle lines drawn. In the sixties we had a common enemy: the government, the system. Lyndon Johnson *was* the government. Now we can see that things are much more complex than that. There is no single answer. Even an answer brings its own problems along with it. That's why Jimmy Carter got elected: He didn't represent anyone else, any single point of view.

"I agree that nuclear power is a problem, but I'm not going to go out and demonstrate the way we once did. That's too simple; it's just one part of something very complex. I'm too busy, I've got more important things to do."

This certainly was his view, *their* view. As we devoured our lunches at Zucky's, Louise sat next to Asa, polishing her nails and brushing on something around her eyes. Occasionally she took out a pen and made a cute little drawing on the corner of a piece of paper, a teddy bear or a cartoon. Later, she said, she would use these for stationery. She ordered only an egg, poached. When it came, she rejected it disdainfully.

"I hate the runny stuff," she said, pointing to it with a long red nail, as if the restaurant had conspired to displease her.

Here and elsewhere, Asa spent a good deal of time catering to Louise, caressing her endlessly in a conscious attempt to be both solicitous of her many needs and firm about their uncertain status.

He was clearly aware of the changes he had embraced. He called himself a "radical conservative," avowing that in recent years the politics of many of our generation had changed.

"You'll still find a lot of people who believe in the revolution," he said, "but now there are revolutionaries who are Reaganites, as well. I'm fiscally conservative," he declared. "Look at the welfare system; it just doesn't work." Money, he maintained, should be used and thought of differently—in a more economically responsible way, not simply as a cure that can be applied directly to problems.

Other beliefs had taken on a new dimension, as well. I was visiting at the time of the Abscam investigations—politicians caught publicly in a web of deceit. Elected officials should be able to resist temptation, Asa said, they *must* be able to. He believes in clean government; it's essential to meaningful politics. In business, on the other hand, financial inducements are all right. "That's the way business is run," he said.

Some of his cultural idols had also come in for reassessment. When he and Louise were in Beverly Hills, they had lived near Timothy Leary.

"His house was around the corner," said Louise. "He's crazy."

"His mind's fried," said Asa, evidencing a somewhat more educated, first-person view of the Pied Piper of the drug movement. Still, they both agreed on this.

"His wife was screaming one night," recounted Louise. "He'd slipped her some drug. They have a kid. Think of him watching all that."

Leary's wife is young and attractive, they said. He'd tried to launch a career in comedy at a local club. It all sounded rather unlikely.

"Can you imagine being entertained by Tim Leary?" said Asa in hurt astonishment. "It just isn't right."

He drives an expensive imported car. They wondered absently, perhaps in their professional capacity, about the source of his income.

Life in the Canyons

Later, Asa and Louise picked me up at Steve's on their way home from work. It was about 8:30 in the evening as we made our way up the Coast Highway to Pacific Palisades. The road was still strewn with dirt from the recent rains. As Asa piloted his new Olds Cutlass with air conditioning and electric windows up into their canyon, he complained bitterly about the dust. He had just had the car washed. He and Louise pointed out scenes of recent mud slides, and Asa continued to talk about housing values.

At home, we had soup and tea. We had a smoke, and I sat down with Asa to talk.

The house was a triplex condominium, adequately large, but not so by local standards. Relating it to the market, Asa said that there are thousands of similar units in Los Angeles—the word "unit" seems to have replaced "house," "home," or "apartment" in his vocabulary. The lowest price is in the range of $250,000, about ten times the amount we paid ten years ago for each of our spacious farms with their many acres of land. In the living room, a gas fire emanated from fake logs. In the bedroom, on the bureau, a stylish contrivance held coins, pocket cash, watches, and jewelry.

"All the latest conveniences," said Asa, wryly, realizing that these were indications of the many changes in his life. In farm days there was little cash and no one believed in watches. Among males, at least, a single pendant, most likely a peace symbol, would have sufficed for jewelry, and could be hung on the doorknob at night.

Outside the house, grass had not yet begun to grow on the surrounding red soil. The units, lined up in a row as they proceeded in uneasy order up the canyon, were so recent that signs of excavation were common. New units continued to be built, extending the settlement farther; several under construction were clearly visible farther up the little valley. Asa said their condo had been built four years ago.

"New," I said.

"Out here," he replied, "it's four years *old.*"

Later in the evening, Louise had a snack fit.

"Where could we go?" she asked distractedly. She called a store she knew, but it was closed. She returned reluctantly to her makeup table, which seemed to hold all the supplies of a well-equipped artist's studio.

"I wish I had some M&Ms," she said wistfully.

When we finished talking, we played some music. Louise had heard that I was an amateur musician, and got out her nylon-stringed folk guitar. We didn't sound too bad, but it was a stretch. I kept thinking: Here I am, up in a canyon condominium in Los Angeles, singing old Joan Baez songs with a realtor's wife.

To join us, Louise got stoned also. For some reason, though, she was unhappy with it.

In the morning, I saw that the sliding glass doors of the living room in which I had slept looked out on the mountainous verge of the canyon. It was a pleasant if limited view.

For breakfast Asa offered a hearty selection from their larder. Louise had one poached egg. "I wish we had some M&Ms," she said.

Although there were condos on every buildable site the eye could see, a closer look revealed that they were not for the elite, but for a comfortably upper-middle-class market. Asa described the Beverly Hills homes he tries to sell: two million each; Rolls Royces are common.

He talked about his time at the farms.

"I wasn't happy there," he reminisced. "I hated it," he added more firmly. Among other things, he said, it was too dirty.

But he values the time he spent there.

"Think of how many people have never farmed, or even planted a garden," he said. "I think it makes us more aware. I don't feel I was sidetracked; it was all valuable."

Interestingly, the brothers he mentioned in *THE BLOOM HIGH WAY* have taken a very different tack from his own. His younger brother studies philosophy at Princeton, and the older is an economist at Yale. Perhaps it was appropriate, after all, that Asa ended up at Grasshopper Farm, the most financially stable and conspicuously upscale of our group of farms.

As realtors, Asa and Louise had a distinctly interested view of one of Southern California's important issues: rent control. Santa Monica, where Steve lives and where they work, is at the center of the movement.

"It's not good," said Asa, a little ruffled at the obvious divergence from the point of view of his earlier radical days. "Landlords won't have enough money to repair their properties. After rent control was enacted, 8,000 units were immediately taken down by owners who didn't want to rent anymore." The whole movement, he asserted dismissively, was organized by Tom Hayden and funded by Jane Fonda, implying that without their backing there would be no valid issues or financial support.

As the visit wound down and we prepared to leave, I stepped out onto the tiny balcony to look at the mountains. Louise came, too.

"This is the fanciest place I've ever lived," she said, and she smiled. "It's so beautiful; I love it. When I had my apartment in Beverly Hills, I couldn't relate to anyone around there. Here I can. Of course, it's expensive—" She glanced around, taking in the hills, the rows of late-model cars, and string of condos, and offered a look of evident satisfaction. "It's called living beyond your means."

As we were leaving, I asked where they were going for the weekend. To my surprise, Asa and Louise's plans consisted of a visit to his parents, in Palm Springs. They had moved several years ago from Long Island, where they had sold the motel and beach resort featured in Asa's novel, to Palm Springs, the affluent suburb of Los Angeles, where they had bought another. Later, they had sold this California property and retired. Asa and Louise were frequent weekend visitors at their new home. After we had gone our separate ways, I gave some thought to how this unlikely peace might have been achieved.

Asa's book had emphasized a return to childhood, a romantic, transcendental vision in which drugs and clean living brought a world in which "no fear, no anxiety, no guilt, no greediness, no embarrassment, nervousness, pain, jealousy, restrictiveness" need be experienced. "There must be a way to get back to that original goodness and innocence," muses Ethen, the protagonist, at one point.

The world he describes is, of course, no newer than the Biblical Eden. Certainly one can say, as Asa correctly did, that the generation of the sixties resisted the challenges of adulthood with great vigor, and on a scale that might even with some justification be called mythic.

But rereading his book, it seemed to me that this transcendental quality—even the word itself is used, especially in connection with drugs—represents a philosophy not of the engagement of Thoreau or Emerson but of the avoidance of some of Asa's other, more contemporary heroes: Kerouac, Leary, Mungo; aspirants to clarity who have tended to leave in their personal wake, instead, a trail of confusion.

This *helpless* quality with respect to events offers a door to worlds other than Asa's own—almost any world, since, as he had told me, and stated often in his book, we should try to loosen up and less often take control. Indeed, it is not unlike the situation of the very soldiers in the war we had all protested; certainly, for the most part, they were not in Asia by their own choice.

Throughout his book there are repeated instances in which Ethen, his friends and acquaintances avoid real solutions to difficulties in favor of salving their personal needs and beliefs, in the hope that all will come out right—"as it should be," they would say—in the end.

At the "wedding freakout," the consistent moral offered is that problems left alone will solve themselves. Earlier, Ethen had created havoc for one of his teachers in order to serve his own needs. He regrets it, but it is not clear that he is ever willing to take responsibility for his actions.

From early on in the book, when our hero gets his first bad mark in school (a surprise for such a good student), a reader gains the distinct impression that Ethen, and thus his progenitor, Asa, emphatically threw away their prodigious talents in the cause of resistance. In contrast with his potential as editor of the high school paper, award-winning writer, attractive and energetic youth, and original intellect, the negative streak in his thinking becomes increasingly clear. Like his mentor, Raymond, he is a bit the provocateur; like our friend Jeannette, he feels he has nothing to lose.

In watching cultural history in the making on the ED SULLIVAN SHOW, he notes in his book that the Beatles shook their hair around "and winked as if they knew something somebody didn't...something about being so big and so famous and so popular that you could get away with anything, *anything.*" This aspect of the sixties is not a prescription for responsibility. Nor is the remark of the Chief Boo Hoo of Timothy Leary's Neo-American Church, an institution much admired in the book, whom Ethen (and no doubt Asa) interviewed at their notorious Millbrook, New York, estate. "I have a permanent open invitation to do anything I want," bragged the Boo Hoo, one of the high officials of Leary's church, while, as the author notes, his bored wife pours him, as necessary, drunk and incapacitated, into and out of his aging Mercedes.

In the late sixties, when Asa was in Boston at the university, both the town and the institution were as repressive and difficult a place as he claims. I know; I was living there myself. "Boston was so straight in those days," he recounts in the book, "that most of its scores of universities and colleges forbade their female students to wear pants in public, refused to allow students to live in off-campus housing, refused to allow members of opposite sexes into each other's dorms, refused students a voice in the decision-making over them, were always telling them where and what they couldn't do..."

Beyond this, as I can attest, it was a city of great intolerance where difference and nonconformity were confused with issues of selfhood and patriotism. This was the world in which, at the time, we all lived.

Becoming a "stoned student activist," as Ethen calls it, was certainly an option, a new choice of which many availed themselves. Under the powerful sway of Raymond—an influential figure on a relatively large scale—and within the stabilizing context of the radical student newspaper, and later the farms, Asa set his new course in this direction.

In this way, Asa, at the time, was extremely fortunate. Underground newspapers and communal culture offered a scene, an alternative way of life still linked to the real world. The Liberation News Service and Asa's stint as a journalist during the Vietnam protests offered him the sort of integrity he respected. Being in the news as well as reporting it supplied an exciting new style of life then gaining the prominence one senses he craved. The farms advanced a welcome prospect of moral clarity.

Later, on the West Coast, on his own and outside that supportive scene, it was perhaps necessary, I speculated, to revert to the causeless, blameless, directionless portion of the world in which as a rebellious youth he had earlier claimed to believe. The surprise was that he was now on the other side. But it wouldn't be that lonely. Besides Louise for company, he now had his parents.

Chapter 5

Steve Diamond

What the Palms Said

Steve Diamond

On their way to Palm Springs, Asa and Louise dropped me back at Steve's. It was a beautiful day. I minded their young daughter Crescent, while Steve and his wife Judy went out to do errands. I sat outside while she played and I went over some notes. After a late lunch with Judy and Crescent, I went for a walk, exploring their neighborhood in the Ocean Park section of Santa Monica, and visiting the local bookstore, a cooperative, politically engaged venture where we later went for a benefit potluck dinner. In the evening they went out to see a movie by a director with whom Steve is in touch; apparently he wants to do a film about marijuana.

During the day I spoke a lot with Judy, a lawyer involved in public service work. She explained that Tom Hayden and Jane Fonda hadn't actually organized the local tenants but that they did, indeed, lend their support to the movement and often associated themselves with its work. Tom is a longtime friend of Judy; the couple lives only a few blocks away. Judy takes them with a grain of salt. Shortly after she and Steve had arrived in California, they all went to a movie together. Judy and Steve were living a life of austerity and had had to overdraw their bank account just to get through the week, of which the movie was to have been the high point. When they got to the theater, Jane—

star of *BARBARELLA* and other distinctly materialist vehicles—didn't have enough money to get in.

What the Trees Said

Hanging with the stars was a role that Steve had always relished, and occasionally attained, but it was a long way from the farm he had written about, where we had met. At the farm, Steve was the premier champion both of our new alternative way of life and of the farm enterprise itself. He had seen it from its beginnings, as a gleam in the eye of Marshall, at the News Service in New York, through all of its various stages up to the time of my current visit. He knew the principal players in our scene, and many more beyond. As a writer and editor influenced by James Agee, Lawrence Durrell, Jack Kerouac, and Hermann Hesse, he had cast a sagacious, somewhat romanticized eye over our activities (including his own) and in the early years of our venture produced *WHAT THE TREES SAID*, a slim but cogent and highly readable volume portraying life on a New Age farm.

Steve was even then a talented and experienced writer, and in *WHAT THE TREES SAID* he did an extremely creditable job of presenting both the overall tone of farm life and some of the critical points in its development. Beginning in what then seemed the Dark Ages of its genesis—only two years before he wrote—he described the farm's growth from Movement news service to rural farm commune. Later in the book he went on to portray its evolution from commune to New Age family, a subject by then of more interest to him. In *WHAT THE TREES SAID*, Steve attempted to plumb what life at the farm was really about, to tout some of its theories and ideals, and by way of an ending, describe its most significant challenge to date: the death of its leader, Marshall Bloom. In between, he offered wisdom, humor, some relevant background, and a bit of playful head-scratching appropriate to the sometimes confusing period we had been through.

Steve wrote easily, in an appreciative, unlabored way. The tone of the book is personal, almost intimate. Often the reader, who is assumed to have some interest in the subject, is addressed directly. Like the times in which it was written, *WHAT THE TREES SAID* is full of revelations to be shared: the "pleasing shock" of recognition between future lovers, the unsuspected joy of milking the cow, the pleasure and distress of a first drug trip. Testing new social and cultural waters, the author's outlook embraces whatever insights a young man in his twenties might be prepared to offer, and a dash of the ready humor our newly invented world supplied. When our first spring order of seeds arrives in the mail, Steve conveys his charm at finding that the garden will be replete with such colorful personalities of the agricultural domain as Spring Gold corn, Green Comet broccoli and Pacesetter onions—the latter, according to the seed packet he quotes, the "Speed King of the Root World!"

Perhaps in part because of these qualities, which offered a low-key, accessible view of new developments in society, along with the

Photo: Christopher Green

Steve Diamond, c.1970.

implicit assumption that you might choose to participate in them yourself, Steve's book, like Ray's first two, *FAMOUS LONG AGO* and *TOTAL LOSS FARM,* was quickly adopted by—and has remained a part of—curricula in schools and colleges dealing with social change and contemporary history in America.

Indeed, as with Steve's other writings, and other places he has lived, there is the distinct sense in this book that he was comfortable at the farm. He conveys this to a reader. It is a non-threatening, user-friendly account of cultural change.

Given the actual condition of the place and the way of life he was depicting, this was a substantial achievement. As he well describes, and we have seen earlier, to its members, life at the farm was all new. In a world of "disorganization and chaos" in which communal farmers slept on floors, in tents, and among bales of hay; in which visitors came and went in no discernible pattern; in which relationships devolved into cross-country separations and occasional reunions, and money was in short supply, the main mission of life at the farm, at the time Steve wrote about it, was simply to try to figure out what life at the farm was in fact supposed to be. In the presence of constant uncertainty and confusion, the search for order and survival took precedence.

In the end, Steve wisely concluded in *WHAT THE TREES SAID* that the significance of the farm in those early days was that it did address these issues and, however painfully, occasionally joyfully, move through them. By taking action and control, a potentially marginalized portion of the New Left became instead a hopeful outpost of a New Age, and a disorganized commune evolved into a tightly knit family. Steve's appreciative descriptions of our fecund garden reveal the farm's strong links to the earth. His narration of the communal farmers happily tearing down the walls of their living room to create new open space in the house displays the empowerment they felt. As Steve points out, in the context of the time, now perhaps hard to remember, the rural commune was a logical next step in life for the culture- and war-torn young of mid-twentieth-century America. The farm, with its strong grounding, emphasis on place, and development of a collective style, was an effort to provide a home for what he called a "homeless, nationless tribe"—the youth of the postwar generation: ourselves.

In Steve and his writings there are also qualities about which I cannot be as sanguine. The centerpiece of the book is a recounting of his first mescaline trip, in which he experiences a vision of Native Americans floating in the air behind the barn, and the conversation with a row of maple trees from which the book takes its title. On one hand, these are genuine elements among the firsthand experiences he relates to us. On the other, his credulous treatment of such adventures betrays an attraction toward the spiritual and the occult that often clouds more disinterested perception. In the world toward which he leans, personification trumps identity, nicknames and epithets replace more strongly etched character, and the presence of ineffable "magic" in the air supplies a set of folkways impossible to adequately confirm or objectively describe.

Steve has a genuine bent toward the mystical. I don't at all doubt that he himself has had the encounters and sensed the sometimes surprising nuances he relates, whether connected with drugs or—just as often—not. Drugs and mysticism were, after all, a perfect fit for the people of the sixties and early seventies, a highly personal, insular form of experience of which only oneself and one's close peers were the appropriate judges. Over the years I have learned to accept Steve's visions and adventures as part of the person I know; in this he is simply on his own recognizance. But for my own part, relying on direct experience and independent examination, I remain convinced that the truly surprising experiences in this world are interpersonal and confirmable. Without this, a certain element of tension necessary to true surprise disappears behind a miasma of imagination, however creative a principle that might be.

As with Asa it concerns me, as one who also experienced that time, that in the name of all the substantial and real novelties of the era, exceptions are conveniently made for lapses in judgment or admissions of inaction that reflect simply on the various individuals and their environment—matters over which we had as much control as others at other times and places in history. In *WHAT THE TREES SAID* Steve enjoys the occasional company of an alcoholic neighbor but claims not to be close enough to him to help him do anything about his habit. He frequently projects his own vision onto social situations, reassuring himself of his private world, while avoiding the obvious public one before him. As a journalist, he is upset as he covers the demise of the historical portion of a New England city, but in the end decides that all he can do is to retreat to the farm to help build a sugarhouse and cut firewood.

There is a difference between withdrawing from a problem temporarily in order to fashion a better solution, and retreating from it completely. At the farm, both were in evidence. The latter type of behavior, however, may be the one that confirms the vision of Steve's trees—with which he conversed along the quiet dirt

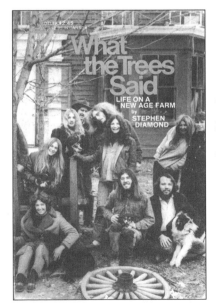

Cover of Steve Diamond's
WHAT THE TREES SAID,
Delacorte, 1971.

Famous Long Ago Archive. Photo: petersimon.com. Courtesy Delacorte Press.

road that ran through the farm—that he and others at the farm might "never get to the main road." At the time this was a comforting and reclusive thought. In light of later experience, it might perhaps be said to constitute a central flaw in their outlook.

This perspective shows up in the language Steve chooses, both in his writing and his conversation. At key moments words emerge such as "weird," "bizarre," or "amazing," words that express notice of people, actions, or events, but are nonjudgmental in regard to their content or character. In this way one remains a participant and an accepted observer, without having to declare the possibly contentious specifics of one's values.

Similarly, irony and contrast are tools frequently used in WHAT THE TREES SAID and other New Age writing and conversation. In looking at farm life, we were all charmed to find, as Steve relates, that we had a stove but that it ran on wood; that poverty helped keep us free; that time could be considered money, making us all, in Raymond's felicitously recycled phrase, "independently wealthy." For us, the words "family trip" conjured up not Yellowstone or Yosemite but mescaline and acid.

There is, of course, a certain humor and mild wisdom to this. We were, after all, mostly in our early twenties and as yet unlearned in the complexities of the world we were beginning to face. Ultimately, however, the truth of this paradoxical point of view was proved in another way. Before long, many of the farmers who had loved to hate New York found themselves living and working there. Asa, who had spurned the materialistic lifestyle of his parents, eventually joined them in Palm Springs, one of its ultimate haunts, and the writers of the farms—he and Steve among them—who had hated Hollywood and the publishing world for their perceived falseness and illegitimate cultural power, all soon wanted in on these scenes themselves.

When Steve says, in a discussion of Marshall, that in the sixties, for all of us as for Marshall himself, "the times went awry," he is certainly correct. On the other hand, for a period—and, in Marshall's case, an individual story—of such extraordinary dislocation, pain, and misunderstanding, this is a rather bland descriptor. More poignant are some of the moments captured in the book's illustrations, and odd observations on the fringes of our lives at that time that appear between the lines of the text. A photo of Raymond cavorting at the farms in the winter snow in a jester's outfit, for example, brought to mind this thought not mentioned in the book: Some in the sixties played at youthfulness and pleasure simply because they hadn't had the chance before. Growing up in a mill town, repressed by Catholicism, achieving his way into the university, crusading editor, News Service founder, New Age farmer and author: When was Raymond supposed to enjoy himself? Smoking dope, investigating sex, talking with his friends, cavorting carelessly in the snow provided an answer. Given the restrictive past of some of our friends at the farms, it is no wonder that life in the New Age was so attractive.

Panama Red

Shortly before I visited in California, Steve had published a second book, a novel, PANAMA RED. For an aspiring writer of the New Age, publishing a 400-page story of love and intrigue based on a plan to legalize marijuana was a vision achieved. Printed by a major publisher in a pocket-size paperback edition for newsstand and drugstore distribution, PANAMA RED had appeared regularly at various locations during my trips to New York. I soon recognized the lurid cover and picked up a copy, wanting to read it before I went west. Since it is largely a work of fiction, it concerns the present story only in its relation to Steve and the elements in the book that are derived from the farm group. For the rest, I can only recommend it as a good read.

As a product of the writer I know, PANAMA RED is highly characteristic. It is well organized and fast paced. But as with other encounters I have had with Steve, my reading of his novel raised questions of content and credence. Cloaked in the adventure, particular quality, and optimism of the plot I saw numerous references to other worlds as the source of solutions I suspect we need to accomplish here on earth. The quota of mysticism was very high, and Steve's affinity for symbols, signs, occult communication, and the supernatural were much in evidence. His upbringing in Panama also provided a defining element of the plot, and his Jewish background a distinctive tone to several of the characters.

Of the characters themselves, a number were drawn from, and their experiences reflected, our friends from the farm. Scenes of the marijuana trade recalled Pete, Phil, and their friends. The life of a pop singer as she emerges into public life from a protected family environment was clearly based on that of a regular visitor to Grasshopper Farm. Touches of rural life, along with an understanding of New York reflected Steve, who had been a student at Columbia and a colleague at LNS. Many other details are recognizable to anyone knowing the story and personalities of the farms.

Putting the two together—the author and his world— *PANAMA RED* would appear to be a serious accomplishment. Like

Cover of Steve Diamond's *PANAMA RED*, Avon Books, 1979.

Famous Long Ago Archive. Courtesy Avon Books.

all such endeavors, though, it reveals as much about its author as it does about what he is trying to say. Its strength is that it is very much of its time—a chapter of the history of the late sixties in fictive form. Its weakness is that it also embodies the credulous aspect of that era: that somehow believing will make it so. In this sense, *PANAMA RED* represents such belief on a rather large scale. I suspect the book was mismarketed. Rather than a newsstand page-turner directed at the romance market (it was advertised in *Cosmopolitan,* among other places), it should probably have been published in the tradition of Tom Robbins and Richard Brautigan, as a cult literary fable of interest to readers of a new and liberated era. This is clearly the readership that its author, who referred to it to me as "the *GODFATHER* of the stoned generation," had in mind.

In any case, at the time when I visited Steve in California, he was still much under the influence of this publishing success, as well as of the ebullience generated by the MUSE concerts and related activities in New York. Although he told me that it had taken him two years and eighteen publishers to get *PANAMA RED* into print, that difficult experience was not stopping him from believing that the book was a key to his future involvement in publishing and film. Indeed, connecting to Hollywood in order to do more with both of his books was the primary motive for his and Judy's move to California, though Judy's own roots in the state played a role as well.

The farms and their extended family on both coasts, whatever may have been their dalliance with nature, were media mavens. Authors, poets, photographers, activists, filmmakers, or journalists, they all needed outlets. Steve told me, eyes lit with enthusiasm, about a visit from Jeannette and Ray to a house in which he and Judy had been staying north of Los Angeles. It belonged to a radical lawyer they knew through Judy, and had a spectacular view of the city. Jeannette and Ray had brought a prerelease tape of the No Nukes recordings, and they sat outdoors on the patio smoking and listening to this secret stash of sound. For farm friends in this era, these were high times.

At moments like these they would share the GMP/No Nukes/Clamshell vision of which I had heard in New York, the Year 2000, 54-year-old fantasy. Again, Steve related it to me. "In the year 2000," he said, *"we* will be the majority." The uniting force would be the culture of the sixties: Dylan, communes, civil rights, the Beatles. It was a shared experience; even those who hadn't participated would remember it from radio, records, television, and film. People like Sam would get elected to public office, and social attitudes that had once gotten us into trouble would be badges of courage and experience. It was a great fantasy. Whether it would prove sustainable we did not at that time know.

In Steve's world, one fantasy leads to another. Soon, in his enthusiasm, he had moved from a vision of the future to one of the past, and he was talking about the roots of today's Movement in ancient Atlantis. We have many lives, he said, looking earnestly at me, referring to reincarnation; the present one is just a learning experience for a higher one in the future. The Atlanteans once reached the point we are at now. They had high technology, but the technologists, advocating nuclear power, won the political battle and ringed Atlantis with nuclear plants. Our class was, as it is now, "into communications," he said, but it did not succeed in adequately spreading the No Nukes message. The result: the melting of the polar ice caps. Fearing the flood that followed, the communicators sent their best people to the highest places: Tibet, the Andes. Their descendants still survive. If we tune in to their wisdom, we may yet have a second chance.

From here, Steve segued into Gurdjieff, *NEUROPOLITICS* by Timothy Leary ("one of the world's most amazing people"), and *THE FINAL SECRET OF THE ILLUMINATI* ("very important"). As I suspected that this was about as far as I would be able to follow him at one sitting, I politely excused myself to take a walk.

Venice Beach

Like those of many Angelinos, Steve and Judy's house is a modest, low bungalow, one of several in a rectangular court in Ocean Park, comfortably off the street, surrounding a garden and a lawn. I suppose this is a vestige of Spanish culture, or perhaps its rebirth in the real estate boom at the turn of the twentieth century. Growth is lush, trees tower over, and of course the air is warm. Bird-of-paradise, other exotic plants, and the occasional garish colors of architectural stucco lend a dreamlike quality to buildings and places otherwise remarkably plain. Walking out of the compound to the street, I stepped over a couple hugging on the steps. "Hi," they each said, as if they were just glad to see another human being and this was the way they usually spent their day.

At the corner, the wide avenues of Los Angeles stretched, palm lined, north and south for miles in each direction. At each end a range of rugged mountains terminated the view. As I walked down Strand toward the ocean, the fragrance of eucalyptus mingled with the smell of barbeque as people enjoyed weekend relaxation in shaded courts. At the end of Strand the view opened up. Across the last avenue was the Pacific. In the space before me were sailboats, palms, and skaters. A light wind blew. The ocean ended in a taut line far out at sea.

Californians love motion. In the large, paved lot at the foot of Strand (parking for the beach) were skaters and skateboarders, some moving by sail power. Bicyclists in old jeans were doing wheelies, while the more competitive breezed past on ten-speeds in goggles and brightly colored Spandex. Joggers of all ages thudded by as hobbyists tinkered with desert buggies and hot rods, then tested their work by taking them for a spin.

It was a tremendous space teeming with life. Everything seemed to be happening at once. Cars dodged skaters, bikers jousted with cyclists. An occasional motorcycle tilted through when a straight line could be found to noisily speed up. There was constant movement. All seemed to be having great fun.

For lunch we walked to Venice Beach. For a New Englander in winter, this was a scene of complete wonder. Its level of activity was a step above the parking lot at Strand, like a busy Breughel in the baking sun. (Later I recognized it as the site of Max Yavno's famous 1949 photograph "Muscle Beach," which gives a good sense of what I saw.) Around me were mimes, jugglers, and clowns. "Whoops, a gust of gravity," smiled a juggler as he stooped to pick up an errant ball. I listened to a white-haired street musician. A young mother in a silver lame tank top cruised through on skates at top speed, pushing a stroller, executing a full turn for good measure—both mother and dizzied child. A young black musician in an Arab caftan glided easily by, skating and playing an electric guitar, a battery-powered amp strapped to his back—Jimi Hendrix on wheels.

The message of Venice Beach seemed to be: Relax, enjoy, take it easy. The eternal childhood and penchant for fantasy for which California has become known were much on display. Skaters wore minimal, tight clothes, headphones, cowboy hats, and an endless variety of T-shirts with monikers such as "Body by Diane," or Brenda, or Jeff—riffs on a popular advertisement of the day. The ocean would have been a stone's throw, if it hadn't been all sand. The only stones in evidence were of the rolling variety. Palms waved languorously overhead. There were thousands of people. I thought I probably was the only one wearing anything as conservative as a Brooks knit shirt and creased dress slacks. Among the street vendors and skate shops, if you didn't have a skintight T-shirt, and either own or feign youth, you were pretty much out of place.

But then there is that other side of California. Ironically, to be truly free requires a certain amount of discipline. Skaters, bikers, and joggers had their own designated lanes. At the entry to beach parking (and much other parking and traffic control in the state) were signs emphasizing correct traffic flow: "Do Not Enter: Severe Tire Damage." Once I saw the clever but vicious metal spikes referred to, and witnessed pedestrians and motorists ticketed for what in the East would have been considered matters of personal judgment, I realized that the spirit of enforcement was genuine. Of course, it needs to be: You can't cruise comfortably on bike, skates or sail board if a car, or truck, or even a pedestrian might unexpectedly interrupt your flight path.

Intrigues and Maneuvers

On the way back we stopped to look at a small cottage Steve and Judy had admired. They were renting and hoped to be able to buy, but even this modest house turned out to be worth about $285,000, way out of their current range.

Tom and Jane had a bigger house nearby, though apparently nothing fancy, and friends of Steve and Judy from the east had bought a similar one in the same neighborhood to start a commune. Both were valued at almost half a million dollars. To paraphrase Woody Guthrie, California is great, if you can afford it:

California's a Garden of Eden,
A Paradise to live in and see,
But believe it or not
You won't find it so hot
If you ain't got the do-re-mi.

The subject of Tom and Jane came up again when we returned to the year 2000 fantasy. One of the current problems with the fantasy, for Steve and the farm crew, was that others had recognized it, too. Among them were Tom and Jane. Their chosen candidate of the future was, however, not Sam but Tom himself, a radical activist of long standing, with considerable connections and credibility.

"If they even *knew* there was another radical thinking about this, there would be big trouble," Steve confided. "They have a candidate, too, but they've also got a thousand people behind them, five hundred of whom have money."

In Steve's view, Tom and Jane were actually relatively conservative.

"Oh, they wouldn't touch Sam for a long time," he said. "To them Sam was a *terrorist.*" He emphasized the word. "They wouldn't have anything to do with him. But then there was Seabrook and Clamshell, and suddenly everybody wanted to be in on the success and get some credit. Sure, they had been anti-nuke before, but very cautiously.

"It was the same with Ellsberg," said Steve—Daniel Ellsberg, source for THE PENTAGON PAPERS. "The focus was on defense. But nuclear power is a much better way of talking to people about radiation," he said. "As soon as you get into defense, people say, 'Well, we *need* defense.'"

Still, perhaps some working arrangement among these potential competitors could be reached. The night before, Steve had taken a proposal for a project called ENS, Energy News Service, over to Tom's "right-hand man."

ENS loomed large in Steve's world at the time. As currently planned, it was to be a weekly packet of columns, news, and cartoons focused on the issue of energy. It would be prepared in ready-to-paste-up form, making it easy to use.

"We polled a thousand newspapers and radio stations," he said. "The public is ready for it. 'Light 'n lively' would be the mode: not too heavy, but between the lines the No Nukes message."

Tom's interest in ENS was obvious. "They want to be in on it so that he can have a column alongside major figures like Barry Commoner and Ralph Nader," said Steve. But," he added, with an enigmatic smile, "Sam would have a column, too." I could see the problem.

As Steve explained, ENS needed them as well. "Through their nonprofit, CED—Campaign for Economic Development—they have $30,000 that has to be put into energy and media. It's from a friend of theirs who recorded a song. It's on his album. The album is doing pretty well, and he assigned the rights to CED. That kind of thing is happening out here much more than it is in the East."

CED is interesting in its own right. Jane has started a health center, possibly to become a chain, with production of videos and other programs to further expand upon it. The profits are to go to CED. This is the equation used by MUSE and other ambitious non-profits. Income is developed on the basis of a name, a product, a performance, or similar influence of some kind. The resulting funds are redirected toward changing the system from which they came. For a generation whose resources are often still small and scattered, it is a plan for leveraging change that makes some sense.

Steve's ties to Tom and Jane came through Judy, who had earlier worked with them on political and social justice projects in the East. She had also known Tom through connections she had had to the trial of the Chicago 8. Steve and Judy themselves had met back in Massachusetts, where Judy had moved with her partner Andy. Both Judy and Andy had been social and political activists in the region of the farms, and we all had mutual friends. Eventually, Judy left Andy to marry Steve. Steve's girlfriend, Betty, later married Andy.

It was a tight world—so tight, I suspect, that the openness and relative anonymity of California eventually looked pretty good. But while Steve tended to see humor in all this, and no doubt the workings of fate, Judy as always saw it with the steely-clear eyes of an attorney.

"Those were the good old days," Steve reminisced one morning over breakfast, speaking mistily about this earlier chapter of our lives at the farm. "We didn't have to get up and go to work, we could stay in bed as long as we wanted."

"Yeah," said Judy, as she continued serving the meal, "—with Betty," and offered an understanding smile.

Steve's Big Break

Tom and Jane and MUSE, as well as other connections to the antinuclear movement, had yielded some genuine contacts in the film industry. Through a producer interested in Steve's principal

[212]

causes, No Nukes and the legalization of marijuana, he had been negotiating for work in the film world, as well as trying to sell his own properties WHAT THE TREES SAID and PANAMA RED. The first he saw as a TV series, the second as a feature film. To my knowledge, neither ever came to pass.

Around dinnertime of the day we went to Venice Beach, Steve burst in to tell us he had gotten his first big break. There was great elation and excitement. On the table he put down SAVE THE PLANET, a film he had worked on with farm friends in Massachusetts, which he had just shown to an antinuclear fund-raising group. Along with it were two screenplays and a film treatment. A producer who was a member of the fund-raising group had agreed to give him $6000 for work on the three pieces he had brought home, and another $4000 for the development of a book and movie idea of his own, though he had shown no interest in PANAMA RED as Steve had hoped.

In those days, for a newcomer outside the industry, and for the newly resettled Steve and Judy, this was very reasonable money. After finishing dinner, during which we stared reverently at the yellow plastic film mailing case that contained SAVE THE PLANET, which had never left the center of the table, celebration seemed to be in order and we trooped over to the West Beach Café. Over delicate tarts and strong coffee, I admired the distinctly West Coast character of the place: flat white walls, elegant, modern, understated appointments, a Mediterranean atmosphere, and a clientele so well groomed as to seem almost caricatures of themselves.

For Steve, celebrating a coup based to some degree on SAVE THE PLANET, this was an occasion to consider the group's success and, as always, where possible, to extend it. Like anyone in or near the farm group who has taken initiative of any kind—in my case research and writing on the farms, and the current trip—I was a prospect for incorporation into the brain trust. During my visit Steve had developed an obsession with reconnecting me in some functional way to the group. A Green Mountain Post Library was the form this particular fancy took at the moment, based, of course, at the college where I was then working. (Annexing the already established authority of another organization is always appealing.) I wouldn't have to do much, Steve said, to come in under the GMP umbrella, just a letterhead and a brochure would be enough to turn me into the institution he presumed I wanted to be, a comfortable subsidiary of the group.

Thus surfaced a conversation we have continued to have ever since, and which really went back to my earliest days at the farm. (Steve had actually written about it in his book.) Some are *not* comfortable joining. I was always surprised by the extent to which this place and this group, dedicated to individual freedom, so often reverted to the law of the clan. It was not one of its most appealing aspects. As always, I resisted. He went on with his pitch. Eventually talk returned to his own trip.

"Getting our ideas into the mainstream, that's what's important," he said, "and we're getting closer now." Steve feels that "the forces" are much in evidence now, doing their part, guiding him. (He is constantly, literally, knocking on wood. Judy, the trained attorney, carries an astrological date book.) His principal mission at this point is something he calls straightening out his karma.

"In my life-reading with Elwood"—the one that had been recorded in Green Mountain Post Films' VOICES OF SPIRIT, a documentary on the Massachusetts trance medium Elwood Babbitt—"he told me I might be in a position to clean up my karma in this life, and I wouldn't have to come back. Right now that's what I'm doing. I run across all kinds of people from earlier parts of my life, people I might have done some disservice to. Now I'm in a position to do something for them. That's what ENS is about. It's the completion of a karmic circuit. I stopped LNS, you know," he concluded, referring to the story of the end of the news service he had told in WHAT THE TREES SAID.

In one way he was talking about himself; in another way he was still angling to involve me, though unfortunately in something in which I had little interest. I tried to imagine slipping under the corporate umbrella of a group whose circle included ties to Pete's escorts and drugs, the alternative life of Greenwich Village, the power of the stars and the magic of Aleister Crowley. It didn't seem promising.

"There has always been a lot of pressure in this group to belong," I said. "But usually I have to resist. That's just the way I am."

"Oh, yeah," nodded Steve. A worried look crossed his face.

The next morning we dashed in Steve's well-worn Volvo down the Santa Monica Freeway. Steve was on his way to work, a part-time gig at a Los Angeles newspaper. I was hoping to catch the 10 A.M. train north toward San Francisco. A brown haze hung over the city and the ocean nearby. In Los Angeles, clean air is a joke.

"A losing battle?" I asked.

"Already lost," said Steve. "You just get used to it."

I thought a bit about my visit. There was a project to get the LNS surveillance files from the government through the Freedom of Information act, but I wasn't sure we would learn anything we didn't already know or suspect. Steve spoke of economic equality and liberating the world from nuclear power, but he was considering working for *Oui* or *Hustler:* Where was the justice there? On the other hand, he and Judy were certainly on the populist side of the fight for rent control (Judy was a judge in the rent control system); Asa had made it clear that he was not.

Steve and Judy didn't trust Asa anymore, despite he and Steve having once been close. Comparing him to our friend Pete, the dope dealer in New York, Steve said, "Oh, I trust Pete a hundred percent more than I trust Asa. His motives are good, I'm convinced of that. But he operates in a tough world, gangsters and all that ..." He laughed at the word. "It's true, he knows all those guys." Steve saw Asa, as most did, as sliding inevitably closer to his parents. In view of the strong opinions voiced in THE BLOOM HIGH WAY, Steve seemed perplexed about what had become of Asa. He seemed vaguely to hope that he might return to the fold. He sighed. "I don't know how it fits together," he said.

We screeched to a stop at the station. I thanked him, grabbed my things, and ran for the train.

Chapter 6

RAYMOND MUNGO

Prisoner in Disguise

Raymond Mungo

The Coast Starliner pulled out of LA, moving by a circuitous route north toward Ventura and the shore. The miles and miles of regular, low housing that make up the city gave way to desert communities. Each house seemed to have a horse and a pool under its prescribed regimen of orange and palm trees. As the housing receded, the land became more prominent; red hills and sandstone boulders: I recognized the locale of the western. Sagebrush grew in abandoned parking lots. Trails over hills shaped by wind and erosion, separated by arroyos, marked the more contemporary playgrounds of dirt bikes and four-wheel-drive vehicles.

Above Ventura was the sultry Pacific. In the distance, mysterious, mountainous, cloud-covered islands loomed. Closer to shore, dull, gray oil rigs stood stiffly in the water; surfers, oblivious, sported in the waves. Santa Barbara appeared, a city of low, housed hills arrayed against the dramatic backdrop of the Coastal Range, with the sea before it. A motorcycle cruised along a freeway parallel to the train, apparently unmoving, the mountains rushing behind. On the ocean side were oil derricks and refineries. In California there is so much nature that man is hardly noticeable, and there is so much of California that this holds true even in a place like Los Angeles, where despite its vast population, endless building, and extensive system of highways, it is the surrounding range of mountains that defines the space.

Beyond Santa Barbara the land turns to pasture. Horses and Black Angus graze under lone, biblical trees shaped by sea winds, in the shadow of poised rocket ships. We pass a prison in which, according to one of the passengers, are "some of those Watergate characters." (Interestingly, we are not far from Whittier, boyhood home of Richard Nixon, and very close to the ranch of Ronald Reagan, soon to gallop onto the national scene to redeem the fortunes of his party.)

Above San Luis Obisbo, in what I later learned was a famous feat of nineteenth century engineering, the train switchbacks up into the hills and we move into farm country. Workers are laying out irrigation pipe. Fields of artichoke and broccoli are dotted with slow moving oil rigs. Row on row of newly planted dark earth go by, fields miles long. On quiet sidings, sun-bleached wooden Southern Pacific cars await produce. It's Woody Guthrie country. In February, for a traveler from the Northeast, the Garden of Eden is a lot to take in.

Salinas, 6 P.M. American Timeless. Through the portals of the railroad station, a town of low buildings is surrounded by miles and miles of fields: big, nondescript frame buildings—feed store, cold storage, farm equipment. Everything looks sunburnt and weather beaten. Across from the station is a wood-frame building of indeterminate age; apartments above, Louie's Lunch below. It is not quite dark. Lights begin to show in the windows. From the open door of the luncheonette, low voices filter out. Over the loudspeaker at the station, "Tammy" is playing. Suddenly, it's 1956.

Guthrie country—also Steinbeck country, Kerouac country, the country of Frank Norris' brawling, rebellious OCTOPUS. The Coast Starliner had delivered me to Salinas. The local bus took me to Monterey, and to Raymond, who conveyed me to the Carmel Center, where for the past two years, when at home, he has hung his hat. A rough ride in the old Volvo he was driving brought us to Henry Miller country, Ansel Adams country, Gertrude Stein country—more recently, the country of Clint Eastwood and Joan Baez.

The past three days had been spent with two other farm friends. Now it was time to visit the new home of one of the original architects of the farms. In an unintended gesture of welcome, and a sign indicative of the personal world I was entering, a letter was poking out from a book under the seat of the car. I looked at it. It was from me. It was the note I had written some time before telling Raymond the day and time of my visit. It was unopened. It was stuck, however, into a copy of one of my favorite books, *LAND AND LIFE*, by Carl Sauer, a California scholar whose catholicity and insight had been much to my liking since my days in college. The aura of coincidence seemed significant.

When I had lived at the farm, it had taken me very little time to recognize that much of the design, and a considerable amount of the spirit of the place, owed its origin to Raymond. Later, in his first book, *FAMOUS LONG AGO,* he had told in classic form the story of the transformation of an underground, urban-based Movement news service to our several new independent rural farm communes in the mountains of southern Vermont and western Massachusetts, registering at the same time one of the key changes of mood in our generation. *FAMOUS LONG AGO* was followed by *TOTAL LOSS FARM,* the completion of that story and the beginning of the long series of more overtly autobiographical tales that have since come to define Raymond's career as a writer.

After publishing these two books, Raymond produced, along with a considerable amount of ongoing journalism, *BETWEEN TWO MOONS* and *TROPICAL DETECTIVE STORY* (both 1972), a screenplay and a novel outlining internal struggles in his own life, and simultaneously continuing the story of the members of the extended farm family who had started to become his artistic "stable," an in-house resident company of characters who assisted him in acting out his story. In these two latter books, he faces and describes his compatriots in a far more personal and direct way.

Not sparing himself, he painfully explores and finally confronts his need to come out into the gay world, and eventually recognizes, sadly, his need to leave the farm that, in a time of higher hopes and spirits, he had helped to found.

Following these works, Mungo moved to Seattle, where he became a bookseller and publisher. Briefly married, he fathered a son and parented a stepdaughter. In *RETURN TO SENDER* (1975), continuing his voyage west, he chronicles a tour of the Orient with the former editor of a rock magazine, a "soul giant," as Raymond calls him, and the sort of appropriately serious, contrarian playmate he most enjoys. During this period Raymond developed an enthusiastic following in Japan, where he subsequently enjoyed a separate career in publishing and media little known in this country.

After Seattle and divorce, he settled in California. His most recently completed book, when I visited in 1980, was *COSMIC PROFIT*, a soon-to-be-published volume marketed as a self-help book about business, but really another volume in his ongoing autobiography. His last venture, or adventure, had been in business in Seattle, which provided a natural setting for this next chapter in his story, and with it the next phrase—"cosmic profit"—in which to capsulize it. From its proximity, it also became the context for much of our conversation.

Prisoner In Disguise

My father had once told me the story of a young bachelor living a life of ease well beyond his means, but very much to his liking, in a small southern town. He was awoken one night by a dream: His creditors were chasing him stark naked down the middle of the town's only street. He was so shaken that he threw a few things into a suitcase and left immediately to join the army, where my father had met him, and where, relieved of his burdensome freedom, he resumed again the carefree existence to which he had become accustomed.

Certainly by the account of himself he gives in his writing, Raymond has had this dream, or something very much like it. His destiny being somewhat different, the army was not open to him. Instead, he joined that other army, composed of writers and artists, who have seen early on that they will never fit in the straight world, and strike out for some other way of doing things. Like our career soldier, our career writer has never regretted his decision.

"Like it or not," Raymond had written in TROPICAL DETECTIVE STORY, valiantly taking the offensive to successfully market the shortcomings of himself and his peers, "my generation has been forced to become pioneers of the soul."

For Raymond this pioneering has always involved writing, first for newspapers, and later in books and magazines.

"I never wanted anything more than to be a writer," he says in COSMIC PROFIT, published soon after my visit, a book ostensibly about business, but really more about a writer writing a book about business.

In COSMIC PROFIT Mungo's own "cosmic profit"—a term he defines in part as "that freedom which permits you to make a living independently doing what you enjoy doing, as long as you don't strive to make enough money to allow you to stop doing it"—is abundantly clear. If we don't keep in mind a picture of the author as a penniless writer, wanderer, and social critic, we might well be puzzled by a book about business in which the heroes are all failures, and success is deemed a dangerous risk; in which the author who has told us early on that "work has become a beautiful word" later confesses—or, rather, proudly declares—that he has never succeeded in holding a job.

For Mungo cosmic profit is a union of means and end, the ability "to stay alive while retaining maximum freedom." In the best tradition of our era, it is a way of turning the prevailing system to one's own more responsible use. Mungo's message, a direct inheritance from Thoreau, has always been clear: The price of success is the loss of your soul. His formulation of this in COSMIC PROFIT is that it is better to lose in business and save your soul than to lose in the more important business of saving the soul itself. "Yes, we're closed," he quotes with relish from a business sign he clearly wishes he had written himself. The reverse reads, "Sorry, we're open."

Mungo was for a long time a Boston phenomenon.

"I never toyed with being a fireman or a doctor or a cop," he goes on in the book. "I never imagined I could do anything else but write."

As the crusading editor of Boston University's student newspaper, the *News,* Mungo turned it from a mere college newspaper into one whose activities were themselves news. Following these days of "youthful passion," he turned down a stint at Harvard to help found LNS. In only its third week, the news service had estimated that its coverage of the "siege" of the Pentagon reached a million readers. By spring 1968, though, internal political and personal struggles were obscuring the higher goals of the Movement, and Mungo dropped another step farther out. Repairing to Vermont, he founded Packer Corners. There he chopped wood, gardened, smoked marijuana, and espoused the post revolutionary style he called "The Life."

From the farm he made his way to the West Coast, first to Seattle and later to California, spending five years selling and publishing books. The move to California is, as Mungo describes it, the most natural thing in the world. He avows that anyone not firmly tied down to the East will eventually "slide" naturally westward to California.

"California's different," says Raymond.

Indeed it is. Remembering the Coast Starliner, as I had made my way north to see him, oil rigs had pumped slowly among fields of produce, and loomed ominously offshore as surfers bobbed carelessly along the beach; horses and cattle grazed beneath rocket ships. In Los Angeles, from which I had embarked, no one had looked twice at a young mother on skates pushing a stroller at the speed of an automobile, while in Salinas, farm country, where I got off, "Tammy" had been playing outside a deserted lunchroom, and time seemed to have stopped altogether.

California is a place where Mungo can live as he likes. At the Center, an artists' colony in Carmel where he was then making his home, his needs were well met.

"There's food in the refrigerator and liquor in the liquor cabinet," he says. "I can get up when I want. I can smoke dope or make love and nobody cares! The company's good. There are five or six houses I can visit at any time of the day or night. I can get easy work at inflated rates, and there's nothing the neighbors would like better than to have an 'author' at their dinner party.

"I've been offered a castle here," he submits, with a sweeping gesture. "The only problem I'd have is choosing the right wine for dinner."

At the Center, Mungo is a star. There is always a ready audience for his prodigious soliloquies. Evenings find him in the common room sharing his thoughts about his next book and

Famous Long Ago Archive. Courtesy Raymond Mungo.

Raymond at Candlestick Park, San Francisco, c.1979.

[222]

gossiping animatedly with the neighbors. Mornings he will be in a "seminar" with other "fellows"—a gathering in his room for the lofty purpose of smoking a joint. While the fellows sit on the bed or the floor, Raymond is at the typewriter talking, writing, and smoking, a drink near at hand. Mornings begin at noon; bedtime is rarely before three.

"This is my daily reality," he says. "I consider it dreadfully cold if it goes down to fifty. I must have chablis for dinner and dope all day."

This is shocking talk for an ex-radical who for years touted the habits of roughhewn New England as The Life, the writer who descended the Concord and Merrimack rivers for *The Atlantic* in the steps of Thoreau. But Mungo does not so much live in California, Boston, or Vermont as he does in a world of myth. At the Center he has found congenial company who appreciate his part in that myth, and who see him in the context of the other mythical presences of the local geography.

"Oh, yes," says Mungo of one of the first people I met on my visit, "Don is in Henry Miller's *BIG SUR,* and more recently *MY BIKE AND OTHER FRIENDS*—have you seen that?" Don's bookshelves are filled with signed copies of Miller, Olson, Creeley, and Dahlberg. He is a widely known artist in his own right.

Still, fame, long ago or otherwise, has its drawbacks.

"You don't like being called an ex-radical," I observed to Raymond, having sat in on a recent phone interview. (Steve Diamond, intrigued by my mission, had decided to pursue the story on his own.)

"Well—it's so journalistic. They have to call you something. What they mean is: people who made a lot of noise in the sixties and then disappeared in the seventies. That makes us ex-newsmakers, so it's convenient to call us ex-radicals; but it isn't really a true definition of who we are, of who I am. I'm no less radical than I ever was. I'm still doing my thing, such as it may be, and my thing goes on, and on, and on. It's a lifetime dance: the five-foot shelf of Mungo's autobiography, every book a new chapter, as if this guy really believes that his life is so interesting that people should pay money to read about it!

"I've often said that I would do anything else for a living that someone would pay me to do, because writing is the hardest thing to do of all. I hate it. If I'm going to sit down to write a story, or part of a book, I will wash the dishes, I will sweep the floor, I will tidy up the beds, I will find every conceivable distraction before sitting down to write.

"I've had offers to do other things. I had an offer from a publisher once. In a way, it was a golden opportunity. I could have issued contracts to all my friends, who were all writing books. But when I looked at the forty-fourth floor of their building in New York, and the secretaries, and the whole sick scene there, I realized I wouldn't last two days.

"And of course there was to be no freedom. All these books I was supposedly going to bring out were 'subject to approval' by the higher-ups in the company." He laughed.

"What it was was an offer from the devil of a sort of middle-range wealth. You know, I would have had a lot of things I didn't have before—like a forty thousand dollar salary—in exchange for my soul, my freedom, and my integrity. *And* my sense of fun. I was going to have to sit around in meetings answering to them why I thought my authors' works were so great when they didn't understand a cotton-pickin' word of them! So I turned the gentleman down.

"I'm better off by far being a writer than I would be being a New York editor. Even my own books have trouble with publishers. I have to sneak my thoughts in around some kind of entertainment in order to get the books through.

"But the thoughts are there, you know, and that's what's important to my readers. I know my readers, because I get letters from them. They are frequently repeaters; they read one of my books and then they want to read another."

"Do you hear from readers of any particular book?" I asked.

"I would say I get more letters from the readers of TOTAL LOSS FARM than any other book, but RETURN TO SENDER has been catching up slowly. It got off to a bad start—the cover didn't really describe the book. It's reaching people for the first time in *MUNGOBUS,* the anthology that came out last year.

"*MUNGOBUS* sells in colleges and universities, because two of the titles in it are used in courses—*many* courses; it's amazing! *FAMOUS LONG AGO* is used in courses on contemporary history and the nineteen sixties; *TOTAL LOSS FARM* is studied as part of courses on utopian societies and modern culture. At this point they're both academic books. I know it's immoderate to praise my own work, but *FAMOUS LONG AGO* is a real slice of history; it's a period piece, it's the soul of the sixties."

"Now, things are very different today than they were in the sixties," he went on as we sat talking in the comfort of the Center. "Take living arrangements, for example. The phenomenon of single households we see today is the opposite of the movement we started in the sixties. In the sixties we said, 'Let's get all of our friends together and live in a big heap.' Then in the seventies I found myself living alone.

"After my divorce I moved into a succession of two- and three-bedroom houses in which I lived alone. I needed the extra rooms for the kids, but a lot of the time the kids weren't there, and I lived alone and liked it. I realized that in a few years I had made a complete transition from living at the farm, where there was no privacy at all, to living all by myself in a big house, with a furnace sending up oil heat—a tremendous amount of energy going into keeping one five-foot, six-inch, hundred and ten-pound writer alive.

"But I found myself pacing around big rooms feeling incredibly depressed. The most depressing thing would be to notice some child's toy. It was soon after my separation, and I was still getting over the fact that I wasn't living with my kids, so it was incredibly haunting and depressing when I'd stumble on some toy, or walk around these empty rooms."

"There are a lot of single households," I said. "Where do you think they come from?"

"It's a kind of selfishness," he answered.

"Well, where did the selfishness come from? It seems odd that selfishness would come out of a time of great idealistic energy."

"In my case, I can only say that I was hurting, and that I wanted to close the door on the world: '*I vant to be alone.*'"

"Do you think that's the typical rationale?"

"I wouldn't be surprised. I would think that most people who live alone are coming off some relationship, so they're hurt.

"Anyway, I arrived at a point where I felt that if I had to live with someone else, I'd go crazy. I didn't want to deal with anyone else in my environment, I just wanted to be 'alone' and heal.

"That lasted a couple of years, but I came out the other end of it desperate for company. What happened was that I was moving out to the country. I needed somebody to rent my house in Seattle so that I could live in the country 'alone.' What I did was to make a compromise. I rented my house in Seattle to a young man who was just moving into town and needed an inexpensive place to stay. Half the time I lived out in the country by myself, and half the time I came in and lived in my own house, which was now occupied. So my tenant was more like a roommate.

"I discovered that it was really pleasant to have somebody to come home to. Every time I pulled into my house in Seattle, I felt this little glow of warmth; the lights were on, music was playing, and there was somebody there who spoke good English, somebody you could have a conversation with. I thought to myself: 'Jesus! I'm over thirty years old and I'm back to this roommate thing that I was doing when I was eighteen in college!' I had gone from the roommate thing to the heavy communal thing, to the nuclear-family thing, to the total 'alone' thing, and then I'd come around full circle to the roommate concept of domestic management."

It was morning at the Center, at which Mungo, as resident author, has the use of a cabin for as long as he needs it. The Pacific was pounding below. On the patio outside were roses; climbing vines shaded the room. A ripe lemon hung against the window. Butterflies and hummingbirds flitted about; tall pines shaded the house. There was a private beach. In one of his many windows, a rose that had inadvertently been trapped between the screen and the glass continued to grow, a live pressed flower that clung to the screen and refused to return to the bush even when the window was open.

"Sure," said Raymond, continuing a discussion we'd been having, "I live in a nice place, I'm not starving, but I'm a thirty-four-year-old American man, viewed as reasonably successful, who doesn't have a bank account, doesn't have any credit, and doesn't have enough income to pay taxes. I'm just a total freak."

"How can you live without having a job, without paying taxes? Won't those catch up with you, eventually?"

"Oh, yes, of course," he said. "There's no free lunch."

"Doesn't it worry you?"

"Not very much. 'If you want to play, you have to pay'; but I don't want to play. I play only as much as they force me to. I'd love to be a millionaire, but only on my own terms."

"But if people refuse to play, don't they put themselves on the fringe? They lose the benefit of the influence that an income can support."

"Benefit? Well, yes, money's important, but what's most important is how you live. If you have enough to eat, if you're comfortable and satisfied, why feel guilty that you don't have the desire to own a sports car? Know what I mean?"

"Sure, but others do. There is war and greed. Is one to assume that they are just conditions of life?"

"Well, they certainly seem to be, don't they? But, being the eternal optimist, I couldn't bring myself to say that there is nothing to be done about it. You can 'study war no more.'"

"Is it a matter of degree," I pursued, "that we could, say, reduce torture, though we could never stamp out dictators or torture as forms of human behavior? Does that seem reasonable to you?"

"I don't accept that, either. I mean, of course it's completely reasonable; what I'm saying is that I hold out for the tiniest fraction of a chance that we *could* stop torture. It's never been done, maybe it never will, but I can't say categorically that it's impossible. That would be denying any hope of improvement in our species.

"All you have to realize is that any bad vibe you put out comes right back to you. It doesn't even take five minutes. Any greed you perpetrate causes you to be victimized by some other greed: You reap just what you sow."

"But people don't seem to realize that their best interests are intertwined."

"Well," he said, "there are religious movements. People go to church to hear about 'Do unto others'—of course, they go to church on Sunday and say the right words, and then go out the next day and gouge their competitors, beat their wives, and push their children through colleges."

"But that's just the human condition?"

"Yes; this life is a vale of tears."

Certainly, Mungo must have been brought very nearly to tears by the five-year misadventure with credit cards and collection agents that he retells in an adapted form in *Cosmic Profit,* and that had appeared originally in *Mother Jones* magazine. In it he recounts his battle for fiscal survival, a foray into overextended credit that backfired, leaving him in a state of "bankless bliss," unwilling and unable to handle even his own checking account.

"In this country," he had concluded, "you're more successful the more money you owe, but the toll on my stomach lining was unendurable."

"Did you see the letters in *Mother Jones* about that article?" I asked.

"Oh, yes, I saw them!"

"Complaining that you were highly unethical?"

"Oh, yes, yes! They got a flood of mail. They got more mail on the bankruptcy piece than on any other article they'd ever published, including the one where they exposed the Ford Pinto. These people were absolutely incensed by my blithe, utterly unguilty attitude toward ripping off the American Express Company. The amazing thing is that the people who wrote in to complain about me were credit counselors, bank vice presidents, credit card executives. I said to the people at *Mother Jones,* 'Do you realize what this means about your readership?'" He laughed.

"I thought I was saying in the article that nobody got ripped off more than me. I was trying to say that you don't get a free lunch: If you don't pay your credit card bill, you gotta pay some other way. I paid by being harassed and pursued by evil forces for a long, long, time, living in fear of those forces, and having to live more or less incognito. I still can't have a phone in my name. Some of these creditors are still active, they call my lawyer every few months."

"How do you keep them from suing you?"

"What's the use of suing someone who doesn't have anything?" he said. "People have sued me. They go to court and get a judgment; I don't even show up, I don't bother to acknowledge the proceeding."

"So you're still an outlaw."

"Oh, yeah, but most of them have gone through the statutory limit," said Raymond. "They can't get me anymore."

"Then it's more an embarrassment and a difficulty than it is a victory, at this point?" I asked.

"There's no victory; I had to pay. But I paid and I learned an important lesson."

"Didn't they teach you the lesson?"

"No, I taught myself. They never meant to teach me *that* lesson. When they give you the card, they don't expect you to go on a six-week vacation!

"But, you see, being a writer, getting sued is no disadvantage, it gives you something to write about. Writers really have a unique advantage. For the price we pay, which is that we're broke and have no credit, we get certain tremendous privileges, one of which is not to give a hoot if we're sued. I might give a hoot if I had lots of money in some bank account that some court could take, but I have no bank account, I have no real estate. I have a business, but it doesn't have any money and *it* doesn't have a bank account. It presents on paper a picture of unfailing, consistent loss. Financially, I'm a total phantom."

"And that's the only way to go?"

"Well, personally," he answered, "I'm the Total Loss Kid, you know, the Cosmic Profit Guy. It may not be the only way to go, but it's the only way for *me* to go."

A day or two later, Raymond returned me to the bus in Monterey. Before continuing my trip—past Cypress Launderland, through Fort Ord, where the driver added to his list of usual and customary admonishments, "No pipes; no cigars; smoking only in the rear of the bus; and *please, no marijuana*"— he showed me Cannery Row and other points of literary and mythological interest.

From the bus I saw him hop into the car, which he uses but does not own, with a characteristic look, closed eyes upturned, the look of a man who is being looked at, and I thought of the rose in his window.

A California couple parted, he a bearded man in his thirties with a knapsack to the San Francisco Greyhound, she a frizzy-haired blonde in tears to a red Toyota pickup with Vermont plates.

"It never ends," Raymond likes to say; "it just goes on and on. I'd like to take one more dance around the floor before I settle down."

A New Life

Settling down was something Raymond had rarely done. At this time it was, it might be said, something he was learning to do. Much of his life had been devoted to breaking away, to leading, directing, discovering, and eventually moving on. Energetic as he was, it had taken some time for the effects of this to catch up with him, to recognize the shortcomings of his way of life, the complement to the positive aspects that had been apparent all along. (Throughout his work, there are many references to leaving people, places, and situations. For Mungo, it would seem, the moment of complete freedom was the one between engagements, when old responsibilities had been left safely behind and new ones not yet developed.)

In *FAMOUS LONG AGO,* a rebellious Mungo had described breaking out of the system and organizing to reform it, turning its energy back on itself for the purpose of change. In *TOTAL LOSS FARM,* he had looked back on that rebellion from the distance of the farms, singing his simple song of The Life and praising the virtues of the country and the earth. Beginning a new chapter in his own life, *TROPICAL DETECTIVE STORY* and *BETWEEN TWO MOONS* had investigated Mungo's dawning mood of dissatisfaction with himself and with the world he has created at the farms. They end with his intention to leave both: change his way of life, and remove himself from the farms. In *RETURN TO SENDER,* we accompany him as he begins to pursue this new life,

Cover of
Raymond Mungo's
RETURN TO SENDER,
Houghton Mifflin, 1975.

Famous Long Ago Archive. Courtesy Raymond Mungo and Houghton Mifflin Co.

abandoning familiar friends and places for a roving existence, a year of constant searching and travel—as the song goes: "address unknown." During the period represented in COSMIC PROFIT, which follows, he attempts to settle—he has a family and a business—but still amply reveals his inability to do so.

While I had known and stayed in touch with him, this was the pattern. It was only when he got to California, where I visited him on this trip, and where he still lives, that his life began to cohere in a way that satisfied him. Still, the old pattern was emerging again.

"There's one thing I haven't done," he said to me hopefully during the course of my visit, "get a husband and have some kids."

Eventually he did find a husband. (Today he describes himself and his partner as "married for twenty-five years.") Children were also much on his mind while we were talking in California, along with a string of related subjects—at least I saw them that way. He spoke a great deal about adoption and foster care, as well as informal, New Age equivalents of these; of friendships with children; of gay life, ethics, and the new postnuclear family. Some of these, I thought, represented new and serious directions for him. They also bore characteristic marks of the radical, freethinking social and political provocateur he had always been, and thus also appeared to be old energy shifted into a new key.

Among the things he said that astonished me, because they seemed new to him, indeed often new by nature, were a thorough consideration of the life of children in the post-traditional world we now inhabited, and had to some extent helped to create. Though entirely devoted to his own young son, and proud of his triumphs—especially at spelling bees and at other accomplishments reflecting Raymond's own influence and strengths—he said he was no longer interested in having more biological children but, rather, in helping those who needed it, whatever their situation or parentage. Living most of the year apart from his son, this echoed his current condition, but like most of the causes he espouses, he had taken it several steps further to embrace the general case. He was now a regular babysitter to local children, and was a mentor of sorts to others. He was a Big Brother to the son of a single mother in Seattle. All of this he placed in the larger framework of changes in our time to relationships and the family. We don't own children, he said, roughly quoting an entire recent school of child psychology; the parents are those who are there. As an emerging gay male, he also directed some of this thinking at promoting the welfare of young boys and men, and to legitimizing the possibility of adult men caring for children.

In addition, there was a purely social, humanitarian side to his concerns. Later, this was played out more fully in the 1990s when he returned to graduate school and earned a degree in social work.

All of this was of interest to me as part of the current story because, while at the farm, Raymond's reputation had suggested that children held little appeal for him. Touting them in song and story and suggesting that they were the promise of the future was fine, but spending time with them, with their seemingly endless questions and demands, was another matter. As recently as a day or two before, Raymond's old friend Steve Diamond, a farm parent himself, had volunteered this opinion about him. It seemed, then, a real change. Part of this, I later surmised, was that many of the children of our generation and group had passed beyond the messy diaper and toddler stage, and entered something more like the age of questioning and Wordsworthian beauty and truth that resembled ourselves at that earlier period, a state Raymond could more easily assimilate and admire.

Personal Narrative

As had been the case with much of his conversation throughout the time I knew him, some of these new subjects would come up in his next book, as those we had been discussing earlier had been present in his last. But it wasn't until I later saw the book he was working on while I was visiting him in California, *CONFESSIONS FROM LEFT FIELD* (1983), that I realized I had once again been a participant in Raymond's ongoing pattern of life and work. Mungo has a clear method to his well-publicized madness. From my stay in Carmel, I could see that it was still in fine, well-honed form.

Mungo's distinct habit is to talk through his writing as part of his daily life, a kind of verbal draft which he conducts during the time that his waking hours coincide with those of the available listeners. Throughout the period of my visit in Carmel, and given the company he was keeping there, this lasted from about noon through the evening hours. Then, as others were fading, he would sit down to write out his thoughts, often staying up till dawn. Since his writing is largely about friends and situations from his own life, what is happening around him, and the comments and experiences of those with whom he spends time, become intertwined with the text on which he is working. The result of writing about the world he inhabits, and inhabiting the world of which he writes, is that he relives each of his experiences several times. And because his writing is true to his daily life and to whatever is then on his mind—which may be the past, and the significant experiences that frequently occupy all of our minds—he is likely to write about them several times, as well.

The issues of the family about which we had been talking in Carmel make a brief appearance in CONFESSIONS FROM LEFT FIELD as part of Mungo's description of his peripatetic year following baseball through its full season around the country, from training camps to World Series. That the subject does appear, and the manner in which it appears, are both significant clues to understanding Mungo and his work. The manner in which it appears is a comment, a sidebar to the main narrative, a sidewise glance at the American family and how it has changed in the postwar years. That it does appear is the result of Mungo's habit of including the narrative of his own life along with that of whatever subject about which he is ostensibly writing. In this case, he is joining the work of itinerant writer with the child-care obligations of a divorced father by camping out with his son along the baseball trail that is his current subject. The joys and trials of such an arrangement easily lead him to thoughts of the more universal condition that this contemporary family experience represents.

His habit of freewheeling narrative, in which life and subject intertwine, vying for our attention, is at once the attraction and the bane to Mungo's readers. On one hand, it is the basis of his easygoing memoirist's style, a literary accomplishment once called, in a perceptive early review, perhaps the most engaging ongoing autobiography of its era. On the other, for readers trying to make sense of Mungo and his thoughts, the informality of his approach can cause opacity in the text that a more methodical approach might easily cure. At this point in his life, however, the development of methodology was a pursuit that Mungo clearly eschewed.

Instead, what we encounter on a regular basis in Mungo's books is the unique mix of public occurrence and personal observation his admirers so much enjoy. Taken together, his first six books up to 1980—and really his later ones as well, though the subject has shifted somewhat—provide an overall narrative of his life and thoughts from the cradle to his latest adventure. Briefly, these may be summarized as: nerdy smartest kid in school; activist college newspaper editor; Movement provocateur and gadfly; New Age communal farmer and author; self-questioning traveler and seeker; proprietor of business and family in Seattle; and, finally, thriving gay *littérateur* in the California haunts of Henry Miller and Gertrude Stein.

One of the distinguishing qualities of this overall narrative is that these individual personal chapters do not sort themselves out according to particular volumes of his work. They loosely overlap from book to book, informally looking forward as well as back. While an individual volume with its distinct subject (the Movement, small business, baseball, the farm) may end, the saga of Raymond Mungo and certain of his preoccupations will continue into the next, as earlier themes will have appeared in the story at hand. Thus, as the subject of some of our conversation over COSMIC PROFIT would appear in his next book, CONFESSIONS FROM LEFT FIELD, so the germ of the following book LIT BIZ 101

(1988), is first seen as a portion of the last chapter in *COSMIC PROFIT*. To Mungo's regular readers, much of this world of ongoing personal myth becomes familiar. For others, to pick up a single volume may be to risk entry into a world of uncertain references and apparently unconnected segments of a longer story.

Throughout this larger personal narrative—which completes itself only over the course of his oeuvre, and requires for its understanding some concerted study and the ability to draw inferences at appropriate points—occur a series of irruptions reflecting the author's experiences, emotions, and observations. These events, like stones tossed into water, represent the insertion of the immediate and personally germane into the larger flowing stream of the account he is giving of himself. Taken together, these irregularly occurring observations provide an entire second narrative rippling through Mungo's ongoing tale. It is here we find close friends and key experiences introduced, remarked, or honored, as well as new ones tendered to us in an experimental mode. Here is something that happened, he might say, but, he

Cover of Raymond Mungo's
COSMIC PROFIT,
Atlantic-Little, Brown, 1980.

Famous Long Ago Archive. Courtesy Raymond Mungo and Atlantic-Little, Brown.

then asks: What are we to make of it? I'm stranded in New York or Tokyo, he might bitterly complain, but remember, he suggests, I have a place to stay.

Through this intimate sharing, we hear of Mungo's life in a direct manner. Paying close attention, and surveying the whole, we can reconstruct his days at the farms, his travels, his group of radical acquaintances, authors, and others he admires, his sympathies and antipathies, his values and beliefs. Through such references we can take in the personal coterie he added to the extended family of the farms—something we all brought in some measure, though Raymond's world was, and remains, one of the largest.

For those who know Mungo, his books yield pictures of old friends, familiar experiences and a consistent point of view. Regular readers eventually get to know these characters, situations, and beliefs as well. While it is a truism that one gets to know an author by reading him or her, Mungo takes this several steps further, revealing not only more than usual about himself but also reaching out to his readers in a more formal way through his highly personal style. (In addition, as he had mentioned to me in Carmel, he engages in considerable direct correspondence with his readers.) Truly, readers get to know Mungo best—even more so, perhaps, than those he encounters casually during his days—because his own world is often to be found more completely recounted in his writing than it ever appears in the outward events of his life.

When I consider the many writers I have known, I think of people who set aside time to think and write. Like painters and musicians, most lead lives of a more or less normal sort— teaching, working, commuting, raising children—and treat their art as something to be done in a certain place or time: regular evenings or the lost holiday weekend; the studio, the library, or the abandoned room. But for Mungo, more than anyone I know, work and life are the same. A confirmed journalist, he reports constantly and effectively on his own life. For this reason, what we experience in reading him is a series of dispatches from the front, from the battle for decency, literacy, humor, imagination, and responsibility, however bizarre a turn the twists his encounters with these ideals may sometimes take. It makes good reading: substantial because the issues it treats are important, engaging because Mungo makes it so.

In this marriage of life and art, this living out of life on the page, Mungo appears to be a direct descendant of his childhood neighbor and longtime mentor Jack Kerouac. Kerouac coined the description "Beat" generation, of which his friend the novelist John Clellon Homes later explained, "It involves a sort of nakedness of mind, and, ultimately, of soul ... it means being undramatically pushed up against the wall of oneself." The recounting of, or release from this pressure can become art. In Mungo's intense world, there is always a leavening place for art. Surprisingly, in the midst of a description of politics, the dangers of consumerism, or the effects of war, he will stop to remind us that there is something more, the thing we are actually fighting for: freedom, peace, beauty. In his books, as in his earlier journalistic efforts, there is always room for other writers and artists—references, pictures, poems, and songs. While fellow student radicals were quoting Marx and Mao, Mungo found room in his editorials to admire D. H. Lawrence.

In this deep respect and earnest familial generosity Mungo reminds me of the lines by the Beat poet Lawrence Ferlinghetti in which he says, the writer "like an acrobat / climbs on rime / to a high wire of his own making / ...performing entrechats / and sleight-of-foot tricks / and other high theatrics / and all without mistaking / any thing / for what it may not be...." For, as the poet later suggests, and Mungo clearly understands, in the practice of writing, as in that of the aerialist, the cost of misperceiving truth can be very high.

As the sculptor David Smith once pointed out, "Art is made by people. What is interesting is the artist, and what is interesting about the artist are his own convictions....Their opinion eventually determines taste, and discovers merit, and elevates its own preferences, which eventually acquire legislative force."

The Raymond Mungo who comes through in his writings is clearly a member of this artistic tribe. He is professional at being alternative or *other*, at offering a different view of life and its possibilities—indeed, he is a prime example of what he himself suggests to us. But while remaining outside the system, he understands it very well. Looking back on his story, we can see the intense effort it takes to command the heights of culture or the media for a moment long enough to achieve effectiveness. It took several years for the young writer to position himself at the head of a university newspaper; numerous conferences, meetings, and appearances to create in LNS a new voice for rebellious American youth; the first volumes of an autobiography to stimulate a demand for more.

This was a persona Mungo developed early. In a 1970 profile in *The Village Voice,* the observant journalist Ron Rosenbaum recognized in its first stages the determining outlines of Mungo's personal style. Relating his entrance into a Boston literary party in 1968, he could see that Raymond was comfortable as a returning hero, a "wise-ass guerrilla celebrity," a quick-witted outsider who "outsmarts rather than outfights his enemy," an outlaw Robin Hood "thinking up new ways to rob the rich...and surviving through intellectual and moral superiority."

Rosenbaum, who went on to develop an enviable journalistic style and career of his own, captured in this article more than Mungo himself. He pinpointed the significance of the writer, his immediate peers, and his followers. Noting that Raymond's birth (Pisces, 1946) placed him on the cusp between two eras and generations, he saw that the choice of Mungo and those who followed his lead was to live life, to write it rather than to read about it. At the same time he foresaw the problem of this group, to which the present writer (Aquarius, 1946) is inextricably linked: that to live out a self-conscious intellectual life, to be constantly in the process of enactment, could sap creative energy and held the potential to turn a time of original thought and action into what Rosenbaum suggests might become "a new Lost Generation self-exiled within our own borders."

Like others of his time, Mungo spent years working out a personal solution to this generational *koan*. The means to manage it he continues to nurture to this day. By now, I think it is safe to say that he has succeeded.

Chapter 7

STEVE LERNER

Villager in Bolinas

Steve Lerner

San Francisco—the name conjured up many of the great scenes of recent years: Janis Joplin, the Grateful Dead, Be-Ins, the Summer of Love; Berkeley, Free Speech, the Black Panthers; Ken Kesey, the Hell's Angels, Altamont. Land of earthquakes, fire, and redwoods; home of the gold rush, instant fortunes and endless opportunity.

Unfortunately, as a traveler, I saw none of this. By 1980 the West Coast had calmed considerably. As my friend Steve Lerner was returning from a well-earned week in Hawaii, we arranged to meet at the airport, the last stop before the city on my bus from Carmel. That was as close as I got to San Francisco. From there, in his bouncy old truck, we made our way across the bridge to Marin County, through the rainbow-painted tunnel in the headlands, past Mill Valley, and over Mt. Tamalpais, a trip I was glad to make but which—the prototype of many later California drives up canyons and along the shore—my stomach would not soon forget.

It was nighttime. It wasn't till morning that I woke to find myself in Bolinas, a town so wary of outside influence that the residents regularly remove all road signs in the hope that casual travelers won't disturb their peace, or even find them at all.

This seemed to be the case. As we walked through the tiny town, Scowley's restaurant on one side, Smiley's bar on the other, the street was filled with scruffy longhairs working on their trucks over opened beers, a scene and way of life that appeared to have remained undisturbed for some time. Diners lounged comfortably at outdoor picnic tables, while children played on the grassy fringes of the street as parents shopped at the health food store nearby. There was a feeling of comfort and ease, as though the town were all just one big backyard, and it was a Saturday afternoon, and the sixties had never ended.

At the far end of the street was the ocean. A large inlet led to a salt marsh. Across the narrow channel was the more fashionable vacation and second-home town of Stinson Beach. Along the shore, people fished, swam, and hunted for shells. One had the distinct feeling that these latter might end up on necklaces, lamp shades, baskets and other items of personal expression and craft.

Earlier Years

Steve was an acquaintance of mine from the farm. Although originally from New York, he was close friends with Jesse and others in our Boston and Cambridge crowd. At that time, the early 1970s, Steve and I still didn't know each other very well. We seemed always to get along, though, and since then, over many years, we have become strong friends.

Steve's father was the writer and social critic Max Lerner. Author, teacher, and a regular columnist for the New York *Post,* Max had the considerable following one might expect of a moral voice of a generation. Their house was always full of interesting people. For his children, Max was a hard act to follow. Eventually, though, each established his own territory. One is a doctor. Steve is a social activist, writer, and investigative reporter. He and his older brother, a fund-raiser and director for non-profits, run Commonweal, a non-profit organization focused on environmental issues, social justice, and holistic health, based in Bolinas.

In the loose manner of the American middle class, Steve's and my families and friends overlapped somewhat. Steve was a product of Dalton, Andover, and Harvard. In New York he had grown up with contemporaries who would be among my classmates at the progressive high school I attended in Vermont. He later saw some of them again in college, and even later a few of them crossed all of our paths as commentators, writers, and activists, often based in New York. Among the best known of our shared friends and acquaintances were the feisty playwright Wallace Shawn, and Jonathan Schell, author of the ponderous THE FATE OF THE EARTH—boyhood and college schoolmates of Steve's, and high school acquaintances of mine. (Schell's brother Orville, a journalist and lifelong friend of Steve's brother Michael, owns a large farm adjacent to Commonweal in Bolinas.) Although we didn't come to know each other till later, Steve and I thus shared the joint world of universities, private schools, and a New York-based culture. One of my closest friends and high school roommates turned out to be the son of the headmaster of Steve's grammar school.

When I later reflected on Steve and those in his sphere, I realized that I could see in them the urban world my parents had left to go to Vermont. It was a world I came to know largely at second hand, but in which, through friends, I was still involved in a tangential way—Dalton, Greenwich Village, and the Upper East Side; Cambridge and Shady Hill; and in summer Martha's Vineyard, Nantucket, and the Hamptons. It was a world to which, from geographical and other considerations, I ultimately related in a different way. In my Vermont high school I had been deeply touched to hear Pete Seeger sing in our hand-hewn rural dining hall. Looking back, I still feel that this was among the most moving live music I have ever heard. Even so, it was years before I heard him again. Steve, however, remembered Pete as the brother of his geography teacher in primary school in New York.

As a young reporter for *The Village Voice* in 1968, Steve had written one of the first dispatches on the departure to the farm of the dissenting members of the Liberation News Service.

"Performed a unique change of address" was the way he had put it, neatly identifying the news but offering it in disinterested journalistic form. In the article, he recounted the seizure of the press, the ostensibly altruistic appropriation of funds, and other exploits that later became staples of the story retold by my fellow farmers, as well as by Raymond in his first two books, and by Steve Diamond in WHAT THE TREES SAID. The tone of Steve's article had been serious but bemused.

We detected his sympathies, though, and he was soon visiting the farms, inaugurating his long association with rural life, a passion that has continued to today. At the farm Steve helped me build the small house I designed there. When I moved back to my hometown in Vermont, we worked together restoring a house. Later, he moved nearby and I helped him build the large, barnlike structure he still uses for vacations and summers in Sandgrove, a tiny, remote, and wonderful community, something of a Bolinas of its own in the mountains of the east.

In the area of Vermont where we lived in the seventies, Steve worked at a tool factory, an industrial pottery, and an orchard. At the pottery he did union organizing, an occupational liability that resulted in the loss of the job. Although we were too involved ourselves to see, he was certainly a sign of the times. During that period he was in the area independently, but two other of his Harvard friends, Jesse and Stephen, were there as well. All merged into the local landscape, as did then, working at restaurants, gas stations, factories, and in the out-of-doors. Today, Stephen is a respected attorney and Jesse the successful writer and editor we met earlier. Steve himself is still a social reformer and investigative journalist, though, like that of his friends, his work has shifted into a considerably more influential, far-ranging mode.

These three were not alone. At that time, southern Vermont and western Massachusetts, like a number of other rural towns, regions, and urban neighborhoods throughout the country, were a warren of underground food co-ops, arts alliances, and group housing arrangements. Like myself, many my age had taken up trades—building, farming, crafts. An acquaintance I befriended only later was known at the time for ranging through our local orchards, in which he was occasionally employed, in a messianic flowing white gown. About the same time a mysterious "family" established itself in an inaccessible location on the back of a nearby mountain; they called themselves a commune.

On Steve's part, much of his trajectory was intentional. Before going to southern Vermont, Steve had written for the *Voice*. Following that, he had traveled extensively in Asia, journeying overland from Turkey to India, and then on to Laos and Cambodia. The trip was paid for by an advance on a book, though in the end, through no fault of his own, it was never published. Returning to this country he, like his compatriots in the area, chose to embark upon a different kind of life. In its physical aspect, it was more solid than that of his parents. (Steve, who has been building and *doing* things since I've known him, mastering chain saws, power tools, winches, and other rural arcana, once told me that in the house in which he grew up there was neither a screwdriver nor a hammer.) Financially, on the other hand, without journalism, teaching, or the great city as a reservoir of potential work, it was far less stable.

In its enlightened, humanitarian principles, his pursuits certainly reflected his upbringing. Steve has always been a reformer, and his life embodies the beliefs of a son whose father had been a colleague of Max Eastman and the New York radicals of our parents' generation. Steve's personal models were writers like Upton Sinclair and Lincoln Steffens, earlier activists whose perceptions and public activities had been put to work to improve the lives of the underprivileged. In college, Steve's thesis had been on Sartre, a world citizen seasoned by the contradictions of the Second World War, and a philosopher, Steve liked to point out, who insisted that we take responsibility for our acts.

From labor and organizing, Steve moved on to building and carpentry. Eventually, though he kept the house he had built in southern Vermont, he relocated to California, where he joined his

brother in the creation of Commonweal. I visited him there on
my trip in the winter of 1980.

The Voice

From the spring of 1968 to the fall of 1969, straight out of
college, Steve had had what seemed to many to be the job of a
lifetime: reporting on the changing scene of the late 1960s for *The
Village Voice.* It was a time of swift transformation, disruption,
violence, and political theater, a period in which cultural icons
were not only extremely active but relatively accessible as well. It
was an era when both youth and established institutions were
under immense pressure to adapt and adjust. Steve took it all in
stride.

Much of this new cultural and political world was on display
in New York. Walking the streets, following his inquiring
instincts, and pursuing the normal routines of an investigative
reporter, Steve wrote weekly articles, appearing often on the
paper's front page, that covered a wide range of prevailing
personalities, folkways, and events of the time. In the summer of
1968, he covered the embattled Chicago convention of the
Democratic Party, in January 1969 the Yippie-inspired protests at
the inauguration of Richard Nixon. In the spring, he reported on
the indictments of the Chicago Eight. During the following
summer, watching with thousands of others on an immense,
futuristic screen in Central Park, he gauged public reaction to the
first moon landing. In August he attended the Woodstock
Festival. Among the personalities he interviewed during this year
were Eldridge Cleaver and Timothy Leary, each at the peak of his
notoriety. He had time to try out for the lead in Michelangelo
Antonioni's radical new film ZABRISKIE POINT. Along with these,
each the subject of a lengthy article, he covered strikes,
demonstrations, and racial, class, and generational strife.
Devoting considerable attention to the counterculture, he
reported on changes of style and political factionalization among
the young, probed the life of teenage runaways, and reflected on

the charged street life in the city, often involving encounters with police. As a social critic he wrote with sensitivity about life on the Bowery, the nearness of violence, and attempts to bring reform to the area's prisons.

Over the course of more than thirty articles, Steve maintained a distinctive voice, point of view, and style. It was a consistent approach—he had written earlier for the Harvard *Crimson* and *The New York Times*—and during the year and a half of his assignment he took it everywhere it could go. Reading through this series of articles, even many years later, one senses the chronology, history, and landscape of the period—the seasons of ongoing activity, the sense of attending, through visits to both known and strange new sites in New York, one of the principal theaters of an era.

Though journalistic and thoroughly professional, as befitted the work of a key correspondent for an important urban paper, Steve's articles also, of course, reflected his own point of view. Advancing his notion of the hero, he profiled a colorful escapee from Soviet Communism who had overcome overwhelming odds to own a successful bar in downtown Manhattan, and admired the novelist Rudi Wurlitzer, author of the cult classic *NOG,* for producing such an idiosyncratic work. Sympathetic to the plight of youth, race, economics, and class, he looked with like sympathy on the young runaways of Judson House and the aging derelicts of the Bowery, pointing out their important relation to less troubled sectors of the society, who in a sense—by ignoring them—had allowed these problems to develop. Reporting from Chicago, Washington, or Woodstock, he found the thick of the action; as readers we feel we are there, benefiting from Steve's prodigious skills with people. Even-handed, he questioned the left, where he clearly felt at home, as well as the right, criticism being part of the responsibility he felt toward even a sympathetic enterprise. Thus, not all radical groups came in for praise. Factionalism and infighting were generally censured. Timothy Leary's comfortable pad in New York was looked at with some skepticism. At a Be-In in Central Park Steve marveled that in the name of freedom a young man should jump mindlessly into the fire that a group was peacefully enjoying, injuring himself in the process.

One of the lessons he implicitly imparts in these pieces is that there are no obvious answers. Occasionally, though, he does betray his own outlook. At the Chicago convention, while focusing on riots, tear gas, and police brutality, he takes time to visit a small group sitting to one side of the action: Allen Ginsberg, William Burroughs, Terry Southern, and Jean Genet.

Looking at these articles today, a reader is struck by the world they represent, their context. The ads, notices, and news that accompany them fill out the world from which they have come, and support the view of the bemused participant-observer Lerner adopted in many of his pieces. Perusing these pages chronicling New York as the sixties moved into the seventies, we recall that Limelight and Max's Kansas City were the places to be, and that the Paradox was making its name on a strict regimen of rice and vegetables. Franz Fanon's BLACK SKIN, WHITE MASKS had just come out in paper, and best sellers in Village bookstores included BEAUTIFUL LOSERS by Leonard Cohen, the DIARY of Che Guevara, and BARBARELLA. At the Fillmore, during one week one could hear the Chambers Brothers, the Beach Boys, the Hollies, Traffic, the Staples Singers and Tim Buckley. Public figures moving through the news included John Lindsay, Eugene McCarthy, and the ill-fated Allard Lowenstein. Future mayor Edward Koch had just succeeded at winning a seat in Congress. The newly christened Baba Ram Dass was giving a talk. Fund-raising events were advertised for Eugene McCarthy and for the Peace and Freedom Party, which really seemed to represent neither of these. Draft counseling was offered, along with "astrology dating" and a new twist on an old Village staple: live nude models who could be painted—themselves. The house cartoonist at the Voice was Jules Feiffer. For only pennies readers could buy a candle representing Nelson Rockefeller, Hubert Humphrey, Ronald Reagan, or Charles De Gaulle, an effigy to incinerate to one's heart's content in the comfort of one's own crash pad or loft.

Marin

Such was the world Steve and the rest of us had shared in the late sixties, when we had all met. When he and I finally arrived in Bolinas, however, from our jarring trip over Mt. Tam and the dirt roads of coastal California, I found myself in a converted tool shed in a backyard in rural Marin County. It was welcoming and clean. In his modest way, Steve had fixed it up to his liking and created a neat, well-organized small space. In its quietness, personal scale, and oriental simplicity, it was calming. It was a long way from the hubbub of Greenwich Village.

The tool shed and small-town manner of Bolinas were one aspect of Steve's life just north of San Francisco, the one reflecting his devotion to independence, contemplation, and an alternative style of life. The other, more public side was Commonweal, where he worked, the organization he had started there with his brother, and an earlier program and organization, Full Circle. At Commonweal and Full Circle, many of the issues about which he had written in New York were addressed through a growing program of exploratory research and practice in social work and health. Supported by the substantial grants garnered by Michael from donors and foundations, the programs at Commonweal and Full Circle, encompassing approaches to such issues as prison reform, mitigation of toxins in the environment, and eventually a holistic approach to cancer, soon received considerable recognition, and over a period of years went on to achieve a high degree of credibility and success.

In the earlier Full Circle, for example, well under way at the time of my visit, inmates from California's Youth Authority, the section of the state's criminal justice system devoted to juveniles, were offered the chance to live together on land in Bolinas adjacent to Commonweal, where they learned to produce their own food and to work at useful tasks, helping in the process to build a small community of their own. This approach to social change, in which environment, community, and health were integrated to create models for larger institutions and systems, reflected the influence of the socially engaged times we had all shared. For Steve, it provided a chance not only to put his ideals into action but to combine them with the kind of hands-on work he had come to enjoy.

Similarly, his first tasks at Commonweal were building and renovating its facilities. Eventually, Steve became Commonweal's Director of Research, putting aside some of the more physical aspects of the job in favor of using his skills in social analysis and writing. As Director of Research, Steve produced a number of publications, began to engage in public speaking, and in a variety of ways worked to publicize and promote the goals of Commonweal. Among the first of these efforts was a magazine called *Working Papers*, (later called *Common Knowledge*), which focused on developments in the fields in which Commonweal took an interest. This was followed by books and studies of their own from the foundation's new Common Knowledge Press.

As Steve recounted to me later, this had been a useful shift of his energies. The physical work had been difficult.

"Sometimes you had to sit on them, literally," he said of Full Circle's youthful charges. "You had to hold them down until they calmed a bit, so they wouldn't hurt themselves or other people. It was tough, it was very hard work."

What Commonweal had since become, and the increasingly responsible role Steve took in it, helped answer some of my questions about New Age energy and idealism in the time since our idyllic days at the farm. Commonweal, launched by the two brothers and a small cadre of associates and peers, was shaping up to be an ambitious research center and practicum for issues of environment, health, and social justice. To bring it into being and make it functional, new roles had needed to be adopted by some of those involved. To achieve his new goals, Michael, a Ph.D. with religious and philosophical leanings, had become an administrator, director, and fund-raiser of formidable stature. To address other specific needs of the nascent organization, Steve had moved from journalism, social criticism, hand labor, and union organizing to a role in which rather than fighting "on the ground" the symptoms of society's ills, he was contributing to rewriting some of the rules of the system itself.

It was this level of engagement that intrigued me about his progress. While I was in Bolinas, we spoke about it in his little tool shed in a backyard near the coast.

Creating Value

"One thing I see out here," I said, as we settled in and began to talk, "is something that looks very familiar. I would have to say that the sixties lifestyle is alive and well. Does it seem to you that in general people have managed to maintain the kind of idealism, or independence from the system, that we had in that time? Is this an isolated enclave, or do you think what's happening in Bolinas is going to have an effect on a larger group of people?"

"No, this is not an isolated enclave," said Steve, "although its culture is certainly different from that of some other places. The impetus toward a self-sufficient lifestyle is increasing with the economic chaos we're moving into. The sixties were not unique. There has always been a counterculture. We are just a reblossoming of something that happens again and again throughout history.

"I think the reason that the sixties were so noticeable was that there had been a boomtime economy in the postwar period, through the fifties and early sixties, and there was also the demographic bubble of the baby boom, so there were many, many young people who didn't have to think about a career. As a result, you got this youth phenomenon, the 'sixties lifestyle', which was much looser, and was not as attached to the traditional roles of making a living.

"People scattered all over the place: They went traveling, they went to the farm, they became artists and poets and musicians. They didn't think about their economic future, because times were good and you could get by on the fat of the land. Over the last ten years, times have gotten tougher. In many areas we've reached the limits. There is a tightening going on, a stiffening of the competition that is forcing a lot of people back into professional roles and the grim competition for financial security. But that bohemian way of life is still going on. This place, I think, is a brave effort to make a living being part of the alternative community."

"Would it be fair to say that Commonweal is one of a number of enterprises similarly pressing at the gates," I asked, "and that it will actually help change things; that medicine, let's say, can actually be turned around, or at least guided in a better direction, by the efforts of well-meaning people? That strikes me as refreshingly idealistic."

"We're certainly working hard to create models that fill a need, and that other people will try out," he replied. "That's a good deal of what we're attempting to do. We also have a world view that I suspect is better than a lot of the older economic explanations at predicting the large trends of the future. As a group I think we're in a reasonably good position to shape an organization responsive to future needs. When you look at the cost of medical care, at the increasing market for unpoisoned food, at the incredibly high cost of living on a piece of beautiful, unpolluted land, you see confirmation of the kinds of things we're trying to do at Commonweal. Our society has reached limits that will put pressure on many of the old institutions, and may even cause them to collapse. So I see the work that we're doing—which is not really highly financed or very professional—being increasingly in demand."

"What you speak of as predicting the future looks to me a lot like creating it," I said. "I think what we're seeing is that the energy that came out of an era of considerable idealism is still functioning, and it's contributing to creating a new world. I'm not surprised that you think you can predict, because you are probably an important part of the new health care in this country."

"Yes, at one level we are," said Steve, "but it's also very fragile. We're not at all self-sufficient yet, but we're among the communities that have managed to come up with more or less self-supporting products and services that serve a public need."

"Do you think that's a good model," I asked, "the self-sufficient, small community, as opposed to cooperation on a larger scale? Can't this communal kind of model, even if it involves hundreds of people, turn out to be a fragmenting force?"

"I'm a federalist myself," he said. "I've recognized it very strongly with all of the talk of tribalism around. I must say, though, to some extent I'm both. Tribalism by itself is quite unrealistic. I'm not into self-sufficiency and isolation alone. Rather, I think I would say that everyone, if he wants to eat, needs to bring something to the table. You know, they can bring the chairs, or the forks, or the art, or the music, or the food—or the table—but they've got to bring something with them. That's the kind of self-sufficiency I'm talking about: not that we're going to make everything we use here but that there is something of value being produced. Welfare, corporate benefits, stocks: Any of those could fall apart tomorrow. I have no faith in any of the legal entities that look so strong today. So, I think that each person and community needs to learn how to perform skills that are really necessary."

"You're not an isolationist, then," I concurred. "In Raymond's campaign for governor, for example—I see a poster there on your wall—he strongly emphasizes the economy of the state of Washington. Our antinuclear friends are very keen on local power generation. But, I'm not clear about the implications of localism. Do you think that those who stress the potential of an insular view constitute an influential lobby?"

"No," he said, "I don't really think so. People think that way, but not many act that way. And, when you get down to it, most people consume all kinds of things that come from all parts of the planet. When you talk about where they get their money, it spreads out even farther.

"I'm always encouraged when I meet people who have their shit together at one level or another, be it a person, a family, a town, a state, or a nation. At every one of those levels we have to make it work—I think that's part of the answer. If you ignore any one of those, there's an imbalance that jeopardizes the whole.

"I've been to places where tribalism operates in a positive way, and I've been to places where it works in a negative way. In Asia I saw the self-sufficiency of tribes undermined by internecine hostilities. There are many people who are enamored of the tribe as a model, who don't have the vaguest notion of the destructive aspect of tribalizing the United States."

I recalled Steve's *Voice* interview with Timothy Leary, who strongly espoused this idealized tribal view.

"In parts of the world where you move from one tribe to another," he went on, "you run into extraordinarily parochial and bigoted groups who are often violent toward the outsider. One of the things that has happened in the United States as a result of a strong federalist program over two hundred years is that we've overcome a great deal of parochial bullshit. It used to be that minorities would be abused in one community after another and

Steve Lerner
traveling in India,
c. 1970.

Courtesy Steve Lerner.

shuttled around like pariahs. I'm very interested in continuing to support the progressive energy that has allowed us to overcome many of those bigotries. It has made people more tolerant. I can drive across the United States and not be asked for a tariff or a passport in order to move from one place to another.

"That's the positive side of federalism. I would like to see that expand to the world, to the planet. That's a long way off, but it's something to aim for. I also think that many of us are so critical of our own history and culture that we fail to see what we've done right. I'm very proud of some of the progress we've made right here in our own country. I hate to see it thrown out the window just because we're part of a capitalist, exploitative, white male system that has been ripping off the peoples of the world for centuries now—because, unfortunately, that's the other side of the picture. I think that it takes realizing both: that we have a lot to rectify, but that we shouldn't ignore that which has made us a more tolerant society."

This sounded very much like the Steve I had known for the last decade, but it still left some questions.

"When you say capitalist, white, male," I asked, "do you have any notion of, for lack of a better word, the enemy, of what needs to be overcome? What about greed, profit over humanity?"

"I guess I think of it in terms of a cycle," he said. "A great deal of my thinking comes out of Buddhist philosophy, and this is part of the world view of Buddhism that I've found very useful. Insecurity, or fear and grasping, express themselves in a chain of events. At bottom we are all afraid that we'll die in some terrible way. That's the oldest, most basic fear I know. To understand people you have to look at the way they protect themselves from the wildest horror of their imagination. One of the best ways people have learned to do that is with money. What they learn through life experience is that they can buy their way out of problems, put up a wall between themselves and trouble, with money. People say 'greed' as if we should do away with it; but in order to do away with greed, you have to eliminate fear and give people enough confidence in their fellow beings that they don't think that they will end up dying starved, abandoned, and unloved.

"Unfortunately, as we look around, we see that there are many people who are starving, unloved, and abandoned, and who are taken advantage of in many terrible ways. At that level our paranoia is legitimate. In a sense, greed is the answer to that. I have my fears about not having enough. If we look at *this* place, versus the home of some other 34-year-old—one who's gone on the executive make and gotten himself a couple of hundred thousand dollars, a beautiful house, and a bunch of stocks—it seems an impossible comparison to this—whatever—shack. But those fears still operate for me. How am I going to put some money aside for when I'm older, not as mobile, not as vigorous? If things go wrong now, I can always plant some vegetables and cut some wood. I'm not always going to be able to do that. Who *will* look after me?

"Unless we begin to create communities where people can feel they will be taken care of, and that others will not leave the old to freeze outside, that will continue. We have to start somewhere to create communities that give confidence. The atomization of our society has led in just the opposite direction. People used to have very hard times, but they had family and neighbors they could expect to take care of them. That was the preindustrial model. It's gone now.

"I've read stories about incredibly poor Russian towns—my father was born in one—where it was understood that if you had extra coin, you went around and left it with the poor. If you had some extra bread, you knew where the starving people were and you left it by their door or window. That was local: you took care of community problems, even during extremely hard times. Times aren't that hard anymore—here, now—but they probably will be, off and on. I'm afraid we've lost a lot of that neighborhood and family stuff that used to be a hedge against fear and want. What we're seeing once again, here in Bolinas and in other communities like it, is a revival. You have the town meeting; you have communal agriculture; you have energy projects starting; you have local people doing medicine—you have all of those basic services beginning to happen again as a community."

"So it's social reform you're focused on," I said. "It's not really aimed at despots or psychopaths, which are perennial problems—"

"No," he agreed, "it's more the neighborhood that we're talking about—people who get together with other people to do things that work. It goes back to creating value. A lot of the problem has been that our society has become so fragmented that many people have been put in the position of creating no value. At Commonweal we're trying to take some of these marginal people and give them an opportunity to create value.

"There are many institutional barriers to that. You can't get any land to grow things on, because real estate values are so high. It's very hard to get money to invest. You need to have a track record so that lenders and the government will deal with you. If you don't, you're just left out. What it comes down to, really, I feel, is: Is anything of value being done here, or not?"

Cooperation or Destruction

"It seems clear to me that you're basing your thoughts not so much on anger at some particular person or entity as on a more positive model," I said. "You don't really seem to have anyone you beat on, like the oil company, the power company, or the bank—or do you?"

"Well, I'd like to say no," Steve said, "but let me give a fuller account, because a yes or no doesn't really adequately explain.

"At Commonweal, I've been mostly interested in the harmful by-products of industry and technology. I focus on those stressors, as we call them, because, essentially, if you don't understand the problem, it's difficult to talk about the solution. We first look at the total load of stressors emanating from our current industrial system, and we try to balance that with the nurturing aspects of our society. Instead of quibbling about the links of cause and effect, which are frequently very hard to prove—often to the tune of millions of dollars—we're trying to look at how you could limit or cut down on those stressors and add instead to the nurturing qualities of our society.

"We've been looking at radioactive and chemical stressors, and then investigating how industry, the government, and ecolobbies deal with those problems. When you ask whether our approach has been positive or cutting down the opposition, I have to say that we go about it both ways. As part of the Genotoxin Survey Project I've been working on, for example, we are going out of our way to learn the names and addresses of those companies that produce chemicals that are known to be toxic to humans and, in fact, to all varieties of species. That will necessarily make them nervous. They will not enjoy reading what we have to say about them.

"But if people know that limited number of chemical compounds to avoid, it will give a greater sense of trust in the industrial system, something I don't intend to dismantle or do without. It will make people feel better about folks who work in the chemical and oil industries. They may begin to feel that these people are choosing among the chemicals that they allow us to be exposed to.

"One of my mentors in this was Lincoln Steffens. He was able to sit down with industrialists and talk to them about working conditions in their factories, and be out front with them and say: 'Now, this isn't good for you either.' That's the message that we have to get across: Pollution is a problem for all of us. We have to show them that they don't need to be afraid, that they can still have some money, and can still live well, and they don't have to poison us to do it."

"Would that be a permanent or an interim step?" I asked. "Some people hope to see income, for example, leveling out. That isn't endemic to your view, it's not a socialist view, let's say."

"No," he said, "I don't see anything leveling out. That hasn't been my experience wandering around the world. I continue to see the most incredible differences in pay scale, if that's the way in which you want to talk about it.

"What I can see happening, a scenario I'm working very hard to avoid, is that the disparity between different income groups becomes so vast that there is massive upheaval and bloodshed, and we are all brought down to a subsistence level again. If that's the revolution—and it has its good and its bad side—I'm one of those who will be happy to avoid it by taking more positive steps: growing pork rather than "offing the pig," so to speak.

"I have to admit, though, that I do go out there and face the big corporations, and get thrown in jail, and get abused and mistreated by that system myself, so I am willing to do what is necessary to change that, and I'm doing everything in my power to do it. But I'm not a violent revolutionary, though I've thought about it."

"So, for you, there's something about the social scale that's pretty well fixed," I summarized. "It's unlikely, or possibly not even desirable, that you could level everything."

"Oh, I think it is desirable. Level, no. Things will never be level. People are different. Even if you try to impose a level system, there are people who know how to manipulate it. That certainly happened in Russia. That was one of the firmest attempts to give everybody the same break, and yet when you go in there now and look at it, they have their hierarchy and their perks and everything else. But communication is such now that people at all levels are more aware of who is getting ripped off, and who is doing the ripping off. That is causing widespread anger and resistance.

"There's a good book on this by Lester Brown of the Worldwatch Institute. I did an interview with him. It's called *THE TWENTY-NINTH DAY*. He looks at the vast differences in wealth and resources, and talks about them in terms of the ecologic limits that we're beginning to reach in a number of fields. He discusses croplands, forests, oceans, and other resources. He shows how much value each of those large ecosystems creates, and how much we're drawing from them. To use the language of bankers and economists, you can see the point of diminishing returns—when you're taking more fish out of the oceans than are breeding, stripping more trees off the hills than are growing, raising more cattle than the prairies can handle. Brown translates where we are overstepping our balance in those areas, to show how that manifests itself as an economic problem, a political problem, or a social problem. Then, when you get into the distribution of the wealth, it creates another whole overlay on the map.

"To me that explains a lot about both the problem we have and the solution. We need to arrive at a population that doesn't overtax the major ecosystems on the planet. That's going to require cooperation and possibly even world government. I have no doubt that we're moving toward either cooperation or destruction. How far we get will tell, I think, whether our history continues or not.

"In my business I talk about a lot of apocalyptic things, but I have reasonable hope for the planet and the species—not that I don't see many threats to them. My father used to say, 'I'm neither an optimist nor a pessimist, I'm a possibilist.' That's the way I feel. There are a whole hell of a lot of things that are threatening; on the other hand, man is a very flexible animal. Giant plagues have wiped out one out of every three people, but mankind has gotten through it. I hold out some hope for our working it out.

"*WORLD ECONOMY* by Herman Kahn, the futures man who works for the Hudson Institute, is similar. His view is that we're in the midst of a four hundred year period of transition in which we will have to reach some kind of stability. What he's shown is that we're now at the peak of population and energy use for all time. The graph goes right up—whoosh!—and 1980 is more or less right there at the top, with two hundred years on either side of it. According to Kahn, we're right at the crest of the energy use and population that this planet can carry—a crisis point. But, as bad as things are, he says that they will necessarily have to change. So, actually, he's an optimist—a possibilist. He says they will *need* to change, so everything will eventually right itself."

"Let's hope so," I said.

Aspects of the Law

Inspired by our mood of optimism, we took a break from our talk. Steve showed me around Commonweal and its neighborhood, and we had some lunch in town. Later, our conversation continued.

"On the way over the mountain we were talking about law," I said, moving into another area of interest to me, "being on both sides of it or playing with it in some way. It seems to me to be one of the things that people of our era have really had to deal with. It has different manifestations. Some kinds of laws are very clear, others much less so.

"At lunch you were saying that we often try to stretch various laws," I continued. "Sometimes you have to look the other way when a law doesn't fit your vision. The system of laws seems a very real thing. How do you see yourself in relation to it? Do you picture it changing vastly, or will people in our position also be making laws which will then become standards to which other people will have to adhere, or from which they will have to look away?"

"I think my basic principle," said Steve, "is that I try not to do things that hurt other people or other species—any species. I also break that rule, but I do the best I can. I swat mosquitoes when they bite me, and I eat meat when I'm hungry. When I deal with man's law, I make an effort to go along with it until I see that it is creating greater harm than good. I guess I'm flexible in relation to the law, but I sometimes break it. Not only do I break it, sometimes I break it very publicly, and when I do, I expect the consequences for breaking it.

"Gandhi is the person from whom I learned the most about the law. He was a lawyer in three countries on three continents— England, India, and then South Africa—and yet again and again he led hundreds of thousands of people on illegal marches. But he told them to expect the consequences of breaking the law. He saw that as a way of changing it.

"I don't look forward to being punished for a bad law. Like many people, I do a number of illegal things simply out of convenience. I've driven a car without a registration. I didn't have the papers to prove it was mine. Sometimes one can't afford to be legal. Insurance: I can't always manage to buy it. I probably could if I sacrificed something that to me is more important. So, I break the law sometimes; but if a cop stops me, I've got to say: 'Yeah, I don't have a registration, take me to jail or give me a fine—whatever."

"It's a calculated risk," I suggested.

"Right, that's a part of it.

"Then, as I say, there are times when I break the law in order to make a point. That's the antinuclear number. At the Diablo protests over nuclear power, I was charged with getting in the way of the lawful operation of a corporation—that was what they busted me for. I got to plead guilty to one out of four charges. It was a delicate moment. At first I said I wasn't guilty. Then I saw what the legal system did when you said you weren't guilty. It put you through a long, expensive trial, and they convicted you anyway. So I decided not to do that. Instead, I did a *nolo contendere* kind of number, saying that, *yes*, I had gotten in the way of the legal operation of this corporation, but that there was a higher law operating here. The corporation was endangering the lives of people, and that was more important than trespassing, or getting in the way of some abstract law. For that breach of the law I served three weeks in prison.

"There are times when laws conflict, and that was one of them. But it seemed to me that it was useful to the judicial system to meet a bunch of people who had thought it out, who said, 'Well, we've considered these conflicting laws, and we're willing to go to jail and take time out of our pleasant lives to point out how important it is that the law change, and that we do something about it, and that you not open a nuclear reactor on top of an earthquake fault,' which seemed pretty stupid to me, and still does.

"There's also that moment when you come into conflict with regulations, and you 'know better,' but it's expedient. It's a very uncomfortable moment; it's a balancing of evils. Some annoying bureaucratic regulation may make a big difference in your program if you're explicit about it. It's the shade between lying and dissembling; it's the way you present it. Fortunately, I have not often been in the position in my work that I have had to lie about things."

"So the law is a kind of tool, it's not anything written in stone?" I asked.

"No, we make it."

"And you go around it, or you go through it, or whatever is necessary—there's nothing holy about it," I suggested.

"Well, there should be. But there are a whole lot of laws that are made simply to protect property; they often come into conflict with other values.

"Sam is very good on this. He talks about the fact that early on—was it the Constitution or the Declaration?—the writers decided on the wording 'life, liberty, and the pursuit of happiness.' Later, for 'happiness,' they inserted 'property.' I think that constitutes an excellent observation about the American system.

"But property in moderation is not such a bad thing. It tends to make people take care of what they own. If this were my land here, it would be better taken care of. But I'm a renter. At any moment I might have to leave, having put several thousand dollars into this land and buildings in order to make a place that I could live. So, even though our system tends to overprotect property, I don't intend to toss it all overboard just because I feel that there is an inequity. In a way, private property is healthy, if it can be administered in a rational, non-polluting, non-oppressive way, using land to create fruits that we all need: privacy and useful goods.

"How people deal with the law is an interesting part of our era. Many in our group, at one period or another in their life, have had a kind of *bandito* aspect to them. Many of us have had to press at the legal boundaries in order to establish our identities. In that post-Second World War era we weren't about to go along with every last aspect of legality. In order to make sure that we weren't being led down the fascist trail, many of us gravitated toward revolutionary or *bandito* roles that were outside the legal structure."

Certainly, I thought, looking back, this was a fair assessment. From civil rights protests, lunch-counter sit-ins and building takeovers to dope, shoplifting, and LNS itself—whose members had felt that, in defense of altruistic cultural and political principles, it was acceptable, perhaps even heroic, to make off with money and goods shared with others—ours had been an era in which laws and mores had been severely tested.

"I have traveled in parts of the world where law was right there on the spot," Steve continued. "You know, the bigger person with the gun establishes the law. I'm very uncomfortable with that. Sensitivity to injustice was part of my upbringing; it's something that I take very seriously.

"The amount of violence in people is more and more on the surface. It's a dangerous world. You know, if you live a quiet existence, protect yourself with money, stay among your close friends, and travel in little bubbles, then it's OK. But as soon as you go outside of that even a little bit, and don't try to pretend to be anything other than you are, you run into a lot of intolerant people.

"That restaurant we were in today in town is tense with that. The street people who run it are *angry,* and at a certain level, righteously so. They see the people who are at the bottom and who are, again and again, unable, even with good motivation and effort, to move anywhere because they don't have the money. You know, to rent a place like mine for a hundred and fifty dollars is a real find, for a toolshed, much less a house. That sort of thing makes people angry. They see somebody come in in their Datsun station wagon, or their fancy convertible, or whatever, and they're angry. *You* have enough money to buy lunch; *you* don't have to wash other people's dishes—you know, they're pissed. I'm struggling to make a living, but I'm doing much more what I want to do. They have jobs they don't want.

"There's an enormous amount of anger around. It's the hardest part of my job not to give up and go off and isolate myself. In that way it was much easier living back in Vermont, because in a sense I was at the bottom. I was a carpenter, and a tree planter, and a pruner, and a factory worker. It was *terrible.* I learned a lot, but in terms of how hard the work was, and how unpleasant, it made me want to change my life.

"On the other side, there's a certain comfort in being able to present yourself as not being part of the exploiting force in the world. Even though I still live in a reasonably humble situation, in a cabin without plumbing, starting to work at Commonweal—even if it's a goody-goody non-profit organization—has put me in a different position. For what it's worth, I'm now an executive. I don't get paid like an executive, but I do that kind of work: I hire, I fire, I make decisions that are important to people's lives. Having that kind of responsibility can put you into conflict with people."

"Well," I said, "that seems to be something that's happening to a lot of people. To take responsibility you have to do things that are unseemly by the standards of ten years ago."

"That's right," he agreed.

"I find that people from our generation who are unwilling to take those measures are often critical of those who are," I said. "'Here I am, raising my own corn,' they will say, or 'I'm on the picket line'; 'what are *you* doing to tone down the pressures of the world?' Actually, in my experience, they might want to consider their views. Because not only should you bring something to the table, as you say, but there are amounts, there is quality and quantity. If you're farming when you could be leading farmers, you're in a sense—no matter what your life may look like—letting other people do the heavy lifting: the thinking, the action, the compromises that go with getting anything larger done."

"Well," Steve said, "I think it depends. I believe there's also a place for the *saddhu*, the wandering holy man who creates a different kind of value. It's a bit like a musician. What are you going to say? Here's this guy who plays the guitar all the time, you know. He's just constantly stoned playing the guitar. Is that value? I'm sure many families have had that argument. But the *saddhu* wanders around, and people wash his feet and give him food."

I thought of Asa's book and the many family conversations in it of this kind.

"The difference," I said, viewing the question more broadly, "is that not many people take that kind of stand, they're more in the middle."

"Right," he said, "I know, they are."

"But I would certainly agree with you about the *saddhu*," I added, "and about the stoned musician, too—though," I ventured doubtfully, "I'd probably want to hear the music before I allowed him too much social credit."

"When you get into this area," Steve continued, glossing over my jaded view and moving back to the realm of concrete social policy, "the question of welfare immediately comes up. What are we doing with all these people with perfectly healthy bodies, and reasonably sound minds, who are on the dole? The industrial system is creating a lot of marginal people. There isn't as much work as there are takers for it. But to say that they should create their own work is rather unrealistic.

"If people are going to be put on the dole, I think that we should have WPA types of programs that everybody is capable of doing. Why should people be given money to do nothing? They could go down to the beach and pick up the litter; they could work with children after school and organize games for them. There are a thousand things that need to be done. I don't think money should just be given out. Support should be given to people who are totally incapable of taking care of themselves, but there are very few of those. Ninety-eight percent of us are capable of doing something of value.

"China is very good at this. They just put everybody to work. Even if you're schizophrenic, they'll put you into a factory. They say, 'I don't care whether you're crazy or not, you're going to staple these things together. If you're going to eat, you're going to staple them together.' Of course there is a down side to this—an overly coercive government—but on the whole, I think it's healthy."

I agreed in an abstract way. I was glad, though, under the circumstances, that I was neither disabled nor living in China.

Privilege and Obligation

"I'm not quite sure how to phrase it," I said, continuing, and venturing into the last area I wanted to cover with Steve, "but in this context, how do you deal with the differential between doing good for others, while still remaining a privileged person? Commonweal has its facilities; your neighbor Schell has his farm. You are all people with altruistic goals. As a group you are looking for a new way to restack the deck, yet you're still benefiting from the old way of dealing it. Your organization can go out and raise a lot of money, while the typical family or community probably can't. This seems to be the kind of conflict that people promoting change have to deal with."

"Yes, it is," he said. "It's very stark, with us, anyway. Commonweal is funded by foundations endowed by wealthy industrialists; and yet *Common Knowledge* often takes positions that attack the industries that have supported it. I don't feel bad about that. The result may be that from time to time we lose foundation money.

"But remember, the reason a lot of foundations are set up is, as I said, that greed comes from insecurity. When people reach the stage where they finally recognize that they have more money than they can do anything with—you know, they can't eat it, they can be on only so many yachts and in so many mansions at a time— then they give it away. They're the ones who are in conflict. They do a lot of greedy things, and then they give away the money. It's their minimal balancing act with society. Of course, it's also a tax break, which is another way of looking at it.

"Many corporations do this: They create a problem, and then they create a foundation to deal with the problem they've created. Now, we are trying to get an organization off the ground. There are a number of ways of doing that. You can borrow money, but you usually have to have something to borrow it against, and we didn't have anything to start with. So, instead, what we did was to raise money with ideas. There had to be a better way of providing medical care for children with learning and behavior disorders. That idea was of considerable interest to a number of foundations. So we got some money together to do Full Circle. Then we broadened it to say: Medical costs are escalating for a whole variety of people who have chronic health problems, and the current medical model is inadequate, so how about giving us some money to try to get preventive health work started? They did. And how about assembling under one roof a series of different diagnostic procedures so that physicians, physicians' assistants, and others in the alternative health field can get together and talk as a group about the best therapeutic approach for a patient? We offered things like that, that are reasonably innovative, though not unheard of. So, through our good ideas about real-world problems, we have been able to get the seed money to start Commonweal.

"That has been a considerable amount of money. But our goal, and we're very serious about it, is to be self-sufficient. In the end, we don't want to have to rely on grants. We expect that the resident community we're planning, when built, on a fees-for-service basis, will be able to support Commonweal. That's also true for the clinic, and for the different parts of Commonweal, but it's the resident community that will really float us.

"It doesn't happen overnight that you build an ambitious resident community. Not only is it assembling the money, it's assembling the right people to do the work, and recognizing what you'd be good at, the focus, and so on."

"I would think," I said, "that that would make you a good deal more vulnerable in some ways—on your piece of land that I know you had to fight for; using money that you had to work hard to get. You're using the advantages of privilege, but I can see how you might get some flak for that from others."

"We do," he said. "You know, Bolinas is Liberty House: Everybody gets to say what they want.

"The real local people here," he said, "and there are a few, feel that there's been a huge invasion from the East Coast, and that we've taken over, and we're wrangling things essentially, as you say, so that it's good for us. But the reality of California, I find, is that most of the people out here are newly arrived—within the past five or ten years—and, you know, when somebody new comes in and does something, it can cramp those already here."

I thought about this, and about how an eastern-born vision had adapted to settle into a home in the west. It was an interesting set of circumstances and surprising turn of events. It gave me much to consider in regard to the lives of my peers and their paths up to the present, and beyond.

Looking Out

On my last day in Bolinas, the final afternoon of my stay in California, I sat on the bluffs overlooking the ocean, at the edge of the western portion of town called The Mesa, where Commonweal had made its home. Below was the beach, a sandy strip north of the mountainous headlands of San Francisco and south of the beautiful forested peninsula of Point Reyes, so spectacularly unspoiled that it would later be declared a national treasure. Below, waves crashed on boulders emerging from the sand. Beyond spread the Pacific. Faintly visible on the horizon was the mysterious presence of the Farallon Islands. It was an exquisitely charmed landscape, sweeping and bold, yet also portentous and dramatically final: the end of the continent. Its role in history was that of a last frontier, the end point of a cycle of American energy. But it was also the locus of something new, a place where novelty thrived and the rewards of invention and hard work could be magnificent. Thinking of the prospects for Commonweal, it was easy to see it as part of this pattern, perhaps the beginning of something new that might bounce back and recross the continent in the other direction.

Turning one's head just a bit, however, this new frontier took on a somewhat different cast. Nearby, the only presences were a few old buildings and a forest of metal trestle towers. What Commonweal had been before its new life was a Second World War era government Loran station, a homely stucco faux-mission structure that still had 'RCA' emblazoned in large letters on its facade, surrounded by the appurtenances necessary for electronic broadcast over the ocean. Certainly a marvel in its day, it now projected the aura of a modern ruin, a lonely outpost replaced by invisible skyborne satellites and other newer technological innovations, and now approachable only by its original rough dirt beach road to the cliffs.

To see how Commonweal was working to adapt this site, striving to return an abandoned piece of industrial detritus to a useful role in the world that surrounded it, was to be moved by the efforts of Steve and his comrades. It was a thought that led to others of its kind: What was next for the founders and staff of Commonweal? For others who espoused the positive, idealistic energy of progress and change? For the former farmers Steve and I knew, and other representatives of the tolerant, reformist views of our time?

On this trip I had seen four people of the same age, and with a shared background, all heading in different directions with their lives. In Los Angeles, Asa was focusing on business and financial

Photo: Copyright R. M. Rufsvold, M.D.

Shoreline, Commonweal, Bolinas, California.

stability, and Steve Diamond on the peace movement, spiritualism, and a push into Hollywood. Raymond seemed happily ensconced in his life as a literary figure in Carmel, while Steve Lerner, with whom he shares aspirations both culturally and politically progressive, was working to build a new world of social systems, environment, and health.

Looking at the windswept, homely shell of Commonweal with its precious freight of idealism and social change, it seemed to me that the openness of California, like that of the farms, earlier, had helped my friends, former farmers, to remake themselves. And just like these structures, recycled for social use, their lives were being rebuilt along new lines, lines not only evocative of their future but reflective of their past.

Along the way, coincidence and intertwining incidents and lives continued to play a role. Steve hadn't succeeded in getting the part in Antonioni's film, but, as it turned out, an acquaintance of his and Jeannette's had. I had gazed out in romantic rapture at the Farallon Islands, but Steve later told me that they had become a toxic dumping site. He had pictures of fish swimming through the islands' ruptured barrels of nuclear waste. Steve spoke of raising money through beliefs and high goals, but, I thought, this was hardly a surprise for brothers whose father had written a book titled *IDEAS ARE WEAPONS*. And while I myself was new to California, it turned out later that work would bring me west to visit Steve and others many times.

When I looked back on Steve's articles for the *Voice*, it was striking how many of the social ills he had observed and reported on were now the subject of his much more far-reaching and effective efforts. Visiting in person, I could see that the bemused, detached observer of those pieces had evolved into an earnest, analytical reformer with command of resources and tools. It was a change as dramatic as the Coast itself. I looked forward to returning home to see what I could make of it.

III

Afterlife

Chapter 8

NEW WORLD

Circa 1981: Transition

By 1980, the time of my visits to California and New York, I had reached a point of change in my own life as well. From 1969, when I had moved to the farm, to 1976, when I took my first office job, I had been engaged in farming, carpentry and other rural pursuits. In 1976, finding that a day of working on my tractor, cutter bar, or flatbed truck did not leave me much energy to write or think, I began the first of five years I would spend in the admissions office of a local college. During this period, up to 1981, I slowly reduced my work time until I had a fairly good balance of income and avocation, the latter being devoted in part to my first attempts to tell the story of the farms. In the world outside we were nearing the end of the Carter administration, in diplomatic war with Iran, and about to enter the Reagan era. The nuclear industry was under attack, and people of my age were beginning to show up in positions of political and cultural influence.

At home, my marriage was under stress, and my job, while financially useful and sometimes fun (the occasional interview with a bright, animated high school senior), was proving to be terminally uninteresting. For different reasons, my wife and I both began to rethink our lives, a process that ended first in a separation and then divorce. For me, her transformation from the poet and philosopher I had married to the health professional she now planned to become reduced our common ground considerably. For her, my own proclivities provided the same sort of obstacle. When, she asked, was I going to stop dreaming about culture and art and get real? While I was out trading old tractors and trying to keep our secondhand VW running, she was dreaming about a new Saab.

As a college employee, I was allowed to take any classes that would fit reasonably into my schedule. My first venture was a year-long rereading of Dante's *DIVINE COMEDY*. I had taken Italian in both high school and college, and had already spent a year reading the *COMMEDIA*. By attempting it again ten years later, I was testing the waters for what I considered to be my more serious interests. The following two years I spent with the same teacher learning Greek. When I could appreciate the character and beauty of the *ODYSSEY* in the original (also portions of Aristotle and Plato), I was moved not only to be in direct contact with such an authentic, primal element of western culture but felt I had proven to myself that my dreams were not out of reach.

With this accomplishment in hand, I set out to determine how I would spend the next few years of my life. I had decided some time before not to attempt to make a living as a writer. I had seen the difficulties encountered by Jesse, Raymond, and other professional writers I knew, and was loath to have anyone tell me what to think about and write. In addition, my own writing was proving to be not of the income-producing variety. My office job at the college had been a step toward work that would support such cultural pursuits; but it was uninteresting, and contributed nothing to the creative side of my life. What I needed, I thought, was to move from the administrative to the substantive side of academic life, to find more rewarding, involving work. The answer was the obvious one I had put off for almost fifteen years: graduate school.

In 1981, combining several interests and abilities, I applied and was accepted into a nearby graduate program in art history. I wrote a strong essay, had a productive interview, and by gaining entry confirmed a pattern for myself of which I became fully aware only later: For me, writing my own ticket was the way to go.

NEW WORLD

*   *   *

I owed my entry into this program to the man then running it, Samuel Y. Edgerton. As I entered the picture, Sam Edgerton was completing his first year as director of the Graduate Program. I was thus a member of the first class he had selected. Sam was a driven scholar and achiever. He had established himself in the field of art history by elucidating some little-known complexities of the history of perspective. He was an Italophile (he later converted to Catholicism) who had found his own way to the work he did. Once a wrestling coach, through his own efforts and imagination he had ended up as a professor of art history at the same university in Boston that had spawned Raymond and his group. From there he went directly to the Graduate Program, which offered him, as it turned out, not only professional advancement but the chance to buy an old pickup truck and a tractor, and the time to farm on the weekends and in the summer.

For these and other reasons—his generosity and perceptiveness—Sam was in a position to discount the lacunae and odd periods of employment in my then brief resume, and focus on my strengths. As he said to me later in his candid if characteristically awkward way, the job of the program, still at that time relatively new and finding its way, was to turn sows' ears into silk purses. There were several students of this description in my class; after we got over the indelicate presentation of the thought, we were grateful for the opportunity it had afforded.

Sam, after all, had written *his* own ticket. He had survived through imagination and grit. He had experienced the sixties in Boston as a teacher at the university. He could respect my work in Italian and Greek: He himself later learned the difficult indigenous languages of Central America to enter a new area of research. Sam obviously loved rural life, and once he realized the connection—which at the time, as I began my new career, I was not eagerly touting—he asked frequently about Raymond and his crew. When his letter arrived in the spring of 1981 inviting me to join the program in the fall, an offer replete with a named fellowship and notice of the program's annual winter trip to Italy, it was probably the first time I felt I had achieved anything of this magnitude entirely on my own. I was thirty-five.

But, it was when I arrived at the program that I realized that my world had really changed. Only a half hour from the small farmhouse in which I was still living—the scene of my encounters with trucks, chickens, buzz saws, and the varied incidents of independent alternative living, as well as my more recent and largely anonymous life as an college administrator—the museum that housed the program welcomed me unequivocally. The library where we attended classes and did our research was a quiet, park-like place with large windows looking out onto a grove of oak and maple. Dark walnut-stained paneling added a tone of gravity. My desk was designated with a small label in handwritten copperplate script. The staff was friendly and helpful and greeted me by name.

The connected museum was a small gem, a private collection bequeathed to a board of trustees who, with the exception of the new program and library, had at that time changed it little. For me, the rows of tools and parts in my shop, and of manuals and other accoutrements of my various trades that had surrounded me daily, were now replaced not only by thousands of volumes on art history but by original works of Dürer, Botticelli, Piero and Degas, and one of the largest collections of Renoir outside France. Walking through the museum, with its generous windows giving onto quiet ponds and fields, to see the newly rearranged pieces from the collection set out occasionally by the museum's director, was only one of the many pleasures afforded by this new environment.

Michael Rinehart

One of the effects of my new milieu was to introduce me to a range of acquaintances and friends whose spheres were far larger and more complex than any I had yet known in my own life.

One of the first people I met was someone to whom I had been referred by a old friend who had worked with him. Michael

Rinehart was a former director of the program I was entering, a professor, and the head of the program's research library used by graduate students, faculty, and visiting scholars.

From a promising academic, Michael had moved on to a career as a librarian—an apparently lower-profile position, but one closer to the source of the materials essential to the field. In the end this proved, for him, to be a fateful decision. Libraries, after all, are repositories of information, and in the particular era in which Michael found himself, information turned out to be a key to significant influence and work in the field.

Clearly an aesthete and a devotee of culture and the arts, Michael had written his doctoral dissertation on a little-known room in the Palazzo Vecchio, in Florence, a room in recent years closed to the public, but for a long time, to cognoscenti in the world of art, a well-known gem of painted decoration. While in Italy, he had also worked at I Tatti, the grand estate of the

Photo: Tom Fels

Library of the Graduate Program.

influential expatriate American connoisseur and collector Bernard Berenson.

Refined, gentle, and aristocratic, Michael radiated an aura of cosmopolitanism. Though reserved, he was not short of self-confidence. Beneath his calm surface one eventually sensed the sterner stuff that had sustained him through his later career. On introducing myself, he was instantly cordial. Occasionally, we would meet to talk or have lunch. Though he was a generation older, we were both in the midst of difficult relationships and divorce, and had found our respective careers relatively late in life, so we already had a certain amount in common. He offered good advice. Later we collaborated on a course. We became friends, though we were never truly close.

We also shared a knowledge of Italian. Michael was multilingual, one of the assets he had put to use in his professional life. To me this appeared to be romantic and sophisticated. Later I came to see it as one of the international aspects of the art community, a small, devoted group who seemed to travel ceaselessly, be at home in almost any part of the world, and capable of conversing and reading in a variety of tongues. (Oddly, despite my own five languages, and the German required for the graduate program, it took me years to think of myself in the same light.) Michael was always off to conferences and meetings—to Europe, to California, to New York. Though he oversaw a library, an information service, and till recently the Graduate Program I was attending, he was almost never there. He had offices in other cities. I wondered, finally: What does he do?

What he did, it turned out, was what in a later era has come to be called information management. As a librarian, a Harvard graduate, and an international scholar of art history, it had not taken him long to perceive that computers would change the way we approached study and information. This had been a prescient observation. The year was 1981. I didn't even own a computer for another six years, and Michael had begun his work more than ten years before I met him.

Librarians, of necessity catalogers and information specialists, developers of the Dewey decimal system, always looking for methodological improvements, were among the first to recognize the value of the computer. In libraries and in fields that generated libraries and other accumulations of data, the advent of the computer—the digital revolution—first seen simply as an organizing tool, had a number of unforeseen consequences. First, one had to understand the computer and its capabilities. Then, software had to be developed to accept the new information for specific fields. Finally, vast amounts of time, as it turned out, needed to be spent inputting the information to create databases and, later, additional time devoted to ongoing upkeep. Eventually, one had a product of some use.

Much of this had been foreseen by developers of digital media. Even so, I think the actual scope of the change was a surprise to most. But it was in fields that truly needed the changes offered by the computer that much of the front line work in dealing with the information revolution was accomplished. Today we would be surprised to find a business that did not computerize its central records, or to receive a handwritten renewal notice for a magazine. Surprisingly, this point was reached in only a few years.

Before long, art history and its libraries joined the movement to employ the computer. Among the challenges to be met were these: The language of art history is very complex and often variable. What one person calls an arch, another might call a gateway, or a door, or a vault. Indeed, the same writer in another context might call the same feature something entirely different. What were things to be called? And, if you arrived at such a name for a feature of art (nomenclature, vocabulary), where would you place it? Is an arch a form, an aspect of architecture, a characteristic of construction, a development of a particular era of design? In judging such matters (subject), whose view would prevail?

Art history is a highly diverse, factionalized field in which feelings on relatively small issues can become very intense. Careers can be made on minor differences of dating or other matters of history, influence, and interpretation. In outlining these areas of the field, who would have the final word (authority)? The international aspect of the arts and their study provided another hurdle to the equitable distribution of information. Any vocabulary developed for the field would need to be applied to the several main languages used in writing and research, especially English and French, and in a diversifying world, eventually perhaps others as well. How would this multilingual aspect (translation) be addressed?

Finally, there were the scholar and the student. How would the clients for this information react to all these changes? How could those engaged in art history (end users), be educated to use, and more importantly, *want* to use, purported improvements to their work approaching with the inevitability of a slow-moving but distinctly unstoppable train? And with the development of these tools, and the resultant explosion of available information, how would those in the field keep abreast of the work being done, most likely produced at a far faster pace than before (publication)?

In the small college town where I went to graduate school, Michael's was one of two important organizations that were facing these national and international challenges to the field of art history. One, the ART AND ARCHITECTURE THESAURUS (AAT) dealt with the vocabulary, subject, and authority aspects of the problem. The other, his own, the INTERNATIONAL REPERTORY OF THE LITERATURE OF ART, or RILA in its better known French acronym, dealt with the translation, publication and distribution of information.

Among the innovations of the *AAT* was the development of some thirty-three hierarchical "trees" of specialized vocabulary, set into seven larger "facets" representing the major areas of knowledge in the field of art. This was pretty heady stuff. To trace the lineage of the simple *campanile,* for example, the bell tower a traveler might encounter in Ravenna or Gubbio, one now considered that it was a leaf on a diagrammatic tree branching from single built works, to works by type, to works by form, to towers, to bell towers. And there it is on the list, surrounded by its fellow towers: clock towers, round towers, watchtowers. Farther out on the branch are other works by form, among them basilicas, kiosks, lean-tos, panopticons and Quonset huts. Across the vocabulary grove, under other structures by type, are those denominated by function, such as those of agriculture, including corncribs, grain elevators, and aviaries.

An even larger controlled vocabulary developed earlier by the Library of Congress, is not limited to the field of art. A look at its multi-volume guide to indexing would be enough to keep even the curious out of the information sciences. Such tools did, however, serve the purpose of addressing the new issues raised by the computer, enabling a librarian anywhere to catalog an article to make it retrievable by anyone understanding the rules of how to find it. This, in our day, is considered progress.

Once that article is written—if it is written in, or translated into, one of the world's major languages—it enters the sphere of Michael's International Repertory of the Literature of Art, an abstracting service that makes brief summaries of articles available to the field, at first in traditional published form and then, later in its history, online. The challenges here include locating all the relevant literature produced by scholars, judging which deserve inclusion, and hiring readers and translators to summarize and present the material. At this point editors then read the solicited articles or books, and writers create abstracts of them for publication. Beyond this, a new publication must accommodate the now much-reduced abstracts. The result: a single volume, or later a disk or online list, of the year's articles and books about art—a great time-saving device for scholars and students in the field.

Clearly, whatever its usefulness, this is a complex and costly enterprise. If from academics Michael had moved to libraries, he soon thereafter moved from libraries to the almost entrepreneurial business of assembling writers, editors, and managers, and of building what amounted to a traditional and eventually an online publishing business in the arts.

Fortunately, both *RILA* (now called *BHA, BIBLIOGRAPHY OF THE HISTORY OF ART)* and the *AAT* were such essential tools to an expanded study of art history that they were quickly taken up by the major new force in the field at that time, the Getty Trust. The Trust, which had expanded vastly after the death of its founder, California oilman J. Paul Getty, now ran not only the museum in California that housed his collections—then a relatively modest, though perfectly appointed campus on the shore in Malibu—but several institutes devoted to aspects of the arts. Among these were research, conservation and the sciences of information. *RILA* and the *AAT* were absorbed into the latter, and many of Michael's trips, if not to the far-flung regional offices of his own publication, or international meetings on developments in information science, were often made to the museum or the downtown Los Angeles suites of the Trust. From this point on, at least within the limits allowed by the corporate outlook of its parent organization, the budgets with which Michael had struggled were no longer an issue.

Michael seemed to take all this in stride. Despite the vast amount he had accomplished over the past few years, his wide network of colleagues, and the work with which he still had to keep up, he remained most at home in his own library, that of the institute where I was studying. He remarried very happily. He again took up the piano, a pastime he had dropped in order to keep up with the growing demands of his work. He helped his son open a state-of-the-art sports shop nearby. He oversaw the merging of his own publication with its French-language counterpart, a nearly overwhelming miasma of electronic, linguistic, and political complexity. As he neared retirement, he spent more time in the office he kept in New York, at the Metropolitan Museum, near the apartment he now shared with his new wife. Eventually, he floated out of my life, leaving, however, substantial traces of shared memories, experiences, and friends in a field for which, I think, we both shared, equally, measures of respect, a certain distance, and a sense that what you do is largely important only in regard to what you do with it, and what it enables you to do.

Rafael Fernandez

The person who undoubtedly aided me the most during these years of transition was the unusual, idiosyncratic head of the museum's department of prints and drawings. Recognizing potential in my abilities, from early on Rafael Fernandez offered me opportunities, motivated me to accomplish them, and supplied comfort and advice far beyond anything I had ever encountered before—indeed, often on a level it took me some time to fully appreciate.

A Cuban exile who had arrived in the United States in the late 1950s with little more than a hastily packed suitcase, Rafael had been trained as a lawyer and educated in Europe. Dispossessed through his change of country, he turned to his love of art, and soon secured for himself a position in the renowned department of prints and drawings of the Art Institute of Chicago. By dint of connoisseurship and his wide grasp of culture, he successfully survived the severe, Old World, intellectual atmosphere of the department's venerable director Harold Joachim, making his mark in the cataloguing of an important set of Italian drawings. He also taught, married into a prominent Chicago clan, and started a family. On the side, he completed most of the work for a Ph.D., although as with many other candidates, circumstances prevented its completion.

Desiring a dominion of his own, Rafael sought and won the position in which I knew him, at which he had remained for many years—in my eventual opinion, too many. For, while Rafael was brilliant, probably one of the two or three brightest people I have ever known, he used the occasion of his comfortable post at the museum not to further scholarship in any great degree, or to produce more than an occasional splendid show, things he did well but rarely, but rather to indulge his endless questioning of the world, his injured sense of himself, his passion for information rather than pursuit of obviously needed organization, and to luxuriate in his highly developed state of ennui.

In his defense, after several years working with him at the museum, collaborating on occasional later independent projects, and eventually filling in for him for two years after he retired, some of the reasons for his disillusioned outlook became more apparent. Shortly after his arrival, a new director replaced the one who had had the wisdom to hire him. Beyond the discouragements he had originally faced—displacement, loneliness, racism—the museum, its new director, and key members of the museum staff during most of Rafael's tenure formed a sleepy, thankless, and isolated club with little ability to understand, or desire to support, someone of Rafael's stature. Of the things that make a curator happy and productive, few were offered to him. Funds were rarely expended on acquisitions or plans laid in advance for complex, exciting exhibitions and publications. With its stellar if small collection and its bucolic setting, the museum needed to do little to attract a steady flow of culture-seeking visitors. Indeed, as Rafael discovered, not upsetting this pattern was a far more important priority for the museum than the risky prospect of attempting to improve it. As a result, he contented himself with a comfortable perch on its periphery.

Toward the end of my tenure another new director came in, and in a brief time the museum changed completely. But by then Rafael had retired. Until that time the Print Room—a lovely, large paneled space with an immense table, views of the mountains, and an extensive vault attached—was his bully pulpit. The Print Room was a small wing adjoining the library and apart from the rest of the museum over which, with one exception, Rafael exercised complete control. The exception was the museum's registrar, or collections manager, an impossible, frustrated woman who used her alleged authority and other imagined powers to intimidate other administration and staff. She and Rafael were an even match. Working in the same building, with a tiny staff, on many of the same projects, attending the same daily and weekly meetings, they managed at one point not to speak to each other directly for several years.

With this exception, Rafael's world was his own. As long as the work of the department was completed, and there was not a great deal of it, the rest of the time could be spent in the pursuit of the subjects he loved. Many an afternoon was occupied in absorbing Rafael's encyclopedic accounts of history, literature, music, and film. (Increasingly, photography, the field to which he felt I was best suited, was added to this list.) Rafael was a master of the segue. As hours wore on, one subject seemed to lead inescapably to another, and one era to the next, from the history of a royal house to the demise of its various descendants, from what had appeared to be a seminal idea back to its original source, until—*voilà!*—the afternoon was gone!

Whatever the misdirection, hidden regrets, or tasks remaining undone, Rafael's was a grand salon. He was a great teacher and superb raconteur. Visiting scholars, if they were not of the hidebound-ideologue variety, always made him their first stop. His acquaintanceship was wide and his command of art and culture virtually complete. It was not uncommon for him to be engaged in activities as varied as entertaining or corresponding with luminaries from great museums or university departments, trading stories about shopping in Italy, reenacting a classic film, demonstrating the complexities of the tango (with gusto), or reminiscing about his experiences in a musty old theater in Paris. He would become animated over the state of a particular drawing or print: who had signed it falsely, how it had become stained or folded, who had copied it, when it had entered a certain collection.

One of the great pleasures of the Print Room was, of course, the prints. Little known to the public, whose interest tended to run to the pastel-hued Renoirs and bottomy Bougereaus downstairs, the museum's collection of prints and drawings far exceeded in number and quality its relatively small group of important paintings. Among its treasures were a nearly complete set of original Dürer prints. A rare example of his drawing, as well as another by Rubens, accompanied a large series of works by masters such as Gauguin, Vuillard, Homer, and Degas. Between these poles of the sixteenth and the nineteenth centuries were several thousand other works on paper by British, French, German, and American artists, many of outstanding quality.

In the Print Room I remembered why I had come to the program. Handling and examining these exquisite works put me in direct touch with their makers: no glass, no frames, no machine-printed reproduction. The sense of entitlement to experience original art fostered by this intimacy—indeed access to quality and authenticity in all the arts—extended a privilege I had enjoyed in lesser degrees before, a legacy of progressive education I have never lost. Later, when I temporarily replaced Rafael after his retirement, I occasionally laughed at the surprising position I found myself in, for walking into the reserved, conservative atmosphere of the Print Room, where only a few people came and went each day, it would have been almost impossible to imagine the treasures hidden behind the simple, dark, unassuming door of the vault. It was an interesting comment on the role I had found for myself that I sat there, alone, as guardian and interpreter to an incalculable wealth of irreplaceable art.

My introduction to Rafael and the Print Room was emblematic of the world I was entering, and while the path down which he guided me was not new, it was certainly new to me.

During my first term in the program, Rafael made my acquaintance, I don't remember how. By the end of the term we had become friends. As a way of vouching for this, and extending it, as my class was preparing for its first-year trip to Italy, he proffered a mysterious errand. In Florence I was to find two art historians he knew, deliver to them a letter he gave me, and report back to him on my visit. My impression of this at the time was that I was to check in on them in some vague way, meet them, get to know them for some reason. I did. Searching out their address on a narrow street in the shadow of the Pitti Palace, I found two aging expatriate gentlemen living in the quiet darkness of a comfortable flat near the Arno. The room in which they offered me tea was accented with the ancient tone of statuary, silver, and textiles They wrote and translated books about art. They were charming and otherworldly. One had an untamed, aggressive, feral presence. The other was gentle and ill, with a faraway look in his eyes that I will never forget. This was a foreign world. I came, we talked, I left. I wasn't sure exactly why I had been there.

When I returned, I dutifully reported on my visit. Later in the second term, after we had come back, Rafael let me know that he was considering naming me as his assistant for the following year. I was stunned. The Print Room assistantship was the best and most desirable at the museum, and currently the domain of a student far more accomplished than I. Looking back, I realized that my visit had not been about looking in on these elders but, rather, that they look at me. It was a mission of intangible intent, an initiation, an experience worthy of Henry James, a glimpse of the brotherhood of intellectuals, art historians, expatriates, and outsiders who made up Rafael's set—a circle into which the appropriateness of my entry was being assessed.

Over the years I learned a great deal from Rafael, among them the routines of curatorial life, proper etiquette with visiting scholars and students, assembling and presenting small exhibitions, and some of the finer points of surviving in a professional, institutional milieu. We completed numerous projects for the department and the museum. Rafael liked me because I was, as he said, a quick study, and could grasp, assimilate and re-present material with promptness and responsibility. We shared an interest in literature and writing, and he was intrigued by my unorthodox past, with its savor of an era during which he had been too busy establishing himself to enjoy the luxury of the adventures he suspected I had seen.

Using the vehicle of these various projects, Rafael supervised me, gently, through the stages I needed to traverse from student to working professional. Even more, he reminded me by example of the respect due to art and artists, and the importance of independent ideas and thought. Eschewing jargon and trendy theories, he was interested only in originality, beauty, and accomplishment, no matter what form they might take. His sympathies were far wider than his personal tastes. With his help I fended off editors who tried to vet my writing, and learned to work with others whose attention would improve it. I absorbed some of the delicate points of presenting art, and sharpened my sense of visual organization and other abilities I had previously put to only modest use.

As graduation approached, with Rafael as mentor and guide, I completed my first exhibition and publication, a substantial endeavor that, however modest in its level of professional achievement, provided important structural elements for the career I was to build, and had consequences he may well have guessed, though I certainly did not.

Not all the lessons were pleasant. We were very different and tolerated rather than truly accepted each other. To me, Rafael was far too self-indulgent; his superior intelligence and stringent training allowed him to get away with a performance only half as good as the one he could really have produced. For Rafael, my artistic leanings and the freedom with which I approached my life were qualities of which, he felt, he could only dream, and my upbringing in mid-twentieth century America represented a background and education too ill-defined to ever bring himself to respect. While I was working with all my power and will to recoup lost years and move ahead, he was gliding easily on cultural waters so familiar that he was rarely challenged. As I struggled to put art and long-neglected files back in order, he wrote lengthy personal letters in the elegant English his correspondents cherished, worked on an unfinished novel, created witty if largely personal collages, and surveyed his collection of *mauvais goût*, a unique accumulation of appallingly inappropriate objects displayed about his office—figurines, postcards, devices of various kinds—a shocking if humorous tribute to the popular culture he both loved and despised.

Eventually we came to blows over some of these issues. When I was hired to run the print department as he retired, my zeal to maintain the standards he had set ran directly into his unwillingness to relinquish the realm he had created. For a long year he lingered, emptying his office, intruding constantly, holding forth while I was trying to complete my work, unwilling to help, blocking me from really succeeding him and making my life in the Print Room impossible. Finally, when I confronted him with this, he became sullen and angry. It was an unfortunate parting. He had meant a lot to me, and still does. Whether I was ever any more to him, though, than the "recycled flower child" he once called me in a conversation with a potential employer, an indulgence in well-intentioned but entirely misplaced rhetorical humor, I will probably never know. But for this lapse of judgment alone, along with other signs I later in retrospect lumped together with it, I would have had to reassess my relationship with him, as he no doubt felt he had needed to do with me. In my turn, then, I felt the cold silence he had once directed at the museum's

Photo: Tom Fels

An early curatorial effort. Works by Edward Hopper and Charles Demuth in an exhibition from 1985.

registrar, and proceeded less hampered, but much chastened, about my appointed Print Room duties.

CCA / PCN

After the Graduate Program, I spent several years looking for permanent work in the field of art. Along the way I held a research fellowship and completed several exhibition and writing projects at the nearby college museum—a second museum in the same town. (There was also a large rare book library to work with and eventually a third, new museum.) In between, I traveled to job interviews and, gathering up my courage, to conferences, academic meetings, and symposia. At one of these, touting my professional abilities as I had learned to do, I gave my name to a young woman working for a nascent museum then housed in New York. Soon after, she called me, and before long, in the winter of 1985, I began the next phase of my life, commuting weekly back and forth to New York City, cataloguing photographs for the future Canadian Centre for Architecture.

At the symposium I had noticed a powerful, severe woman hovering on the fringes of the room, doing her best to contain the impatience she obviously felt. She was involved as a participant but gave the distinct impression that she was at the same time pulling crucial but invisible strings, like a puppeteer, to direct the action around her. Eventually she called inescapable attention to herself by hounding one of the speakers off the stage entirely for presenting too long and unfocused a talk. She turned out to be the founder of the new museum for which I would work, whose growing collection was the subject of the symposium, and of the ambitious exhibition and book *Photography and Architecture* on which it had been based.

The critical and exacting founder and director of the future Canadian Centre for Architecture (CCA) was Phyllis Lambert, a Canadian graduate of Vassar and a figure of growing importance in the world of architecture, collecting, and museums. As a Bronfman and scion of the Seagram's liquor fortune, Phyllis was free to direct her full attention to her passions. Her principal passion was architecture. She had studied with Mies van der Rohe and had designed an elegant art center. But it was images of architecture—photographs, drawings, prints, books—that had for several years begun to occupy her. She was a forceful woman, strong and authoritarian. Until the activity surrounding the founding and opening of the museum, her most widely known accomplishment had been the substantial one of turning what was to have been another uninteresting corporate headquarters on Park Avenue into the modern classic that is the Seagram Building. A devoted student of Mies, who was then working and teaching in Chicago, Phyllis had convinced her father, the head of Seagram's, to hire the stern founder of the International Style to create an emblematic monument of the times, an icon of the era to which the company could attach its name. This successful bit of persuasion, facilitating the creation of one of the key works in the career of one of the most important architects of the twentieth century, suggests the power and imagination wielded by Phyllis Lambert, not to mention the almost unlimited scope of the sphere in which she was able to bring them to bear.

(Another province of activity for Phyllis was the conservation and reconstruction of her native Montreal. Channeling her energies into civic and broadly social projects in historical preservation, urban design, and building, over the years she has had a lasting effect on the environment in which she lives. While few in New York were yet familiar with her name, certainly everyone in Montreal was.)

Soon I was commuting to New York to help catalog Phyllis's growing collection of photographs. It was a new sort of life. Starting in Vermont, I would pack my things and then drive my aging car an hour or more to the train. Cruising along the Hudson on Amtrak's Empire Corridor, I would work or doze or draw the landscape, quietly composing myself for the week ahead. At about nine I would arrive at Grand Central, where I would collect my bag and whatever else I had brought for the week, and hike the ten blocks up Park Avenue to 52nd Street, where an elevator whisked me up to the museum's New York offices on the Seagram Building's 24th floor.

I was one of several cataloguers of the museum's fast-growing collection. Numbering a photographer, a graduate student, an artist, a wandering scholar (myself), and a few others, we gathered there each morning from our various modest corners of the city, being usually the only ones crossing the building's austere, elegant plaza in backpacks and jeans. (It was also one of the entrances to the building's best-known attraction, the exclusive Four Seasons restaurant.) Once on the 24th floor, we spent most of the day in a freezing-cold vault Phyllis had had built for the photographs, conditions far better suited to the well-being of the pictures than ourselves. Being used to this from northern climes, I arrived for work even in warm weather supplied with mittens, hats, scarves, and a down vest. My urban colleagues scoffed, but I was the only one who survived the experience without contracting a cold or the flu.

As I soon found out, Phyllis's display at the symposium had been a typical performance. Though based in Montreal, she visited regularly, times when all hands were alerted to look sharp, tensions ran higher than usual, and many photographs arrived to be considered for acquisition. Literally boxes and boxes, stacks, and fat portfolios of pictures filled entire rooms. Together, Phyllis and her principal curator, Richard, a British-born photographer with a felicitous resemblance to the dancer Rudolf Nureyev, would go through them, sometimes with the assistance of the dealer proffering them to supply information, or one of us to help handle the often large original pieces. Purchases were made, but tempers ran high, explosions of piqued emotion were occasionally heard, and a large portion of the offerings were invariably rejected.

Phyllis did, of course, on these occasions, have the longer view. Among the unique guidelines developed by Phyllis and Richard was that they preferred to buy documents and art in series, rather than as isolated elements. Hence, not a picture or two would be bought but entire albums, not a single volume but entire sets, not isolated works but, if possible, complete portions of an artist's oeuvre or estate. New series of architectural photographs were commissioned as well. The approach was different from that of most museums, and so were the results. When the Canadian Centre opened several years later in its beautiful new building in Montreal, designed in part by Phyllis, it held, despite the youth of the collection, unparalleled resources for the study of building, architectural and urban history, and design, and was instantly of unique importance, one of only a very few high-quality museums and study centers for architecture in the world.

I smiled again at Phyllis' role when, arriving one morning at work, I found a movie being filmed on the plaza and in the lobby of the Seagram Building. The structure, I could now see, exemplified a certain urbanity and sophistication. This turned out to be an appropriate starting point for the movie being filmed, BABY BOOM, with Diane Keaton, a story involving issues such as quality of life, rural living, and a baby boomer's relation to marriage and career, themes with which I was very familiar.

At this point, the lines of my life were beginning to cross in just such new, interesting, and in some instances unsettling ways. Again, patterns continued to be illuminated or newly set.

On another day, I was working as usual in the vault. At home and in evenings in the city, I had begun to write and publish more widely. Some of my exhibitions and publications had been seen by people I could never have known. At the same time, when I left the city, I returned to the relative anonymity of a small town unconnected with my life in museums or New York. Emerging into the light this particular day from refrigerated stacks of images of Italy and Greece in the nineteenth century, be-mittened, - hatted and -scarved, I encountered a prominent dealer in photographs who was delivering a portfolio to Phyllis for consideration. We had never met. Seeing us all, the vault crew, in a relaxed mode as we took a break, he offered some small talk on photography as he waited for Richard to complete the paperwork for the packet he had brought. He turned out to be Jeffrey

Fraenkel, from San Francisco. The talk turned to Carleton Watkins, the photographer on whom I had done my graduate school exhibition and publication, an important figure in the arts in San Francisco in the nineteenth century. Eventually, Jeffrey realized that I was the one who had organized the exhibition and written the catalog.

"*You* are Tom Fels?" he asked, somewhat shaken.

"Well, yes," I replied. There really wasn't anything else I could say. I did take off my mittens, though, as I could see that this meeting was taking on dimensions I had not anticipated. Later we became friends and colleagues. I continue to respect Jeffrey as a great judge of photographs and one of the most astute connoisseurs and businessmen in his field. The effect on me, though, was to open a certain window I had not till then suspected. Apparently I had a national life, a presence in the field of which I was unaware. I was almost forty and only then finally sensing through occasional comments, reviews, and encounters of this kind that there were people out there somewhere who liked what I did. It was a good feeling, though many more hours were to pass in the vault, at the typewriter, and in the installation of numerous museum galleries before I felt anything resembling comfort in this new role.

During the period when I was in New York, and beginning shortly before, I expanded another area of my life that, like art, combined both my personal and my professional interests: writing. While, at the time it was shown, my graduate exhibition had provoked only modest comment, a year later a review appeared in a national magazine that seemed the answer to all my dreams. Like my meeting with Jeffrey Fraenkel a few months later, it left me in complete astonishment. At the time of my show on Watkins there had been another, much larger one, with its own much more lavish publication. Another book on him had also recently been brought out by a major photographic press. Reviewing all three publications one long and silent year later, the writer, one of the few genuine scholars to have then emerged in the new field of photography, concluded that the modest three-dollar publication I had produced exceeded the other coffee-table books by all measures I considered important: meaningful approach, grasp of cultural history, and insightful interpretation of the art. "This essay," the author wrote, "is intellectually ambitious in a way that the others are not." I couldn't really have asked for more.

I dropped a note of thanks to the author. I also wrote a brief letter to the editor of the magazine, *The Print Collector's Newsletter,* Jacqueline Brody, explaining my interest in prints and photographs and asking that she keep me in mind for future projects. Some time later I received an assignment from her to review a new book on landscape photography, a subject I knew well. Jackie liked it, and for the next ten years I wrote regularly for this small but influential publication, read mostly by museum professionals, teachers, graduate students, and collectors.

During graduate school Rafael had alerted me to the quality of the *Newsletter*—known to its devotees as *PCN*—a modestly produced, low-key, but authoritative publication which he read religiously and kept prominently visible in its characteristic three-ring bound volumes on a Print Room shelf. With his encouragement, I was prepared to pursue an opportunity he felt was unusually propitious, given my particular abilities and interests. What I hadn't expected was the bonding I experienced with its editor. The success of *PCN* was no coincidence. As I worked over the years on reviews, features, and occasional reports from afield, I came to realize the important directorial and editorial role played by Jackie in shaping the life of the magazine, and thus of its writers. It worked for me as well.

Before going to *PCN* I had resented editing. I polished to a high finish everything I submitted, and was regularly appalled at the changes with which these pieces were returned to me, or in some cases directly printed without even my consent to the alterations. In my naiveté, and far from the center of the publishing world, I had considered these to be conditions of writing and editing themselves. In Jackie, however, I had finally found a good editor, and the difference was immense. I learned that published writing is often the result of teamwork. When I got things back from Jackie or her competent assistants, they were always better than when I had sent them in. The organization and flow of the writing was improved, yet the ideas I presented, however critical or contentious, were never questioned or tampered with. Jackie was the best editor I ever had. We worked together well.

For me, the exposure afforded by my regular contributions to *PCN* offered a chance to speak out and to develop a voice at a

Cover feature for PCN, Spring 1986.

national level. For Jackie, I became one of a stable of competent, versatile writers with more of a penchant for opinion than most magazines would encourage. No one at *PCN* took things lightly, and my critical approach fit well. Though I sometimes lost sleep over who might be offended by my views, the positive response I sometimes received more than compensated for these occasional fears. When the magazine was sold and changed its editor and publisher, an era of my life was distinctly over. After a few further attempts to continue under the magazine's new, less sympathetic regime, I turned my attention to other outlets for my thoughts.

The Met

With the new distinction of my work for *PCN*, and the increasing visibility of the Canadian Centre where I was working, I began to grow somewhat into the position I had been, in a rather backward way, creating for myself. When I had returned to graduate school, all I had wanted was a steady job at a museum. Three years out of the program and five years later, what seemed to work for me, instead, was still the same combination that had gotten me admitted to, and helped me survive in that program: independence, focus, imagination, and hard work. As the Canadian Centre was slated to eventually move to its new home in Canada, taking no Americans with it, and *PCN* and other small publications for which I occasionally wrote did not provide a steady income, I decided to try to leverage my achievements to date in a different direction.

On my visits to *PCN* to drop off or pick up manuscripts and illustrations or meet with the editors over corrected page proofs, I couldn't help but notice the imposing building at the end of the street—the Met. The magazine, which later moved a few blocks east to Jackie's newly renovated building adjacent to Park Avenue, was housed at that time in a little brownstone literally in the shadow of the great museum. With the growth of the field of photography over the past ten years—roughly since the mid-seventies—a fledgling department of photographs had recently been established there. Its new curator, who had arrived only a short time before, was an ambitious, energetic woman whom I thought might be interested in testing her wings in the battle for notoriety and funding within the museum. Together we put together a proposal for a project to work with a neglected part of her collection. It was accepted, and for the next year I came and went regularly from the Metropolitan Museum of Art in an attempt to accumulate enough information to attribute some 350 photographs of the Civil War.

Unfortunately, this turned out to be one of the few, but highly noticeable, of my projects to substantially founder. They always seemed to be among the large and important ones. (Later, the draft manuscript for a book over which I stumbled was not accepted, and another on which I did an outstanding job was never published.) The problems of attributing several hundred pictures believed to be by Mathew Brady came to be far more complex than either the curator or I had envisioned. The foremost problem turned out to be that Mathew Brady was less a war photographer than an entrepreneur and director, in the sense of a film director. Most if not all of the pictures in the museum's group had been taken by others on Brady's mobile and highly itinerant photographic teams, and returned to his studio only for printing and distribution. Attributing them definitively (attribution, in art history, signifies identifying the author or artist of a work) entailed, among other considerations, tracking the whereabouts of Brady's many photographers throughout the course of the war, as well as determining the publishing history of their negatives after they were returned to the Brady studio to be printed. Other complexities included disentangling long lists and printed booklets of the published works, in which duplications, substitutions, and changes of title were difficult to trace in the absence of actual pictures with which to compare them. Was "Tents, Bull Run" in a list of 1863, say, the same as "Bull Run, Tents" in a different publication two years later? Was "A.G." Alexander Gardner or some other photographer with those initials?

To some extent, this was the same sort of information that needed to be addressed in any art history project. What we learned in the process of this particular effort, however, was that the scale of Brady's work—cadres of photographers and assistants, thousands of photographs, many levels of reproduction from originals to rotogravures—combined with the expansion of publication and printing in the nineteenth century, added tremendously to the difficulty of assigning authorship to artwork of this kind in the modern era. In addition, the history of Brady's negatives themselves was complex—they had been lost, found, lent, broken, copied. (During this era pictures often appeared in different formats—prints, stereos, reproductions—with entirely different attributions, as one company bought a series of images from another and published them under its own name.) Add to this the internecine warfare among the Washington institutions that held them today—conflicting, difficult to translate systems of organization; political maneuvering among civil employees and competing professionals—and the story became more and more difficult to reconstruct.

As I shuttled from New York to Washington, Chicago, Boston, and other locations holding source material on Brady and these particular prints, I accumulated far more information than the year I had been given would allow me to unravel. Eventually, the curator and I differed: I wanted to finish the project, she wanted me to simply report on what I had done. She took the initiative by not advocating support for the project's continuation. I, of course, was not willing to complete an effort which could not be adequately funded. This stalemate was never resolved, and in my subsequent career I have, unfortunately, never been able to seek the support of this important curator and great museum.

One of the causes of this parting of the ways was the advent of other projects. Traveling, talking with colleagues, spending time in New York and other cities—along with a measure of the growing self-assurance that interesting work and its connected anecdotes will produce—all contributed to bringing me to the attention of others who could use my skills. While I was at CCA and the Met, several other opportunities arose; some grew into important projects, others did not. All, however, fostered my movement away from association with a single museum and edged me toward the prospect of an independent career, toward what used to be called freelance work and is now euphemistically described in the business of culture as the role of the "content provider."

Over these several years I wrote a number of articles, organized two more exhibitions, and added another publication to the three I had already produced. By the time I had been out of school five years, my resume was becoming difficult to contain. Finally, nearing the end of the eighties, two opportunities arose that conspicuously raised the visibility of my career. One was an important exhibition and publication done in 1989, the other, which started shortly before that exhibition and continued well after it, was the opportunity to do some work in California. To work on the exhibition, which came to be called O SAY CAN YOU SEE, I returned to my home territory and increased my professional independence to an extent not allowed to me before. It was also the occasion of meeting one of the more interesting figures I have encountered in the world of photography and art.

George Rinhart

While I was working in New York, I had heard stories of a reclusive collector living in the woods of rural New England. The reports I heard described a difficult man with a mind of his own, one of the founders of the then new photography market who had retreated from the urban scene to a private life divided between collecting and dealing in photographs. This was intriguing but didn't mean much to me until a museum for which I had organized a previous exhibition approached me with the opportunity to work with him. He was everything I had been led to believe, and more.

After some discreet diplomatic arrangements, I drove to meet the elusive collector. The business at hand was to lay the groundwork for an exhibition and publication based on a selection from his collection. It was 1989, the 150th anniversary of photography, and everyone, it seemed, was organizing an exhibition of some kind in homage to the field. Since I was not currently connected to a museum, the opportunity to work with the collector held several advantages. First, there was his collection, which would provide the art. Second, working with an individual, for whom the artwork, permissions, and shipping would not be a problem, the project could move much faster than one for which outside loans were necessary. Third, since this was to be the public debut of his collection, its owner was willing to underwrite the publication of a substantial book, a goal I was eager to accomplish as well. Last, his forbidding reputation having kept others at bay, I was the first to work with him and could make of this opportunity whatever I was able. We also had a certain natural kinship. What looked to those in the city like the deep woods of the north were to me only fashionable suburbs and weekend-house territory: I lived much farther from the city than he did.

To visit, I drove almost two hours south toward New York to a pristine town in the northwest corner of Connecticut. When I arrived, I found that George Rinhart lived in a large, well kept turn-of-the-century Adirondack-style mansion. It was, indeed, far out in the country, but no farther than the houses of most of his neighbors, and it was civilized to an almost baronial degree. Everywhere were fine furniture and art. In winter a fire was always roaring in the immense stone fireplace, and in all seasons tea and lunch were served in impeccable style. Behind this facade of civility, however, was evidence of Mr. Rinhart's passion and business: American photographs. In every chest and cabinet, in closets and files, in entire separate houses dotted along the town's country roads, as I discovered, were stacks and stacks of photographs. Rumor had ventured that Mr. Rinhart had a million photographs. As far as I could see, that guess might be conservative.

To obtain the masterpieces we were to show, Mr. Rinhart had culled many other collections. He toured the country constantly in search of material and maintained contact with a team of runners, as they are called in the trade, to investigate auctions, estates, and sales as they came up. He and his longtime assistant had assembled, and frequently consulted, an extensive research library, including, when necessary, such common, everyday tools as phone books and local business guides of various eras, with which to help him locate photographers and the descendants, businesses, friends, and clubs in whose hands an artist's work might remain. More than once I heard stories of surprised families receiving a letter or a call from Mr. Rinhart inquiring about treasures they themselves had forgotten, or on which they now placed little value. By buying entire estates and bodies of work, Mr. Rinhart made the task of choosing easier—he just bought them all. The obverse of this habit was that, in order to secure its tip, the bulk of the pyramid he had acquired had to be housed, resold, or in some cases simply given away—often donated to a library or museum.

Over the course of the period we worked together, in which I drove down regularly to look at pictures and talk about the exhibition and the publication, I began to get a sense of Mr. Rinhart as a collector, historian, and man of means. His devotion to American photographs (and, indeed, other entire areas of American art that he collected, as well) was absolute. In the essay I wrote for the book we produced, which focused on the first one hundred years of American photography, I was influenced by his views and by the tremendous amount I learned from working with him. Its subject became the importance of photography as an American art, a perspective I had already developed, but which through my experience with him sharpened considerably.

One of the important things I learned working with Mr. Rinhart was the difference in approach between art professionals and academics. Because I had spent the past several years with art historians, my standard for information had become verifiability and documentation. In this view, pieces of art were specific, had individual histories, and were considered acceptable links in the great chain of art history only to the extent that their origin and path could be traced with certainty. Mr. Rinhart, on the other hand, trafficked not only in the firm information he had acquired through accepted channels of research but in far more casual stories, anecdotes, and inferences. What was interesting to me, which I have since seen many times, was that this more personal form of knowledge, despite its drawbacks, often yielded results far beyond anything of which most art historians would even dream. Given a set of information, the academic will use only what is firmly established. This provides a necessary base for ongoing

Courtesy George R. Rinhart.

William Dassonville, *Ship's Deck*, c.1926.
From the exhibition and book O SAY CAN YOU SEE, 1989.

research and the founding of a factual grid important in creating a reliable context for works of art. Given the same set of information, on the other hand, the art professional will use it all. Judgments are made, of course, as to its veracity, but in general, if a cousin or a friend of an artist has been heard to say that he produced a certain work, or was influenced in some particular way, now lost, the art historian, for lack of further documentation, will be reluctant to admit this informal report as evidence. The art professional, in contrast, is the sort who will go out and try to find the cousin or his descendants or the work. Mr. Rinhart's world was full of such stories. He knew all about the lives of the photographers in whom he took an interest, their families, their odd habits and foibles, their frequent moves, their now forgotten great successes. As a result, he could put together pieces of puzzles larger than those that documentation alone could provide.

In practice, these approaches lead in quite different directions. For the art historian, documentation provides the ultimate matrix for new facts, and the library (full of such hard-won facts) is the primary backdrop for his or her work. For those engaged in seeking out art itself, a much more informal, probing, exploratory approach works best. Working with Mr. Rinhart, I could see the extensive knowledge of individual artists, families, trends, friendships, discrete historical events, and even rumored meetings he had accumulated. While the information he savored was often unverifiable, the collection he had amassed, and its quality, proved unequivocally that this form of knowledge could also be productive.

Of course, good art historians and good art professionals often combine the best of these qualities. A former neighbor of mine, Julius Held, whom I first met in the course of my graduate work, was a good example of this. An expert in the history of Rembrandt, Dürer, Rubens, and other northern European artists, Julius was also a highly perceptive analyst of style and technique, and a writer in his second language, English, whose ability would shame many who learned it at their mother's knee. When I once sat in on the first lecture of Mr. Held's annual course, he approached his subject in a way that showed his outlook, catholicity, and humor—as well as his knowledge. Using the blackboard and a piece of chalk, he started to outline some odd shapes. As he continued, he would ask periodically if we, young American students, recognized what he was drawing. We didn't. Eventually, he completed his strange, wiggly shapes. A dot went in here and there. Still no response. Finally, a few names helped us: Dresden, Aachen, the Rhine, Berlin. Continuing, he pointed: Here was the home of Dürer, here was the center of court life, here was the original site of the Isenheim altarpiece. It was Germany and its environs. To him it was home. Although I didn't take the course, and still know little about either Germany or northern European art, I have never forgotten the lesson that art and artists come from a culture, a people, a location, a time, and that to understand them fully one needs to learn their context either at firsthand or from someone who has immersed him- or herself in it, as was true of both Julius Held and Mr. Rinhart.

Mr. Rinhart's other distinguishing characteristic was his avidity. He was utterly driven in his passion to uncover as much as possible about American photographs, and of those he considered to be of importance, to acquire as many as possible. His pursuit of this grail was never-ending, and woe to those who might stand in his way. The result, of course, was that he found and acquired much that was exceptional and unique. His best pieces, if they did not remain with him, now populate the most outstanding collections of photography, both public and private. His methods, though, along with his highly inflammable passions, did not make him many friends, as the rumors I had heard had shown. He had a strong dislike for a number of others in the field, and I think felt little compassion for those he could best. The irony was that though he sat on a mountain of extraordinary, literally epoch-making material, few were aware of it, and of those who were, most chose not to venture near enough to see for themselves.

Because of the quality of work it contained, much of it little known at the time, and because of the beautiful volume Mr.

Rinhart's subvention had enabled the museum to produce, *O SAY CAN YOU SEE* (1989) became a much sought-after volume and a key departure point in my career. Even before it appeared, however, the second development of a similar kind occurred.

Go West

While in New York, I connected with a number of old friends and made several new ones—especially in the areas of photography and museums in which I was working. I was also, of course, far more available than I was at home in Vermont to visitors and travelers who might find themselves in the city. Simply being in New York, even for the year or two I was there, afforded me opportunities and provided contacts from which I would benefit for many years.

Probably the biggest change in my life at this time, though, was that through a complex set of circumstances I began a series of research, exhibition, and writing projects in California. As I had envisioned a role for myself at the Metropolitan Museum, I now looked at the changing, expanding scene in the world of photography and saw what many others at the time saw as well: the West. The reasons were clear. It was not only the tremendous growth of the arts in the Southwest, particularly among galleries, artists, and craftspeople, or the expanding cultural milieu of the Northwest Coast. It was not even the forbidding impenetrability of curatorial life in the east, where jobs were scarce and most of the important positions were either already filled or closely guarded. It was rather, in various parts, the long history of appreciation of photography in California, my own history with western photographs through my work with Watkins, and especially an event that occurred just at this time: the founding of a department of photographs at the J. Paul Getty Museum in Los Angeles.

The founding of the department at the Getty was news for several reasons. First, it was a surprise. Negotiations for the original purchases that formed the core of the new department's collections had been conducted in such secrecy that few knew about them until they appeared in the daily papers and art magazines as a *fait accompli*. Beyond this, the scale of these purchases dwarfed the activities of other museums, and the quality of the work that was acquired was breathtaking. The scope of the quest had been global, gathering in a single gesture one of the foremost collections in the world. There were other considerations. Photography was a growing field, yet because serious collecting had started only recently, there were still masterpieces to be obtained. Because it was a young medium, prices were also still relatively low. Combining these factors, those behind the Getty deal had realized that for the price of one important painting, probably less, they could purchase a substantial portion of what remained in private hands of the world's best photographs, guaranteeing themselves a place at the table in the life of a medium whose history was only beginning to be appreciated—and, of equal interest to me, beginning to be written.

This place at the cultural table came to be occupied largely by Weston Naef, the new curator who had helped assemble the collection. In the east, Weston had been known as an ambitious, high-strung man with a strong allegiance to the fine arts. He had first worked with prints, and had developed a taste for photography before going to New York, where he was a curator at the Metropolitan in the era in which its photographs still fell under the oversight of the museum's department of prints. By the mid-eighties, Weston had produced several important exhibitions and publications relating to photography. He was an influential figure and, despite his demanding presence, or perhaps in part because of it, an acknowledged authority in the field.

The missing piece in this picture, I came to see, though no doubt not the only one, was that Weston had ties to California. One of his best-known publications, which I had used in research for my exhibitions, was on photographers of the Far West. As I later learned from him, he had gone to college in greater Los Angeles. Although he was perceived as part of the eastern museum establishment, the opportunity to return to California, judging by subsequent events, was no doubt very appealing—especially arrayed in the new professional garments in which he had arranged to clothe himself. It was a return advantageous in several ways. In the west, as I discovered, the credibility of easterners is increased several fold, so Weston presumably gained through this aspect of his return. But having worked in the east, and especially at the Met, he indeed had considerable connections and influence to bring to bear. The twist he gave to his career and to the institutional history of photography, and the boost these contributed to the West Coast do, certainly, lend him credit. To hear him tell the story of his return to California—as it appeared to him at dawn at the end of the long flight he took in the large jet hired by the Getty Museum to transport its newly acquired photographs to Los Angeles—is to experience a modern tale of mythic proportions, in which some vast cultural imbalance between the east and the west is corrected, and a new chapter in the study of art begun.

The Metropolitan itself, where he had been working until the eve of this announcement, was not as delighted as some others with these developments. To those outside its immediate sphere, the events surrounding the formation of the department of photographs at the Getty suggested that the aura of one institution had been enlisted, however informally, in heightening the radiance of another. The taste of loss, felt by the Metropolitan and other eastern institutions, at sensing the success of the maneuver the Getty had accomplished, clouded for some time a number of Weston's connections in the east and, to an appreciable extent, the standing of the Getty Museum itself. Though largely orchestrated through a New York dealer, the entrepreneurial, frontier justice approach to what had been done definitely had a western ring. The Met responded by strengthening its own department of photographs and hiring the curator I worked with there, a scholar with a strong track record of research, someone who would appreciate the advantages of stability, credibility, and New York and would presumably build the department and the collection—as, indeed, she did—rather than be wooed away.

The Getty deal, however, represented a once-in-a-lifetime circumstance. No one truly blamed Weston for taking advantage of the extraordinary opportunity that had offered itself, and many simply marveled at the temerity he had displayed in pulling it off. In establishing himself in Los Angeles, though—as he unpacked photographs, began to hire staff, and chart his course—Weston unveiled some novelties that reflected changes in the way he would approach photography, and thus how his department would be run, that separated him in more substantial ways from his new peers in the field.

Among these was that rather than build a department of in-house specialists, he chose to rely on visiting experts. After the initial unpacking, indeed, well before it was finished, commenced a long string of visiting scholars that would continue for years. Experts in early or modern work, in French or German work, in the daguerreotype, in the various schools of photography—naturalism, pictorialism, modernism, were invited to look over works in their area of specialization. Connoisseurs of particular geographical areas—America, the Middle East, and students of particular masters—Stieglitz, Talbot, Le Gray, all began to make a stop in Los Angeles, filing through the department, at this time, for lack of adequate space at the old museum, and many years before the completion of its magnificent current new facility, housed in a high-rise bank building in Santa Monica.

I looked at this with some interest. Of course it made sense to hire only the best scholars for a particular type or body of work. The Getty could afford this level of specialization on a regular basis, while most other institutions could not. It was also a shrewd management ploy, of which we have seen much more since: Visiting scholars were not full employees needing salaries, desks, and insurance; the institutional base remained small and the visitors, when finished, simply returned home. The Getty department did attract and develop some full-time scholars, but for years the model was that those employed there principally facilitated the work of others who came as visitors to do the bulk of the scholarly research.

Fortunately, I had a card to play here. My graduate exhibition and publication had been on California photography. I knew from Weston's book on the subject that this was a favored topic. Reading the fine print about the assemblage of prints that now formed the Getty collection, I realized that the photographs on which I had worked were among those bought by the museum. I was thus the kind of expert Weston was seeking.

The line at the door, however, was growing. I was early enough, though, that when I wrote to Weston, whom I had yet to meet, he responded, showing some interest in my proposal to help catalog his photographs. As a recent graduate with only a masters degree, though, I suspected that I didn't have the professional profile, the academic allure of older, more experienced scholars. How was I to make my case?

I knew from Weston's work that he respected competence and experience. I knew from his history that institutions and influence were important to him. But I was now seasoned myself, and knew how to respond. In my answer to his letter I included a few carefully crafted lines noting my fellowships, projects, and publications to date. By that time they were linked to some of the most important institutions and authorities in the field. Instantly, the tenor of our correspondence changed. Before long, I was in California on the first of several trips to catalog the works of Carleton Watkins. Eventually, I got to know Weston better. Under his aegis I organized an exhibition at the Getty Museum, and the contacts I made while in Los Angeles and Santa Monica involved me in several later projects with the museum and the trust. Even at the time, though, I realized that my future had depended largely on those few lines.

I was not the obvious choice for this assignment. There were others who knew more than I did. It was important to me, though, and I did my best to make it work for Weston and the museum. Most significantly, for me, it became a part of my life. As the cataloging proceeded over a period of time, I explored Los Angeles and southern California, reconnected with lost friends, and through them and my new colleagues made a number of new ones. Despite the stress of regular cross-country travel, it was a fruitful period of my life, a time in which I was increasingly judged only by who I was and what I did, and I have always been grateful to Weston for that. As I get older, though, and see in events more ancient, mythical themes, I think of the lure that power in New York held first over another institution in the west, and then its new curator, and recall, as one then beginning to make his professional way, the satisfaction of the fabled fox as the crow's cherished cheese fell at his feet.

Arriving in California was like arriving at the Graduate Program I had attended, only at a higher level. As a consultant to the Getty, I traveled at their expense. On arriving, I was whisked to a nearby villa kept by the museum for visiting scholars. My rooms constituted a small suite. The colors were of a warm, modern, neutral hue. There were long French doors, sea air, and lots of sun. The low living room table was graced with a bouquet of stunningly beautiful flowers that I later learned to recognize as bird-of-paradise. In the refrigerator was a bottle of cold California chardonnay. Palms lined the streets. The air was fresh and the ocean near. It was midwinter. Now I could see what Weston had had in mind.

I immediately set up the room for my visit, arranging the dining room table for work and the living room sofa as a reading area. The rooms were within easy walking distance of the department's offices. I had brought with me a recently acquired Zenith laptop and Diconix printer, my first computer and one of the earliest such combinations to be truly portable. During the days I would review photographs at the department a few blocks away and type in my notes. In the evening, I would return to my rooms to edit and print out what I had done. It was a great way to work. I was very happy with what I could accomplish, and the department was amply satisfied with the progress we made.

Over the period of my visit, I moved through a great deal of material, but there was more to do, and the museum continued to acquire additional photographs, so several return trips were necessary. During these visits, days were spent in the department's print room, a library-like space with a view of the San Gabriel Mountains to the west of Los Angeles, toward Pasadena. I got to know the staff, with whom I still stay in touch. The one break in the otherwise busy and very intense day was lunch time. Two blocks to the west, beyond the Pacific Coast Highway, was the ocean. There were restaurants in that area, but most were too tony and expensive for an office lunch break. Two blocks to the east, however, a short way down Wilshire from the department's quarters, was the perfect spot, the one that the staff seemed to favor, a busy sandwich shop that we visited frequently. It had a familiar look. It was Zucky's, the place where I had had lunch with Asa seven years before.

Over the course of these stays, Weston and I had gotten to know each other better. He was a highly organized person. When we discussed anything of importance, especially something that affected his calendar or his budget, he would reach into his pocket and pull out a small book to record it. I could see why. One day he might be in his office at the bank on Wilshire or over at the museum in Malibu. On another he might be in New York for a meeting, or in Paris looking at photographs for possible acquisition, or conferring with colleagues at another institution. Once I ran into him in San Francisco. Seeing some photographs of interest, he asked me to research them and send him a report. We discussed a timetable and a budget, and he entered it into his book. Five minutes later he was gone.

One of these encounters I distinctly remember. We were sitting outside for lunch in the outdoor marketplace on Santa Monica's Second Street, a paragon of enlightened city planning and one of the pleasures of life in that charmed northwest sector of Los Angeles. (The street was bounded at the south end by an early work of Frank Gehry, then virtually unknown.) Weston rarely invited me to lunch on my own, usually it was with members of the staff or other visitors. He was busy, and lunch, if not connected to business, was an indulgence he could rarely afford. Delicately, as it did at some point in the course of each of my visits, the conversation came around to the future. We had shared some thoughts. I had told him of the projects on which I was working. He had confided that his ambitious work on photography and art was still in progress (it still is). He pulled out his book.

"Tom," he said, "I think you should do a show for us."

This made some sense. I was familiar with the material, we had discussed it extensively, and I had ideas about how it should be presented and described. Still, it was one of those surprising moments you feel you have worked for and yet do not expect. I looked around me at the congenial life of Santa Monica—bookstores, galleries, an open-air market—took in the sun and the palms, thought about future visits.

"That would be a privilege," I said. He made a note in his book.

The exhibition I organized for the Getty Museum was shown in 1990. A little later I had a similar lunch on State Street in Santa Barbara with one of the Getty's editors, a woman I came to greatly like and respect. We agreed over enchiladas and beer, on the restaurant's shaded outdoor patio, that a book about Watkins would be a great addition to a new series of monographs the museum was developing. Regarding these two events together, I can see that, though there was still a great deal of work to be done, a certain new level in my professional life had been reached.

Chapter 9

OLD FRIENDS

Circa 1990: Michael Curry

One of the advantages of my new work at the Getty Museum was that it put me back in touch with my old friend from the farm, Michael Curry. A newly minted Ph.D., Michael had taken a job in the geography department of UCLA, one of the best in the country. From the sketchy reports I had heard, I gathered that he lived in Los Angeles near the university, only a few minutes by car from where I was working and staying. On my arrival in California, I immediately got in touch with him.

In some ways, my impression of Michael was typical of those I had of the early farmers. In other ways, they were separate and distinct. As a member of the farm community, Michael had engaged in woodworking, a popular activity, though as a serious, careful cabinetmaker, he was especially good at it. He also took part in the farming and machine repairs we all did. We had common memories of our mutual friends and of the frontier life we all shared in western Massachusetts and southern Vermont. But beyond this, he and I shared specific interests in architecture, design, and building; in music; and in recondite intellectual pursuits that were far from the mainstays of farm life. He also distinguished himself for me by establishing a long-term relationship with my former girlfriend—although it was someone else who had actually first run off with her—a bond that both unites and occasionally divides us even now.

Michael had come to the farm from New College, an experimental school in Florida, as a friend of a collegemate who had moved to the farm with Liberation News Service. After his time at the farm, Michael had lived in the Midwest, where he had worked in architecture in Minneapolis, married, and eventually gone to graduate school in Madison, where he studied with Yi Fu-Tuan, a luminary in the field of geography.

At the farm I had gotten a sense of Michael as bright, responsible, and highly principled. He always saw things through. I remember we worked together on a building I had designed that included a semicircular window below the peak of the roof—a nice touch, I had thought. Our building plans were interrupted by a trip I needed to make. I handed the plans over to Michael. He looked at the drawings: all rectangular and straightforward. "No problem," he said. Then he saw the semicircular window. Introducing curves into their buildings was something hippie farmers rarely had the energy or expertise to do. The look he gave me as he calculated how he might make the complicated cuts needed to complete the job has stayed with me over the years.

Nonetheless, in the time we have known each other, we have become close friends. For him that incident is no doubt long forgotten. When he married a second time, to Joanna, a Polish geographer living in New Jersey, I served as their best man. Not long after, as part of their ongoing, highly mobile international life, they bought a summer house near me, in the hills of Sandgrove, where they remain neighbors of Steve Lerner and others in our sometimes reclusive, always tight-knit tribe.

In Santa Monica, Michael was my first friend and guide. As I got to know this new territory, and began to embark upon what would be a number of regular visits to California, he and I would have a Thai dinner after work near the shore and talk, over beer and various pungent Eastern sauces, about old times and the surprises of our new lives. News from the farm in these later years was complex, politically charged, and often tumultuous, part of a lengthy, at times apparently interminable process in which many of the festering legacies of our earlier days eventually emerged, and finally came to be resolved—a process in which Michael played a large part. Michael and I were each also beginning a new portion of our careers, so there was plenty of news on that front. Personalities, opportunities, the stresses of achievement, the occasional professional fiasco or political wrong turn provided us with ample entertainment as we sat at sidewalk tables in the cool evenings and watched the comings and goings of street life, from late model Maseratis to the wandering homeless with their pirated shopping carts, in Los Angeles' most habitable corner.

When possible, we used the occasion of my visits to reconnect with other farm friends. Steve Diamond was now living in Santa Barbara and Raymond near San Diego. On a weekend or a free day, I could persuade Michael to go up to Santa Barbara, or later, if I was working there, Michael would come up and see both Steve and me. There were several ways to get to Santa Barbara: along the coast; on the freeway; through the mountains. On these drives, and later ones with Michael and Joanna, I learned about the landscape I had seen from the train in 1980, and later in the nineteenth century photographs I had studied, and began to understand more about California life. In Pasadena, I saw there was art and culture of an almost East Coast character. In a dry, open valley on the way to Mt. Wilson, to see the observatory, we encountered one of California's recurrent brush fires. Helicopters came and went, dropping water, as traffic stopped and clouds of smoke billowed from the scrubby chaparral. In the large space the event looked tiny. I could see, though, how it would appear represented through the telephoto lenses of newspapers and television, the only way I had ever seen such a thing before. In a canyon, near a small-town museum of the petroleum industry, on the way to Santa Barbara, oil actually oozed from the rocks along the road, like slow-moving water. In Ojai we admired displays of crystals and visited a spacey bookstore with a Spanish patio in the back where you could take your book (or theirs) and read all day undisturbed. It was the land of Krishnamurti and things really were different.

At the time of these visits, in the late 1980s, Raymond was at work on BEYOND THE REVOLUTION (1990), an effort to bring his readers up to date on the scenes on which he had reported in his early books almost twenty years before. Hearing that some potential subjects were in town, he was persuaded to leave his partner and desert retreat to join Michael and me in the high-rise hotel to which I had graduated, just off the Coast Highway. Together, overlooking the Santa Monica Mountains from the twelfth floor, we devoured a substantial room-service dinner, and over a tape recorder and ample drinks (and possibly other inducements, though at this point I can no longer remember), we discussed the changes we had all been through and the differences in our lives since the times at the farm. The results became a lengthy segment of the book's eleventh chapter, on the farm family and its former members. However eclectic the approach, we were in good company. Besides others from the farm group, those of its extended family interviewed about their transition from a militant or idealistic past to a generally more comfortable, more relaxed present included the publisher and writer Paul Krassner, comedian and activist Dick Gregory, and radical historian Howard Zinn.

As a geographer, and as a resident with genuine needs, Michael actually knew his way around Los Angeles. Driving with him from one place to another on our various errands and appointments, I visited streets, and places like the Watts Towers, I would never have seen and could certainly never find again. Later, when I would be in town on independent projects, I often stayed with him to lower expenses and to visit. Over this period he had a series of apartments in Westwood, near the university, always filled with bikes and various other accoutrements of life both for himself and for his absent children, who visited on vacations, and the serious stereo and video equipment he needed to pursue his own interests in music and film. Although he was fully employed, he still seemed attached to camping out, a sort of bachelor-pad life for which Joanna had only great disdain. Given the cross-country, international nature of their relationship, though, he felt, I think rightly, that he had adjusted well. He still dreams of restoring a period house in the hills. Meanwhile, he speaks more realistically about a colleague at the university who has no apartment at all, and camps out, too, in his time in LA—under his office desk.

What has always been appealing to me about visiting with Michael, along with his warmth and sense of humor, and the friends we both share, are his diverse interests and experience. He is unceasingly curious about the world, and is as well read as anyone I know. Over our shared meals and occasional travel, we explore the nuances of national and international news, and I catch up on developments in technology and information science, and trends in demography and culture. He is always involved in depth in some new area about which he is eager to talk. His department and tenure battles have taught me much about the academic world I resisted entering. In recent years, he has been traveling extensively. With family still in Arkansas, where he was raised (along with other locations; his father was a career officer in the Air Force), he was working in California, where I often visited. His children were living in Texas with his ex-wife. Joanna teaches and lives in New Jersey and travels regularly, as a consultant, to Poland, Washington, and any number of other places. Both Michael and Joanna attend numerous conferences and lecture on geography, politics, public policy, and other fields in which they are involved. Their itinerary in any given month, especially around the holidays, is dizzying. Papers for academic symposia and publications are always due, and of course there is the basic regimen of teaching, correcting papers and tests, and departmental duties, that provides the mainstay of their professional and financial life.

Visiting with Michael humanized California for me. In the seemingly endless city of Los Angeles, in one of the largest and busiest states, after crossing an immense nation by air, looking down on America's varied assortment of fields, towns, roads, and mountains, it made a difference to me to know one person, someone I liked, with whom I actually looked forward to getting together.

Michael was one of the first of my old friends to whom I reconnected in my new life. In the succeeding years, our paths crossed often, and our friendship only strengthened. When we visited we discussed the fate of the farm and the destinies, sometimes unexpected, of our many friends. We shared the urban experience in California and rural life in Vermont. When he and Joanna were looking for a summer house in Vermont, Steve Lerner and I found them the one they now have in Sandgrove, nearby.

Beginning as a fortuitous meeting connected with a business trip, we graduated to a closer-knit weaving of our present and past. Sitting with other refound friends outdoors in summer, or by the fire in winter, enjoying each other's music, adventures, acquaintances and talk, my experience with Michael began, for me, to confirm the truth of a remark our mutual neighbor Steve Lerner had once made. Sitting on my porch with him one summer, I was lamenting my distance from the city and the difficulties it created in finding work and staying in touch with colleagues and friends in the larger world.

"I don't know, Tom," Steve said, thoughtfully, considering the town, our lives, and the habits of the people about whom we were talking. "I think, if you're patient enough, the world will come to you."

Travers Newton

As with other important projects I had done, my work in California and new connection to the Getty had what is called in economics a multiplier effect. While I felt comfortable with the level of work I was doing, it became clear to me that what often mattered more was not what I had accomplished but for whom it had been done. Thus, as I began my cross-country treks to work in California, and my professional profile continued its abrupt ascent, it occurred to friends of mine that since I was working for a museum in Santa Monica, I might be available to work for one in nearby Santa Barbara as well.

This connection was made by my friend Travers Newton, a colleague and close *confrère* from my days in graduate school. At that time we were both new in the town in which I had gone back to school. I was beginning studies in art history, and he had recently arrived with his wife Melissa to work at the museum's large regional art conservation laboratory. Together, as outsiders in a cloistered New England academic milieu, we supported each other and made the best of the resources we had. Travers introduced me to the conservation lab, where I completed an internship and, working with him, learned the fine points of art restoration, especially painting. I introduced him and Melissa to the local environment and its inhabitants. We shared parties and road trips and generally did our best to enjoy our hours away from our work.

Besides his career in conservation, Travers was also an artist and a serious art historian. On weekends or evenings we would spend time in his studio looking at paintings and talking about art. When I had a show myself, in the days when I thought I might succeed as a practitioner as a part of my life in art, he helped me mat and frame the pieces, and he and Melissa came to the opening, though it was almost a day's drive away. (Although I sold only one piece, it was an important experience for me to see some twenty years' work hanging together at one time.) Through long examination of their work, Travers became an ardent student of Gauguin and van Gogh, whose idiosyncratic, highly individualistic lives and strong personal visions appealed to him. Today he is one of the world's experts on their lives and work.

Travers was originally from Santa Barbara, where his family had lived for many years—indeed, since the nineteenth century, something relatively unusual in California today. They had deep roots in the area. Travers' great-grandfather had drilled the first oil well in California—one of the keys to its future—and had been a U.S. senator under presidents William McKinley and Theodore Roosevelt. (Interestingly, Travers had even earlier roots in the area in which we lived in the east, family papers and portraits taking them back as far as the Revolution.)

In Santa Barbara, Travers' parents had long been involved with the local museum, an outstanding regional institution, directly in the center of town, with an ambitious program of exhibitions and publications. Through Travers I was put in touch with them. The museum was experiencing problems with one of its curators, an artist who had gone off to pursue his own work, leaving several of his museum projects unfinished. The Newtons wanted to know if I might be available to come out and finish an uncompleted exhibition and related publication, as well as some additional work on the collection. A meeting was arranged in New York. Robert, the museum's flamboyant chief curator, a thorough professional well versed in his work who was in the city to look at

Illustration from feature article about Travers and his work, *Sunday Times Magazine*, London, 1979.

Courtesy Travers Newton and the Sunday Times, London.

paintings for acquisition and loan, set out for me what would be involved in finishing the projects. It looked feasible. I signed up, and before long I was on my way out west again to what turned out to be the first of another long series of assignments for a single museum.

These two saints of the southern coast, Santa Barbara and Santa Monica, are very different. The latter, Santa Monica, full of culture and education, not far from the great university in Westwood, a haven for aging radicals, and a short hop into town for the artists, musicians, and producers hiding in the canyons near Malibu, has developed a civilized style of life perhaps akin in some ways to that of bohemian France, including a sizable portion of urban sophistication. The former, Santa Barbara, farther north along the former mission trail, is more isolated, more contained; a more rigid, almost Mediterranean social structure prevails. Beginning above the town, its upper portions, in well-recognized demarcations, descend the foothills of the Santa Ynez Mountains from the affluent villas of Montecito, on the upper ridges, with vistas far out into the ocean and to the Channel Islands, through a middle range near the freeway. Below, and sometimes interspersed, the less prosperous areas stand just behind the valuable waterfront, and in isolated enclaves nearby. There is a great deal of wealth in Santa Barbara, and this affluence seems to buy, as it does along the Mediterranean, the clearer, higher air that all enjoy, as well as the expansive properties on which to build, and—in southern California—the tank loads of water trucked in to maintain them.

I remembered Santa Barbara from my day-long train ride north ten years ago, in 1980, from Steve Diamond's in Los Angeles to my final stop near Raymond, in Salinas. It was an exceptionally dramatic setting: snowcapped mountains behind, the descending town, and on the other side of the tracks the blue water of the Santa Barbara Channel. At that time, though, I hadn't gotten out; the train was just passing through.

This time, my arrival was different. Disembarking in Los Angeles from the cross-country flight, I got into a small prop commuter plane for the brief hop north. I watched below as we skirted the jagged mountains and sweeping shoreline above Los Angeles. It took me a while to orient myself to this view, for while Santa Barbara is part of the northward trip along the coast, it is actually sixty miles west of the westernmost point of Los Angeles, a city that easterners think of as the end of the continent. When one looks out from the beaches of Santa Barbara, thinking one is gazing west toward Hawaii, he is actually looking south toward the waters off Los Angeles.

At Santa Barbara I emerged from the tiny plane onto the flats near the water, to an airport about the size of a large suburban ranch house. Everything was open; there were few walls. Robert was there to meet me, opera vibrating from the car radio. I found my bag in the unguarded, open-air luggage area, and we headed into town.

Town was, at its center, a busy but tightly managed upscale tourist area. There were galleries, high-end clothes stores, good restaurants, sidewalk cafes. It was clearly a day-trip and weekend destination for travelers from Los Angeles. It was also a large second-home and retirement community. For these latter reasons, the downtown, despite its heavy traffic by car and on foot, was neat and well kept. In short, it was a resort, but one with a regular, civic-minded year-round population to keep an eye on it.

Behind the traditional facades, often modern adaptations of Spanish design, were shopping malls, supermarkets, and other less picturesque necessities of village and tourist life. Beyond these were the places one actually wanted to visit: tiny ethnic restaurants, hidden crafts studios, small urban squares, and the occasional theater or other civic appurtenance. What distinguished Santa Barbara for me were the many small courtyards and shaded places, also descendants of Spanish architecture and history. In one of these—often the Café Bianco, hidden behind a theatre, or Andersen's restaurant, on Main Street, which served outrageously large and delicious breakfasts—I would meet Steve Diamond in the mornings over a cup of latte. He would peruse the paper and smoke his morning joint. An early riser, he was already running at full tilt, while I, even with the benefit of an eastern schedule, would sit there somewhat groggy until the strong coffee finally opened my eyes.

Santa Barbara was a like a large small town, intimate and personal. People knew each another and greeted one other on the street. Although it was busy, the scale was human. When I first visited, Steve was working in a social service agency in a low building next to the small hotel where I was staying. Later his office moved to a local landmark, a very visible art nouveau brick office building with a movie theater below.

"It's the tallest building in town," he said proudly, pointing it out. The mountains loomed over it. It was all of seven stories high.

My share of this Old World comfort in a New World guise was embodied in a small inn called The Upham. Only a few blocks from the museum, and paid for as part of my role as a consultant, The Upham was a stately though low-key example of nineteenth-century California architecture, a simple, broad-porched clapboard house of the Victorian era that had been expanded for public use through the addition of a few discreet cottages. Arriving at The Upham after a cross-country flight, or after a long day's work at the museum, was like coming home. Unlike many of the newer buildings in California, it was surrounded by venerable plantings of flowers, trees, and bushes. Located away from midtown, it was quiet at all hours and dark at night. As it turned out, Steve worked next door and lived, during my later visits, down the street. Each morning, from my cabin, I would awake as if on vacation, and go to work at the museum. In the evening, I would return and sit quietly on its small enclosed patio, enjoying the cool California white wine and welcome snacks set out by my hosts. Later, I would saunter out to find dinner, or meet with a friend or colleague at The Upham's own comfortable restaurant. As professional engagements went, this was a charmed setting.

OLD FRIENDS

*   *   *

Besides Steve to see in Santa Barbara, there was also, of course, Travers. Since I had last seen him, Travers had been divorced from Melissa and set up a studio in New York's Chelsea section, before higher rents and increased visibility made new settlement there much more difficult. Eventually, he moved his base of operations back to Santa Barbara, where he converted a building on his parents' property to his own use. His work had become increasingly national and international. His motive in moving back was to lower his costs between jobs, as well as to spend time with aging parents. Where he started from on his long flights to Paris, Washington, Amsterdam or Brazil was less important than finding himself in a familiar community when he was able to be at home.

At this point, Travers was much in demand. He was a painting conservator of prodigious ability—what used to be called, before a scientific revolution in the field, a restorer. As a painter and scholar as well, he was unusually conversant with the historical and artistic issues of the work with which he dealt. Others in the field respected this, and among his colleagues and friends were curators, collectors, historians and conservators from important institutions throughout the world.

When I had first met Travers and Melissa, they were a luminous couple. Radiant with California vigor and health, sporting long, well-groomed hair and carefully tailored clothes, they were the secret idols of the staid New Englanders and academics around them. At that time they had recently returned from Italy, where Travers had been involved for several years in conservation projects. Melissa had spent some of this time in California as a young actress in film and television. They still had that stunned, otherworldly air of those who have been forcibly separated from primary sources of culture or inspiration.

In Italy, Travers had worked at the highest levels of restoration. Originally introduced to Italian art by Carlo Pedretti, his art history professor at UCLA and a distinguished scholar in

Italian Renaissance art, Travers had risen in the field through the intelligence, study, and hard work that have been the hallmark of his career. As science came more and more to dominate the field of conservation, he mastered the many techniques, including obscure chemical and electronic tools, that allowed one to understand the history of a work and how it had been painted, permitting a responsible treatment to be developed for damaged or aging works of art. For an American working in art in Italy—frequently a closed, nationalistic setting—such progress was unusual. By the time he came home, Travers had worked on Leonardo da Vinci's *Last Supper* in Milan and made important technical contributions to the long, ongoing academic debate over the artist's famous lost fresco *The Battle of Anghiari,* believed by some to still be hidden in Florence's Palazzo Vecchio. Later, he was invited to speak at a meeting of the Leonardo Society in Milan, an unusual honor for a young American. He wrote and gave the talk in Italian.

For a conservator to have worked on such touchstones of western culture was remarkable enough, but as I got to know Travers, I thought that the main effect it had had on him was on his personal life and on his life as an artist. As time went on, he took his painting more and more seriously, even when it competed with his work in conservation. His hair grew longer and an edgy mustache appeared. At one point when I was traveling for one museum and he for another, we arranged to meet in Pont-Aven, in western France, a picturesque coastal town that was a gathering place for an important group of nineteenth-century French artists in whom he had a particular interest. In true bohemian style Travers showed up with a French girlfriend.

Like some I know—like myself, to some degree—Travers has led a divided life. Exposed early to Leonardo, working intimately with the direct hands of van Gogh, Gauguin, Pissarro and other painters of highly accomplished individuality and vision, he feels close to them and shares the intense level of their creative experience. Indeed, he truly knows more about them, knows them better, than most. He is an important contemporary link to their history.

But for a painter, writing about painting or repairing it clearly constitutes a secondary role. The thirst, always, is to produce one's own work, to live the life that occasions these mysterious miracles of human imagination. Hence in his work he always champions the artist. For Travers, the repair of a key self-portrait of van Gogh (at the Fogg Museum in Cambridge) thought to have been mutilated either by the artist or by Gauguin, to whom the artist had given it, provided not only a close view into van Gogh's work but the incentive for an intense study of the lives of both of these artists, leading him to further significant research and writing. A plan to repair an undistinguished Spanish devotional painting at the college museum near us in western Massachusetts led instead, through his own study and over institutional doubt, to its complete removal, revealing a far more interesting earlier work hidden below.

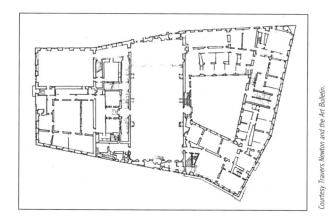

Courtesy Travers Newton and the Art Bulletin.

Palazzo Vecchio, Florence, First Floor plan.
From Newton and Spencer, "On the Location
of Leonardo's Battle of Anghiari,
The Art Bulletin, March 1982.
Redrawn by R. Trotter after Lensi-Orlandi.

The life of van Gogh or of a medieval monk didn't offer a very hopeful model, but as time went on, as he read Gauguin's *NOA-NOA* and the artist's journals, and visited me in the Print Room to look at original works by Gauguin, I felt Travers increasingly took on aspects of the life of the artist himself. He spoke glowingly of the South Seas—for a Californian, what California is to those of us in the East. He cultivated a cosmopolitan, international life of which his French girlfriend, Maud (with whom he eventually became very serious), was only one prominent element, and, indeed, with his long hair and mustache literally began to look like the famous artist.

Unfortunately, as I saw it, this was the artist of the late self-portraits in which Gauguin looks diabolical and wasted by his life in the Pacific. This was what I feared for Travers. Always helpful, Travers and I have for years exchanged professional information, worked occasionally on each others' projects, introduced each other to colleagues and friends. We have shared life in California, New York, New England, Brittany and Paris. He is unfailingly generous and openhearted, as well as incisively canny and experienced concerning the world of museums and art. Still, like Raymond and others I have known, he is always quietly agitating for complete subversion—freedom, the bar, a wild affair, desertion to a desert island seem often not far from his thoughts. Perhaps because of the wide range of responsibilities he bears, he has always been among the first of my friends to dream of escaping them.

Of recent years, his work has taken him all over the world. When I can find him, we are in touch. Always, I am the one to play the conservative, but together we share a history of continual, increasingly successful efforts to open the doors to the sources and means to create. At times it can be a painful experience.

Once, when I was visiting with Travers and his family in Santa Barbara, his mother took me aside as if to address some long-standing, important issue.

"You know," she said, almost questioningly, gazing off into nearby space, and speaking to me as if I were an old friend, "Travers was always such a nice boy—"

I'm not sure what I answered, though I am sure it was as civil and intimate as the question itself and the strong support they had always offered me, but my own opinion was certainly different.

"Well," I thought, "we all were. Have you noticed our generation? Have you noticed that we've grown up? Have you noticed that, unlike life within the sacred precincts of Montecito, in which we ourselves cannot afford to live, we have had to make compromises, find ways to support our visions, create a framework in this difficult world through which to live and to survive?"

I thought back to my own mother and father, and also of their similar relation to their families as well. I doubted that Travers would ever be able to satisfy his parents, but I was quite sure that in a disinterested world he would be judged eminently successful by any standard he elected to choose.

By this time, like Travers, I had realized that I would probably never be attached to a single institution, and that independent, freelance work was where I was most likely to succeed. Under such circumstances, my ear for possible projects had become much more closely attuned. While I was still working for the Getty and completing my temporary duties at Santa Barbara, around 1990, I began to hear of such a project. A large, ambitious exhibition on the history of California photography, with a substantial publication, was being planned by the museum at Santa Barbara. It would be divided into three sections—early, middle, and late. I was well qualified to assemble the early section of the exhibition and write the accompanying essay, a good next step, I thought.

At this point, in my limited niche in the field—an expert on two or three early photographers of the American West, with a basic knowledge of California history and arts and a regular presence in the state—I was one of the few people most likely to be considered for this role. I did my best to ensure that I was the one chosen.

Through lobbying and some direct talk about my abilities, I got the job. As work for the exhibition and publication unfolded, it afforded great opportunities for both research and travel in California, and to meet the people—curators, librarians, collectors, researchers, and writers—who then made up the relatively small world of California photographic history. For this exhibition, eventually called WATKINS TO WESTON: 101 YEARS OF CALIFORNIA PHOTOGRAPHY (1992), I was given a generous budget and a set of criteria: California pictures from California collections, 1849-1990. From this I was to weave a history of the early years of the medium. There were two other curators. David Travis, curator of photographs at the Art Institute of Chicago, was to handle the modern era, which was his own strength. Therese Heyman, the longtime curator of prints and photographs at the Oakland Museum, outside San Francisco, was given the task of outlining the intervening years, from the invention of the Kodak in 1888 to the onset of modernism in the early twentieth century, an era in which she had long specialized. Both David and Therese were highly respected professionals. As the only independent curator on the project, I was very pleased to be included.

To complete my part of the work, I traveled to a number of archival collections, panning for pictures (after all, this was California), assembling from them an overview of the era, and assessing the possibility of borrowing a selection of these works for the show. In Sacramento, I visited the State Library, whose photo archivist and historian proved very helpful, and has remained so over the years. In San Francisco and Berkeley, as well as Oakland, there were libraries and museums with important repositories of work. At UCLA I got to know the university's pictorial resources, a separate branch of its Research Library. Other specialists and institutions were helpful as well. In my rental car, holed up in various motels and bed-and-breakfasts with a traveling library and a growing accumulation of notes, my work on WATKINS TO

WESTON was a crash course in both the history of California and its current state.

With its three out-of-town curators, travel expenses, numerous loans, and a lengthy, well-illustrated publication, this was a very ambitious exhibition for a moderate sized regional institution. The reason the museum could take on a project of this scope was that it was in the process of forming a new partnership. The more I heard about this, the more intrigued I became. My curiosity was resolved over the course of the original meetings to outline and then plan the work to be done.

I had at first been wary of the group doing this planning, as it was to make the decision of hiring the curators for the show. It was a powerful group. But as I came to see, I knew almost everyone in it. Robert and Karen, his new curator, represented the museum in Santa Barbara. Weston, from the Getty, was included; his museum's large fund of California work would certainly provide a key source of loans. Later, Therese and David attended also, and I knew them as well. But there was one person I didn't know. This was the museum's new partner. He was described to me as someone in the film business, and a collector of photographs. He was also the principal underwriter of the project. With only this relatively inauspicious introduction, I arrived for the first meeting at the Topanga home of Michael Wilson.

Michael Wilson

Topanga is a legendary enclave of Los Angeles, a haven for artists, writers, musicians, and producers, a canyon just north of the city reachable only by a narrow twisting road from each end. Topographically too varied to be entirely ostentatious, it is also too close to the city to have escaped development. As I wound my way up Topanga Canyon Boulevard, past trailers, long-parked VW buses, scrubby old farms, and the occasional gate of a comfortable modern house, I could see, on my first trip to Michael's, the mixed character of the neighborhood in which he had chosen to settle. In many ways, as I later saw, it was typical of a certain type of

California landscape and environment. Michael, on the other hand, to me, was something entirely new.

Up to this point, my experience with the film industry had been limited to disappointed screenwriters such as Steve Diamond and Asa Elliot. The one successful person I knew in the business, Jesse, was a New Yorker, though he did spend a lot of time in Los Angeles. (A college friend had also become a well-known writer and producer for television, but my few visits and reports from friends indicated that most of his profits—as the phrase then had it—went up his nose.) Of course, I occasionally saw a movie, though not often, and was exposed to the ads, reviews, and profiles of Hollywood that appear in the press. From this distant, public view, I expected Michael, a producer, to be an aggressive, overbearing, manipulative type with a cigar.

Instead, at the end of my tortuous drive, I was welcomed by a trim, healthy man into an airy, well-appointed but low-key modern house, set on a small rise above the canyon. The windows looked out on the dry, bald, chaparral-filled meadows characteristic of the Santa Monica Mountains. The walls held a choice selection of framed vintage photographs. There were a fireplace and animals, and the kids, from their downstairs rooms, were preparing for school.

As I was to find out, Michael and his wife, Jane, were of a decidedly domestic cast. For as long as I have known them in their complex, cosmopolitan life, they have always maintained a warm, welcoming home, and put their children, friends, and personal lives before anything else. Even their annual Christmas letter, outlining in their quiet way the high-profile work and accomplishments of their extended family, reveals an outlook that, against all odds, strikes me as remarkably normal. When it was time for lunch and we commented on how fresh and good the bread was, Michael acknowledged that he often gets up early to bake.

This eminently sane way of life appeared to be in stark contrast to his daily work in business. Trained as an attorney, but with strong creative leanings, he descended each day from the canyon to do battle at the MGM studios in Century City. His family holds the rights to the James Bond films—indeed, to everything having to do with the roguish British agent. In Michael's family, the biennial ritual of making and releasing the next Bond movie is a matter not only of planning, work, and investment, but of history, passion, and honor. Michael's stepfather, now viewed as the progenitor of a small Hollywood dynasty, had been the producer and popularizer of the original Bond movies. Eventually, Michael, even at a relatively young age, had been given increasing responsibility for them. Today, in conjunction with a family consortium, he helps to oversee the entire effort.

Such plums are not, however, always easily held. During the course of the first few years I knew the Wilsons, much of Michael's time was devoted to defending the family escutcheon from a series of intruders, most notably the Sony Corporation, in ongoing legal skirmishes that absorbed immense amounts of his energy and time. The copyright and trademark issues involved—films, books, syndication, foreign rights, spin-offs, products—offered enormous potential benefits to the winner. In this battle, though the foe was notoriously powerful, the Wilson clan had the advantage not only of its history with the Bond enterprise but of a family *esprit de corps* and staying power that even rapacious corporate lawyers couldn't match. Eventually, thanks to legal strategies developed by Michael and his team, the giant Japanese corporation backed off.

From film it was not a great leap to photography. Michael and Weston had known each other in college. Their then girlfriends, now wives, were themselves college friends, and over the years the couples have remained in close touch. Like Weston, Michael led an international life: The Bond films were made in a studio outside London, as well as in the far-flung locations that made them so attractive and romantic to viewers. He spent a great deal of time traveling: scouting sites, interviewing actors, counseling technicians, directors, and screenwriters—setting the stage for the next production and managing the legacy of those that had come before. (In recent years, though still maintaining offices in Los Angeles, the family has largely abandoned Topanga for London.) As Michael tells the story, he was at one point in a city in which some photographs Weston wanted were at auction. Weston called him and asked him to bid for the museum. None of those pictures turned out to be within the budget given him, but, as he likes to say, he came home with a big stack of material of his own.

Michael was interested in photography for a variety of reasons. He admired creativity, and as a producer, writer, and playwright himself, appreciated the artistic aspect of the work. Through his involvement in the film industry, he recognized the relation between the two media, photography and film—one of his favorite photographers was Eadweard Muybridge, the precocious nineteenth century inventor of one of the first successful methods of serial photography, an early progenitor of

The roguish British agent as he appeared on the Op-Ed page of *The New York Times*, Fall 2006.

the motion picture, about whom Michael had written a play. Being a Californian, he valued the high quality of regional work often not widely known or appreciated outside the west. Michael also had already displayed some of the distinctive qualities of the collector: Earlier, he had gathered a large set of French lithographs and given them to the museum in Santa Barbara.

In many ways the coincidence of his interests and his timing was perfect. In the 1980s, photographs were still available in great numbers. Spurred perhaps by Weston's own progress, Michael's knowledge of photography and photographic history grew quickly. (Both shared a particular interest in California and early photography.) Because of his travel, he could visit galleries and auctions, and because of his means, he was able to buy. He was soon, in his own right, a scholar and collector of the first rank. Because of their closeness, Michael and Weston sometimes worked together, as they did in helping organize the exhibition in which I was involved. Later, they joined forces with another collector to produce an exhibition and book about California Pictorialism, a popular style of the late nineteenth and early twentieth century, that was a landmark in the field.

Working with Michael was probably as close as I have ever come to actually living in Los Angeles. The trips to Topanga, the visits to United Artists/MGM at Century City, the late-evening dinners in wild, all-glass postmodern restaurants where tables were lozenge-shaped and nothing was square: There was a sense of enjoyment, of living life to the full. Still, through all of this Michael and Jane maintained a very warm, accessible mien. We all shared what we were doing. They were always interested to hear news of the project: new information uncovered, a mutual friend encountered, long-lost pictures found.

Later I visited them in London and New York. There was one thing I didn't understand. Why, I asked Michael, as we sat in the living room of his family *pied à terre* off Fifth Avenue in New York, after all his work to collect and study pictures, did he have them stored in Topanga, in a remote house in the midst of territory known for earthquake, mud-slides, and fire? His answer has always struck me as characteristically Californian. Oh, he said, they had considered this. They had built the house with an ample vault beneath. Should fire come, they would take the few pictures on the wall and flee. The photographs below would be safe—but the house would burn to the ground.

Other Friends

While in California, working on various projects over the years, I encountered old friends and met many new ones. From my farm days I sought out Laurie, whose communal farm in Vermont I had helped her to find and whose comrades there had included several of my high school and college friends. Laurie was originally from San Francisco, and after the demise of the farm, near Rutland—a typical breakup of the time, in which the participants simply had had enough of caring for goats and chickens and wanted to get on with their lives—she sold the farm and returned to the West Coast, settling across the Golden Gate Bridge in Mill Valley, where I would sometimes stay in her guest room, the percussion studio of her teenage son, already a serious drummer.

In the course of the *WATKINS TO WESTON* project, I again came in touch with Therese Heyman, whom I had met through Rafael five or six years before and with whom I had since been in contact over jobs, organizations, projects, and other professional matters. Therese was a very bright, well trained, Smith College educated print curator with children my own age, whose research, writing, and exhibitions had helped expand the world of prints to include photography. She was active nationally in professional groups, through which she knew not only Rafael but a number of my other future colleagues. Therese worked hard to maintain her professional independence, though her husband, former chancellor of Berkeley and later head of the Smithsonian Institution, had a set of connections and interests that sometimes overshadowed her own. Together, Therese and Karen and I worked together, exchanged ideas, saw one another at professional meetings, and found each other congenial company when others were too busy on the professional make, or partying, to join in the civilized, literate, humorous talk we enjoyed. (Karen, the new photo curator at Santa Barbara, was also married to a former chancellor from the UC system. My father had been a college president as well, giving us all a bond.) From Therese I learned important things about curatorial, museum, and institutional life. She was a good judge of people, and like Jackie, my editor in New York, a good teacher, counselor, and friend, and a thorough professional in all concerning art and related work. Later, I was fascinated to find that from Therese's weekend house in Stinson I could see across to Bolinas, where Steve Lerner and his brother lived and worked, as though looking from one part of my life into another.

Through Weston, Michael Rinehart, and especially my neighbor Julius Held, who had been his teacher, I also came to know John Walsh, the director of the Getty Museum. From someone I thought I should know, as a friend of other colleagues and head of the museum for which I was working, he soon became someone I enjoyed seeing and was glad to know. On visits for conferences or work, I looked forward to our lunches at the Getty's delightful outdoor café in Malibu. Not afflicted by the distancing superciliousness and ostentation that is the regular habit of some directors, John, an expert in Dutch painting whose wife was an artist, showed genuine interest in art, culture, and intellectual life. His enormous duties—which included not only overseeing the Getty Museum in Malibu and its many programs but the years-long process of coordinating the conception, design, and building of its monumental new campus in the hills of Westwood—never seemed to stop him from taking time to discuss the far more modest, far-flung projects and interests of others. When, on inviting me to lunch one day, I found him serving me a meal himself in his own office (it had appeared on a handy wheeled cart), I knew I had encountered a person comfortable with himself, unaffected, and graced with an outstanding natural ability to put others at ease.

Later years also brought increased or renewed relationships with venerable western organizations such as the Oakland Museum, the California Historical Society, and the California Society of Pioneers. (To qualify for membership in this exclusive latter group, one's family must have arrived—Neil Young's metaphor notwithstanding—before the Gold Rush.) A recent project brought me into contact with Phil Wood, the legendary founder of the Ten-Speed Press, in Berkeley, whose astoundingly successful *WHAT COLOR IS MY PARACHUTE* was for years the bible and creative support of the unemployed. Phil, an irresistible character whose Mr. Natural-like image graces the pages of all Ten-Speed catalogues, someday deserves a portrait of his own.

Outside California, new colleagues and friendships also continued to grow. Among those I came to know in more than a passing way through work or related travel were Keith Davis, who oversaw the extensive though little known art holdings of the Hallmark company in Kansas City (although at the time he was living in London and California), and Mark Haworth-Booth of the Victoria and Albert Museum, whose imposing name and reputation masked a charming, alert and fun-loving peer, who like a number of others in my field, enjoyed life in all its variety and depth.

Of those I worked with more extensively, I especially came to enjoy the friendship of Sally Pierce and David Farmer. Sally had interviewed me for a job early in my career. She was the curator of prints and photographs at the Boston Athenaeum, a thorough and practiced professional who enjoyed the research and history necessary to tie the graphic arts into the intense traditions of both Boston and the Athenaeum—an institution whose founders and members included some of the luminaries of American culture.

Sally spoke with me one fall afternoon at the Athenaeum. I had lived and worked in Boston, but I had never been to the Athenaeum. I was charmed by the nineteenth-century atmosphere of the place. Behind the padded leather doors at 10½ Beacon Street, the stacks, probably marvels of their time, today appeared crowded and quaintly old-fashioned. The reading lounges were filled with comfortable stuffed leather chairs. There were huge portraits on the walls, and busts of Emerson, Thoreau, and others punctuated spaces that virtually defined the popular idea of the athenaeum as an educational and cultural forum of the nineteenth century. We sat outside on a tiny porch overlooking the ancient burial ground behind the Athenaeum. During the hour or so that we talked, our conversation was not limited to photography or prints, the subjects ostensibly at hand, but ranged over the arts in general, people's attitudes toward them, and surviving in the field we were both in. I wasn't right for the job, but we became great friends. Later she helped me with key loans for an exhibition, and at her invitation, I gave a lecture at the Athenaeum that helped define some of my future directions in writing and research. We continue to visit, and her husband, who is both an artist and a therapist, has at times advised both Travers and me.

My introduction to David Farmer dated from my days in New York, but our ties went farther back. At the time when I was cataloging photographs in the Seagram Building and the Met, David was directing the exhibitions program of the American Federation of Arts, an organization in New York that prepared and coordinated traveling exhibitions for museums. Earlier he had been the director of the art gallery of the University of California at Santa Barbara. He knew Travers and his family and the staff at the Santa Barbara Museum, as well as others I would meet in California and elsewhere in the field of art. Travers introduced us, and after that David and I met several times to discuss possible projects. Again, as with Sally Pierce, little at first came of this, but we liked each other, and when David became head of a new small museum in New York, I proposed two exhibitions that did very well there—my first forays on my own into the treacherous waters of the New York museum world. After David retired, we continued to stay in touch, visiting each other and developing together projects of our own for exhibitions in other museums.

FARM FRIENDS

David, Sally, Therese, John: For me these and a few others were the bright lights in the field in which I found myself. The number was never very large. Strong friendships are rare, and I continue to value those that endure and the new ones that occasionally emerge. I would probably be considered only normal in saying that in most cases they mean more to me than much that I encountered in the larger field through which we met.

Themes, Motifs

My projects in photography and art were largely comprised of exhibitions and writing, with occasional lectures, the cataloging of collections, and similar related work. I helped Travers research the restoration of an immense, two-story-high painting in Boston's Faneuil Hall. For a while I ran a cooperative art gallery. Now and then I had administrative or clerical assignments, but the whole thrust of my entry into the field having been to move away from such work, these were never my favorites.

The advantage to projects was that they were all interesting and frequently focused entirely on essentials. Usually, the important part of my work was the substantive portion. If possible, the museum for which I was working arranged to handle the paperwork, transportation, and other difficult-to-coordinate parts of the job that were really not a very good use of the time of a specialist in history and interpretation. This was not always the case, but in contrast to an institutional position with its rigid roles and administrative obligations, I had freedoms that were the envy of full-time curators. On the other hand, unlike work at an institution, some projects required that I accomplish whatever I had to do entirely on my own. In my home office, or in travel, there was no team, no additional support, and in order to compete for the job, the budget in relation to the work to be done was typically small. In the cases where I was responsible for an entire project—its conception, arranging loans, writing, publishing, publicity, installation of an exhibition, sometimes even matting and framing and the transportation of art—between my home computer, laptop, fax, phone, e-mail, express mail, and the regular daily post, I actually more often felt like an institution than an individual.

While it was the mechanics of these projects that kept me employed, in that institutions and collectors had work needing to be done, it was the ideas behind them that interested me. A museum simply wanted an exhibition or a publication to fill a certain need in its programming; I, on the other hand, had something specific I wished to say or show. In some ways, I realized, this was what Raymond had meant when he described having to sneak in the content of his books that his readers actually craved, between the lines of entertainment his publishers thought were necessary to sell it.

In the study of photography, in which to some surprise I found myself in the early eighties, I discovered that in regard to museums and art history, it was a relatively open field. As a new area of study, there were few rules and much work to be done. Interesting challenges in research abounded, and as museums often served as their own publishers—happy simply to see a well-written manuscript of any kind—I found I could often say what I wanted, or felt needed to be said, in whatever way seemed best. Under these conditions, I could develop or adapt projects to move into new territory where definition and statement addressing whole sectors of the field were needed. In addition, projects themselves often took me into new territory: Immersion or investigation into the nature of a particular subject could lead to perspectives on it that I had never imagined.

Thus, in my first exhibition and publication, under the guidance of Rafael and a key book by one of my former college professors of which we were both aware, my study of the two sets of photographs I had been assigned to present led me to see the larger context that connected them. One, a set of views of western landscape, was picturesque and romantic; the other, a series of views of mining, was a testament to industrialism. To see these divergent activities successfully represented, through the art of photography, as entirely different worlds, though geographically they virtually bordered each other, was to grasp their defining cultural significance: In the American West, these activities were not connected. Development went on irrespective of its effect on land and life, while the admiration of beauty was pursued as an isolated province unaffected by troubling economic activities nearby. To me, the discovery of such expansive and influential concepts emerging from objects I could handle and study, and whose significance I was able to unravel myself, was very exciting. In this case, from hundred-year-old photographs of two neighboring locations in California, I had uncovered visible evidence of attitudes toward nature, preservation, land use, and wealth that were still recognizable today. From these I drew conclusions about American history and about California and the west that have continued to inform my views. The direction for the exhibition and the essay, by far the longest I had written up to that time, thus arose from the material itself, a precedent I have followed, whenever possible, ever since.

At the same time, through studying pictures, reading, research, and observation, I began to understand the importance of nineteenth-century photography and its relation to the history of the United States. Both the medium and the land in which it had been used were among the most significant developments of the modern era; that they occurred together, I saw, helped define a period of history and art. As part of this larger picture, I also began to discern the special role of California and the unique place it holds as a bellwether and testing ground in the process of our national development. In addition, as I learned more about photography itself I could see, though few knew of him, how good the photographer I was dealing with, Carleton Watkins, really was. Putting these together, I concluded that the art and history with which I was concerned represented a chapter whose full outlines were only beginning to be understood. As the quality of the work of great artists like Watkins appeared to me to be self-evident and not in need of further discussion, I turned more often to the elucidation of the social history that surrounded it, which seemed to me to be far less clear and—when properly understood—to offer keys to the significance of the art itself, as well as of the larger family of media to which it now belonged.

In this spirit, I then moved on, after a year or two, from my first subject, Watkins, to his contemporary, the extraordinary figure Eadweard Muybridge, whom I later found to be a favorite of Michael Wilson. Watkins and Muybridge, both prominent San Francisco photographers in the heyday of post-Gold Rush California, were often compared. Curiously, some of their work was so similar as to be indistinguishable by all but experts, yet, as personalities and artists, they were as different as two contemporaries could be. In dealing with Muybridge, then, I was eager to distinguish him in some meaningful way from Watkins. In the end, taking its place among the many other such questions competing for attention in my work, it took me several years to arrive at an adequate way to articulate this: Watkins could best be understood as Platonic, idealistic, and formal in outlook, while Muybridge, in his thirst for mechanism and detail, was clearly a descendent of Aristotle.

Meanwhile, I contented myself in my essay on Muybridge, the first of several as it turned out, with calling attention to what seemed to me to be his unique and inarguably intrinsic qualities. The most important of these was that unlike Watkins, who was an artist by nature and tied by necessity to his medium, a man who over the course of his life had given ample proof that he was good at nothing else, for Muybridge photography appeared to be largely a tool. Having embarked on it after several other careers, and continuing with it through remarkable reinventions of his life, he went on to use it in ingenious ways, the best known of which are his epoch-making studies of motion, which—120 years later—remain in print today. Being attached to the medium in this entirely different way, which crossed only at one point—their careers as photographers of landscape and cultural life in the west—it became clear that while Watkins was a classic artist in the timeless mode, whose vision would have been of interest in any medium, Muybridge was a man of his time, indeed so much so that his work consciously helped shape the future as well. From Watkins' influence would come great photographers of clarity and simplicity, such as his admirer Ansel Adams. From Muybridge emerged the legacy of film, television, and now today's even more advanced use of imaging, with which he—perhaps the world's first true geek—would certainly have felt at home. They were thus members of entirely different traditions, and in stating this, and pointing out Muybridge's quintessential modernity, I felt my work in this area was done.

With A. J. Russell, the third of the unsurpassed photographers of this era with whose work I dealt, my time was shorter and my relation less close. I could see, though, the extremely high quality and unique artistic character of his work, and highlighted these in an exhibition and essay exploring the connection between photography during the Civil War, when his career began, and that of the later work of Russell and others who continued that tradition in recording the building of the railroads in the American West.

In working with Russell, though, I had a professional experience that has stayed with me and provided a cautionary lesson. Having traced the photographer's career to the end of the line—California, where the transcontinental railroad ended, and thus so did his pictures—I arranged to visit the museum that, miraculously, I thought, still held his original glass negatives, now well over one hundred years old. This was the center of scholarship on Russell. More was said to be known about him here than anywhere else. Under the aegis of the museum, a biography was being written, and the curator was interested to know more about what I myself was doing on the topic. When I got there, however, I found that information was to flow only in one direction. I was welcome to contribute to the museum's store of knowledge concerning Russell, but they had little interest in offering anything helpful to me. I thought this an odd attitude. Sharing often seems to work better than exclusion. I also felt that as a public institution, and as stewards of artistic and historical work, it was not only uncivil but unethical not to assist a colleague in scholarly work. In any case, I left somewhat disillusioned about the profession, though certainly enlightened concerning the power of those who have cornered the market on valuable intellectual or artistic property. In the end, though, while the modest exhibition I produced proved very popular and I continue to answer requests for the catalog I wrote, little further work that I know of has been done on the subject by that museum, and the biography has, after some twenty additional years, yet to appear.

Articles and talks provided another outlet for my ideas about photography, history, and art. In 1989 the opportunity arose to organize a small exhibition on Samuel Butler. Known as the author of the important novels *EREWHON* and *THE WAY OF ALL FLESH,* the British writer, as few knew, had also been a scholar, composer, and painter. As I found out, he had been a photographer as well. The small museum exhibition I organized, mounted as a collaborative effort with the rare book library that owned the material, amply showed Butler's employment of photography in his scholarly publications, and as an amateur pursuit in its own right representative of the time—the late nineteenth century. What interested me, however, was the character of Butler himself. As a subject not central to the exhibition, this was pursued in a separate article. Here I set out the qualities I believed made him of enduring interest and relevant to the present day. Butler was a strong individualist, a crusading nonconformist whose mission seemed at times largely to challenge established orthodoxy. Hewing to his own research and discoveries, he was entirely unyielding to those he believed to be in thrall to unthinking tradition or misguided belief. Responsive to his own unconventional visions, he understood the necessary independence of the arts and thought, and accepted their frequent unpopularity. One piece of his writing included extensive musical quotations from Handel and recounted visions of souls blowing like clouds of dust through the Alps. All of this I found stunningly original in a man raised among severe school- and churchmen of the Victorian era. Finding myself deeply sympathetic, despite the notion that we almost certainly would not have gotten along, I celebrated the irascible Butler by describing him as best I could, a service I felt would be of use to all those of our joint cultural persuasion.

Further occasions of this kind came in the form of lectures, independent articles, and adjuncts to other projects like the Butler show. Early on, while I was working on an exhibition of American paintings, I was offered the chance to publish a lost debate between the crusty American Regionalist artist Thomas Hart

E. S. Schaffer and Bolton Museum and Art Gallery. Courtesy Elinor Schaffer.

Samuel Butler, Tabachetti's *Sta. Veronica*
(ca.1599), Varallo, Italy, 1888. One of Butler's
unusual photographs for use in illustrating
his writing on art history.

Benton and the unswerving modernist architect Frank Lloyd Wright. This was an unlikely couple, but in reviewing the material I found points of similarity as well as divergence that had not been addressed before. I discussed them in an afterword to the publication. In talks written for a variety of museums, I explored other subjects outside the relatively straightforward presentations necessary for the research and exhibitions on which I worked. In a talk at Andover, Massachusetts, I looked at the legacy of the American athenaeum in the nineteenth century, in another, in Boston, the place of photography among the traditional American arts. At the Metropolitan Museum I gave a lecture exploring the ties between early photography and the theater of the nineteenth century; and for a talk at the Getty Museum, in conjunction with the exhibition on Watkins I organized there, I pursued an inquiry into the formal aspects of photographic style, especially the elements of composition and the juxtaposition of certain pictorial elements, that helped define the unique qualities of Watkins' work.

Through friends and colleagues came other, different opportunities. Though I continued to write more on art, I used these separate occasions to expand the writing voice in which I felt most comfortable, but which was not always appropriate to my professional work. Often, these became low-key commentaries on matters of personal or general interest. Through these less traditional, more journalistic and literary venues I wrote on subjects such as landscape, architecture, drawing, history, and travel—topics on which I held passionate opinions and observations, but lacked any authority other than my own experience and informal study. Eventually I found a small magazine willing to support these more personal ventures. Through this literary journal I began to publish pieces approaching more closely what I wanted to produce: essays in a personal tone about the areas for which I cared the most. The positive response I received to these pieces gave me the courage to approach the larger projects of my own on which I wanted to work.

FARM FRIENDS

*   *   *

A further area into which I moved was reviews. Freelance reviewers work largely on assignment and I did not have much choice about what I reviewed. I did believe that, whatever the subject, if possible, supportive reviews were best. I used reviews to point out what in a particular show or a book was novel, insightful, or in some other way important to a potential reader or viewer. If something wasn't worth endorsing, I didn't see why it would be worth reviewing. The exception was work I considered dangerously off base, so egregiously erroneous in conception or execution that I felt the public or the profession should be warned about it. Among these, three come to mind, though I know there were more. The first was a book about landscape photography that seemed to prove that its authors—however eminent— understood little about either. A second pointed out that a vast, complex, and expensive exhibition on an important subject, and its related publications, did not remotely live up to the promise it offered, nor to the substantial resources with which its organizers had been entrusted to complete the effort. A third was a review of a book simultaneously so bad and so pretentious that I took the unusual step of disputing a number of its major theses and methods point by point to show how much could have been done with the material if viewed and interpreted in a more judicious way.

Efforts of this kind made me very uneasy. As a freelance writer with no permanent institutional affiliation, I had more freedom than some to speak my mind. I also, in the event that my views were contested, had nowhere to hide—no regular salary, no tenure, no professional peer group, no classes to which to attend and so divert my attention. Whatever credibility I had was thus the result simply of outspoken opinions, competent analysis, or cogent style—all qualities to which, partly for my own good, I adhered as closely as possible. The latter book, above, sat on my desk for a year while, along with other work, I made various attempts to assimilate and appreciate it. Only then did it dawn on me that this was exactly the problem. How could a book by a widely known, aggressively assertive scholar, on an important subject, from a major university press, be so bad? This was, I realized, in addressing this book, the subject on which I ought to write. Sending off the review with some trepidation, my only consolation was the advice I remembered in such cases from Rafael: When hunting lions, shoot to kill. The unusual number of phone calls I received over the first few days after the article's publication, thanking me as though I had finally attacked the neighborhood bully, reassured me that I had taken the right approach.

Frontiers

In other ways as well as these, the ideas with which I was working diverged in directions quite unexpected, even breathtaking. Spending so much time in California, among historic photographs, and regularly crossing and recrossing the country, I began to see American history, as others had, as the westward movement of the frontier. The opening of the transcontinental railroad in 1869, as I had seen in my exhibition on Russell, and the continuing growth of the West ever since, provided ample pictorial and historical evidence of this. As I had witnessed for myself earlier, in Bolinas, the American frontier ended with some finality at the Pacific. Once I had come to assimilate this, however, I looked across the vast western ocean and saw something unexpected: another frontier headed the other way. It was the mid- to late 1980s. The Soviet Union was still a dominant world power. As I looked at it—the continent, the union of disparate peoples, the vast geography, the challenges of developing a nation in the industrial age—I thought: This is just our own experience geographically reversed.

In regard to the nineteenth century, at least, that turned out to be indeed what it was. But at first, lacking any knowledge of Russian history or art, what I set about looking for—photographs that might represent this idea—were works about which I was theorizing but had never seen. I had no assurance they even existed. Pursuing various hunches, though, I searched for them. When visiting collections, I always asked about Russian work. I kept my eyes open for books on the subject or experts who might know something about it. Before long, with the help of colleagues, I had identified and seen a wide variety of Russian photographs in American collections. The result confirmed my expectations. Photographs of nineteenth-century Russia included albums about mining, exploration, and the building of railroads—exactly what those of the United States at the same time showed. The settlements pictured were full of log cabins, dirt roads, and churches, staples of Americana. The history I read indicated that the Russian frontier had been populated by individualistic people who led a challenging life of farming, trapping, and the commerce of regional towns. There were parallels in cultural history as well—outpourings of nationalism, folklore, music, youth rebellions, and civil wars. With borders from Europe through the Middle East to Pacific Asia, Russia was also a "melting pot." I concluded that, despite the tremendous difference in history and culture, the two superpowers at loggerheads in the late twentieth century actually shared much more in their national experience than most Americans—and presumably most Russians—were aware.

This was an idea that drew considerable support. The collections that held the different groups of virtually unknown Russian photographs were intrigued to know that there might be a place for them in international cultural history and art. Institutions that could display an exhibition of these works, or use them in educational programs, were impressed with the importance of the idea they represented. I received several grants for the development of an exhibition and a publication, and was well on my way to producing them when the widespread budget cuts of the early nineties eliminated funding for the project. Although the exhibition and the publication never appeared, it is an idea in whose strength I continue to believe.

OLD FRIENDS

*   *   *

The excluded middle—as philosophers say—of this proposition of East and West was the Pacific itself. Moving west to the American coast, then turning to view the question of continental development from the other direction, as coming to the Pacific moving toward the East, for a while I saw only the connection between the two. Since the annexation of California to the United States, Alaska had been added as well. American culture had thus spread north and west toward Russia. As I discovered, Russian culture had done the same, moving east into North America, though at a much earlier time. Southern Alaska, even northern California, were, I found, full of vestiges of Russian influence. Fort Ross, a former Russian trading post, the southernmost point of this earlier chapter in international history, is only an easy day trip north of San Francisco. Attracted by trapping and trading, the Russians had explored the American coast long before the Americans got there. By 1620, while Europeans were learning the significance of turkey, pumpkins, and corn, and the development of the West was more than two hundred years away, the Russians had already crossed their own continent, founded towns, and moved out into the Pacific rim.

There was thus a circle of Russian-American culture, mixed with that of indigenous native American and Asian tribes, surrounding the northern Pacific. But what, indeed, did it surround? Regarding this portion of the circle, and looking farther south, to China, Japan, and southeast Asia, with its current explosive growth, great needs, and new economic power, and at California, which faced Asia from across the ocean, it seemed to me that the Pacific might again be the new American frontier.

To an easterner steeped in European-based history, this came as something of a shock. At the same time, it made a great deal of sense. The growing globalism of our times suggested that the European theater of economic and cultural operations was changing, and its relative importance moderating. As history, of course, it would not change. American roots in Europe would always be relevant to its culture and life. But the increasing relative importance of other areas of the globe, and the impending period of their own development, apparently close at hand, suggested that for our future we might again begin to look west—the direction from which our cars, computers, clothing, product services, and even new religious and philosophical leanings were beginning to emerge.

As with other areas into which I stumbled, the Pacific had, of course, been discovered before. Looking at its relevance as we see it today, it seemed to me that for Americans and Europeans its new importance had begun during its life as a laboratory of late-eighteenth and early-nineteenth-century thought. Exploration, scientific research, commerce, and whaling (Captain Cook, Sir Joseph Banks, Admiral Perry and Herman Melville, for example, among the best known) had opened the Pacific to travel and to European and American eyes. Before long, though, this had given way to religious proselytizing, colonialism, and general trade. Later these activities metamorphosed to investigations of culture, artistic experimentation, tourism, and, in some cases, feats of pure adventure.

A prime model of this, I saw, was Travers' hero Paul Gauguin. In the Pacific, Gauguin had been able to live a life largely outside the constraints of European social and artistic expectations. In Tahiti he abandoned these to adopt portions of native culture. In addition, however, perhaps despite himself, Gauguin and other travelers projected their own views and beliefs onto the life they found, forming in this distant place a new and useful adjunct to European culture and art. While, geographically, Gauguin could not have been farther from home, in a cultural and historical sense he and other Europeans in the Pacific helped transform this vast area, so far away, into something more understandable to Europeans, a region they could see as a displaced part of their own mythology, somehow lost and now fortuitously rediscovered. In this way, the Pacific came to be a sphere not only of scientific discovery but also of intellectual and artistic invention, and the locus in which important aspects of the broadening dream life of Europe could be played out.

Others had also held these views. In 1890, the American painter John La Farge traveled to the Pacific with the writer and geologist Clarence King (coincidentally, a patron of Watkins). Their accounts of bronzed, statuesque men and women living in primitive simplicity echoed the prevalent views of their time. Others came as well to this land of scattered islands—geologically only the tips of submerged volcanoes or reefs emerging from deep beneath the surface of the sea. In one brief era Gauguin, La Farge, King, Robert Louis Stevenson, and Jack London were all in the Pacific in search of an age of myth still abroad in the world. Often, I found, their stories shared common elements: the same ports, dissipated characters, legends, and local gods. The resulting amalgam of allegory and tradition, I saw, had offered a new context in which intellectually and artistically adventurous Europeans and Americans might think and work.

Like many others of my culture, I had always seen the Pacific of this era as different and remote. Looking at it through the eyes of Gauguin and other Europeans of the era—along with Africa, the Caribbean, Central America, and similar unfamiliar, newfound areas of the globe, and of the psyche itself newly encountered or admired (think of Freud)—I suddenly understood the appeal of new lands, new mythologies, new folkways that might supplement and perhaps leaven the rigid patterns of European life.

There was little early Pacific photography that I could find. (No doubt there is some. There are stunning early views of Hawaii. A peripatetic French photographer took photographs in both the Pacific and other remote locations that capture the geography and low coastal settlement then characteristic of island regions.) The paucity of known images and the limitations on subject matter lead me to think that photography is not the art to which we will turn to understand this region. It is more likely native arts, illustrations, written records from travel and science, and the work of the occasional painters and writers who visited there that will provide the important links. Although the chapter of European visitation and colonization is important, I suspect that in a globalized world it will be the indigenous experience of these regions that will provide its principal history. If the diary of one of the mistresses of Gauguin were to be found, it would be an instant classic of the new global culture, showing the way the world viewed us when we were too busy at our narcissistic occupations to notice that, to others, we ourselves were the other.

Finally, returning to the theme of photography and frontiers, my foray into Russian photographs alerted me to an issue beyond the mere comparison of East and West. If photographs of Russia could resemble those of America, such different and apparently contrasting nations, I thought, what of the many other locations

Photo by Andrey Osipovich Karelin. Courtesy Arnika publishers.

Andrey Osipovich Karelin: Fishing in a local pond, Russia, 1870s.

in which similar chapters of economic development and cultural change had occurred? My experience suggested that there might be considerable similarity among the photographs of these places. Further research supported this perception. In pursuing its proof, I learned something that, again, seemed entirely new. Critics and scholars tended to see photographs of their own nations as geographically and historically specific. Invariably the many photographs of a new bend or cut for the transcontinental railroad in America, which show tracks constructed through an excavation in a small hill in Utah or Wyoming, are described as images of Manifest Destiny: Beyond, on the horizon, new lands beckon. Similarly, a desolate outpost along the rail line will be taken to be emblematic of the indomitable American spirit.

On investigation, these views turn out to be almost entirely interchangeable with views taken in South Africa, Russia, India, Brazil, and other developing nations. Photographs of the Australian gold rush are virtually indistinguishable from those taken in California. Instead of the many purported national readings of photography, it would seem that there is one international style reflecting the state of the medium and the stage of international development at the time. The professional importance of this is that terms other than reductivist adulation must be found to describe the meaningful qualities of some important bodies of work. The personal message was that disinterested inquiry in a subject is an important ingredient in understanding it. In perceiving the international style, I was leaving the world of photography and reentering the larger intellectual and artistic sphere of which it was but a single part. I was more comfortable there, and I thought I would stay.

Paris, Pont-Aven, Fontainebleau

By this time, the early to mid-1990s, independent projects provided most of my living. All were interesting in some way, but increasingly I was attracted to issues such as those concerning Russia, the Pacific, and an international style, for which only extremely ambitious exhibitions and publications would suffice to introduce them properly to the public and the profession. Doubting the possibility of achieving this on my own, I turned more often toward accomplishing the work I wanted to do myself. One other brief chapter remained, however, before that proved possible.

When the economy temporarily slowed me from pursuing Russian photography and other institutionally based exhibitions and publications, I retrenched by taking several staff jobs and independent projects in the art community of the region. The best of these was my brief term replacing Rafael in the print department. During that period my perks included travel for the museum. Thus, in the mid-nineties, I found myself able to arrange to return to Paris, where I had not been for almost twenty-five years, and to London, which I had visited only briefly since I had been there as a boy. For me this was an important opportunity. I was a great devotee of Paris and had much to learn about London, with which I was far less familiar. The museum, and what was for me an unusually ample budget, offered a chance to reconnect to places I valued, from which I had been separated for many years.

I was not the first to admire Paris, but I can say that, earlier, it had played a singular role in my life. In the fall of 1970, frustrated with the farm and yearning for a larger world, I had embarked on a lengthy voyage of discovery. Of the succeeding four months, I spent three in Paris and one in Scotland with friends I had made in Paris. Traveling with a heavy load of books and an unwieldy guitar, I read Eastern philosophy, tried to make my way as a musician, and suffered the lonely tortures of the damned until, without sufficient money, and yearning for friends and a familiar land, I finally headed home. During this time, despite my difficulties, I came to really appreciate Paris and to know it fairly well. I found an inexpensive room, shopped in the nearby markets, and enjoyed *café au lait* every morning in an outdoor *tabac*. The architecture, the sense of age and history, and the connections everywhere to culture and art sealed my involvement with this city once Roman, still medieval, lingeringly nineteenth century, and modern only in the oddest, frequently unappealing manner of the French. The endless stone, the variety of bridges, the river, the delicate spires, the strange street life of post-1968 Paris all conspired to attract me.

Some basis for this had been formed ten years before, in 1960, when Paris had been one of the first stops on the only trip my family had ever taken together to Europe. It was a giddy, idealistic time. My parents, like many of their generation, were successfully rebounding from the Depression and the Second World War. In that summer, John F. Kennedy was campaigning for a presidency that would come as close to myth as my country had seen for some time. Activism was budding into an era in which people believed they could make a difference, and that good works could change the world.

What I saw in Paris, southern France, Italy, and other stops on our extended family trip was a culture of beauty, history, substance, and grace that my own country lacked. I saw folkways that in America had long been lost, and textures that had accrued from times far more ancient than anything whose remains I had experienced. My palate expanded to include new tastes, and I experienced at firsthand tics to a cultural life I had previously known only at a distance from books and art. In addition, since I was fourteen at the time, Europe, and especially France, alerted me to sensual life in a way entirely concealed at home, or at least deeply disguised or repressed.

Even beyond this earlier strong personal savor of another culture, my ties went further back. My mother was a confirmed Francophile. Her own family had summered on the French shore when she was a child, and she has since returned whenever possible. Her grandparents had toured there a generation before. My sister was also moved, and like myself has maintained an enduring interest in Paris. Later, the tradition would be continued by our children.

What I liked about Paris ten years later, in my twenties, was its unique liveliness and style. It had a vibrancy, a sense of material reality, and a human scale that made life within its borders feel meaningful and full. In a way this was, of course, something of a constructed experience. As I learned later, the city with its low buildings had been carefully preserved, even as necessary rebuilt, while modern intrusions had been expressly excluded or, like the great avenues and the Eiffel Tower, carefully placed and controlled. Its aging culture had been conscientiously tended, while features that might attract and retain tourists, scholars, artists, and other admirers of its culture had been steadily expanded and discreetly housed. Still, in 1970, the city seemed made for the sort of searching, learning, and living that I—and others my age—needed to do. I was grateful to find it, happy that finding meant rediscovering, and exhilarated that among the new discoveries were friends who could help me make it real.

Returning now in the 1990s, twenty-five years later, I brought with me much of the warmth I felt for the city. Circumstances had changed, though, allowing me both freedoms and responsibilities I had not encountered before. I now had my own contacts, and with them work to do. Having brushed up on my languages, I survived reasonably well on my own, providing a more functional independence than I had felt earlier. Visits to galleries, dealers, and curators were often conducted in French. My training in art history, combined with the vast recent growth and redevelopment of French cultural institutions (I. M. Pei's renovations to the Louvre, for example; the new Pompidou Center where in my memory had been Les Halles; and the eclectically refurbished Musée d'Orsay), gave new depth to my visits to museums. A clearer sense of French history in the nineteenth century helped me understand the city in a way I had not been able to before.

In addition, there were aspects of my experience that were entirely new. Through Travers I had learned of a design library of which I had been unaware. I visited it with great interest and enjoyed its unusual collection of clippings and other ephemera with a sense of its relevance to intellectual and artistic concerns of my own. At the Musée Carnavalet, through one of its curators I had met, I took new pleasure in the exposition of the history of

Paris it offered, to which earlier I had paid little attention. Most important in this new equation, during the years I had been away I had raised a daughter. Now approaching her twenties, she, too, had adopted Paris as a place to live for some time, and on later trips during this period, we enjoyed the city together, even making a day trip to Fontainebleau to satisfy my need to see the unusual landscape and unique geological formations that had influenced generations of painters and now photographers.

I visited Paris in the summer with a friend who didn't really enjoy it. I visited in the winter, when I went with my daughter to celebrate New Year's Eve among hoards of drunken and carousing French. (They jammed the metro and the roads above, alike, in a scene whose overwhelming bacchanalian exuberance challenged the imagination of a citizen of the puritan American Northeast.) I visited with Travers, made friends with the family of his girlfriend, Maud, haunted the flea market at Clignancourt and generally made my own way.

One of my first trips for the museum was to Pont-Aven, in Brittany, a gathering place for French artists during the late nineteenth century. At Pont-Aven, Paul Gauguin had been at the center of a small but influential group of artists, including his close friend Emile Bernard, but eventually a number of others as well. Among the better known were Maurice Denis, Armand Seguin and Paul Sérusier. The nearby village of Le Poldu, a tiny, scruffy fishing town, held the odd little inn where they had often stayed. Today, as Travers showed me, its walls and cabinets are still painted with the homemade masterpieces the artists exchanged for room and board.

I was able to go to Pont-Aven because the museum was lending a painting to a show there. While traveling to France was not a necessity, museum representation at the opening of an exhibition to which it is lending is always desirable. I made the case that I should go, adding the prospect of some judicious visits to galleries and museums regarding the museum's potential expansion into photography, which was then under consideration.

The trip was approved. I was also assisted in this venture by Rafael, who had introduced me to the mysteries of departmental budgets. Our own was small, but as the end of the fiscal year approached, he alerted me to a concept unknown to me for some time: extra money. If I didn't use the travel budget, he said, it would just revert to the museum's ample stores, where it wasn't really needed. (The museum, as it was then run, constituted the rare case of an institution with minimal needs and abundant resources, a condition that was to change under a new director with more ambitious plans.) I could take a hint.

Pont-Aven was a beautiful little seaside town, not itself on the ocean but connected to it by a long, deeply forested saltwater inlet. There were comfortable hotels, and boats at the small town *quai*. I could see why artists would have wanted to visit there to paint. In honor of these earlier visitors and their subsequent notoriety, the town had built a small museum highlighting their work. My own museum's picture, a Gauguin canvas with Tahitian themes, set in southern France, fit right in.

And so did I. Catching the express train from Paris, I changed once, took a long cab from the station, and arrived easily at Pont-Aven. Along the way I read my *MICHELIN* and took in long stretches of French countryside. The pace of life in Brittany was relaxed. Travers and Maud were there, making me feel more at home. We walked together around the quaint village, which included among its attractions a woods called enticingly the *Bois d'Amour*. Travers knew all about the artists and their work, and expounded on the era of Postimpressionism and the tortured lives of the painters he admired. For all my assertions at home of the importance of the trip, I was glad to be hardly noticed, and enjoyed the art and the scene in a way I couldn't have had I been more than a casual visitor.

The occasion for the exhibition was the hundredth anniversary of Gauguin's last visit to Pont-Aven, in 1894, one of his last stops in Europe before departing for his final stay in Tahiti. For years Gauguin had been inspired by the primitive, and before embarking on his Tahitian journeys, he had spent time in Brittany, considering it culturally distant and comfortably "other" in comparison to the cosmopolitan life of the capital. (Earlier, for the same reasons, he had visited the Caribbean island of Martinque.) In 1894, returning from Tahiti and encountering again the chaotic art world he had willfully left, he repaired from Paris to Pont-Aven, where, characteristically, he broke his ankle in a fight with seamen, sued his innkeeper, and otherwise made his visit memorable. Enhancing his exotic status, he was accompanied on his trip by an Oceanean woman called Anna the Javanese.

At the same time, however, Gauguin attracted a group of followers who were eager to work with him again, and he put his own time to good use in ways that furthered his career and his art. During this time, he completed important canvases. While sidelined by his broken ankle, he worked at editing his personal account of the South Pacific, *NOA-NOA,* and produced a series of monotypes that remain among his most characteristic work.

Gauguin was rightly admired by advanced artists of his time. He offered new approaches, a fresh palette, and exotic experiences that influenced the art of not only his own era but subsequent ones as well. His strong emphasis on the element of imagination was described at the time in a way that today seems quaint and hardly unusual, but was then a radical proposition: that he would rather consider the sky to be red than to accept it as blue along with the rest of the world.

I knew about Gauguin. I was intrigued, though, with the artists he had attracted. These were the surprise of my trip, and lent some identifying qualities to Pont-Aven, a place I had never visited before.

The premise of the exhibition at Pont-Aven was that everything in it had been painted one hundred years ago, in 1894, by Gauguin and his circle. This quick sketch of the master and his followers during his last stay in France revealed a group of artists of diverse individual styles, in whom the flame of imagination showed, though often in a manner more restrained than in Gauguin. Adding them up one could see on the one hand the departures from the norm that might indicate a time of change, and on the other the kinships that when connected, could justify the name of a school. In the former group, some characteristic novelties were the Cézanne-like brushstrokes of Chaudet, the imaginative color and Japanese-influenced flatness of Maurice Denis, the internationalization and modernization of Breton themes seen in Dezaunay, and the idiosyncratic affinity for sinuous line in the work of Gauguin's Irish follower Roderic O'Conor. In the latter group, the similarities formed themselves around such matters as the new color brought to traditional subjects and themes by Emile Jourdan and the British painter Eric Forbes-Robertson; the tendency toward cloisonne-like outline in Filiger; and the medievalism of Lacombe and Sérusier.

While for these artists, for the most part, blue was not red, the change from earlier, traditional work was apparent. Some, indeed,

Courtesy Musée de Pont-Aven.

Robert Bevan, *Maison bretonne au bord de la route*, c. 1894.
Pencil on paper. Private collection.

had already developed a style resembling that of Gauguin himself. Although the master was clearly the best by far, the painters Bevan and Seguin had adopted a similar use of imaginative line, and Chamaillard and Maufra a related sense of color. The canvases of Henry Moret and Georges Rasetti showed a sensitivity to the excitement of color and form that resembled that of their mentor, though in the case of Moret, his smaller brushstrokes, almost Pointillist, and for both painters a lack of fluidity of composition, made the overall effect very different from that of Gauguin.

What I could see, then, was a new direction in art that I found very congenial: Rural themes and traditional folkways were favored as subjects, and color and line combined to present images of graphic interest engaging to the modern eye. In these canvases russets, violets, yellows, oranges, dusty blues, and intense greens were used in combinations not seen before. The effect was of a dreamworld, a shy portent of Fauvism.

The day trip I took to Fontainebleau, near Barbizon, with my daughter, provided another illuminating experience for me in this era of European travel. Painters in the nineteenth century had made the forests and parks around this small outpost of royal life—essentially a vacation cottage and hunting lodge of imposing proportions—an important subject in their work. Early French photographers had also found it intriguing, and had produced images of forests, marshes, and stone formations that made me curious to see the area for myself. I wanted to know what constituted the allure of these strange, almost otherworldly landscapes that produced images so compelling and yet so different from much of the art that had gone before.

After tracking down the errant merchant who ran the tourist stand at the Fontainebleau railroad station, we rented bikes, consulted our map, and headed for one of the many paths through the woods, the former royal hunting grounds. It was fall. The air was crisp and there were fewer people in the forest than there would have been in the busy summer season.

I soon found some of the differences that made Fontainebleau so engaging. For one thing, it was not raw nature. The forest had been tended for generations. The paths were well established. Particular locations and rock formations were identified and well known. The finest trees, often ancient gnarled oaks and other venerable monarchs of the forest, had individual names. Clearly, this was not merely a random location but a place to which artists (and travelers, vacationers, and writers) repaired in full knowledge of its specific, unusual qualities.

The land and artists' reaction to it reminded me of something I had seen in Italy when I had gone there with my graduate school class some fifteen years before: The art of a region often resembles the place itself. While this might appear to be self-evident, what we often see when we look at a painting is the artistic work that created it. Unless we have seen the subject itself—landscape, city, the sitter for a portrait—we have no way of judging the relation of a work of art to the actual world from which it comes. Seeing the subject—one of the best reasons for travel and learning—we understand that it was not, for example, an artist's idealized view of a tree that accounts for its unusual shape on a canvas, but the tree itself, unfamiliar to us, which has simply been adapted, often with few physical changes, from the original. Thus, on that earlier trip, the land around Florence had looked to me like Florentine painting, and the monuments of Rome truly exuded the sense of age and eponymous Romantic ruin with which they are often represented.

I also remembered a conversation I had been fortunate enough to have with the great historian and psychologist of art Ernst Gombrich, whom I encountered one evening on the quiet patio of a museum where he had come to speak. Looking out, we marveled at the beauty of the landscape and talked about the ways in which land was interpreted by artists. In parting, he gave me a small booklet with an essay he had written about landscape. Reading the essay and speaking with Gombrich, I came to understand something simple but essential: that in painting, as in all media, the artist needs to respond emotionally to the subject represented—to color, to form, to character, to land. Without this the art is inert and without animating qualities. Translating the source of this emotion into something others can perceive, enjoy, or understand, depending on the motives of the artist, is what constitutes his work.

A visit to Fontainebleau enabled me to understand artists' reaction to its landscape: They had been moved by it. It was truly strange and different, it had specific qualities, a personality, though it was varied, that called out to be contemplated, understood, and communicated. Although artists have always been interested in anomalies—manifestations of beauty and awe, the sublime—I thought that the attraction of this particular place during the nineteenth century might have had something to do with the growth of science. Here nature seemed to offer forms so unusual, yet so orchestrated, as to arouse emotions simply in their very presence. Why were these unusual places and objects as they were? What sort of messages did such phenomena offer? What did they signify? The artists' response to such questions was to depict these subjects, to portray them in all their physical oddity, rare majesty, or intense ordinariness. In this atmosphere of almost personal inquiry, stones looked as if they might move, and a humble marsh could be seen as one aspect of a multifaceted world of nature.

Returning to Paris, I made appointments to visit the Bibliothèque Nationale and the Société Française de Photographie to see their peerless collections of original Barbizon photographs. The acknowledged expert at the time in this rarefied field was Bernard Marbot of the Bibliothèque, who grudgingly guided me through a quick review of the material—carts full of it—before leaving me on my own for several days with his assistant to finish the job. (The French did not think much of American scholars, especially ones like myself without advanced degrees or university affiliations.) In the bookshop of the Bibliothèque, I bought Marbot's monograph on the subject. This, along with my Fontainebleau guides and maps, and later a new catalog on the subject, provided me with material with which to pursue my inquiries at home.

Looking later at Marbot's book and the materials I had collected, I could see that others had focused on the same themes I had uncovered. Marbot demonstrated that "portraits" of nature had appeared first in painting, and that not only had personifications, such as trees baptized with names like "Jupiter" and "the Emperor," flourished in the forest at Fontainebleau, as I had seen, but they shared a history in French and European culture. In the protected clefts of some of the great trees of the French woods, miniature chapels had been established, and in one case a small home. Evidently, the attachment to such unusual places was deep and complex.

Trying to understand this, I looked into the history and prehistory of the forest. Known in Roman times as a rocky desert, the forest at Fontainebleau has since grown to cover or disguise some of those early features. The land itself was originally constituted of drifted sand from the floor of an ocean of the Tertiary Age. Emerging from these waters, it was subsequently shaped by winds. It was then compressed and further modeled by glaciers, whose liquid retreat left immense masses of rock cemented by alluvial deposits of calcium. Other natural incursions broke and shaped this material, producing what one writer called a "picturesque chaos of sandstone"—the final product that gives the rocky landscape around Fontainebleau its unique character.

Some one thousand years after Caesar had civilized this barren territory during his Gallic Wars, it had become forested, and as early as 1067 had been made a royal preserve. Its first official foresters arrived in 1316. In the 1660s, the woods had received the earliest of its ongoing planning, divisions, and redesigns. After the Revolution, it became public property, and following 1832, having reached a size of some 50,000 acres, was developed intensively as a park. By the 1860s, it was so heavily used that 4,000 acres were set aside as *réserves artistiques,* one of the first acts of modern forest preservation. Indeed, its physical presence was so charged that artists had been known to uproot and prune areas of the forest to their taste, feeling that the many trees grown in the course of its biological development obscured the geological and topographical views they valued.

Such singular qualities and history encouraged the projection and mythologizing that created the modern sense of Fontainebleau. It was a locus of retreat and meditation, a place to connect to the childhood of the world—as the nineteenth century had come to understand the past as it was present in geology and nature. As a result, I could finally see, Fontainebleau was a place where nature had stimulated imagination, a landscape that had been consecrated by artists, a scene of natural process that had generated intense response. While in its essential features it was nature in a wild, unadulterated form, over a long period its surface

Private collection.

Eugène Cuvelier, *Sables des Macherin,* (Fontainebleau), salt print, c. 1863. Private Collection.

had been carefully civilized and interpreted, yielding what an earlier author termed "a forest for people from the city."

These, of course, were qualities that could also be ascribed, with some allowances for cultural difference, to Yosemite, Central Park, or Niagara Falls. I was thus, to my surprise, able to place Fontainebleau more easily than I had thought from my own experience in studying the era and background from which its recent popularity had arisen.

Such adventures were the grist of my days. I enjoyed the stint at the museum that allowed occasional travel and the opportunity to pursue ideas in exhibitions, teaching, and talks. At that time I also visited London, where I saw the Wilsons and the beginnings of what is now an important study center for photography adjacent to their home. My editor from the Getty was then also living in London, and we caught up with each other over an animated reunion lunch at the National Gallery, overlooking the great square in which it is housed. I visited Mark Haworth-Booth at the Victoria and Albert Museum, and dropped in on London photo dealers I thought might have material of use to the museum.

My work at the museum was supported by members of its board who took a broader view of its direction and purpose. Among those who became friends to whom I could turn for endorsement or understanding at key moments were the art journalist Grace Glueck, and two directors of institutions of their own, the presidents of the Rhode Island School of Design and of Williams College. Access to colleagues such as these was one of the benefits of my work at the museum. It was a great pleasure to spend time with people committed to ambitious cultural goals, and well versed and articulate enough to make collaboration and conversation always interesting.

In reality, though, my privileges were quite limited. By habit outside the system, I was serving only in an interim position at a museum soon—under a new director—to enter a period of transition. When Rafael's replacement was hired, I returned full time to independent work. A book on collecting photographs was the first of a new series of projects. Others were further exhibitions, articles, and publications. Finally, to better pursue my own writing, I settled into a regular position running a small new museum near my home, a task which required only part-time work.

Reconnecting with the Farm

During these years of museums, travel, and art, I continued to stay in touch with my farm friends, and to collect material for a book on my generation and our experiences since the postwar era in which we had been raised. Eventually, I felt the time had come to begin to weave the story together. I worked to put aside some money and time to devote to it, and began to organize both my work space and the materials—an archive of interviews, pictures, publications, letters, and clips—to be able to focus on what had become the monumental task of making sense of myself and my times.

Others were thinking along these lines as well. In the summer of 1993, the farm celebrated its 25th anniversary. I worked with the organizers of this reunion to make its week of events productive and useful. There were large meetings in the barn, in which our now very extended community attempted to come to terms with its legacy. It was a dynamic, involving time. Many believed that during these August days we had laid the groundwork for a new, cooperative, healing era in the history of the farm. After all, by now we had a cadre of lawyers, doctors, teachers, parents, and administrators—responsible adults who could address some of the difficulties we had avoided for years. Who owned the farm? To what use should it be put? Did former residents have any rights there, though they may have left it twenty years before? Should present residents hold sway, though they possessed only a tenuous relation to the farm's founding, its mission, or the crucial early days in which its identity had been forged?

Unfortunately for the lofty goals of the reunion, lawyers, teachers, parents, and administrators were exactly the responsible adults from whom we had all fled, and behaved little differently than they had a quarter century before. Ten years after the reunion, following long periods of infighting, animosity, and maneuvering, the farm's problems were only belatedly resolved. This was a tortuous process in which Michael Curry, Jeannette, Sam, Cathy, Susan, Harvey, Steve Diamond, and others from early farm days were closely involved. As an object lesson on those times, these labyrinthine negotiations someday deserve more attention. In brief, the legal owners of the farm no longer living there, and its current tenants unwilling to pay its full value, it was sold at a moderate price to a successful nonprofit spiritual group from—of course—California. All were fairly satisfied. Most were wounded, but none severely gored, and the life of that earlier, formative time now continues in its new guise only under our own

Famous Long Ago Archive. Photo: Emmanuel Dunand. Courtesy Emmanuel Dunand.

Discussion in the barn, Montague Farm reunion, 1993.

many separate roofs, with the farm itself no longer either a bone of contention or a land of free retreat.

This might seem a surprising ending to a story that had begun in idealism and sharing, and was grounded in a style of life that emphasized personal freedom and broad cultural and social goals. Yet, looking back on the times we had been through, and the way we reacted to them, perhaps it was not.

A cogent and sympathetic overview of those early years is provided by one of the farms' writers. In the early 1980s Marty Jezer, a longtime activist and one of Packer Corner's most able and productive writers, published THE DARK AGES, LIFE IN THE UNITED STATES 1945-1960 (1982), a study of the background of the era in which we had been children and students, up to the time of high school and college. Being several years older and a serious student of history, he reached back farther than most of us remembered to provide the context for the events that followed. In Marty's analysis, probably typical of many of the farms' persuasion, the ethos of the sixties began in the unsettling social turmoil of the Depression and Second World War, and America's extraordinary recovery from them—efforts often seen as redemptive and heroic on a global scale. In the flush times that followed, affluence and success were perceived as signs of progress. At the same time, however, corporate influence led to cultural homogenization, and the Cold War and McCarthyite anti-communism laid a blanket of repression and conformity over social and political life. As we grew up, credit was plentiful, advertising and marketing stoked the fires of commerce, and living room television came to replace more interactive forms of social life. I well remember in my early years my enthusiasm to participate in the market economy he describes, eagerly seeking out the hula hoops pictured in *Life* magazine, the coonskin caps I saw on television, and the latest 45-rpm records heard on radio or in the houses of my peers—dutifully following every rise and dip in styles of music, behavior, and dress. During this period of apparent contentment, however, as Marty points out, monopolization grew at a tremendous rate, paved highways edged out more sensible forms of mass transportation, and automation contributed to a drop in employment. In addition, the quality of both the urban fabric and family life, by most objective measures, declined.

As youth awakening to the end of this era, in our early teens, it was not surprising that the questioning gene that makes itself felt at that period of life prompted a different reaction to it than that of our parents. No longer a captive audience, we followed the newly developed influence of our inclinations; the force-feeding ended, we sought a diet of our own. As young adults with some ten years of schooling and experience on which to draw, we knew and saw more. Looking around us, we awakened from the dream.

To the dangerous phenomenon of homogenization we offered stiff resistance; why shouldn't we be individuals, colorful and unique? Toward its progenitor, the corporation, there was anger that profitability and comfort should exceed the value of balance, compassion, and care, and there was strong questioning of the economic, social, and political structure that methodically reduced these prerogatives. To the primary tools of this leveling—television, advertising, marketing—we reacted with revulsion, often foreswearing them for life, and at the least reducing our consumption and participation to a minimal level. Looking at the nation around us, we saw that the prosperity we enjoyed penetrated little below the affluent surface of society, and that the silent problems with which others were afflicted were ills we might help cure.

The resulting condemnation of affluence and challenge to repression, however, overlooked some important considerations. We were products of the world we rejected, formed by its habits and predilections, and prey to its needs. Affluence, even its periphery, suited us, and comfort, although moral over physical, still played a strong role. While repression was abhorrent, the views and the tools used by some to fight it were themselves often narrow and uncompromising. And while we saw ourselves as free individuals, our generation constituted a large group and asserted a power of its own.

When the farm family came together to solve its problems in 1993, it no longer represented the apparent unanimity of a quarter century before. Instead, its behavior revealed some of the underlying, hidden fault lines we had all brought to that time we had shared, as well as the accentuation of them—or occasionally even further departure from them—that years of outside adjustment had wrought. Because we had become relatively comfortable, there was less tolerance for the extremes among us. Still convinced of our own particular ways, it was difficult to accept those of others. As veterans of the fight for individual paths, the likelihood of achieving good for the whole group could be questioned.

More than this, the time for the farm as it had been had simply passed. Admittedly, some, having few other options, still clung to it. For others, it represented matters of principle and faith, but unfortunately far beyond anything their means would allow them to support. For those who might be able to arrange support, personal missions and the exercise of power seemed to cloud the altruistic rhetoric in which their offers of accommodation were presented. As the impasse at which we had arrived after the reunion seemed to announce, the farm itself was no longer essential to anyone; if it had been, presumably some way would have been found to keep it. Instead, the discussion of its fate devolved into the factionalism in which it had been born, now raised to a new level that bespoke our increased differences, experience, abilities, and age.

Indeed, the directions people had gone from the farm were many. Tony, a builder, and Dan Keilly, of Green Mountain Post Films, are among those who have chosen to remain nearby. Susan, now the head of the art department at a private school in New York, maintains her house only a mile from the farm as a summer and weekend studio, though she still runs it with the spare charm that has always marked her style. Aaron, our woodsman, married an Irish colleen, but refusing to abandon his handmade house, divides his time between two continents. Sam, consistent with his word, returned from New York to become a selectman and focus on regional and local issues. Now an attorney, and married to a former New Yorker won over from Phil's staff, he is, however, not above occasionally returning to the city for work that helps float his public spirited causes to the north.

In the city, Andrea abandoned internal medicine and the hospital for the more stable life of the psychiatrist. Her husband, Jack, likewise, making use of his experience writing and editing, has founded his own publishing firm. Alex, who showed me the beauty of New York from her editor-in-chief's corner window wall, followed him away from books to magazines and was for years an influential editor at *The New Yorker*. Jesse, moving from entertainment to the next big thing, spent a number of years as director of cultural affairs at America Online (AOL), his income rising (and then falling) with the fortunes of the digital revolution. With the burst of that bubble shortly after the opening of the millennium, he returned full time to writing and the tending of his new web site, having recently achieved several of the important goals in his life: Happily married and father of one of the youngest children in the farm group, he and his family are now secure veterans of the momentous move from the Upper West to the Upper East Side.

Of Jesse's friends, Stephen continues as a brilliant criminal attorney. His personal focus is on conservation and environment. He was considered recently for a position on his state's supreme court. Steve Lerner, still associated with Commonweal, remains an effective writer and activist. Among his projects was assisting in the preparations for the Earth Summit in Brazil, in 1992, two books on those meetings, and an important volume on innovators in the field of sustainable growth. Other subjects he has addressed through activism or writing range from the Bhopal disaster to the persistence of racism in America.

Raymond is a social worker specializing in terminal AIDS patients. On the side, he continues the chapters of the five-foot shelf of his life, the more candid the older he becomes. (The ex-radical was recently welcomed back to his hometown in

Massachusetts as an honored speaker in a college lecture series.) Laurel married an Italian sculptor and divides her time between Italy and New York. Irv ran for mayor of a small New Jersey city, and almost won. Susan's brother Michael, whom I visited on Wall Street, helped found Ireland's new commodities exchange and now makes his home in Spain. Jeannette, still on Carmine Street, continues to turn out discs of classical music. (Her hero, former governor and presidential candidate Jerry Brown, judiciously trimming his sails, became the mayor of Oakland, California, and more recently the state's new attorney general.)

Of course, my post-farm friends were already well established when I met them. The astute Mr. Rinhart moved South in pursuit of lower taxes; the curator Keith Davis returned to Hallmark home base in Kansas City. But what of others from the early days? Grasshopper denizen Stephen Davis has written books for, about, or with Jim Morrison, the Rolling Stones, Michael Jackson and a dozen other rock celebrities. Carl, who lived both at the farm and with Jesse and me in Vermont in 1969, has written successfully both for publication and for television. For the last several years he has been in San Francisco, dividing his time between his career in journalism and his life-long passion for performing flamenco. Peter Gould, author of BURNT TOAST, has spent thirty years as a mime. Branching into more conventional drama, he teaches summer Shakespeare, runs a small youth theater, and has recently earned a Ph.D. in comparative literature. His son, who attended Yale, married the daughter of a local farmer. Cathy, who broke dishes against our stone wall because we had too many, became the dean of a medical school.

The mystical Steve Diamond still is. Uprooted after nineteen years in Santa Barbara, he spent some time editing a New Age magazine in Sedona, Arizona, before taking up with one of its like-minded readers in Holland. Recently, I saw them in Amsterdam, where I was traveling on art-related business. Others, less happy, roam the planet desperately trying to fit in. There seem to be all levels and degrees of failure and success. Some have fallen out of sight. (Asa, for example, was difficult to find. His brother, however, whom he, the zealous dropout, disparaged in his book as a pedantic, conformist college student, appears frequently in the news as one of the nation's most influential economists.) Problems of health and aging increase (a mild stroke has slowed even Steve Diamond's international pace); a few, like our great friend Doug, designer of magnificent magazines and record covers, have died. A new generation, our children, is now approaching its thirties, older than we were when we moved to the farm. My alter ego Tim and I remain as close as ever; his thoughts, as always, remain mine as well.

On first encounter, this seems an overwhelming panoply of trajectories and lives. It appears not necessarily related to the farms—more like the world itself. Actually, this resemblance constitutes one of the important points of significance of the farm group. In the time we all shared, in the late sixties and early seventies, we came together in a relatively joyous, unquestioning mode of cooperation and learning. As we left that social space and moved out into our many separate lives, these bonds and lessons were often preserved. The farms are thus a kind of cultural switchboard to which we, and others, can look back as a reference point. Regarding this group today, it encompasses both the macrocosm it has inevitably grown to join, and the microcosm in which its many potential new experiences were once united. As I type, I sit looking out on the smoky-blue hills of Vermont, in a town in which I have lived for many of the past fifty years. Yet, on the outer edges of the farm group, I know that Steve Lerner is finishing a book on social justice, that Harvey is investigating voting irregularities in recent elections, that Anna pursues her organizing in Germany and Africa on behalf of women and peace. Susan and Verandah produce writing and art, various businesses are conducted, doctors and attorneys attend to the needs of the public. Teachers go to school every day, households are managed, meetings of the PTA are attended and probably run.

I feel very privileged to have been able to know at first hand so much of the world in which I live. For me, it has been important to try to understand it. At the same time, when I look around me, some questions come to mind. How is it, with so many people our age doing so much of social, economic, cultural, and political bearing, that in the time since our heady days as bellwethers of the culture (so we thought), much of the world we inhabit has, in fact, gone back the other way? Looking at the farms as part of the larger postwar population boom, one has to ask: For a generation that has produced so many teachers and devotees of knowledge, how is it that our schools are in desperate decline? To dedicated doctors: What is the explanation for the disintegration of the nation's system of health care? To political theorists, even activists, of a distinctly altruistic turn: How could so much of the social progress apparent on the horizon a generation ago have evaporated, if not been reversed, in the years of our greatest energy and activity?

Such concerns constitute one of the troubling puzzles of our time. Looking back on the shared past we have seen, though, perhaps it is not such a mystery.

In my own case, I would have to say that I had already disengaged myself from direct political action before my last full year of college, 1967. To advocates who had registered voters, worked in alternative political campaigns, fought academic paternalism, sensed the power of labor and music, and recognized the rising new role of women, the events of those years—years of battle, one might almost say—were dispiriting in the extreme. Heroes fell. Hard-won gains were reversed. Matters of substance and meaning were corrupted beyond recognition. 1964: Freedom Summer (civil rights). 1967: Summer of Love (personal freedom). 1969: Woodstock (countercultural solidarity). But in between: 1963: the assassination of John F. Kennedy. 1965: the murder of Malcom X. 1966: early Vietnam protests. 1968: Martin Luther King, Jr., Robert Kennedy. 1973: Watergate. 1980: Ronald Reagan. In the face of such blows to society's core, other activity seemed, and often was, pure hype. Woodstock? Why would any of the farm family go to Woodstock? We already had most of what that momentary nation stood for and wanted: peace, freedom, music on our front porch. The lesson for us was not to join half a million other people going in search of these things, and paying for the privilege, too; it was to produce these necessities of the civilized life ourselves. Morning in America? Not by any definition we understood.

Looking at others, I see much the same. Success in forging our own world had the corollary effect, as journalist Ron Rosenbaum had foreseen, of creating a lost generation alienated within its own borders. We do our best to write, to paint, to create music, to raise educated children, to encourage a culture of inquiry, invention, and originality. But who has been minding the larger shop? Where are the politicians to advocate the public good: not just to advocate—we do have some—but to succeed? Where are the administrators of vision? Planners, chemists, executives, engineers?

Yet, if I didn't do these things, I think to myself, perhaps I can't expect others to have done them either. In such a troubled time, with new tools available for rebellion and dissent, and attitudes geared more to conflict than cooperation, my generation has been fragmented in ways that are proving difficult to repair. As in the books of Steve and Asa, we have often placed ourselves apart. The results are obvious.

In Sandgrove, as we sit around the fire, we talk about such things. Steve Lerner is in from Washington and California to spend some time in the house I helped him build. Michael and Joanna are here from California, New Jersey, and Krakow, enjoying the rebuilt silo we found for them. The attorney Stephen drops in from next door, where he has lived with his wife, a teacher, for many years. Other guests, neighbors, might include a filmmaker, a psychotherapist, a builder, a music teacher, proprietors of a small inn. The spirits of two artists are with us: Lothar and Karl, a sculptor and a painter from New York, immigrants who saw in America possibilities we were too engaged with it to see for ourselves. Several years older, they led us to this place that we now make our own.

(When I once asked Lothar how he managed to take care of the 150 acres of woods around his house, he smiled and said, "They take care of *me.*")

Lothar and Karl can no longer join us. Many others are absent as well. A passage comes to mind from Hawthorne's *BLITHEDALE ROMANCE,* which I have been reading. Published a century and a half before, and based on the celebrated utopian community at Brook Farm, it is word for word, I tell my companions, the story of the farms. Glossing from the opening of the second chapter, I recite the following:

Montague Farm, the upper field, 1972.

Famous Long Ago Archive. Photo: Tom Fels.

There can hardly flicker up again so cheery a blaze upon the hearth, as that which I remember at Blithedale. It was a wood-fire in the parlor of an old farm house. Vividly does that fireside re-create itself, as I rake away the ashes from the embers of my memory. Vividly, for an instant, but, anon, with the dimmest gleam. The staunch oaken-logs were long ago burnt out. Around such chill mockery of a fire, some few of us might sit on withered leaves, spreading out each a palm toward the imaginary warmth, and talk over our exploded scheme for beginning the life of paradise anew.

Sobering thoughts, mingling warmth and cold, ideals and history, memory and pain, and reminding another of our literate band of these lines from Raleigh:

Whosoe'er hee bee to whom fortune hath been a servant and time a friend, let him but take th'accompt of his memory, for wee have no other keeper of our pleasures past.

For the farm family it is, of course, the twenty-first century and not the sixteenth or even the nineteenth. Still, as we peer into the ashes of our own exploded schemes of paradise, memories are certainly almost all we have. (*PARADISE NOW*, declared the Living Theatre in the title of one of its flagship productions, which I attended for several memorable if lengthy hours in the late sixties, a time that now seems distinctly long ago.) Noting the efforts of Hawthorne and Raleigh themselves, though, we must remember that we do have other keepers of our pleasures past—and of our accomplishments, and, naturally, our failures, disappointments, and misguided initiatives, as well. Representing the farm group alone we have books, articles, films, catalogs of art shows, poems, and songs. There remain many buildings and other physical signs of our life and work. There is the new generation of children. There are students influenced by the teachers we have become, work accomplished at the jobs we have held, organizations and businesses founded and functioning. Over time, no doubt, journals, letters, and other traces of this era will surface as well.

Though the prognosis has not changed, and is not likely to (as comforting as these public attainments may be, they do not, after all, extend our actual lives), certain legacies endure that might speak for the values and goals of that time. Foremost among these, I believe, are the roots of this era in the idealism of the Romantic movement. Without the Enlightenment, Rousseau, and the Age of Revolution few of the figures of the nineteenth and twentieth centuries who influenced us, nor their ideals, could have appeared at all. Fortunately, ideas do not die, and certainly one of the signal gifts of our era will be the optimism and conviction reflected in the cultural, social, and personal battles of the time.

Idealism, however, soon collided with reality. The reactions of the postwar generation to the issues of politics, changing styles of life and work, relationships and marriage, family, education, and other matters of social and cultural concern have been as divergent as the situations and personalities of its many members. As always, change and adaptation have been key indicators of survival. That the world that will emerge from this era will reflect these diverse actions is not in doubt. What it will take to couch them in the overall principles in which we once believed, however, is less clear. Will we pay more to buy products that employ our neighbors and friends? Are we willing to reduce our expectations in order to expand those of the less fortunate? Will the horror and injustice of killing others of our species overcome the desire to gain their resources and power? Are we willing to care for the aging lover of our former spouse?

For myself, I can say that whatever answers I see to these questions lie in the lives of those in this book, and the many others like them. I speak about them because they are what I have seen. I tell my own story because it is (to quote Thoreau) the one I know best. If there are inaccuracies, as seems unavoidable, few of them, I believe, are of outlook, perspective, or intent. The story is told as I saw it, and now I leave you to rejoin my friends by the fire.

Selected Bibliography

The list below is a partial collection of books and publications suggesting the range of activities of the extended farm family. Journalism has been included if relevant to the farms and their members, or helpful in clarifying the career of the writer or the subject of the piece. The lists following "The Farm Group" outline a selection of secondary sources directly relevant to the group, as well as materials mentioned in "Afterlife."

The Farm Group:

Abrams, John. THE COMPANY WE KEEP. (White River Junction VT: Chelsea Green Publishing, 2005).

Blinder, Catherine. "Did We Get It Right?" (*Northeast Magazine*, [Sunday supplement of the *Hartford Courant*], April 4, 2004), pp. 5-9.

_____. "This Is Not Your Mother's Feminist Movement." (*Northeast Magazine [Hartford Courant]*, August 29, 2004), pp. 5-7 and ff.

Bloom, Marshall. (*Amherst Student*, London School of Economics, United States Student Press Association, Liberation News Service / LNS).

Clamshell Alliance. (News coverage, publications).

Curry, Michael. (Reviews editor for: *Ethics, Place, and Environment*).

_____. THE WORK IN THE WORLD: GEOGRAPHICAL PRACTICE AND THE WRITTEN WORD. (Minneapolis: Univ. of Minnesota Press, 1996).

_____. DIGITAL PLACES: LIVING WITH GEOGRAPHIC INFORMATION TECHNOLOGIES. (New York: Routledge, 1998).

Davis, Stephen. (*Boston Phoenix, Boston Globe, The New York Times, Rolling Stone*).

_____ (author) and Peter Simon (photographer). *REGGAE BLOODLINES*. (New York: Doubleday/Anchor, 1977).

_____ (author) and Peter Simon (photographer). *REGGAE INTERNATIONAL*. (New York: Random House, 1981).

_____. *BOB MARLEY*. (New York: Doubleday, 1985).

_____. *HAMMER OF THE GODS*. (New York: William Morrow, 1985).

_____. *SAY KIDS! WHAT TIME IS IT? NOTES FROM THE PEANUT GALLERY*. (New York: Little, Brown and Co., 1987).

_____ and Michael Jackson. *MOONWALK*. (New York: Doubleday, 1988.

_____ and Mick Fleetwood. *FLEETWOOD*. (New York: William Morrow, 1990).

_____. *JAJOUKA ROLLING STONE*. (New York: Random House, 1993).

_____ and Levon Helm. *THIS WHEEL'S ON FIRE: LEVON HELM AND THE STORY OF THE BAND*. (New York: William Morrow, 1995).

_____ and Aerosmith. *WALK THIS WAY*. (New York: Avon Books, 1997).

_____. *OLD GODS ALMOST DEAD*. (New York: Broadway Books, 2001).

_____. *JIM MORRISON*. Gotham Books, New York, 2004

Diamond, Stephen. (*New Age Journal, New Times, Dock of the Bay, Los Angeles Herald Examiner, Sedona Journal*.)

_____. *WHAT THE TREES SAID*. (New York: Delacorte, 1971).

_____. *PANAMA RED*. (New York: Avon, 1979).

_____. "Sam Lovejoy's Nuclear War." (*New Times*, October 1974), pp. 30-36.

_____. "Back to the Land" in Karen Manners-Smith and Tim Koster, eds., *TIME IT WAS: AMERICAN STORIES FROM THE SIXTIES*. (Upper Saddle River, NJ: Pearson Prentice Hall, 2007).

BIBLIOGRAPHY

Donham, Parker. (*Harvard Crimson; Boston Globe; Cape Breton Post, MacLeans; Canadian Broadcasting Corporation, Halifax Daily News.* Assistant press secretary, Eugene McCarthy Campaign).

_____. "The Seal's in No Danger of Extinction." (*San Francisco Sunday Chronicle,* May, 1978). Republished in Deanne K. Milan and Naomi Cooks Rattner, FORMS OF THE ESSAY: THE AMERICAN EXPERIENCE. (New York: Harcourt Brace Jovanovich, 1979), pp. 288-290.

Elliot, Asa. (LNS).

_____. *THE BLOOM HIGH WAY.* (New York: Dell, 1972).

Fels, Tom. "Economy: Thoreau at the Turn of the Millennium." (*The Mind's Eye,* Massachusetts Coll. of Liberal Arts, 2001), pp. 29-40.

_____. "Narrative of Surprising Conversions: Irv in New York." (*The Mind's Eye,* Massachusetts Coll. of Liberal Arts, 2003), pp. 40-56.

_____. "Troubled Prophet: The Life and Death of Michael Metelica." (*The Mind's Eye,* Massachusetts Coll. of Liberal Arts, 2006), pp. 5-39.

Gould, Peter. (Gould & Stearns, New England Youth Theatre).

_____. *BURNT TOAST.* (New York: Alfred A. Knopf, 1972).

_____. *A PEASANT OF EL SALVADOR.* (Brattleboro, VT: Whetstone Books, 1983).

Green Mountain Post. (First issue: *New Babylon Times*; sixth issue: *Farm Notes*), various authors, Montague, MA, 1969-93.

Gyorgy, Anna. (Clamshell Alliance, Public Citizen, Women and Life on Earth. Environmental advisor to Jesse Jackson campaign).

_____. *NO NUKES: EVERYONE'S GUIDE TO NUCLEAR POWER.* (Boston: South End Press, 1979).

_____. *ECOLOGICAL ECONOMICS IN ONE WORLD.* (Bonn: Die Grünen (Green Party), 1991).

FARM FRIENDS

_____. "Globalizing Peace, Love, and Understanding" [Review of the book EARTH DEMOCRACY by Vandana Shiva]. (*Peacework Magazine,* Cambridge, MA, 2006). Electronic version retrieved August 1, 2007 from www.peaceworkmagazine.org/node/206.

Jacobson, Nora. (Off the Grid Productions).

_____ (Producer/Director). DELIVERED VACANT [Motion picture]. (Norwich , VT: Off the Grid Productions, 1992).

_____ (Producer/Director). MY MOTHER'S EARLY LOVERS [Motion picture]. (Norwich , VT: Off the Grid Productions, 2000).

_____ (Producer/Director). NOTHING LIKE DREAMING [Motion picture]. (Norwich , VT: Off the Grid Productions, 2004).

Jezer, Marty. (*WIN* magazine, LNS)

_____. THE DARK AGES: LIFE IN THE UNITED STATES, 1945-1960. (Boston: South End Press, 1982).

_____. RACHEL CARSON: BIOLOGIST AND AUTHOR. (New York: Chelsea House, 1988).

_____. ABBIE HOFFMAN: AMERICAN REBEL. (New Brunswick, NJ: Rutgers Univ. Press, 1992).

_____. STUTTERING: A LIFE BOUND UP IN WORDS. (New York: Basic Books, 1997).

Keller, Daniel and Charles Light. (Green Mountain Post Films).

_____ (Producers: Daniel Keller and Charles Light; Directed by Daniel Keller). LOVEJOY'S NUCLEAR WAR [Motion picture]. (Turners Falls, MA: Green Mountain Post Films, 1975).

_____ (Directed by Daniel Keller). VOICES OF SPIRIT [Motion picture]. (Turners Falls, MA: Green Mountain Post Films, 1975).

_____ and Dr. Helen Caldicott. RADIATION AND HEALTH [Motion picture]. (Turners Falls, MA: Green Mountain Post Films, 1976).

_____. TRAINING FOR NON-VIOLENCE [Motion picture]. (Turners Falls, MA: Green Mountain Post Films, 1977).

BIBLIOGRAPHY

_____ (Producers: Daniel Keller and Charles Light; Directed by Daniel Keller). *THE LAST RESORT* [Motion picture]. (Turners Falls, MA: Green Mountain Post Films, 1978).

_____ (Produced by Charles Light and Daniel Keller; Directed by Daniel Keller; Music by Jackson Browne, Bonnie Raitt, John Hall, Pete Seeger). *SAVE THE PLANET* [Motion picture]. (Turners Falls, MA: Green Mountain Post Films, 1979).

_____, Dick Gregory and Pete Seeger. (Producers: Daniel Keller and Charles Light; Directed by Daniel Keller; Music by Jackson Browne, Pete Seeger, & John Hall). *EARLY WARNINGS* [Motion picture]. (Turners Falls, MA: Green Mountain Post Films, 1981).

_____. *ECOCIDE* [Motion picture]. (Turners Falls, MA: Green Mountain Post Films and E.W. Pfeiffer, 1982).

_____. *VIETNAM: THE SECRET AGENT* [Motion picture]. (Turners Falls, MA: Green Mountain Post Films, 1983).

_____ and Country Joe McDonald. (Directed by Daniel Keller and Joe McDonald; Produced by Daniel Keller and Charles Light). *THE VIETNAM EXPERIENCE* [Motion picture]. (Turners Falls, MA: Green Mountain Post Films and Rag Baby, 1988).

_____ (Produced and Directed by Daniel Keller, Charles Light, and Rob Okun; Music by Patty Carpenter & Richard Corey). *UNKNOWN SECRETS* [Motion picture]. (Turners Falls, MA: Green Mountain Post Films and Rosenberg Era Art Project, 1990).

_____ (Producers: Daniel Keller and Charles Light. Director: Daniel Keller). *ABE AJAY: DIMENSION X 3* [Motion picture]. (Turners Falls, MA: Green Mountain Post Films, 1990).

_____. *THE GULF BOWL CABARET* [Motion picture]. (Turners Falls, MA: Green Mountain Post Films and Blue Angel Arts, 1992).

_____. *RIBBON CANDY* [Motion picture]. (Turners Falls, MA: Green Mountain Post Films, 1994).

_____ (Produced and Directed by Daniel Keller and Charles Light; Written by Steve Diamond; Music by David Bromberg, Scott Shetler and Patty Carpenter). CANNABIS RISING [Motion picture]. (Turners Falls, MA: Green Mountain Post Films, 1996).

_____ (Produced and Directed by Daniel Keller, Charles Light, and Steve Diamond; Music by Judy Collins and Peace Links). PEACE TRIP [Motion picture]. (Turners Falls, MA: Green Mountain Post Films, 2000).

Kopkind, Andrew. (*Time, New Republic, The Nation, New York Review of Books*).

_____. WASHINGTON, THE LOST COLONY. (Washington, DC: New Republic, 1966).

_____. DECADE OF CRISIS: AMERICA IN THE '60s. (New York: World Publishing, 1968).

_____. AMERICA: THE MIXED CURSE. (New York: Penguin, 1969).

_____ (author) and Joann Wypijewski (ed.). THE THIRTY YEARS' WARS: DISPATCHES AND DIVERSIONS OF A RADICAL JOURNALIST, 1965-1994. (New York: Verso Books, 1996).

Kornbluth, Jesse. (*New Times, New York, The New York Times Magazine, Esquire, Vanity Fair*, headbutler.com).

_____. NOTES FROM THE NEW UNDERGROUND. (New York: Viking, 1968).

_____ and Luigi DiFonzo [authored as "Peter Chandler"]. BUCKS. (New York: Avon, 1980).

_____ and Jack Osborn. WINNING CROQUET. (New York: Simon and Schuster, 1983).

_____ and Roger Enrico. THE OTHER GUY BLINKED: HOW PEPSI WON THE COLA WARS. (New York: Bantam Books, 1986).

_____. PRE-POP WARHOL. (New York: Random House, 1988).

_____. HIGHLY CONFIDENT: THE CRIME AND PUNISHMENT OF MICHAEL MILKEN. (New York: William Morrow, 1992).

_____. AIRBORNE. (New York: Macmillan, 1995).

_____. *Now You Know.* (New York: Newmarket Press, 1999).

_____ and Jessica Papin. *Because We Are Americans.* (New York: Warner Books, 2001).

_____. "This Place of Entertainment Has No Fire Exit: The Underground Press and How It Went." (*The Antioch Review*, Spring 1969), pp. 91-97.

_____. "Play It Alone Brickman." (*The New York Times Magazine*, February 24, 1980), pp. 28-35 and ff.

Lerner, Stephen D. (Commonweal, *Village Voice, New Republic, Audubon*).

_____. *Earth Summit: conversations with architects of an ecologically sustainable future.* (Bolinas, CA: Common Knowledge Press / Friends of the Earth, 1991).

_____. *Beyond the Earth Summit: conversations with advocates of sustainable development.* (Bolinas, CA: Common Knowledge Press, 1992).

_____. *Eco-pioneers.* (Cambridge, MA: MIT Press, 1997).

_____. *Diamond.* (Cambridge, MA: MIT Press, 2005).

Lovejoy, Sam. (News coverage: *Greenfield Recorder* (MA), February 1974 ff.)

_____. "Somebody's Got to Do It." in Karen Manners-Smith and Tim Koster, eds., *Time It Was: American stories from the sixties.* (Upper Saddle River, NJ: Pearson Prentice Hall, 2007).

Mareneck, Susan. (See Through Books Press).

_____. *Beyond a Unifying Light.* (Hanover, NH: Dartmouth College Press, 1990).

_____. *Packaged Views, Lower East Side Printshop.* (New York: See Through Books, 1990).

_____. "Ben Frank Moss, Painter." (*Kansas Quarterly*, Kansas State Univ., 1983).

_____. "Double Dedication." (*Spence School Centennial Bulletin*, New York, 1992).

Maslow, Jonathan. (*The Atlantic, The New York Times, Boston Globe, Herald News* (NJ)).

_____. THE OWL PAPERS. (New York: E.P. Dutton, 1983).

_____. BIRD OF LIFE, BIRD OF DEATH. (New York: Simon and Schuster, 1986).

_____. SACRED HORSES. (New York: Random House, 1994).

_____. TORRID ZONE. (New York: Random House, 1995).

_____. FOOTSTEPS IN THE JUNGLE. (Chicago: Ivan R. Dee, 1996).

Mungo, Raymond. (*Boston University News,* LNS, *The Atlantic, Mother Jones,* Montana Books).

_____. FAMOUS LONG AGO: MY LIFE AND HARD TIMES WITH LIBERATION NEWS SERVICE. (Boston: Beacon Press, 1970).

_____. TOTAL LOSS FARM: A YEAR IN THE LIFE. (New York: E. P. Dutton, 1970).

_____. BETWEEN TWO MOONS. (Boston: Beacon Press, 1972).

_____. TROPICAL DETECTIVE STORY. (New York: E.P. Dutton, 1972).

_____. RETURN TO SENDER. (Boston: Houghton Mifflin, 1975).

_____. MUNGOBUS. (New York: Avon, 1979).

_____. COSMIC PROFIT: HOW TO MAKE MONEY WITHOUT DOING TIME. (Boston: Little, Brown & Co., 1980).

_____. CONFESSIONS FROM LEFT FIELD. (New York: E.P. Dutton, 1983).

_____. LIT BIZ 101. (New York: Dell, 1988).

_____. BEYOND THE REVOLUTION: MY LIFE AND TIMES SINCE FAMOUS LONG AGO. (Chicago: Contemporary Books, 1990).

_____. PALM SPRINGS BABYLON. (New York: St. Martin's Press, 1993).

_____ and Robert H. Yamaguchi. NO CREDIT REQUIRED. (New York: Penguin/NAL, 1993).

_____. YOUR AUTOBIOGRAPHY. (New York: Macmillan, 1994).

_____. LIBERACE. (New York: Chelsea House, 1995).

BIBLIOGRAPHY

_____. *SAN FRANCISCO CONFIDENTIAL*. (New York: Carol Publishing, 1995).

MUSE (Musicians United for Safe Energy).

_____. *THE MUSE CONCERTS FOR A NON-NUCLEAR FUTURE*. [Concert Performances]. (New York: MUSE, September 1979).

_____. *NO NUKES* [Music LP]. Producers: Jackson Browne, Graham Nash, John Hall, Bonnie Raitt. (Los Angeles: Elektra/Asylum Records, 1979).

_____. (Directors: Schlossberg, Goldberg, Potenza). *NO NUKES* [Film]. (New York: MUSE/Warner Bros., 1980).

Nagin, Carl. (*Frontline*/PBS, *The New Yorker, Common Ground, San Francisco Weekly*).

_____ and Francis Caro. *CHANG DAI-CH'IEN*. (New York: Frank Caro Gallery, 1984).

_____. *BECAUSE WRITING MATTERS*. (San Francisco: National Writing Project / Jossey-Bass, 2003).

_____. "Paper Dragons." (*Art & Antiques,* November 1988).

_____. "The Peruvian Goldrush." (*Art & Antiques,* May 1990).

_____. "Master of Deception." (*Art & Antiques,* May 1992).

_____. "Ely de Vescovi, A Life Discovered." (*Art & Antiques,* January 1999).

_____. "The Ballad of Gypsy Davy." (*East Bay Express*, March 2000).

_____. "Said Nuseibeh." (*Black and White*, October 2004).

Parker, Douglas. (*Bostonia,* Rounder Records, On the Vineyard Gallery.)

Porche, Verandah. (LNS, *Ms., The Atlantic, The Village Voice, New Boston Review*).

_____. *THE BODY'S SYMMETRY*. (New York: Harper & Row, 1974).

_____, Susan Mareneck and Cathy Rogers. *GLANCING OFF*. (North Leverett, MA, See Through Books, 1987).

_____. *LISTENING OUT LOUD: A HUNDRED DAYS IN PARKVILLE*. (Hartford: Real Art Ways, 2003).

Rogers, Cathy. (American Association of Naturopathic Physicians, Bastyr University).

_____ (contributor) in Dr. Peter DiAdamo, *EAT RIGHT FOR YOUR BABY*. (New York: G.P. Putnam, 2003).

_____ (associate editor). *THE HEALING POWER OF NATURE: THE FOUNDATIONS OF NATUROPATHIC MEDICINE* and *THE ECOLOGY OF HEALING: PRIMARY CARE FOR THE TWENTY-FIRST CENTURY*. (New York: Elsevier, in press).

Saltonstall, Stephen. (*Boston Review*).

Schweid, Richard. (*The Tennessean, Los Angeles Times, Barcelona Metropolitan*).

_____. *CATFISH AND THE DELTA*. (Berkeley, CA: Ten Speed Press, 1992).

_____. *BARCELONA*. (Berkeley, CA: Ten Speed Press, 1994).

_____. *THE MAVERICK GUIDE TO BARCELONA*. (New York: Pelican, 1997).

_____. *THE COCKROACH PAPERS.*. (New York: Four Walls Eight Windows, 1999).

_____. *HOT PEPPERS*. (Chapel Hill, NC: Univ. of North Carolina Press, 1999).

_____. *CONSIDER THE EEL*. (Chapel Hill, NC: Univ. of North Carolina Press, 2002).

_____. *CHE'S CHEVROLET, FIDEL'S OLDSMOBILE*. (Chapel Hill, NC: Univ. of North Carolina Press, 2002).

_____. *HEREAFTER: SEARCHING FOR IMMORTALITY*. (New York: Thunder's Mouth Press, 2006).

Simon, Peter. (LNS, *The New York Times, Newsweek, Rolling Stone*).

_____. *MOVING ON/HOLDING STILL*. (New York: Grossman, 1972).

_____. *CARLY SIMON COMPLETE*. (New York: Alfred A. Knopf, 1975).

_____. *ON THE VINEYARD*. (New York: Doubleday, 1980).

_____. *I AND EYE: PICTURES OF MY GENERATION*. (Boston: Bulfinch Press, 2001).

BIBLIOGRAPHY

Wasserman, Harvey. (*Michigan Daily,* LNS, Greenpeace, freepress.org).

_____. *HARVEY WASSERMAN'S HISTORY OF THE UNITED STATES.* (New York: Harper & Row, 1972).

_____. *ENERGY WAR: REPORTS FROM THE FRONT.* (Westport, CT: Hill/Meckler, 1979).

_____ and Norman Solomon. *KILLING OUR OWN.* (New York: Delta, 1982).

_____. *AMERICA BORN & REBORN.* (New York: Collier, 1983).

_____. *THE LAST ENERGY WAR.* (New York: Seven Stories Press, 1999).

_____ and Bob Fitrakis. *HOW THE GOP STOLE AMERICA'S 2004 ELECTION.* (Columbus, OH: CICJ, 2004).

Williams, Paul. *(Crawdaddy).*

_____. *OUTLAW BLUES.* (New York: E. P. Dutton, 1969).

_____. *TIME BETWEEN.* (New York: Entwhistle Books, 1972).

_____. *PUSHING UPWARD.* (New York: Links Books, 1973).

_____. *DAS ENERGI.* (New York: Elektra Books, 1973).

_____. *BACK TO THE MIRACLE FACTORY.* (New York: Forge Books, 2002).

Wizansky, Richard. (Greenfield Community College, Vermont Humanities Council).

_____, ed. *HOME COMFORT: LIFE ON TOTAL LOSS FARM.* (New York: Saturday Review Press, 1973).

Selected Secondary Sources

Anderson, Terry. *THE MOVEMENT AND THE SIXTIES*. (New York: Oxford, 1995).

Aaron, Daniel, ed. *AMERICA IN CRISIS*. (New York: Alfred A. Knopf, 1952).

Bloodworth, Sandra, William Ayres and Stanley Tucci. *ALONG THE WAY: MTA ARTS FOR TRANSIT*. (New York: Monacelli, 2006).

Carlyle, Thomas. *ON HEROES, HERO-WORSHIP AND THE HEROIC IN HISTORY (1840)*. (New York: Frederick A. Stokes, 1891).

Gitlin, Todd. *THE SIXTIES: YEARS OF HOPE, DAYS OF RAGE*. (New York: Bantam, 1987).

Goldberg, Hillel. "Tragic, Magic Marshall: The Anatomy of a Suicide." (*Intermountain Jewish News*, Denver, May 1986), pp. 1-15.

Houriet, Robert. *GETTING BACK TOGETHER*. (New York: Coward, McCann & Geoghegan, 1971).

Jerome, Judson. *FAMILIES OF EDEN*. (New York: Seabury, 1974).

Kittredge, Clare. "Group Returning to Radical Roots: reunion planned for members of '60s 'virtuous caucus' group." (*Boston Globe*, July 1993), p. 28 and ff..

Leppzer, Robbie. *AN ACT OF CONSCIENCE*. [Documentary film]. (Wendell, MA: Turning Tide Productions, 1997).

Lerner, Max. *IDEAS ARE WEAPONS*. (New York: Viking, 1939).

Laffan, Barry. *COMMUNAL ORGANIZATION AND SOCIAL TRANSITION*. (New York: Peter Lang, 1997).

Lorenz, J. D. *JERRY BROWN: THE MAN ON THE WHITE HORSE*. (Boston: Houghton Mifflin, 1978).

Lynd, Robert and Helen Lynd. *MIDDLETOWN: A STUDY IN AMERICAN CULTURE*. (New York: Harcourt, Brace, 1929).

Manners-Smith, Karen and Tim Koster, eds. *TIME IT WAS: AMERICAN STORIES FROM THE SIXTIES*. (Upper Saddle River, NJ: Pearson Prentice Hall, 2007).

BIBLIOGRAPHY

McLane, Daisanne. "MUSE: Rock Politics Comes of Age." (*Rolling Stone*, November 1979).

Precht, Paul. "Fertile Fields for the Sixties: Montague Farm looks back 25 years." (*Hampshire Gazette*, Northampton, MA, August 1993), pp. 9-10.

Rodale, Robert. "Young People–Are They America's New Peasantry?" (*Organic Gardening and Farming*, May 1971), pp. 30-33.

Rosenbaum, Ron. "In Search of Ray Mungo: Robin Hood in Vermont." (*The Village Voice*, July 1970), pp. 5-6 and ff.

Sale, Kirkpatrick. *SDS*. (New York: Random House, 1973).

Schell, Orville. *BROWN*. (New York: Random House, 1978).

_____. *THE TOWN THAT FOUGHT TO SAVE ITSELF*. (New York: Pantheon Books, 1976).

Stevens, Amy. *DANIEL SHAYS' LEGACY? MARSHALL BLOOM, RADICAL INSURGENCY & THE PIONEER VALLEY*. (Amherst and Florence, MA: Collective Copies, 2005).

Surbrug, Robert E., Jr. *THINKING GLOBALLY: POLITICAL MOVEMENTS ON THE LEFT IN MASSACHUSETTS, 1974-1990*. [Manuscript]. (Amherst, MA: Univ. of Massachusetts, 2003).

Section III: Afterlife

"Bibliography of the History of Art" [Online subscription database].
Produced by Getty Research Institute in Los Angeles and the
Institut de l'Information Scientifique et Technique (INIST) in
Paris. http://www.getty.edu/research/conducting_research/
citation_databases/databases.html#bha).

Butler, Samuel. *ALPS AND SANCTUARIES OF PIEDMONT AND THE CANTON
TICINO.* (London: David Bogue, 1882).

_____. *EX VOTO.* (London: Trubner, 1888).

Fels, Thomas Weston. *CARLETON WATKINS, PHOTOGRAPHER.*
(Williamstown: Clark Art Institute, 1983).

_____ and Robert J. Phelan. *EADWEARD MUYBRIDGE: ANIMAL
LOCOMOTION.* (New York: SUNY/Albany, 1985).

_____. *O SAY CAN YOU SEE, AMERICAN PHOTOGRAPHS 1839-1939.*
(Cambridge, MA: MIT Press, 1989).

_____, Therese Thau Heyman and David Travis. *WATKINS TO
WESTON: 101YEARS OF CALIFORNIA PHOTOGRAPHY.* (Santa
Barbara, CA: Santa Barbara Museum of Art in cooperation with
Roberts Rinehart Publishers, 1992).

_____. *FIRE AND ICE: TREASURES FROM THE PHOTOGRAPH COLLECTION
OF FREDERIC CHURCH AT OLANA.* (New York: Dahesh Museum
of Art in association with Ithaca and London, Cornell Univ.
Press, 2002).

Getty Art History Information Program, (Toni Petersen, Director). *ART
AND ARCHITECTURE THESAURUS.* (New York: Oxford Univ. Press,
1990).

Hawthorne, Nathaniel. *THE BLITHEDALE ROMANCE.* (Boston: Ticknor,
Reed and Fields, 1852).

Marbot, Bernard and Daniel Challe. *LES PHOTOGRAPHES DE BARBIZON.*
(Paris: Hoebeke / Bibliothèque Nationale, 1991).

Moyers, Bill. *HEALING AND THE MIND.* (New York: Doubleday, 1993).

BIBLIOGRAPHY

Naef, Weston and James N. Wood. *ERA OF EXPLORATION: THE RISE OF LANDSCAPE PHOTOGRAPHY IN THE AMERICAN WEST, 1860-1885.* (Buffalo: Albright-Knox Art Gallery; New York: Metropolitan Museum; Boston: Distributed by New York Graphic Society, 1975).

Newton, H. Travers, Jr. and Vojtech Jirat-Wasiutynski. *TECHNIQUE AND MEANING IN THE PAINTINGS OF PAUL GAUGUIN.* (New York: Cambridge Univ. Press, 2000).

_____ and John R. Spencer. "On the Location of Leonardo's Battle of Anghiari." (*The Art Bulletin*, LXIV, March 1982), pp. 45-52.

_____. "Leonardo da Vinci as mural painter." (*Arte Lombarda*, no. 66,1983), pp. 71–88.

Pare, Richard. *PHOTOGRAPHY AND ARCHITECTURE, 1839-1939.* (New York: Callaway Editions for the Canadian Centre for Architecture, 1982).

Print Collector's Newsletter / On Paper, New York, 1985-1997

Puget, Catherine, Caroline Boyle-Turner and H. Travers Newton, Jr. *LA CERCLE DE GAUGUIN EN BRETAGNE.* (Pont-Aven, France: Musée de Pont-Aven, 1994).

Wiedemann, Henning and Daniel Challe. *EUGÈNE CUVELIER.* (New York: Cantz / DAP, 1996).

Wilson, Michael and Dennis Reed. *PICTORIALISM IN CALIFORNIA.* (Los Angeles: Getty Museum / Huntington Library, 1994).

Credits and Permissions

Generous thanks are offered to photographer Peter Simon (petersimon.com), who allowed a number of his works to be reproduced here, and to Dr. Robert Cox of the Famous Long Ago Archive at the University of Massachusetts, Amherst (http://scua.wordpress.com), for equally gracious cooperation. Photographs have also been contributed by Emmanuel Dunand, Christopher Green, Ira Karasick, Steve Lerner, and R. S. Rufsvold, MD. The author's own photos are credited in the text. Full references to books and articles relating to the farm mentioned either here, below, or significantly in the text, are listed in the Bibliography.

The overview of the farm and its history which makes up much of Chapter 1 is based on the author's experiences there, and conversations with farm members. For further information on the early history of the farms, see *WHAT THE TREES SAID* (1971) by Steve Diamond and Ray Mungo's *FAMOUS LONG AGO* and *TOTAL LOSS FARM* (both 1970).

Photo, p. 26, by Peter Simon. Famous Long Ago Archive. Courtesy petersimon.com.

Page 33. Description of Packer Corners Farm from Judson Jerome, *FAMILIES OF EDEN*.

Photo, p. 36, by Peter Simon. Famous Long Ago Archive. Courtesy petersimon.com.

Photo, p. 43, by Peter Simon. Famous Long Ago Archive. Courtesy petersimon.com.

Photo, p. 52, by Ira Karasick. Courtesy Ira Karasick.

Photo, p. 55, by Peter Simon. Famous Long Ago Archive. Courtesy petersimon.com.

Profiles of farm members in Chapters 2 and 3 are based on visits and conversations with the author, as noted in the text.

Illustration, p. 73. Courtesy of the author.

The profile of Irv beginning on page 81 appeared in slightly different form as "Narrative of Surprising Conversions: Irv in New York," in *The Mind's Eye*, Massachusetts College of Liberal Arts, North Adams, MA, Spring 2003.

Photo, p. 87. Courtesy Ira Karasick.

The profile of Sam Lovejoy beginning on p. 95 is based on the interview with the author noted in the text. Expanded versions of Lovejoy's often quoted public statement on pp. 102-103 can be found in MUSE (Musicians United for Safe Energy), *Official Program* for the MUSE Concerts for a Non-Nuclear Future; Steve Diamond, "Sam Lovejoy's Nuclear War"; and Lovejoy's own version of his story in Manners-Smith and Koster, *TIME IT WAS*.

Photo, p. 104, by Christopher Green. Courtesy Christopher Green.

Illustration, p. 110. Famous Long Ago Archive. Courtesy Clamshell Alliance.

Illustration, p. 115. Famous Long Ago Archive. Courtesy MUSE, Inc.

Pages 120-122. For Jesse's comments on the underground press and the sixties, see: "This Place of Entertainment Has No Fire Exit: The Underground Press and How It Went," *The Antioch Review,* Spring 1969; and Jesse Kornbluth, "Bark When the Man Says Dog," *Fusion Magazine,* undated.

Photo, p. 121, by Sandy Noyes. Famous Long Ago Archive. By permission of Jesse Kornbluth. Courtesy the photographer and Viking Press.

Photo, p. 126. Famous Long Ago Archive. By permission of Jesse Kornbluth. Courtesy *New Times.*

Page 132, Jesse's article on John Cheever appeared as "The Cheever Chronicle," *The New York Times Magazine,* October 21, 1979.

Photo, p. 133. Famous Long Ago Archive. Copyright © *The New York Times,* by permission of Jesse Kornbluth.

Jesse's article on Marshall Brickman, discussed on pp. 133-134, subsequently appeared as "Play It Alone Brickman," *The New York Times Magazine,* February 24, 1980.

Page 135, Jesse's "Women of the Ivy Leagues," appeared in the September 1979 issue of *Playboy.*

Photo, p. 137. Famous Long Ago Archive. Copyright © *The New York Times,* by permission of Jesse Kornbluth.

Illustration, p. 146. Famous Long Ago Archive.

Photo, p. 153, by Dorothy Tanous, After-Image. Famous Long Ago Archive. Courtesy of the photographer and Random House.

Illustration, p. 162. Famous Long Ago Archive. Courtesy MUSE, Inc. and Electra/Asylum Records.

The profiles of Asa Elliot, Steve Diamond, Ray Mungo and Steve Lerner that make up Part II, "Garden of Eden," are based on the visits and interviews referred to in the text, as well as discussion of their written works.

Quote from Ernest Van Den Haag, p.184, can be found in Asa Elliot, *THE BLOOM HIGH WAY,* page 268, as well as in Van Den Haag's *THE JEWISH MYSTIQUE,* from which it is quoted there.

Photo, p. 188, by Peter Simon. Famous Long Ago Archive. Courtesy petersimon.com.

Steve Diamond's classic of communal life *WHAT THE TREES SAID,* discussed in Chapter 5, has recently been republished by Beech River Books, Center Ossipee, New Hampshire (www.beechriverbooks.com).

Photo, p. 199, by Christopher Green. Courtesy Christopher Green.

Illustration, p. 202. Famous Long Ago Archive. Photo: petersimon.com. Courtesy Delacorte Press.

Illustration, p. 205. Famous Long Ago Archive. Courtesy Avon Books.

Page 210. Lyrics from Woody Guthrie's "Do-Re-Mi," 1937.

Photo, p. 222. Famous Long Ago Archive. By permission of Raymond Mungo.

Page 228 ff. Ray Mungo's account of his days of "bankless bliss," appeared originally as Raymond Mungo, "The Repossession of Ray Mungo" *Mother Jones,* Sept/Oct 1978, pages 20-24.

Illustration, p. 231. Famous Long Ago Archive. By permission of Raymond Mungo. Courtesy Houghton Mifflin Co.

Illustration, p. 236. Famous Long Ago Archive. By permission of Raymond Mungo. Courtesy Atlantic-Little Brown.

Page 238. Lines from Lawrence Ferlinghetti's "Constantly risking absurdity / and death" from his *A CONEY ISLAND OF THE MIND,* New Directions Books, 1958. Remarks on art by David Smith from Gene Baro, "David Smith," in *Contemporary Sculpture,* undated.

Page 239. Ron Rosenbaum's early assessment of Ray Mungo appeared originally as Ron Rosenbaum, "In Search of Ray Mungo: Robin Hood in Vermont," *The Village Voice,* July 1970.

Bolinas, California, in the era recounted in Chapter 7, is well described in Orville Schell, *THE TOWN THAT FOUGHT TO SAVE ITSELF.*

A later assessment of the Commonweal programs discussed in Chapter 7 forms the concluding chapter of Bill Moyers' *HEALING AND THE MIND.*

Articles by Steve Lerner chronicled on pp. 246-248 can be found in *The Village Voice,* Spring 1968 -Fall 1969.

Photo, p. 254. Courtesy Steve Lerner.

Photo, p. 270, by Dr. Robert Rufsvold. Copyright © R. M. Rufsvold, M.D.

The profiles and autobiographical overview which makes up much of Part III, "Afterlife," are based on the author's experiences, as well as conversations and communications with those depicted.

Complete bibliographic references to *RILA/BHA* and the *AAT,* Chapter 8, are listed in the Bibliography.

Page 292. Pare, Richard. *PHOTOGRAPHY AND ARCHITECTURE, 1839-1939.*

Illustration, p. 298. Cover feature by the author in *Print Collectors Newsletter,* 17.1, March-April,1986. Copyright © 2004 Darte Publishing LLC, by permission of *Art*

On Paper magazine. Photo: Timothy O'Sullivan's *Ancient Ruins in the Canyon de Chelle,* 1873.

Page 305. Photo by William Dassonville. Courtesy George R. Rinhart. Related discussion: Thomas Weston Fels, *O SAY CAN YOU SEE, AMERICAN PHOTOGRAPHS 1839-1939.*

Pages 308-315. My experiences at the Getty Museum described in working with its curator of photographs Weston Naef, are based on my part-time work there, as recounted in the text.

Pages 321 ff. Relevant bibliographic references for Travers Newton are listed in the Bibliography.

Photo, p. 323. From "Leonardo's Lost Masterpiece," *Sunday Times Magazine,* London, 1979. By permission of Travers Newton. Courtesy the *Sunday Times Magazine.*

Illustration, p. 329. Original floor plan by Lensi-Orlandi, redrawn by R. Trotter for Travers Newton and John R. Spencer, "On the Location of Leonardo's Battle of Anghiari," *The Art Bulletin,* LXIV, March 1982. By permission of Travers Newton. Courtesy *The Art Bulletin.*

Pages 332 ff. Thomas Weston Fels, Therese Thau Heyman and David Travis, *WATKINS TO WESTON: 101 YEARS OF CALIFORNIA PHOTOGRAPHY.*

Page 335. The outcome of the Wilsons' fight with Sony Pictures is recapped in "Sony Gives Up on 007," *The New York Times,* March 4, 1999.

Illustration, p. 336. Drawing by Michael Kupperman from Simon Winder, "Her Majesty's Sacred Service," Op-ed page, *The New York Times,* November 18, 2006. Courtesy *The New York Times.*

Page 342 ff. Relevant references to the author's work in nineteenth century photography, discussed in "Themes, Motifs," and in other places in *FARM FRIENDS,* appear in the Bibliography.

Pages 347-348. The exhibitions mentioned here were *SAMUEL BUTLER, PHOTOGRAPHER* and *PHOTOGRAPHY AND ART HISTORY* (the latter co-curated with Rafael Fernandez), Clark Art Institute, MA, 1989.

Photo, page 348. See Elinor Schaffer, *SAMUEL BUTLER: THE WAY OF ALL FLESH,* Bolton Museum and Art Gallery, England, 1989. Courtesy Elinor Schaffer and Bolton Museum and Art Gallery.

Page 355. On artists and writers in the Pacific, see: Gauguin, *NOA-NOA;* La Farge, *AN AMERICAN ARTIST IN THE SOUTH SEAS;* King, *LETTERS;* Stevenson, *THE BEACH AT FALÉSA;* London, *TALES OF THE PACIFIC.*

Photo, page 356, by Andrey Osipovich Karelin. See *ANDREY OSIPOVICH KARELIN,* Arnika Publishers, Nizhnii Novgorod (Russia), 1994. Courtesy Arnika Publishers.

The exhibition on Gauguin and his followers described on pp. 361 ff. has been published as Puget, Boyle-Turner, and Newton, *LA CERCLE DE GAUGUIN EN BRETAGNE,* Pont-Aven, France, 1994.

Illustration, p. 364. Drawing by Robert Bevan. Private collection. Courtesy Musée de Pont-Aven.

Pages 365-370. For further information on the issues of Fontainebleau mentioned here, see the works by Marbot, and Wiedemann and Challe, in section III of the Bibliography.

Illustration, p. 369. Photo: Eugène Cuvelier. Private collection.

Page 371 ff. Coverage of the farm reunion includes Paul Precht, "Fertile Fields for the Sixties: Montague Farm looks back 25 years," *Hampshire Gazette,* August 1993; and Clare Kittredge, "Group Returning to Radical Roots: reunion planned for members of '60s 'virtuous caucus' group," *Boston Globe,* July 1993.

Photo, p. 372, by Emmanuel Dunand. Famous Long Ago Archive. Courtesy Emmanuel Dunand.

Pages 373-374. For more on Marty Jezer's view of the 1950s see his *THE DARK AGES: LIFE IN THE UNITED STATES, 1945-1960.*

Pages 381-382. Hawthorne's *THE BLITHEDALE ROMANCE* has recently been reprinted in *NATHANIEL HAWTHORNE: NOVELS,* The Library of America, New York, 1983.

Pages 382. Raleigh's remark on fortune and time appears in Virginia Woolf's essay on him in her *COLLECTED ESSAYS,* Volume 3, Harcourt, Brace and World, New York, 1967.

Photo, pp. xxv and 385, by Peter Simon: May Day, Packer Corners, c.1970. Famous Long Ago Archive. Courtesy petersimon.com.

Cover photo by author: Barn and trucks, Montague Farm, c.1970. Famous Long Ago Archive.

Photo of author, p. 407, by Jennifer Ann Fels, 2007.

Tom Fels is a curator and writer specializing in American culture and art. Some of his many exhibitions have been presented at the van Gogh Museum, in Amsterdam, and the J. Paul Getty Museum, in California. His most recent book was nominated for the Alfred H. Barr, Jr. Award, the Philip Johnson Award, and the Wittenborn Memorial Award. In 1986 he was named a fellow of the Metropolitan Museum of Art and in 1998 a fellow of the Huntington Library. A veteran of communal life (1969-73) and long committed to the counterculture and alternative living, he is the founder of the Famous Long Ago Archive at the University of Massachusetts, in Amherst, which focuses on the extended family of Montague Farm and its times. He lives with his wife in North Bennington, Vermont.

Photo of author: Jennifer Ann Fels.

Carl Oglesby has been a leader in the anti-war movement and an early president of Students for a Democratic Society (SDS), as well as a dramatist and musician. His books *CONTAINMENT AND CHANGE* and the *NEW LEFT READER* remain classics of modern American political discourse. His later *YANKEE AND COWBOY WAR* melds his interest in conspiracy with a larger overall theory of American political history. Oglesby's important speech at the November 1965 March on Washington was recently republished in *DISSENT IN AMERICA: THE VOICES THAT SHAPED A NATION*. His memoir of the Vietnam years is forthcoming from Scribners.